THE EVOLUTION OF THE WORLD ECONOMY

THE EVOLUTION OF THE WORLD ECONOMY

Editor

Tristan Peak

Socialy Press
AN IMPRINT OF SCITUS ACADEMICS

The Evolution of the World Economy

Edited by **Tristan Peak**

This Book is Printed on Acid-Free Paper. ♾

ISBN: 978-1-68117-757-1

Library of Congress Control Number: 2017938769

Socialy Press

(An Imprint of Scitus Academics),

616, Corporate Way, Suite 2, 4766,

Valley Cottage, NY 10989

www.scitusacademics.com

Notice

Printed in United States of America.

PREFACE

A hundred years ago, the international economy was entering the 20th century with the freest flow of goods, services and capital in human history. The previous century had witnessed expansion of global output and trade, and rising living standards in Europe and North America at a pace never before seen in human history. China's rapid growth and its growth model have accelerated important existing structural trends in the world economy and made them decisive characteristics of the global economy. In particular, China has ensured that this will be the era of the global market economy; the super-industrial economy; the post-industrial economy; the ecologically constrained economy; the complex economy; the highly globalized economy; the innovation economy; an economy with a new moral consciousness about the global supply chain; and an economy with an emerging new monetary system.

The Evolution of the World Economy explains how capitalism has changed industrial structures around the globe. Using structural development economics and political economy analytics the clarifying changes in the global industrial landscape are examined.

In both the 19th and 20th centuries, technical change played an important role. But, paradoxically, in the 19th century it was the dramatic decline in transport costs that enabled the rapid expansion of global trade and real incomes, whereas in the second half of the 20th century, it was a dramatic decline in policy-induced trade barriers that had the same effect. And whereas the reversal of globalization in the early 20th century resulted from political hostilities, the major threat to continued economic success at the beginning of the 21st century appears to be economic nationalism.

This Book will be of valuable to many, particularly those specializing in international business, economics, political science, and international relations. Academics and practitioners alike will find this an invaluable resource.

TABLE OF CONTENTS

1

THE EVOLUTIONARY TRAVERSE: A CAUSAL ANALYSIS

David Haas

Graz Schumpeter Centre, University of Graz, Universitatsstrasse 15/FE, Graz, A-8010, Austria

ABSTRACT

This paper explores the process of adaptation to new methods in a simple model where the growth rate of labour supply is exogenously given and constant. It shows that competition for a primary input in short supply changes the mechanism of adaptation and its consequences: If surplus labour exists, differential capacity accumulation effectuates adaptation and leads to a logistic replacement pattern; but if labour is in short supply, 'growth predation' undermines the former mechanism and leads to an exponential replacement pattern. The consequences of the quantitative adjustment mechanisms for aggregate growth are discussed by means of a 'causal analysis', which focuses on the properties of the traverse between two full-employment steady states. The analysis reveals that different types of new methods lead to different adaptation paths and results. Overall, adaptation entails unsteady growth and it is not always the case that the diffusion of a new method boosts aggregate growth.

Keywords: Technical change, Diffusion, Competitive selection, Adaptive growth and employment, Resource constraint

1 INTRODUCTION

We study the evolutionary traverse in a one-commodity model where labour is supplied inelastically. The aim of this exercise is to clarify the consequences of a resource constraint for the evolutionary adjustments triggered by the arrival of new methods of production.

In the evolutionary approach to technical change adaptation is recognized as a selection process, where differences in the efficiency of used methods, certain routines of firms and the economic as well as the institutional environment determine the rise of superior methods and the decline of inferior ones. This 'restructuring' is seen as a vital source of growth and technical change and typically exhibits a logistic pattern (Metcalfe 1998, 2008).

In simple variation-cum-selection models which prefer a macroeconomic interpretation, such as Nelson and Winter (1982, chap. 10) and Silverberg (1984), labour supply conditions play an important role for the selection process and its effects. For example, Englmann (1992) shows that the response of the real wage rate to selection dynamics shapes the overall employment effect of the diffusion of a new method.

Although different wage adjustment mechanisms are explored, the common assumption made in simple variation-cum-selection models is that there always is enough labour to fully employ the capital stock. In this context, Metcalfe and Steedman (2013) argue that this implicit assumption of surplus labour is not as innocuous as it may seem. They draw attention to the fact that the nature of adaptation depends on whether surplus labour exists or not: If the supply of labour is unlimited, adaptation is driven by the differential abilities to invest by means of retained profits. But if the supply of labour is fixed and in short supply, a different mechanism called 'growth predation' here effectuates adaptation. It relies on the idea that firms using the superior method can attract workers employed elsewhere through offering wages that are higher than what firms employing inferior methods can pay. Through this the superior method displaces the inferior one not only in relative but also in absolute terms through depriving the inferior one of the basis of its very existence. A further important difference between the two cases is that in the surplus labour case the amount and distribution of capital limits total output, whereas in the labour shortage case the amount and distribution of labour limits total output. This has important implications for the growth effect of competitive selection, which depends both on the bias of the innovation and the state of labour supply; see Haas (2015) for a typology of new methods and their growth effect for the case of surplus labour.

The paper develops the idea of 'growth predation' in a simple model in order to put into sharp relief the effects of a resource constraint that potentially limits output at the population level. A causal analysis helps to shed light on the crucial forces and features of what may be called an 'evolutionary traverse', i.e. the path from one full-employment steady state to another when the original steady state is disturbed by an innovation. With minor differences, this approach resembles Schumpeter's (1934) analytical scheme for understanding economic development based on the concept of what he called the circular flow (Kurz 2008).

In line with Metcalfe and Steedman (2013), adaptation is brought about by output share dynamics only; the problem of imitation is not discussed. In contrast to Metcalfe and Steedman (2013), we assume that capital is not circulating but perennial and non-malleable. This means that capital does not depreciate and cannot be transformed to serve other purposes. Thus in the case of a labour shortage some firms have to accept that part of their equipment lies idle. Note that under-utilisation of capital results from a lack of complementary means to employ it and not from a lack of effective demand; the latter problem is neglected in this paper.

The main findings include: (i) The implementation of certain types of new methods causes unemployment which is relieved through the above-normal growth potential of 'new' firms; (ii) as long as unemployment prevails, adaptation through differential accumulation features a logistic replacement pattern, a typical feature of evolutionary models, whereas adaptation through 'growth predation' leads to an exponential replacement pattern; (iii) the aggregate growth rate depends both on the question of whether there is full employment or not and the bias of the innovation. Growth is unsteady and the diffusion of an innovation is not always expansionary.

The paper is organized as follows: Section 2 presents a simple growth model with two rival firms. In Section 3 the relation between adaptation and growth for different types of innovations is explored by means of a causal analysis. Section 4 concludes. The Appendix shows that the traverse towards a fully automated system differs fundamentally from other cases.

2 A SIMPLE EVOLUTIONARY GROWTH MODEL

This section presents a simple 'macro' selection model, where labour supply grows at an exogenous rate and firms use distinct technologies. For analytical convenience we deal with the simplest case of two rival groups of firms, namely users of the 'old' technology and users of the 'new' technology. For a greater ease of reading, we will call the former group 'old firm' (indexed by 1) and the latter one 'new firm' (indexed by 2).

As we are concerned with basic relationships in evolutionary selection models and how certain assumptions drive results, we work with a set of premises that is typical for such models. In particular, it is assumed that variety in terms of methods is not renewed through innovation and that there is no imitation.[1] Rather, economic change at the macro level results exclusively from changes in the economic weight of rival technologies. Through this process of competitive selection the economy as a whole is able to adapt even though there are strong inertial forces at the micro level.[2]

2.1 Production

We assume a closed economy in which firms produce a single good which serves both as an investment and as a consumption good. Output of firm $i \in \{1, 2\}$ is determined by the fixed-coefficients method of production

$$x_{i,t} = \min\left\{\frac{L_{i,t}}{l_i}; \frac{K_{i,t}}{b_i}\right\}, \tag{1}$$

where $x_{i,t}$, $K_{i,t}$ and $L_{i,t}$ are the output, the stock of perennial capital ('machines') and employment of firm i in period t. Because the two rivals use distinct technologies, labour coefficient l_i and *full-utilisation* capital coefficient b_i are firm-specific parameters.

Before production starts, firms hire workers. To avoid the problems of heterogeneous labour and of skill formation, workers are treated as homogeneous in skills and efficiencies and both methods are assumed to require the same type of labour. This is crucial here, because the two rivals compete for the same primary input which is not in unlimited supply. Rather, labour supply N grows at a given and constant rate $n > 0$ such that[3]

$$N_t = (1 + n)\, N_{t-1}. \tag{2}$$

Assume that firm i wants to produce full capacity output, which means that its labour demand, or desired employment, is given by

$$L_{i,t}^{d} = \frac{K_{i,t} l_i}{b_i}.$$

Because the quantity of labour available is limited and inelastic, *total actual* employment, which we denote by $L_t = \sum_i L_{i,t}$, in any case must satisfy the inequality condition

$$L_t \leq N_t.$$

Clearly, if the firm population demands more labour than is available, i.e if $\sum_i L^d_{i,t} >$ Nt, this condition binds in such a way that at least one firm is rationed on the labour market and hence must produce below full capacity.

How could this be resolved? We follow Metcalfe and Steedman (2013) who argue that an input shortage, faced by the firm population as a whole, may influence different firms differently. The argument is this: Firms which use distinct technologies in general yield different rates of profit; and because of this they differ in their ability to attract workers by offering a wage that is higher than what rivals can pay.

Assume that the 'new' firm 2 pays a slightly higher wage rate than firm 1 and as a result is able to satisfy its labour demand. The extent of this wage differential depends on the perfection of the labour market. If workers are fully informed and perfectly mobile, a negligibly small premium will attract enough workers (Metcalfe and Steedman 2013; see also Nelson and Pack, 1999).[4] For simplicity both nominal wage rates, w_1 and w_2, are rigid and hence stay constant. Because $w_2 > w_1$, there is an asymmetry in the determinants of firm employment levels given by

$$L_{1,t} = \min\left\{L^d_{1,t}; N_t - L_{2,t}\right\}, \tag{3a}$$

$$L_{2,t} = \min\left\{L^d_{2,t}; N_t\right\}. \tag{3b}$$

Equation 3b states that new firm 2 is rationed only if its *own* labour demand exceeds total supply. For the old firm 1 matters are more complex. It is rationed if *total* labour demand exceeds total supply. If this is the case, its employment depends on the accumulated stock of machines of the new firm. This interaction that results from competition for a limited quantity of labour is the basis for the mechanism of 'growth predation' (see Section 3) that effectuates diffusion.

Because we focus on this mechanism, we exclude the possibility that firm 2 is rationed on the labour market by an additional assumption on firm investment behaviour, to which we turn now.

2.2 Investment

After production has taken place, firms pay their workers and decide on investment. In order to simplify the analysis, we assume the extreme von-Neumann-hypothesis: Workers consume their entire income and capitalists do not consume.[5] Further, firms only invest in their own business, an assumption that Silverberg (1984) terms 'auto-catalytic self-reproduction'.[6]

For the investment process of firm *i*, its 'individual' expected rate of profit plays a decisive role, which depends (i) on the goods price it expects and the nominal wage rate it pays; (ii) on its technology; and (iii) on its capital utilisation rate:

$$r^e_{i,t} = \frac{1 - \frac{w_i}{p^e_{i,t}} l_i}{b_i} u_{i,t}, \tag{4}$$

where $u_{i,t} \leq 1$ is firm *i*'s current capital utilisation rate, which is the ratio of actual output $x_{i,t}$ to potential output $K_{i,t}/b_i$. Further, pei,tpi,te is the price firm *i* expected. Assuming that all firms have *static expectations*, it follows that pei,t=pt−1, where p_{t-1} is the last period's uniform price. Clearly, a firm which is rationed on the labour market exhibits a rate of capital utilisation that is smaller than unity, or, stated differently an *actual* capital coefficient that is larger than it could be on purely cost-minimizing grounds. As a consequence, its 'individual' rate of profit is lower compared to the case in which it is not rationed. This detrimental effect of 'new' technology on 'old' capacity may be taken as a reflection of the process of creative destruction (Schumpeter 1934, 2010 [1942]); this is ultimately enforced by a lack of complementary inputs in the presence of a more profitable opportunity to employ them.

Further, firms take into account that the supply of labour limits the amount of capital which can be fully utilised. If firms are assumed to know the growth rate of labour supply, they can adjust to it by respecting the following inequality constraint:

$$K_{i,t+1} \leq \frac{(1+n) N_t}{l_i} b_i. \tag{5}$$

where the right-hand side of the weak Eq. 5 gives the amount of capital needed to fully employ *all* workers available in period $t + 1$ using method *i*. For our case of just two rivals, this condition means a constraint on investment for the new firm 2 and implies that it is never constrained on the labour market in the way firm 1 is. For the old firm 1, constraint (5) is never binding because of Eq. 3a.

It follows that investment levels are determined by

$$I_{1,t} = r^e_{1,t} K_{1,t}, \tag{6a}$$

$$I_{2,t} = \min\left\{ r^e_{2,t} K_{2,t};\ \frac{(1+n)\,N_t}{l_2} b_2 - K_{2,t} \right\}, \tag{6b}$$

where $I_{i,t} = K_{i,t+1} - K_{i,t}$ denotes *real* investment of firm *i*. Because the two firms differ in their technical conditions of production, they also differ in their 'individual' profit rates. And via Eq. 3a this difference translates into differential capacity accumulation of the two rivals. This is the basis for the well-known mechanism of differential growth (see Section 3).

The investment functions show that a lack of complementary inputs slackens capital accumulation in two different ways: If old firm 1 is rationed on the labour market, its lower rate of capital utilisation depresses its individual profit rate; this 'de-valuation' of its capacity results in decelerated accumulation. New firm 2 would face this problem only after it has become 'too big' and if it grows too rapidly. Because firms are treated as knowing the growth rate of labour supply but not the accumulation plans of rivals, the new firm avoids being rationed by adjusting its investments according to condition (5).

What has become visible so far is that the problem of a lack of complementary inputs may affect different types of firms in different ways. And that while some implications of an input bottleneck may instantly show economic effects, others remain in the shadow and enforce economic movements only after the system has passed some turning point. The third element of the model is goods market interaction, which is explained next.

2.3 Goods market

In the goods market firms sell the part of their production which they do not use to grow capacity. It is assumed that all firms sell at the same price which is determined by *market clearing*.

At the time of market interaction total *real* supply S_t and total *nominal* demand D_t are given magnitudes determined by prior decisions on production and investment: The amount of goods supplied to the market equals total output minus total investments; and total *nominal* demand is the total wage bill since workers do not save and capitalists do not consume. Market coordination thus can only be brought about by a variation of the price.

For the goods market to clear, the price p_t adjusts such that real supply S_t and real demand D_t/p_t coincide:

$$p_t = \frac{D_t}{S_t} = \frac{w_1 L_{1,t} + w_2 L_{2,t}}{x_{1,t} + x_{2,t} - I_{1,t} - I_{2,t}}. \tag{7}$$

Figure 1 illustrates this: As the amount of goods supplied is fixed, the supply curve (the line *S*) is a vertical line. The aggregate real demand curve (the line *AD*) shows the relation between the amount of goods workers are able to purchase and the market price for their *given* nominal income. If the price rises, the quantity of goods a worker can buy falls. The price at which the two lines intersect clears the market and is the one at which all supplied goods change hands. Note that because the *Law of One Price* holds on the goods market but not on the labour market, employees of firm 2 receive a slightly higher real wage than employees of firm 1 such that there is inequality within the group of otherwise homogeneous workers.

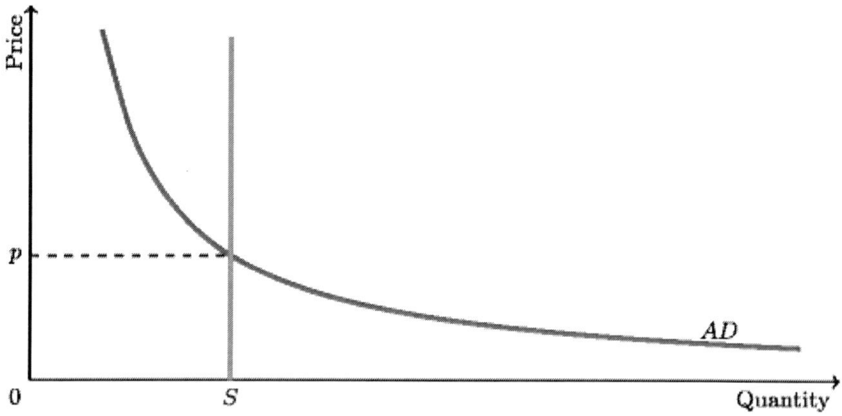

Figure 1. Aggregate real demand curve *AD*, aggregate real supply *S* and the market clearing price *p*

One implication of this pricing rule greatly simplifies our analysis of the evolutionary traverse (see Section 3): As long as both firms' investments are purely profit-led, the price does not change. This can easily be verified by applying Eq. 4 together with Ii,t=rei,tKi,tIi,t=ri,teKi,t for $i \in \{1, 2\}$ to the pricing rule (7). As long as the price does not change, the growth rate of the new firm is constant and the rate at which the old firm accumulates changes due to rationing only. The stylized 'mechanics' at hand may thus put quantity adjustments unfolding in the course of adaptation into sharp relief.[7]

But this is not to say that price dynamics are not important here. To the contrary, as will be shown below, condition (5) sooner or later gets binding and the resulting price movements play a decisive role in restoring equilibrium. The fact that the price does not gradually adapt reflects one central theme of this study, namely that the forces which move the system may not remain the same over time. Rather, one force may shape economic movements in one phase, but at the same time it may pave the way for new forces. And if they gain momentum and prevail, the behaviour of the system may change and new phenomena may arise. Thus something can be learned from the study of the sequence of mechanisms and their interplay.

2.4 Summary

Before we deal with this question, let us summarise the model in order not to lose sight of its data, variables and (behavioural) relations. Figure 2 illustrates the basic structure of the model. The givens consist of the set of firm-specific data $\{l_i, b_i, w_i\}$ where $i \in \{1, 2\}$ and the rate at which the labour supply grows, n. The endogenous variables are the aggregate stock of machines $K_t = \sum_i K_{i,t}$, aggregate employment $L_t = \sum_i L_{i,t}$, aggregate output $X_t = \sum_i X_{i,t}$ and the market share of firm 2, denoted by $q_t = x_{2,t}/x_t$, which shows the economic weight of the innovation.

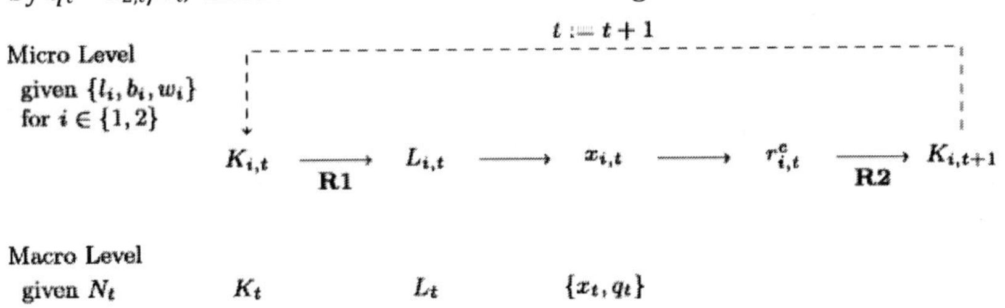

Figure 2. Logic of the model

Firm variables $\{K_{i,t}, L_{i,t}, x_{i,t}\}$, where $i \in$ 1, 2} from which aggregates are built, evolve according to two *micro rules*, which establish relations between firm variables: the method of production (1) and the investment functions (6a). The *macro rule* (2) determines labour supply, describes the environment in which firms act and defines channels through which they interact. There are two *interaction rules*: Eq. 3a establishes a functional relationship between firm variables yielding firms' employment levels as outcomes of labour market interaction; and through coordination rule (7) firms interact via the market-clearing output price.

As already mentioned, for the case that labour supply grows at an exogenously given rate, two forms of rationing can occur, which are referred to as **R1** and **R2**:

R1

Firm 1 is rationed, if total labour demand is larger than supply. This implies that its capacity-determined employment level is strictly larger than its labour-supply-determined level $(L^d_{1,t} > N_t - L_{2,t})$.

R2

From condition (5) it follows that firm 2 is 'investment rationed' if its profit-determined level of investments is larger than its labour supply-determined full-utilisation level of investments.

3 ADAPTATION AND GROWTH

This section turns to the dynamic process of adjustment in order to clarify the central forces and features of the evolutionary traverse. To put them into precise terms, we perform a 'causal analysis'. For this purpose we compare the path of the adapting economy with its reference path. The adaptation path starts when some particular innovation disrupts the 'old' steady state and ends when a 'new' steady state is reached. Along the reference path no innovation takes place such that the economy remains in its 'old' steady state. The causal effect of the innovation then is the difference between the two paths.[8] We assume that in the 'old' steady state all firms use the same method, namely 'old' method 1 with l_1 and b_1 as unit requirements and pay the same uniform and constant real wage rate w_1/p; the price of the good equals unity in the old steady state. Further, there is full employment and the system grows at rate $g_1 = r_1 = n$. Consistency requires that $n \leq 1/b_1$.

Unlike most evolutionary selection models which start with given variety of methods, this approach requires us to not only consider the diffusion process, or the process of variety destruction, but also the process by which variety is created. For the study here, two questions of the innovation process are important. The first question concerns the conditions that the new method must satisfy in order to trigger a successful traverse (see Section 3.1). The second one pertains to the way in which the new method could emerge within a system where there are no unemployed resources and the effects this produces (see Section 3.2).

3.1 Types of new methods

We distinguish between different types of new methods based on both their innovation bias and their economic superiority or inferiority.

Potential new methods, i.e. those not (yet) used, are grouped according to their *innovation bias*. The capital bias and the labour bias of the (new) method 2 compared to the (old) method 1 are given by the measures

$$\Theta_b = \frac{b_2 - b_1}{b_1} > -1 \quad \text{and} \quad \Theta_l = \frac{l_2 - l_1}{l_1} > -1.$$

where Θ_b (Θ_l) is the relative gain in physical efficiency with respect to capital (labour). Note that both measures are assumed to be strictly larger than −1 so that both inputs are necessary to operate the new method.[9] The bias of an innovation is defined by the combination of signs of the two measures. For example, new methods for which $\Theta_b = 0$ and $\Theta_l < 0$ are pure labour saving innovations. Table 1 lists all types innovation that are possible in a one-good model given the above condition. Below we show how the features of the innovation in terms of physical efficiencies, not just absolutely but relative to what is already there, crucially shape the path of diffusion and aggregate growth of the traversing economy.

Table 1. Causal effects in the innovation period.

Innovation type	Bias	RI	$\Delta_{X,0}/X_R$	$\Delta_{L,0}/L_R$
Capital saving and labour using	$\Theta_b < 0,\ \Theta_l > 0$	Yes	−	0
Labour saving and capital using	$\Theta_b > 0,\ \Theta_l < 0$	No	−	−
Pure capital saving	$\Theta_b < 0,\ \Theta_l = 0$	Yes	0	0
Pure labour saving	$\Theta_b = 0,\ \Theta_l < 0$	No	+	−
Combined factor saving	$\Theta_b < 0,\ \Theta_l < 0$			
Neutral	$\Theta_b = \Theta_l < 0$	No	+	0
Dominantly capital saving	$\Theta_b < \Theta_l < 0$	Yes	+	0
Dominantly labour saving	$\Theta_l < \Theta_b < 0$	No	+	−

Second, we distinguish between methods which are economically superior to the old method and methods which are inferior. In contrast to an inferior method, a superior method is defined as one that would successfully spread and displace the old method along the traverse, if it were implemented. In our model a method is superior if it yields a rate of profit which is strictly higher than that of the old method and yet pays a wage rate that is sufficiently above the wage rate of the old firm (see Eqs. 3a and 6a).[10] This condition implies that some (new) method 2 is superior to the (old) method 1 if

$$r_1 b_1 \left(\frac{b_2 - b_1}{b_1}\right) + \frac{w_1}{p} l_1 \left(\frac{e l_2 - l_1}{l_1}\right) < 0. \tag{8}$$

We see that the new method yields a higher rate of profit only if at least one of its two unit requirements is strictly smaller compared to the old method. Although a greater physical efficiency with respect to one input is necessary for a new method to be superior, in some cases it is not sufficient: If either one of the two unit requirements is higher for the new method and/or if its labour costs per unit of output are higher because of the wage differential, the ruling income distribution in terms of the wage share and the profit share determine the superiority or inferiority of the new method.

Hence, economic and institutional conditions play an important role for the success of new methods (Kurz 2008). The institutional conditions that play a role here are those which determine the size of *e*. As already noted, the size of *e* depends on the perfection of the labour market in terms of information and mobility of workers (Metcalfe and Steedman 2013, p. 169-170).

In the remainder of this study only the case of a superior method is studied. Notice that we also exclude 'dynamic re-switching' where a new method is superior initially but becomes inferior because the income distribution changes in response to its diffusion.

3.2 The implementation period

At the beginning of the implementation period, which is period 0, firm 2 using the new method 2 is set up. By assumption it grows out of existing resources and comes into being through the 'mutation' of some small fraction of the 'old' capital stock. This 'mutation' is taken to be a singular, exogenous event and to some extent violates our assumption that installed machines cannot be transferred as between firms. But, in the words of Schumpeter, the important point is that an innovation requires "a 'withdrawal of goods' from their previous uses" (Schumpeter 1934, p. 108) as there are no unemployed resources available in a steady state. This is crucial because this influences the aggregate quantity effects of implementing a new method.[11]

In order to determine the effects of implementing a new method on aggregate output and employment, total output x_0 and employment L_0 of the adapting economy are compared to the reference economy, where in both cases the same stock of capital K_0 and the same amount of labour N_0 are available. The difference between the two cases is that in the adapting economy some fraction $K_{2,0}$ is used by the new firm. The instant employment and output effects are described below. The findings are summarised in Table 1 for different types of new methods.

The effects of implementation on aggregate output and employment depend first of all on whether firm 1 is rationed already in the innovation period (**R1** holds) or not. **R1** holds in the innovation period if

$$\frac{l_2}{b_2} > \frac{l_1}{b_1} \qquad \text{or} \qquad \Theta_l > \Theta_b .$$

We see that **R1** holds if the labour intensity is higher for the innovating firm than for the old firm.

The instant employment effect is defined as the relative deviation of the implementation period's aggregate employment L_0 from the reference level $L_R = N_0$ and is given by:

$$\frac{\Delta_{L,0}}{L_R} = \frac{L_0 - N_0}{N_0} = \begin{cases} 0 & \text{if } \mathbf{R1} \text{ holds } (\Theta_l > \Theta_b) , \\ \frac{K_{2,0}}{K_0}\left(\frac{\Theta_l - \Theta_b}{1+\Theta_b}\right) & \text{if } \mathbf{R1} \text{ does not hold } (\Theta_l \leq \Theta_b) . \end{cases} \tag{9}$$

Because a full employment reference path is assumed, the employment effect is either zero or negative. It is zero in cases in which the innovation is more labour intensive than the old one. Hence, if **R1** holds, full employment prevails in the implementation period, but some of firm 1's machines lie idle. If a neutral innovation ($\Theta_l = \Theta_b$) gets implemented, the employment effect is zero, but the capital stock remains fully employed in this period. If the innovation is less labour intensive ($\Theta_l < \Theta_b$), installed capacity is fully utilised but some workers are unemployed.

We also see from Eq. 9 that the extent of what may be considered technological unemployment does not only depend on the innovation bias but also on firm 2's initial capital share. For example, if the innovation is capital using and labour saving with $\Theta_b = 0.25$ and $\Theta_l = -0.25$, the employment effect is $\Delta_{L,0}/L_R = -0.1$ for $K_{2,0}/K_0 = 0.25$. But if the whole capital stock mutates instanteneously ($K_{2,0}/K_0 = 1$), the employment effect is $\Delta_{L,0}/L_R = -0.4$.

The instant output effect is the relative deviation of the implementation period's aggregate output x_0 from its reference x_R:

$$\frac{\Delta_{x,0}}{x_R} = \frac{x_0 - x_R}{x_R} = \begin{cases} -\frac{K_{2,0}}{K_0}\left(\frac{\Theta_l}{1+\Theta_b}\right) & \text{if } \mathbf{R1} \text{ holds } (\Theta_l > \Theta_b) , \\ -\frac{K_{2,0}}{K_0}\left(\frac{\Theta_b}{1+\Theta_b}\right) & \text{if } \mathbf{R1} \text{ does not hold } (\Theta_l \leq \Theta_b) . \end{cases} \tag{10}$$

As we can see, the direction of the instant causal output effect is determined by the two dimensions of the innovation bias and how these compare with each other: If the innovation is more labour intensive than the old one, we know that **R1** holds. It follows from Eq. 10 that the labour bias Θ_l determines the direction of the output effect in this case. But if the innovation is less labour intensive and hence causes unemployment (**R1** does not hold), it is not the labour bias Θ_l but the capital bias Θ_b that determines the direction of the effect. It follows that in both cases the causal effect can be positive (or negative), although for different reasons (see Table 1).

The next section shows in what way economic circumstances, in particular whether there is full employment or not, interact with the process of differential growth that is initiated by the implementation of the new method and shapes its path of diffusion.

3.3 The diffusion period

In this section we study the diffusion period during which the new method gradually gains weight in terms of its output share. This quantitative restructuring drives aggregate output and employment growth. The exercise below shows that the type of innovation under consideration crucially shapes the way its diffusion is effectuated and the effects this entails. As shown above, the implementation of some types of new methods makes workers redundant. It will turn out that the *instant* employment effect shapes the adjustment path.

The argument is the following: In case the new method is less labour intensive than the old method, i.e. if $\Theta_l < \Theta_b$, implementation causes technological unemployment. This means that there is a phase during which no firm is rationed. As long as this situation prevails, diffusion is effectuated by differential capacity accumulation. Through this the new firm gradually gains economic weight in terms of its output share. This adjustment mechanism shapes things in the *re-absorption phase* where neither **R1** nor **R2** holds (see Section 3.3.3).

The re-absorption phase through which the system moves only if $\Theta_l < \Theta_b$ eventually ends because the new firm grows at an above-normal rate and by doing so re-establishes full employment. The system then enters a different phase, during which firm 1 is rationed on the labour market, while firm 2 still expands at an above-normal rate by attracting workers from firm 1. This kind of predatory interaction shapes things during the *predation phase* where **R1** holds but **R2** does not (see Section 3.3.2).

Also this phase ends, because the new firm eventually exhausts its potential to grow at an above-normal rate by luring away workers from firm 1. If then condition (5) becomes binding and not only **R1** but also **R2** holds, the system enters the *restoration phase*, in which the innovator adapts his accumulation speed to the growth rate of labour supply. This leads to a strong fall in the output price as a consequence of which the system enters a new steady state (see Section 3.3.1).

3.3.1 *The re-absorption phase*

During this phase technological unemployment prevails because an innovation which is less labour intensive than the old method has been implemented. We call it the re-absorption phase, because jobless workers are gradually re-employed.

The reason why this happens is that the innovation yields an above-normal rate of profit because the market price does not change (see Section 2.3). As no firm is rationed their output growth rates are given by

$$g_1 = \frac{x_{1,t+1} - x_{1,t}}{x_{1,t}} = r_1 = n \qquad \text{and} \qquad g_2 = \frac{x_{2,t+1} - x_{2,t}}{x_{2,t}} = r_2 > n.$$

The growth rate of aggregate output is the weighted average of firm growth rates, where the weights are the output shares of firms. It can be expressed as

$$g_t = \frac{x_{t+1} - x_t}{x_t} = n + \underbrace{q_t\,(g_2 - n)}_{\text{(re-absorption effect)}} > n, \tag{11}$$

where q_t is the market share of firm 2. We see that the aggregate growth rate is larger than n, which is the rate at which the reference economy grows, because of a positive 're-absorption effect'. The same holds for employment growth, which is the weighted average of firm growth rates with firms' employment shares as weights. Isolating the re-absorption effect gives

$$g_{L,t} = \frac{L_{t+1} - L_t}{L_t} = n + \underbrace{q_t \frac{1 + \Theta_l}{1 + q_t \Theta_l}(g_2 - n)}_{\text{(re-absorption effect)}} > n,$$

and shows that its extent also depends on the innovation's labour bias Θ_l: The more the innovation saves on labour, the slower job growth is. This indicates that the length of the re-absorption phase depends on the type of innovation.

The structure of production in terms of output shares of the two rivals changes due to the mechanism of differential accumulation at a rate which is proportional to the difference in profit rates:

$$\frac{q_{t+1} - q_t}{q_t} = \frac{g_2 - g_t}{1 + g_t} = (1 - q_t)\,\frac{(r_2 - r_1)}{1 + g_t}. \tag{12}$$

Equation 12 defines the diffusion path and shows that the new method displaces the old along a sigmoid curve. This logicstic replacement pattern is a typical result of evolutionary models of the variation cum selection kind for the case of two rival methods (Metcalfe 2008). However note that it is not a simple 'S'-shaped logistic curve, because the aggregate growth rate g_t is not constant but increases over time (Metcalfe and Steedman 2013, p. 164).

Summing up, the re-absorption phase appears bright and prosperous: The economy grows at a rate which is always above of what was feasible before the innovation occurred. But note that this is only possible if the emergence of the innovation at first caused unemployment. Further keep in mind that the mechanism of differential growth shapes economic movements and causes a logistic pattern of diffusion.

3.3.2 The predation phase

As differential growth eventually restores full employment, the system enters the predation phase, which is defined by the fact that **R1** holds but **R2** does not. This implies that a new force sets in and shapes the course of things.

As now full employment prevails, the causal employment effect is zero. We thus focus on the causal output effect. The explanation of the causal output effect begins with the remark that also in the predation phase the market price does not change. Hence firm 2's rate of profit remains constant and above *n*. Yet, firm 1's position is less favourable as it is no longer able to maintain full capital utilisation. Idle capital in turn forces down its individual rate of profit such that $r_{1,t} < n \quad \text{and} \quad r_2 > n.$

This detrimental effect of 'new' technology on 'old' capital ensures that the speed at which firm 1 accumulates capacity abates.

But this is not all that happens. Predatory interaction on the labour market by Eq. 6a implies that the growth rate of the old firm now depends on the growth rate of the new firm:

$$g_{1,t} = n + \underbrace{(-1)\,\frac{q_t}{1 - q_t}\,(1 + \Theta_t)\,(g_2 - n)}_{\text{(predation effect)}} < n. \tag{13}$$

Since $g_2 > n$, this equation shows that the faster the innovator grows the slower the old firm expands in terms of output. By predation of workers, firm 2 pushes down firm 1's rate of output growth and thereby continues to be able to realize an 'above-normal' growth path. The mechanism of 'growth predation' thus leads to a situation in which

$$n > g_{1,t} \qquad \text{and} \qquad g_2 > n,$$

where $g_2 = r_2$.

This direct and one-sided dependency shown in Eq. 13 is a novel feature in the context of variation-cum-selection models. What difference does it make for adaptive growth and the path of diffusion?

For the system as a whole, growth predation affects aggregate output growth by

$$g_t = n + \underbrace{(-1)\, q_t \Theta_l \, (g_2 - n)}_{\text{(predation effect)}} . \tag{14}$$

We see that adaptive growth may differ from reference growth n due to the 'predation effect' of Eq. 14. Since $g_2 > n$, the sign of this effect is determined by the innovation's labour bias Θ_l only. Hence innovations do not necessarily entail an expansionary tendency in the predation phase: Only if the innovation saves on labour ($\Theta_l < 0$) the economy experiences 'above-normal' growth; but if a labour-using innovation ($\Theta_l > 0$) gains economic weight, 'below-normal' growth results; and if $\Theta_l = 0$ the economy grows at its normal rate n. Therefore there are cases in which the aggregate output growth rate flips from an above-normal to a below-normal level, since re-absorption growth is always above the normal level.

The reason why the labour bias of the innovation is a major determinant of aggregate growth is that the economy hits the full-employment ceiling as it passes from the re-absorption to the predation phase. This means that total output is given by xt=Nt/l¯ where l¯tl¯t is the average labour coefficient, defined by l¯t=(1−qt)l1+qtl2 l¯ Taking the growth rate of the average labour coefficient reveals that output growth rate is smaller than n if a labour-using innovation gains economic weight.

The fact that the system hits the full-employment ceiling does not only change the determinants of adaptive growth but also the adaptation mechanism. Because growth predation breaks the one-to-one relation between the profit differential and the growth differential, it undermines the 'pure logistic law' as a driver of restructuring. To see this, let us turn to the evolution of employment shares, which are more informative than the corresponding output shares here: Let employment share of firm 2 be $q_{L,t} = L_{2,t}/L_t$ and let Λ_t denote the rate at which it changes.[12]The rate of change in employment shares for the re-absorption phase and the predation phase then are:

$$\Lambda_t = \frac{q_{L,t+1} - q_{L,t}}{q_{L,t}} = \begin{cases} (1 - q_{L,t}) \frac{(r_2 - r_1)}{1 + g_{L,t}} & \text{in the } \textbf{re-absorption} \text{ phase,} \\ \frac{g_2 - n}{1 + n} & \text{in the } \textbf{predation} \text{ phase,} \end{cases} \quad (15)$$

where $g_{L,t}$ is the rate at which total employment grows in the re-absorption phase ($L_t < N_t$). From Eq. 15 it follows that the same logistic process effectuated by differential growth as in Eq. 12 shapes employment shares in the re-absorption phase. In contrast, in the predation phase the problem of labour shortage offsets this mechanism and causes a different adaptation pattern. Economic movements now result from growth predation, a mechanism which shows an exponential pattern of restructuring, where the rate of change is constant.[13]

One may infer from this finding that if bottlenecks and predatory interaction on input markets play a role, the pure logistic law of replacement may not always hold if looked upon from a purely theoretical perspective. For example, in a world in which industries are interconnected, imbalances of supply and demand of complementary inputs may shift the probability in favour of exponential replacement patterns rather than logistic ones.

3.3.3 The restoration phase

So far we have treated the case in which the old firm is not rationed and the case in which it is rationed and showed how the re-absorption phase paves the way for the predation phase. This section now turns to the case in which not only firm 1 but also firm 2 is affected by the labour inflexibility assumption. Hence both **R1** and **R2** hold.

In Section 2 we argued that the new firm is able to avoid being rationed in the way the old firm is. This assumption resides in constraint (5), which enters firm 2's investment function (6b). Then, **R2** holds if firm 2's profit-determined level of investments is larger than its labour supply-determined full-utilisation level. In the first period where **R2** holds, say T, firm 2's real investment therefore is given by

$$I_{2,T} = \frac{(1+n)\, N_T}{l_2} b_2 - K_{2,T} < r^e_{2,T} K_{2,T}.$$

This implies that firm 2 is 'investment rationed' in the sense that the evolution of labour supply de-motivates the realisation of potential growth determined by the profit rate. Hence the innovating firm's profit-led growth regime ends during the passage from the predation phase to the restoration phase.

That the system necessarily passes over from one to the other is due to the fact that the potential for firm 2 to grow at an above-normal rate by luring away workers from firm 1 eventually exhausts. That firm 2 is 'investment rationed' implies that its growth rate is

$$g_{2,T} = (1+n)\,\frac{\bar{l}_T}{q_T l_2} - 1, \tag{16}$$

where $q_T < 1$. Because in period $T + 1$ firm 2 owns exactly that amount of capital required for employing all workers, output of firm 1 in period $T + 1$ is zero and $g_{1,T} = -1$. This implies that in period $T + 1$ the innovation is fully absorbed into the system. 'Old' capacity now is economically obsolete in the sense that 'new' capacity has grown big enough to employ the whole labour force.

What completes adaptation is the fact that in the restoration phase the output price erodes: If **R2** holds, $g_{2,T} < r^e_{2,T}$,Te, which means that the amount of goods supplied is greater than the amount which would maintain a stable nominal price. Given the assumption of perfect coordination by Eq. 7, a price p_T is established which is smaller than the price which prevailed during the re-absorption and the predation phase. Because the price 'jumps' to a lower level, the real wage rate and the real costs of production increase. The distributional consequences of innovation now affect not only workers employed by the new firm (through the wage differential) but also workers still employed by the old firm, which therefore is at risk of losing its economic viability.

As noted above, output of firm 1 in period $T + 1$ is zero. Its capital stock is economically obsolete and hence ready to expire physically. If free disposal is assumed, the problem of getting rid of it will not have significant economic effects. Because firm 1 vanishes ($q_{T+1} = 1$), it follows from Eq. 16 that $g_{2,T+1} = n$. Also for this period **R2** holds which means that the price drops again; the price which gets established, say p_2, re-establishes a new steady state path along which the profit rate equals n and the real wage rate is given by $(w_1 e)/p_2 = (1 - nb_2)/l_2$.

We may conclude the discussion of the restoration phase by pointing out that one theme of this study, namely that adaptation forces may not remain constant but change conditions such that new forces set in and new phenomena arise, appears here in the form of non-steady price dynamics: The price is stable first, but strongly reacts after the system passed some turning point, which is reached due to the inner logic of change. Above all, this hints at the uneven nature of economic change we ought to explain.

4 CONCLUSIONS

In this paper we clarified the role of a resource constraint for the evolutionary adjustment process triggered by the arrival of new methods of production. By means of a causal analysis we have obtained two main results.

First, the nature and effects of adaptation to a new method crucially depend on whether surplus labour exists or not. Concerning the nature of evolutionary adjustments we have shown that if there is surplus labour, differential accumulation leads to a logistic pattern of restructuring. But in the case of a labour shortage, growth predation through which firms' output growth rates become interdependent, leads to an exponential replacement pattern. Through a comparison of re-absorption growth and predation growth the state of labour supply in relation to demand has also been shown to play an important role for the effects of new methods on aggregate growth along the traverse.

Second, different types of innovations lead to different adaptation paths and effects. Some innovations cause technological unemployment, which is eventually removed through the new firm's above-normal ability to accumulate. Overall, adaptive growth is not steady and it is not necessarily the case that innovations boost aggregate growth.

By way of a conclusion, even in simple models like the one studied here the effects of innovations are hard to assess. From the objectivist position taken up here, this is so because diffusion is a time-consuming process such that effects extend over time; and because effects depend on the features of the innovation, not just absolutely but relative to what is already there, as well as on the economic circumstances into which they are born and spread. Hence, without taking economic circumstances into account we cannot expect to know how innovations will change the system. And even if the diffusion of an innovation causes some pattern to persist for some time, it may prove a bad guide for the future because forces behind patterns may revise the economic circumstances on which they rely.

FOOTNOTES

[1]The first evolutionary diffusion model dates back to Nelson (1968). Further important contributions include Nelson and Winter (1982, chap. 10), Soete and Turner (1984), Silverberg (1984), Englmann (1992), Metcalfe (1997, 1998), Nelson and Pack (1999), Metcalfe and Steedman (2013); see also Haas (2015). See Metcalfe (1998) for a concise elaboration of the economic theory of selection. For an overview of the

evolutionary perspective on growth and technical change see Santangelo (2003) and Silverberg and Verspagen (2005).

[2]Evidence suggests that the case of strong 'incumbent inertia' is not purely hypothetical; see for example Gilbert (2005) and the references he gives.

[3]Note that the assumption of an exogenous population growth rate is quite at odds with the classical perspective, in which the workforce endogenously adjusts to the pace of capital accumulation (Kurz 2008, 2010). It may be motivated by the idea that the structure of productive activities changes faster than the factors which determine population growth.

[4]Note that here the explanation of the wage differential has nothing to do with the skills of workers or the quality of jobs; see Kurz and Salvadori (1995, chap. 11) for an analysis of persistent forces which regulate the structure of relative wages in the long run.

[5]The classical saving hypothesis according to which workers do not save and investments depend on capital incomes is a typical assumption made in evolutionary growth models; see e.g. those cited in footnote 1 and Dosi et al. (2010).

[6]See Soete and Turner (1984) for a discussion of investment flow adjustments in the context of diffusion and selection.

[7]This feature of the model mimics the hypothesis of Metcalfe and Steedman (2013) who treat the real wage rate, except for a small wage premium, as constant during the adjustment process on the basis of the principle of the marginal firm.

[8]This method has been employed by Kalmbach and Kurz (1992) in their empirical study of employment effects of diffusion of new methods of production. Hicks (1983) describes the *causal analysis* as follows:

We compare two alternative paths that extend into the future. Along one of those paths some new 'cause' is not operating; along the other it is. The difference between the paths is the effect of that cause. The difference itself extends over time [and] it is the *whole* of the difference between the paths which is the effect of the cause (p. 109; *Hicks's italics*).

[9]The appendix on page 19 discusses the case of a fully automated method ($\Theta_l = -1$) and shows that it differs fundamentally from cases where the new method requires labour.

[10]In the following, $e = w_2/w_1 > 1$ denotes the ratio of the two wage rates and reflects the assumption that the new firm pays a higher wage rate in order to compete away workers from the old firm; the size of e is assumed to be constant and given.

[11]The argument that broader economic conditions play an important role for the process of innovation and effects has been emphasised by both Schumpeter (1934, 1939) and Spiethoff (1925). Whereas Schumpeter assumed that innovations are introduced into a situation of full employment, i.e. what he termed a 'circular flow', Spiethoff argued on empirical grounds that innovations normally are born into a world in which some economic resources lie idle. This difference led them to put forth different views on innovation-driven change (Kurz 2015a).

[12]The employment share relates to the output share by qL,tl¯t=qtl2qL,tl¯t=qtl2.

[13]Note that in terms of capital shares $K_{2,t}/K_t$ and $K_{1,t}/K_t$, the logistic law remains intact, although the adaptation speed is higher than in the re-absorption phase. But the point is that the change in capital shares no longer drives structural change.

ACKNOWLEDGMENTS

Open access funding provided by University of Graz. I am very grateful to Heinz Kurz and Christian Gehrke for various valuable suggestions and discussions. I further express my appreciation to two anonymous referees for their helpful comments and recommendations. All remaining errors, misconceptions and inaccuracies are, of course, mine. An earlier version of this paper was presented at the 19th annual ESHET conference in Rome in May 2015. I gratefully acknowledge the financial support from the Austrian Science Fund (FWF): P24915-G11.

CONFLICT OF INTERESTS

The authors declare that they have no conflict of interest.

FUNDING

This study was funded by the Austrian Science Fund (P24915-G11).

REFERENCES

1. Dosi G, Fagiolo G, Roventini A (2010) Schumpeter meeting Keynes: A policyfriendly model of endogenous growth and business cycles. J Econ Dyn Control 34(9):1748–1767

2. Englmann F (1992) Innovation diffusion, employment and wage policy. J Evol Econ 2(3):179–193

3. Gilbert CG (2005) Unbundling the structure of inertia: Resource versus routine rigidity. Acad Manag J 48(5):741–763

4. Haas D (2015) Diffusion dynamics and creative destruction in a simple classical model. Metroeconomica 66(4):638–660

5. Hicks JR (1983) Classics and Moderns. Collected essays on economic theory, vol III. Blackwell, Oxford

6. Kalmbach P, Kurz HD (1992) Chips und Jobs. Zu den Beschäftigungswirkungen des Einsatzes programmgesteuerter Arbeitsmittel. Metropolis, Marburg

7. Kurz HD (2008) Innovations and profits: Schumpeter and the classical heritage. J Econ Behav Organ 67(1):263–278

8. Kurz HD (2010) Technical progress, capital accumulation and income distribution in classical economics: Adam Smith, David Ricardo and Karl Marx. The European Journal of the History of Economic Thought 17(5):1183–1222

9. Kurz HD (2015a) The beat of the economic heart. Joseph Schumpeter and Arthur Spiethoff on business cycles. J Evol Econ 25(1):147–162

10. Kurz HD (2015b) David Ricardo: On the art of elucidating economic principles in the face of a labyrinth of difficulties. European Journal of the History of Economic Thought 22(5):818–851

11. Kurz HD, Salvadori N (1995) Theory of production: a long-period analysis. Cambridge University Press, Cambridge

12. Metcalfe JS (1997) The evolutionary explanation of total factor productivity growth: Macro measurement and micro process. Revue d' économie industrielle 80 (1):93–114

13. Metcalfe JS (1998) Evolutionary economics and creative destruction The Graz Schumpeter Lectures. Routledge, London

14. Metcalfe JS (2008) Accounting for economic evolution: Fitness and the population method. J Bioecon 10(2):23–49

15. Metcalfe JS, Steedman I (2013) Exploring Schumpeterian dynamics: innovation, adaptation and growth. Evolutionary and Institutional Economics Review 10(2):149–178

16. Nelson R (1968) A diffusion model of international productivity differences in manufacturing industry. The Am Econ Rev 58(5):1219–1248

17. Nelson R, Pack H (1999) The Asian Miracle and modern growth theory. Econ J 109(457):416–436

18. Nelson R, Winter S (1982) An evolutionary theory of economic change. Cambridge, Belknap Press of Harvard University Press

19. Ricardo D (1951) The works and correspondence of David Ricardo, 11 vols, edited by Piero Sraffa with collaboration of Maurice H. Dobb. Cambridge University Press, Cambridge

20. Santangelo G (2003) The evolutionary perspective on growth. In: Salvadori N (ed) The theory of economic growth. A 'classical' perspective, Edward Elgar, Cheltenham, UK, Northhampton, pp 205–221

21. Schumpeter JA (1934). The theory of economic development: An inquiry into profits, capital, credit, interest, and the business cycle Transaction Books, New Brunswick

22. Schumpeter JA (1939) Business cycles. McGraw-Hill, New York

23. Schumpeter JA (2010 [1942]) Capitalism, socialism and democracy. Routledge, London

24. Silverberg G (1984) Embodied technical progress in a dynamic economic model: The Self-Organization paradigm. In: Goodwin R, Krüger M, Vercelli A (eds) Nonlinear models of fluctuating growth. Springer, Heidelberg, pp 192–208

25. Silverberg G, Verspagen B (2005) Evolutionary theorizing on economic growth. In: Dopfer K (ed) The evolutionary foundations of economics. Cambridge University Press, Cambridge, pp 506–539

26. Soete L, Turner R (1984) Technology diffusion and the rate of technical change. Econ J 94(375):612–623

27. Spiethoff A (1925) Krisen. Handwörterbuch der Staatswissenschaft 6(1):8–91

28. Steedman I (2001) Consumption takes time: Implications for economic theory The Graz Schumpeter Lectures. Routledge, London

2

MARKET CHOICES DRIVEN BY REFERENCE GROUPS. AN EVOLUTIONARY APPROACH

Michał Ramsza

Department of Mathematics and Mathematical Economics, Warsaw School of Economics, Al. Niepodległosci 162, Warsaw 02-554, Poland

ABSTRACT

The present paper tries to answer analytically how much the reference group influence can affect an actual market share of a particular brand or product. It is found that the increase of the size of a reference group and the probability of following the majority within the reference group may lead to the temporary modest prevalence of one brand. This result requires a relatively large size of a reference group and a high probability of following the majority within the reference group. If these conditions are not satisfied the effect on the market share is negligible.

Keywords: Reference groups influence, Population games, Learning

1 INTRODUCTION

The concept of a reference group and its potential influence on an individual has been know at least since the landmark publication of

Merton (1949), but its beginnings can be traced to Cooley (1902). A brief definition of a reference group is given in Park and Lessig (1977):

> "(...) a reference group is defined to be an actual or imaginary individual or group conceived of having significant relevance upon an individual's evaluations, aspirations, or behavior."

The present paper uses the concept of a reference group in a very broad sense as defined above. The general discussion regarding the concept of a reference group is beyond the scope of this paper. A brief discussion of the history of the concept of a reference group and its relevance can be found in Dawson and Chatman (2001).

This short note concerns the choices between two alternatives made within a large population. Suppose that each individual in the population uses a product of one of two alternative brands. Once in a while the product breaks and needs to be replaced with a new one. At this time, an individual tries to determine which brand is used by the majority of a population. He selects at random a group of k∈Nk∈N individuals. This group becomes his reference group. He chooses a brand used by the majority of those in the reference group with the probability $\alpha \in (0,1)$, referred to as the follow-up probability. This procedure is repeated in time and leads to fluctuations of the share of each brand in the market. The market share of the first brand at any given time t is denoted by $x(t) \in [0,1]$.

The two parameters, the size of a reference group k and the follow-up probability α, are exogenous. The size k of the reference group governs the precision of information that an individual gets while choosing a brand.[1] The follow-up probability α is the measure of affect's strength of an individual for the group. The strength of the influence of the group on the individual thus measures how strongly an individual wants to be associated with the majority of a population. The value $\alpha = 1/2$ is referred to as the neutral position — larger values indicate the positive attitude to the information, while lower values indicate the negative attitude to the information.

The main issue investigated in the present paper is the *isolated effect of the reference groups on the market share of a particular brand*. Specifically, there are two main points investigated. The first point concerns the existence and (local) stability of equilibrium. The second point concerns the dependence of equilibrium on the follow-up probability α and the size of a reference group k. It is shown that, depending on the follow-up probability, there are two distinct types of model behavior, i.e. the model is not structurally stable for any k. The (pitchfork) bifurcation occurs for relatively high values of the follow-up probability provided that the size of a reference group is small, which may be interpreted as the negligible effect of the reference group in certain circumstances.

The rest of the paper is organized in the following way. In Section 2, the model is constructed and analyzed. Section 3 offers discussion and conclusions.

2 THE MODEL AND ANALYSIS

2.1 The model

A large but finite population of a size N∈NN∈N of individuals is assumed. Each individual may choose one of two alternatives (brands). At each period $t = 0, \delta, 2\delta, \ldots$, where $\delta>0$, there is a fraction of the population using the first brand. This fraction, as mentioned above, is denoted by $x(t)$. The share of a population using the other brand is $1-x(t)$.

The learning algorithm employed by members of the population is very simple. At each period t, a single individual is selected at random.[2] This individual randomly chooses a group of k persons from the population, referred to as the reference group.[3] An individual in question determines which alternative is in the majority in a reference group and chooses this alternative with the probability $\alpha\in(0,1)$. The probability of following the majority in a reference group is called the follow-up probability. This process is repeated during every period.

In the above construction, the time is assumed to be discrete, $t = 0, \delta, 2\delta, \ldots$, and the size of a population N is finite. The state of a population can be described in several different ways, but because the model is concerned only with the market share of each brand, it is described by the share of a population $x(t)$ using the first brand. Given that the size of a population N is finite, the set of possible states of a population $\{0, 1/N, 2/N, \ldots, (N-1)/N, 1\}$ is also finite. The procedure of brand selection defines the transition probabilities between the states of a population. These probabilities are denoted by $p_{ij}(x)$, that is, $p_{ij}(x)$ is the probability that a single individual changes the brand from the i-th alternative to the j-th alternative, $i, j = 1,2$, given the state of a population x.

The above model is, in fact, a finite Markov chain. This Markov chain can be studied directly, but it is easier to consider a system of differential equations of the form

$$\begin{cases} \dot{x} = p_{21}(x) - p_{12}(x), \\ 1-\dot{x} = p_{12}(x) - p_{21}(x). \end{cases} \quad (1)$$

System (1) approximates[4] the average behavior of the Markov chain; cf. (Benaim and Weibull 2003). The induced system of differential Eqs. (1) is derived by taking the limit $N \to \infty$ with $\delta = 1/N$ but for the approximation to hold, it is enough to have the size N of a population finite and large enough.

The size k of a reference group defines, together with the follow-up probability α, the transition probabilities and is not related in any way to the size of a population but only to the state of a population, that is, as long as the state of a population is x and both k and α are fixed, then the size N of a population can be arbitrary. It is assumed only that N is larger than k. In fact, in the context of the background story, it is better to think of k as a much smaller number than the size N of a population.

It is clear that, for two alternatives, one of the equations in Eq. 1 can be dropped and from now on it is assumed that the second equation is dropped and only the following equation is used

$$\dot{x} = p_{21}(x) - p_{12}(x). \tag{2}$$

The intuition behind the Eq. 2 is that the change in the share of a population supporting the first alternative is the difference between the rate of inflow into the first alternative and the outflow from it. The approximation (2) is considered in continuous time and solutions take values in the interval [0,1]. However, for large N, the grid of states of the Markov chain is very dense and, with a slight abuse of notation, the same notation is used for both.[5]

2.2 Small reference group

For any given k, it is simple to calculate the probabilities $p_{ij}(x)$. However, for simplicity, it is assumed[6] in this section that $k = 3$. With this assumption the probability $p_{12}(x)$ reads

$$\begin{aligned} p_{12}(x) = x \Big(\alpha \left((1-x)^3 + 3(1-x)^2 x\right) \\ +(1-\alpha)\left(x^3 + 3(1-x)x^2\right)\Big) \end{aligned} \tag{3}$$

and the probability $p_{21}(x)$ reads

$$\begin{aligned} p_{21}(x) = (1-x)\Big(\alpha\left(x^3 + 3x^2(1-x)\right) \\ +(1-\alpha)\left((1-x)^3 + 3(1-x)^2 x\right)\Big). \end{aligned} \tag{4}$$

The probability p_{12} is the product of two probabilities. They are the probability that the supporter of the first alternative is selected and the conditional probability that the second alternative is followed. The probability that the supporter of the first alternative is selected, given the state x of a population, is simply x. The conditional probability that the second alternative is followed is the sum of probabilities of four events: every individual in the reference group uses the second alternative and the majority follows what happens with the probability $\alpha(1-x)^3$; two individuals in the reference group use the second alternative and the majority follows with the probability $\alpha 3(1-x)^2 x$; only one individual in the reference group uses the second alternative and the minority follows with the probability $(1-\alpha)3(1-x)x^2$; and finally all individuals in the reference group use the first alternative and the minority follows with the probability $(1-\alpha)(1-x)^3$.

Symmetrically, the probability p_{21} is also the product of two probabilities. They are the probability that the supporter of the second alternative is selected and the conditional probability that the first alternative is followed. In the considered model, it is assumed that the probability of following a given alternative is independent of the currently supported alternative. Thus, the conditional probability of following a given alternative is the same for both currently supported alternatives, i.e. the probabilities $p_{12}(x)$ and $p_{21}(x)$ differ only by the first term x and $(1-x)$, respectively, and switching every occurrence of α to $(1-\alpha)$ and the other way around.

Ultimately, given the above assumptions, the differential equation describing the evolution of the share $x(t)$ reads

$$\dot{x} = f(x) = (1-2x)\left(x^2(2\alpha-1) - x(2\alpha-1) + 1 - \alpha\right). \tag{5}$$

The first thing to notice about Eq. 5 is that the right hand side $f(x)$ is a polynomial. Thus, for any initial conditions, there is a unique solution defined for $t \geq 0$. Second, the interval [0,1], which is a projection of the two-dimensional simplex, is forward invariant because $f(0) = 1-\alpha > 0$ and $f(1) = \alpha - 1 < 0$.

For any follow-up probability α, there is an equilibrium x^a=1/2x^a=1/2 and because

$$\frac{df(\hat{x}^a)}{dx} = \frac{6}{2}\left(\alpha - \frac{5}{6}\right)$$

this equilibrium is stable for $\alpha < 5/6$ and unstable for $\alpha > 5/6$.

For $\alpha > 5/6$, there are two additional equilibria, namely

$$\hat{x}^b = \frac{1}{2} - \sqrt{\frac{5-6\alpha}{4(1-2\alpha)}} \quad \text{and} \quad \hat{x}^c = \frac{1}{2} + \sqrt{\frac{5-6\alpha}{4(1-2\alpha)}}.$$

Both equilibria are stable for $\alpha > 5/6$ because

$$\frac{df(\hat{x}^b)}{dx} = \frac{df(\hat{x}^c)}{dx} = 5 - 6\alpha < 0 \quad \text{for } \alpha > \frac{5}{6}.$$

At $\alpha_0 = 5/6$ a pitchfork bifurcation occurs.[7] Figure 1 shows the behavior of f for various values of the follow-up probability α and the bifurcation diagram for (5).

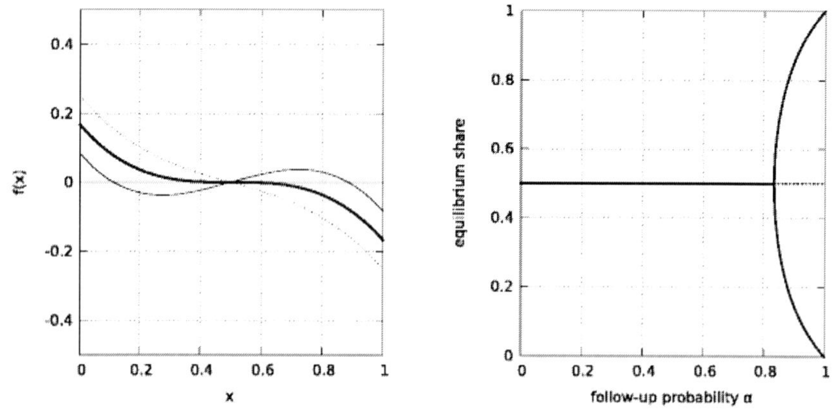

(a) Behavior of f for various values of α (b) Bifurcation diagram

Figure 1.a Behavior of f for various values of the follow-up probability α. The *dotted line* is for $\alpha = 9/12$, the *solid bold line* is for $\alpha = 5/6$ and the *thin solid line* is for $\alpha = 11/12$. **b** Bifurcation diagram for (5). *Solid lines* are for the stable equilibriums, the *dotted line* is for the unstable equilibrium

2.3 Large reference group

The analysis in the previous section is done for a small reference group where $k = 3$. The obvious question is what happens for larger values of $k>3$. It is possible to derive exact formulas for p_{ij} for any fixed k. However, the polynomials describing the probabilities of transitions become large and unwieldy very quickly. Therefore, it is easier to approximate these probabilities by the central limit theorem.

Let l be the number of people supporting the first alternative in a randomly selected reference group of a size k; l is a random variable following the binomial distribution with parameters k (a number of trials); and x is the probability of a success. Let w denote the probability that $l>k/2$, that is, w is the probability that the majority of individuals in the selected reference group supports the first alternative given the state of a population x. For large values of k, the probability w is approximated by the standard normal cumulative distribution function Φ as follows

$$\begin{aligned} w &= \Pr\left[l > \frac{k}{2}\right] = 1 - \Pr\left[l \le \frac{k}{2}\right] \\ &= 1 - \Pr\left[l - kx \le \frac{k}{2} - kx\right] \\ &= 1 - \Pr\left[\frac{l - kx}{\sqrt{kx(1-x)}} \le \frac{k/2 - kx}{\sqrt{kx(1-x)}}\right] \\ &\approx 1 - \Phi\left(\frac{k/2 - kx}{\sqrt{kx(1-x)}}\right) \\ &= 1 - \frac{1}{2}\left[1 + \operatorname{erf}\left(\frac{k/2 - kx}{\sqrt{2kx(1-x)}}\right)\right], \end{aligned} \tag{6}$$

where erf() is the standard error function, given as

$$\operatorname{erf}(x) = \frac{2}{\sqrt{\pi}} \int_0^x e^{-\tau^2} d\tau$$

and the approximation follows by the central limit theorem.

The transition probabilities are

$$\begin{aligned} p_{12}(x) &= x(\alpha(1-w) + (1-\alpha)w) \\ p_{21}(x) &= (1-x)(\alpha w + (1-\alpha)(1-w)). \end{aligned} \tag{7}$$

Taking into account (2), (6) and (7) the equation analogous to Eq. 5 reads

$$\dot{x} = g(x) = \left(\frac{1}{2} - x\right) + \left(\alpha - \frac{1}{2}\right)\operatorname{erf}\left(\frac{\sqrt{k}}{2\sqrt{2}}\,\frac{2x-1}{\sqrt{x(1-x)}}\right). \tag{8}$$

The right hand side of Eq. 8 is not defined for $x = 0$ or $x = 1$. However, the limits at these points are

$$\lim_{x\to 0^+} g(x) = 1 - \alpha > 0 \qquad \text{and} \qquad \lim_{x\to 1^-} g(x) = \alpha - 1 < 0.$$

These limits are taken as the values of $g(x)$ for $x = 0$ and $x = 1$. Since $g(0)>0$ and $g(1)<0$, the interval [0,1] is forward invariant under g. Also, g is a C^1 function. Thus, for any initial condition, there exists a unique solution defined for $t \geq 0$.

For any $\alpha \in (0,1)$, there is an equilibrium x^a=1/2x^a=1/2 because erf(0)=0. The derivative at $x = 1/2$ reads

$$\frac{dg(x)}{dx} = \frac{(2\alpha - 1)\sqrt{k}\, e^{\frac{k(1-2x)^2}{8(x-1)x}}}{4\sqrt{2\pi}(-(x-1)x)^{3/2}} - 1 \quad \text{and} \quad \frac{dg(1/2)}{dx} = \sqrt{\frac{2}{\pi}}(2\alpha - 1)\sqrt{k} - 1.$$

Further, $dg(1/2)/dx = 0$ for

$$\alpha_0 = \frac{1}{4}\left(\frac{\sqrt{2\pi}}{\sqrt{k}} + 2\right).$$

For $\alpha < \alpha_0$, the equilibrium x^ax^a is stable and, for $\alpha > \alpha_0$, the equilibrium x^ax^a is unstable. At α_0, the pitchfork bifurcation occurs.[8]

The behavior of a model for large reference groups is qualitatively identical to the simple model with $k = 3$. However, the particular value of the critical follow-up probability α_0 depends crucially on the size of a reference group. The larger the reference group, the smaller the critical follow-up probability α_0. Eventually, for $k \to \infty$, the critical follow-up probability would converge[9] to 1/2. Figure 2a shows the behavior of g for various values of α and $k = 20$. Figure 2b shows the dependence of α_0 on the size of a reference group.

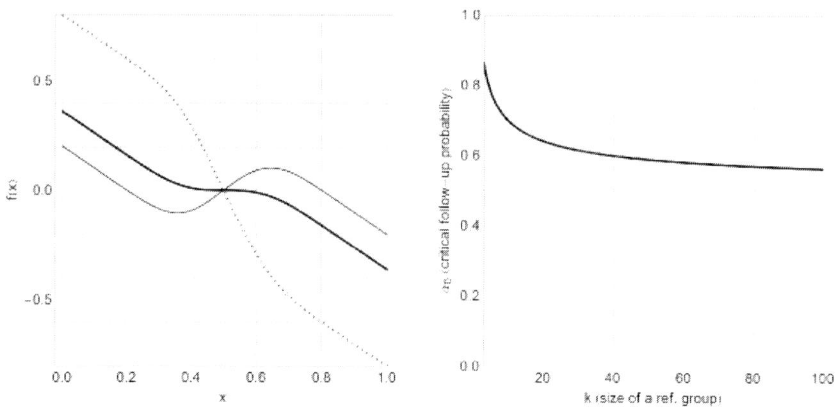

(a) Behavior of g for various values of α **(b) Critical follow-up probability**

Figure 2.a Behavior of g for various values of the follow-up probability α. The *dotted line* is for $\alpha = 2/10$, the *solid bold line* is for $\alpha = \alpha_0$ and the *thin solid line* is for $\alpha = 8/10$. All plots for $k = 20$. **b** Behavior of the critical follow-up probability α_0 with respect to the cardinality of the reference group k

3 DISCUSSION AND CONCLUSIONS

The presented model is concerned solely with the isolated effect of the assumed algorithm of choosing a brand. As a result, any potential characteristics differentiating the brands are not part of the model and, consequently, the results are symmetric about the equal split of a market between two brands. The results of a model should be interpreted as the potential edge that one brand can have due only to the reference group influence and not the actual preferences of population's members, since those are absent from the model. The main result of the model is that this potential edge should be relatively small if the size of a reference group is small and the follow-up probability is not too large. This behavior results from the imprecise information from the reference group and is amplified if an individual is not certain how to act upon the information.

It is very important to remember that the differential Eqs. 5 and 8, for k = 3 and k>3, respectively, are only approximations to the actual Markov chain. It is clear that the Markov chain approximated by the Eqs. 5 or 8 is ergodic for any $\alpha \in (0,1)$ and so there is a unique stationary distribution depending on k and α. This stationary distribution is symmetric about x = 1/2. For $\alpha < \alpha_0$, the stationary distribution is a single peak distribution. For $\alpha > \alpha_0$, the stationary distribution becomes a bimodal distribution with peaks aligned with the stable equilibria of a differential equation. As the value of a follow-up probability $\alpha \to 1$, these peaks converge to 0 and 1. For $\alpha = 1$, these states of the Markov chain are absorbing.

The interpretation of these results is the following. The market share of the first brand fluctuates around $x = 1/2$ as long as $\alpha < \alpha_0$, with increasing variance for $\alpha \to \alpha_0$. Once this critical value of α is crossed, the behavior changes. Any realization of the Markov chain spends most of the time near the stable equilibria of a differential equation, with occasional switches between them. The time spent near one of the equilibria depends on the size N of a population. The larger is N, the longer the time[10] spent near the equilibrium before switching to the other equilibrium.

The setup of the presented model is somewhat similar to other models, in particular to the models where the population is identified with the set of nodes of a graph and the reference group of a player (node) is then identified with the set of its neighbors, as in DeGroot (1974), Watts (2002) or Acemoglu et al. (2011). The present model also can be fitted within this general setup, provided that the graph is the Poisson graph[11] with the average degree equal to the size of a reference group. In this setting, Eqs. 5 and 8 are usually referred to as the mean-field equations or the master equation; cf. (Helbing 1995).

There are two modeling choices made in the present paper. The first concerns the random choice of a reference group. This is the typical choice for evolutionary game theory, population learning theory and other similar models such as the ones mentioned before. It allows for rigorous analytical analysis of the model. The compromise is the structure of a network of connections and the type of results (average behavior) that can be achieved. The random choice procedure used in the model can be thought of as reflecting an individual observing other randomly selected people and choosing a brand accordingly.

The second modeling choice concerns the follow-up probability. There are other choices possible, e.g. the threshold rule used in Watts (2002), best-reply type rules or rules based on imitations. All these rules have one thing in common: they do not allow for innovations in the sense that, if all members of a population use the same brand, then every individual making the switch decision chooses the brand used by all members of a population.[12] In terms of the Markov chain, it means that these two states (everyone uses the first brand and everyone uses the second brand) are absorbing (and consequently asymptotically stable equilibria).

The concept of a reference group is used in the present paper in a very broad sense as introduced in Section 1. The speculations on the precise meaning of the presented model for theoretical sociology and economics is left for future research. It is, however, clear that, in the light of recent papers such as Kramer et al. (2014), it is important to try to understand if it is possible to construct and to provide a product that, through the manipulation of the follow-up probability, can swing the brand shares in favor of a particular brand.

Ultimately, the main insight from the presented model is the interplay between the precision of information and the strength of reaction to this information. If the information is not precise (small k), then, even for a relatively strong reaction (large α), the result for the market share is slim (realizations of the Markov chain wander about $x = 1/2$). It takes precise information and a strong reaction in a large population to influence the market share of a given brand for a longer time. Whether this can be achieved in reality is not clear at this time.[13]

FOOTNOTES

[1] The parameter k is essentially the sample size. The larger the sample size, the more precise information about the majority in the general population that can be obtained by an individual. For small k, there is high probability that the majority within a sample is different than the majority in a general population.

[2] This is the standard setting for evolutionary game theory and the theory of learning in population games. In the context of the presented model, the choices of individuals are done when a device being used breaks. For all individuals, these events may be modeled by independent Poisson processes. Thus the probability that two devices break at the same time is zero. Consequently, at any given time, there is only a single individual making a decision.

[3] It is assumed that the reference group is selected at random at each time, which is typical for evolutionary game theory. The main reason for this assumption is that it makes the analytical analysis of the model

possible. More detailed discussion of this assumption is postponed to Section 3.

[4]The thorough explanation of the relation between solutions of the system (1) and realizations of the Markov chain is certainly out of the scope of the present paper; cf. (Benaim and Weibull 2003). Consider the solution of the system (1) and a realization of the Markov chain both starting from the same state. It can be shown that, for any ϵ and any time interval, there exists the size of the population N large enough that the probability of a realization of the Markov chain deviating from the deterministic solution of the system (1) by more than ϵ is arbitrary small. (Cf. (Benaim and Weibull 2003), p. 880, Lemma 1.) The basic intuition behind this result is that, in a single step of the Markov chain, the average change in shares is exactly $(p_{21}(x)-p_{12}(x))/N$. The actual realization in a single step differs from this value (since it is always $\pm 1/N$) but for large populations, this difference is arbitrary small. If the probabilities $p_{ij}(x)$ are continuous in x, then the propagation of the difference between the actual realization of the Markov chain and the system of differential equations is mitigated because the values of $p_{ij}(x)$ do not change too much if the values of x do not change much and, with high probability, a realization of the Markov chain remains in a vicinity of the solution of the deterministic system of differential equations.

Consider the realization of the Markov chain starting from a state in a neighborhood of a stable equilibrium of the system (1). It can be shown that the probability of the exit time from the neighborhood being smaller than some time t is arbitrary small for the appropriately large size of the population. In other words, the realizations of the Markov chain will stay arbitrary long in a vicinity of a stable equilibrium of the system (1). (Cf. (Benaim and Weibull 2003), p. 895, Lemma 3.) It can be also shown that, for large populations, the Markov chain almost surely spends almost all the time, in the long run, in the vicinity of a set of stable equilibria of the system (1) or, more precisely, in the intersection of the finite (but very dense) grid of states of the Markov chain and the neighborhood of the set of stable equilibria of (1). (Cf. (Benaim and Weibull 2003), p. 884, Proposition 4.) It is much harder to provide a precise intuition behind those results because they require definitions of certain mathematical objects that are beyond the scope of this paper.

[5]However, in Section 3, a clear distinction is made between the approximation and the actual Markov chain.

[6]For $k = 1$, the model is even simpler but it lacks any interesting features. Any realization of the Markov chain for any $\alpha < 1$ wanders about $x = 1/2$ and increasing α leads to increasing volatility. For $k = 2$, the results are identical (the transition probabilities are identical). The value $k = 3$ is the lowest value that produces the behavior observed for all higher values of k.

[7]The Eq. 5 can be rewritten as

$$\dot{z} = -z\left(z^2 + \frac{5-6\alpha}{2}\right),$$

where $z = (x - 1/2)\sqrt{4\alpha - 2}$. Formal proof is moved to Appendix A.

[8]Formal proof is moved to Appendix A.

[9]The differential equation (8) is an approximation, the better the larger the size N of the population. It is assumed that $k < N$, so technically the limit of α_0 as $k \to \infty$ is only possible once the limit $N \to \infty$ has been taken. However, in the context of the background story, only relatively small values of k are considered and the limit is just provided for completeness.

[10]Using formulas from (Benaim and Weibull 2003, p. 895, Lemma 3), we know that the average exit time from the neighborhood of an equilibrium is longer than $\exp(\gamma N)/4-1$ for some positive constant $\gamma>0$ not depending on N.

[11]The Poisson graph is the type of a random graph introduced in a series of papers (Erdos and Renyi 1959; 1960; 1961).

[12]For rules based on the best-reply mapping, a payoff function must associate higher payoffs with the brand used by the majority of a population (leading essentially to the coordination game).

[13]There are other questions concerning ethical and legal issues. Also, it is not quite clear if it is possible to manipulate the follow-up probability, despite the claims made in Kramer et al. (2014).

REFERENCES

1. Acemoglu D, Dahleh MA, Lobel I, Ozdaglar A (2011) Bayesian learning in social networks. Rev Econ Stud 78:1201–1236
2. Benaim M, Weibull JW (2003) Deterministic approximation of stochastic evolution in games. Econometrica 71:873–903
3. Cooley CH (1902) Human nature and the social order. Schocken Books, New York. (reprint)
4. Dawson EM, Chatman EA (2001) Reference group theory with implications for information studies: a theoretical essay. Information Research 6, (available at, http://www.informationr.net/ir/6-3/paper105.html)

5. DeGroot MH (1974) Reaching a consensus. J Am Stat Assoc 69:118–121

6. Erdos P, Renyi A (1959) On random graphs. Publ Math 6:290–97

7. Erdos P, Renyi A (1960) On the evolution of random graphs. Publ Math Inst Hung Acad Sci 5:17–61

8. Erdos P, Renyi A (1961) On the strength of connectedness of a random graph. Acta Math Acad Sci Hung 12:261–67

9. Helbing D (1995) Quantitative sociodynamics. Stochastic methods and models of social interaction procesess. Kluwer Academic Publishers

10. Kramer ADI, Guillory JE, Hancock JT (2014) Experimental evidence of massive-scale emotional contagion through social networks. Proc Natl Acad Sci USA 111:8788–8790

11. Merton RK (ed) (1949) Social theory and social structure. Free Press, New York

12. Park CW, Lessig VP (1977) Students and housewives: Differences in susceptibility to reference group influence. J Consum Res 4:102–110

13. Watts DJ (2002) A simple model of global cascades on random networks. Proc Natl Acad Sci USA 99:5766–5771

14. Wiggins S (2003) Introduction to applied nonlinear dynamical systems and chaos. Springer

3

DEPARTMENT OF MATHEMATICS AND MATHEMATICAL ECONOMICS, WARSAW SCHOOL OF ECONOMICS, AL. NIEPODLEGŁOSCI 162, WARSAW 02-554, POLAND

André Lorentz[1] · Maria Savona[2]

[1] Evolutionary Economics Group, Max Planck Institute of Economics, Kahlaische Strasse 10, 07745 Jena, Germany

[2] Faculté des Sciences Economiques et Sociales, Université Lille 1, Lille, France

ABSTRACT

The paper aims to account for the empirical stylized facts related to changes in sectoral structures that have led to the growth of services in most advanced countries over recent decades. A growth model with evolutionary micro–founded structural change is developed, which formalizes the role of technical change and changes in intermediate demand as they affect the evolution of the sectoral composition of the economy and macro-economic growth. The simulated results are based on the use of the actual data, including Input–Output coefficients in the case of Germany. Three scenarios are identified, which account for the effects of a set of key parameters on changes in the structure of the economy.

Keywords: Economic growth, Structural change, Growth of services, Evolutionary micro–foundatio, nInput–output

The authors are grateful to M. Valente for suggestions and technical advice. The paper benefited from comments and suggestions from E. Andersen, R. Schettkat, U. Witt and participants in the 11th International J.A. Schumpeter Society Conference held in Nice in 2006, and those of two anonymous referees. This work was carried out during Maria Savona's stay at BETA, Université Louis Pasteur, Strasbourg as a *Centre National de la Recherche Scientifique* Post-doc Fellow. The usual disclaimers apply.

1 INTRODUCTION

The debate around the determinants and economic impact of tertiarization is age–old (Fisher 1935, 1945; Clark 1940) and has always been somewhat controversial. On the one hand, the 'optimists' (for instance Fourastié 1949) looked at the growing employment share of services as being an indicator of a further stage of development in advanced economies following mass industrialization, as well as a symptom of an increasing income– and consumption– capacity. On the other hand, a later, large community of 'sceptical' scholars (Baumol and Bowen 1966; Baumol 1967; Kaldor 1966; Fuchs 1968) pointed to the 'collateral effects' of the growth of services in terms of de–industrialization, which translated into (s)lower aggregate productivity growth.

Since the beginning of this debate, the growth of services has become an empirical stylized fact, which represents the most relevant case of change in the economic structure. (For a recent reassessment, see Parrinello 2004; Schettkat and Yocarini 2006). Yet, it is still the object of lively debate, as far as its determinants are concerned.

A recent collection of contributions on the economics of services (ten Raa and Schettkat 2001) in fact refers to the 'service paradox' as a still unresolved issue in the economic literature. (See also Appelbaum and Schettkat 1999; Baumol 2001; Pugno 2006). The 'paradox' consists of the empirical fact that advanced economies are still experiencing sustained growth rates in real output and employment in the service industries, despite the trend towards increasing input costs and prices.

Baumol recently confirmed his position with respect to the 'service paradox' (p.1 Baumol 2008):

> I have repeatedly argued that the rising real prices that constitute the cost disease that is named in my honour cannot

> force society to give up the patterns of consumption to which it is habituated and that it prefers now or used to. Neither health care nor education are condemned to deterioration in quality and decline in quantity by their rising real prices. For the nearly universal phenomenon of rising productivity means we *can* afford them, indeed, that we can even afford steady expansion in the amounts supplied and consumed, despite their disturbingly persistent and substantial rates of cost increase.

Further, he points to the very essence of the process of structural change– cross-sectoral differences in productivity growth rates – by reformulating the concept of 'cost disease' named in his honor in terms of 'Baumol's Fourth Tautology' (Baumol 2008):

> 'Since rates of labour–saving productivity growth are uneven, the growth in some activities *must* be below average'

Baumol refers to the two specific empirical facts that represent the main drivers of tertiarization processes. On the one hand patterns of (final) consumption of services have been shown to be rather price–inelastic. On the other hand, the uneven rate of productivity gains across sectors are behind the existence of a 'paradox'.

Indeed, since the debate around tertiarization started, the growth of real output shares in services has been mainly attributed to shifts in private domestic consumption, which in turn has been claimed to be mainly sustained by a positive income effect, more than compensating for a negative price effect. However, the demand for services overall has been steadily growing, whereas average real income growth rates have been slightly declining from the mid–1970s onwards (ten Raa and Schettkat 2001). As a consequence, ten Raa and Schettkat (2001) refer to what they call a more general 'change in demand conditions', which is claimed to dominate over the pure income and price effects in driving the 'service paradox'.

The 'service paradox', and particularly the black box of the 'change in demand conditions', is likely to be related to changes in the composition of intermediate demand. These latter might complement—and in some case dominate—the role of income– and price–led changes in final demand in accounting for structural change. The 'change in demand conditions'—namely the role of intermediate demand—is argued here to be overlooked in the Baumolian and post–Baumolian literature.

More generally, much effort has been devoted in the empirical literature to the identification of the sources of structural change, particularly in the contributions in the Input–Output (I–O) tradition, starting with Leontief (1951) and Leontief (1953). Within the I–O framework, and in the economic literature more generally (Pasinetti 1973, 1981), a full empirical account of structural economic change relies on the assessment of changes in sectoral interdependencies.

In line with this literature, in earlier work (Savona and Lorentz 2005) we decomposed sectoral output growth into the relative contribution of changes in intermediate coefficients and final domestic and foreign demand. We applied an I–O Structural Decomposition Analysis (SDA) technique[1] to 13 selected macro-branches of the economy over the period from the end of the 1960s to the end of the 1990s for four Organisation for Economic Co-operation and Development (OECD) countries (Germany, Netherlands, UK and US).

The empirical evidence thereby identified can be summarized as follows:

- Real output growth since the beginning of the 1970s in most of the OECD countries has been positive for most of the service branches considered, and particularly for the Knowledge Intensive Business Services (KIBS).[2] Further, this seems not to have crowded out the manufacturing branches, except in the UK and USA, between the end of the 1970s and the beginning of the 1980s.

- The contribution of changes in intermediate coefficients to real output growth is much higher for service than manufacturing branches. The sources of structural change leading to growth in services are linked to both intermediate and final demand, whereas the output growth of manufacturing branches is mainly due to final (private and public) consumption. Unlike what has occurred in manufacturing branches, foreign demand has played a marginal role in the output growth of services, and this trend continued in the 1990s.

Our empirical findings are in line with those in recent work on the relative contribution of KIBS to aggregate performance, in terms of both output and productivity growth (van Ark et al. 2002; Peneder et al. 2003; Cainelli et al. 2006; Kox and Rubalcaba 2007). This supports our main conjecture that the role of changes in intermediate demand in driving the most dramatic changes in the sectoral structure of developed economies has been overlooked throughout the long debate on tertiarization, and particularly within the Baumolian literature.

The present work aims to reconcile the two-sided extended debate on the determinants of tertiarization, by considering ‘Baumol’s disease’ as one possible—and time-specific—scenario, among others. To do so, we start from the ‘service paradox’ and the empirical stylized fact identified above, and account for the main sources of structural change of the economy by considering the role of technological change and changes in intermediate demand. To achieve this, we develop a formal model of economic growth with evolutionary micro-founded structural change.

The model developed is in line with attempts to embrace, within a unifying framework, both neo-Schumpeterian[3] and Keynesian lines of thought in explaining economic growth (Verspagen 1993, 2002, 2004; Fagerberg 1994; Montobbio 2002).

The model extends that proposed in Llerena and Lorentz (2004) by providing an evolutionary micro-foundation for structural change in the economy. First, we provide a micro–foundation for the Kaldorian Cumulative Causation mechanism (Kaldor 1957, 1966).[4] Second, we account for (demand–related) macro-constraints as affecting the micro-behavior of firms when adopting technology. Further, we account for the mechanisms transmitting the effects of micro-behavior on aggregate growth, via changes in the intermediate linkages.

The remainder of the paper is organized as follows. Section 2 develops a model of economic growth with evolutionary micro–founded structural change. In Section 3 we explain the methodology employed to simulate the model (Section 3.1); we identify three simulation scenarios (Section 3.2) and finally discuss the simulation results, the coherence between the empirical evidence found for the case of Germany and the simulated results (Section 3.3). Finally, Section 4 summarizes the main findings, draws some conclusions and proposes directions for future research.

2 A MODEL OF EVOLUTIONARY MICRO-FOUNDED STRUCTURAL CHANGE

2.1 The macro–economic framework

Drawing on an I–O framework (Leontief 1951), we decompose the sectoral output ($Y_{j,t}$) into three components: intermediate consumption ($I_{j,t}$), final domestic consumption ($C_{j,t}$) and (net) foreign final consumption ($X_{j,t} - M_{j,t}$). The aggregate output is therefore a function of the sectoral structure of the economy, which in turn is determined by the intermediate and final components of demand.

$$\begin{pmatrix} Y_{1,t} \\ \vdots \\ Y_{j,t} \\ \vdots \\ Y_{J,t} \end{pmatrix} = \begin{pmatrix} I_{1,t} \\ \vdots \\ I_{j,t} \\ \vdots \\ I_{J,t} \end{pmatrix} + \begin{pmatrix} C_{1,t} \\ \vdots \\ C_{j,t} \\ \vdots \\ C_{J,t} \end{pmatrix} + \begin{pmatrix} X_{1,t} \\ \vdots \\ X_{j,t} \\ \vdots \\ X_{J,t} \end{pmatrix} - \begin{pmatrix} M_{1,t} \\ \vdots \\ M_{j,t} \\ \vdots \\ M_{J,t} \end{pmatrix} \qquad (1)$$

Intermediate consumption for sector j is defined as the sum of the firms' demand of sector $j$product and is characterised as follows:

$$I_{j,t} = \sum_{k=1}^{J} Y^D_{j,k,t} = \sum_{k=1}^{J} a_{j,k,t} Y_{k,t} \tag{2}$$

where $Y^D_{j,k,t}$ represents the demand for sector j products by the sector k; $Y_{k,t}$ represents the level of production in sector k, and the coefficients $a_{j,k,t}$ are computed as follows:

$$a_{j,k,t} = \sum_{i} z_{k,i,t} a_{j,k,i,t} \tag{3}$$

where $z_{k,i,t}$ represents the market share of firm i belonging to sector k; market shares are defined by Eq. 18 and $a_{j,k,i,t}$ represents the coefficient of intermediate consumption of firm i (belonging to sector k) for sector j products.

The vector I_t of intermediate consumption can therefore be represented as follows:

$$\mathbf{I_t} \equiv \begin{pmatrix} I_{1,t} \\ \vdots \\ I_{j,t} \\ \vdots \\ I_{J,t} \end{pmatrix} = \begin{pmatrix} a_{1,1,t} & \dots & a_{1,k,t} & \dots & a_{1,J,t} \\ \vdots & \ddots & & & \vdots \\ a_{j,1,t} & \dots & a_{j,k,t} & \dots & a_{j,J,t} \\ \vdots & & & \ddots & \vdots \\ a_{J,1,t} & \dots & a_{J,k,t} & \dots & a_{J,J,t} \end{pmatrix} \begin{pmatrix} Y_{1,t} \\ \vdots \\ Y_{k,t} \\ \vdots \\ Y_{J,t} \end{pmatrix} \tag{4}$$

Final consumption is a function of the aggregate real income level. Final consumption for sector j ($C_{j,t}$) is a share $c_{j,t}$ of the aggregate real income level:

$$C_{j,t} = c_{j,t} Y_t \tag{5}$$

Real income is linked to real GDP and is given by the sum of sectoral nominal output deflated by the aggregate price index. The level of consumption devoted to each sector j can therefore be expressed as follows:

$$C_{j,t} = c_{j,t} \sum_{k=1}^{J} \frac{p_{k,t}}{\bar{p}_{t-1}} Y_{k,t}$$

where \(\bar{p}_{t-1}\) represents the aggregate price index.[5] The vector C_t of final consumption is computed as follows:

$$\mathbf{C_t} \equiv \begin{pmatrix} C_{1,t} \\ \vdots \\ C_{j,t} \\ \vdots \\ C_{J,t} \end{pmatrix} = \begin{pmatrix} c_{1,t}\frac{p_{1,t}}{\bar{p}_{t-1}} & \cdots & c_{1,t}\frac{p_{k,t}}{\bar{p}_{t-1}} & \cdots & c_{1,t}\frac{p_{J,t}}{\bar{p}_{t-1}} \\ \vdots & \ddots & & & \vdots \\ c_{j,t}\frac{p_{1,t}}{\bar{p}_{t-1}} & \cdots & c_{j,t}\frac{p_{k,t}}{\bar{p}_{t-1}} & \cdots & c_{j,t}\frac{p_{J,t}}{\bar{p}_{t-1}} \\ \vdots & & & \ddots & \vdots \\ c_{J,t}\frac{p_{1,t}}{\bar{p}_{t-1}} & \cdots & c_{J,t}\frac{p_{k,t}}{\bar{p}_{t-1}} & \cdots & c_{J,t}\frac{p_{J,t}}{\bar{p}_{t-1}} \end{pmatrix} \begin{pmatrix} Y_{1,t} \\ \vdots \\ Y_{k,t} \\ \vdots \\ Y_{J,t} \end{pmatrix} \tag{6}$$

For each sector the level of imports $(M_{j,t})$ corresponds to a share $m_{j,t}$ of the total domestic demand of the sector $(I_{j,t} + C_{j,t})$. This share can be a proxy for the international competitiveness of the economy. Sectoral net exports are defined as follows:

$$X_{j,t} - M_{j,t} = X_{j,t} - m_{j,t}(I_{j,t} + C_{j,t})$$

Using Eqs. 4 and 6 we define the vector of net exports $(X_t - Mt)$ as follows:

$$\mathbf{X_t} - \mathbf{M_t} \equiv \begin{pmatrix} X_{1,t} \\ \vdots \\ X_{J,t} \end{pmatrix} - \begin{pmatrix} m_{1,t}\left(a_{1,1,t} + c_{1,t}\frac{p_{1,t}}{\bar{p}_{t-1}}\right) & \cdots & m_{1,t}\left(a_{1,J,t} + c_{1,t}\frac{p_{J,t}}{\bar{p}_{t-1}}\right) \\ \vdots & \ddots & \vdots \\ m_{J,t}\left(a_{J,1,t} + c_{J,t}\frac{p_{1,t}}{\bar{p}_{t-1}}\right) & \cdots & m_{J,t}\left(a_{J,J,t} + c_{1,t}\frac{p_{J,t}}{\bar{p}_{t-1}}\right) \end{pmatrix} \times \begin{pmatrix} Y_{1,t} \\ \vdots \\ Y_{J,t} \end{pmatrix} \tag{7}$$

By substituting Eqs. 4, 6 and 7 in Eq. 1, we obtain the following expression for the vector of sectoral demand:

$$\begin{pmatrix} Y_{1,t} \\ \vdots \\ Y_{j,t} \\ \vdots \\ Y_{J,t} \end{pmatrix} = \begin{pmatrix} \alpha_{1,1,t} & \cdots & \alpha_{1,k,t} & \cdots & \alpha_{1,J,t} \\ \vdots & \ddots & & & \vdots \\ \alpha_{k,1,t} & \cdots & \alpha_{j,k,t} & \cdots & \alpha_{k,J,t} \\ \vdots & & & \ddots & \vdots \\ \alpha_{J,1,t} & \cdots & \alpha_{1,k,t} & \cdots & \alpha_{J,J,t} \end{pmatrix} \begin{pmatrix} Y_{1,t} \\ \vdots \\ Y_{k,t} \\ \vdots \\ Y_{J,t} \end{pmatrix} + \begin{pmatrix} X_{1,t} \\ \vdots \\ X_{j,t} \\ \vdots \\ X_{J,t} \end{pmatrix} \tag{8}$$

with

$$\alpha_{j,k,t} = (1 - m_{j,t})\left(a_{j,k,t} + c_{j,t}\frac{p_{k,t}}{\bar{p}_{t-1}}\right)$$

We obtain the reduced form of our model from this last equation, assuming the short-run macroeconomic identity holds:

$$\begin{pmatrix} Y_{1,t} \\ \vdots \\ Y_{j,t} \\ \vdots \\ Y_{J,t} \end{pmatrix} = \begin{pmatrix} 1-\alpha_{1,1,t} & \dots & -\alpha_{1,k,t} & \dots & -\alpha_{1,J,t} \\ \vdots & \ddots & & & \vdots \\ -\alpha_{k,1,t} & \dots & 1-\alpha_{j,k,t} & \dots & -\alpha_{k,J,t} \\ \vdots & & & \ddots & \vdots \\ -\alpha_{J,1,t} & \dots & -\alpha_{1,k,t} & \dots & 1-\alpha_{J,J,t} \end{pmatrix}^{-1} \begin{pmatrix} X_{1,t} \\ \vdots \\ X_{k,t} \\ \vdots \\ X_{J,t} \end{pmatrix} \quad (9)$$

The vector of sectoral demand, therefore, is obtained as a function of the demand parameters only, given in the short–run (but evolving over time), and of exports. The latter are assumed to be exogenously defined.

2.2 The micro–behaviors

At the micro–level firm output is determined by its share of sectoral demand. The production technology of a firm consists of a combination of products from all sectors (including the one to which the firm belongs) and labor, as defined by the production function (Eq. 10).

The labor productivity dynamics for each firm are assumed to follow a Kaldor–Verdoorn Law (Verdoorn 1949; Kaldor 1966). A technological shock is represented by changes in firms' labor productivity, on the basis of a Kaldor–Verdoorn mechanism and, simultaneously, by changes in the structure of the intermediate coefficients.

A firm i active in sector k is defined by the following production function:

$$Y_{k,i,t} = min\left(\frac{1}{a_{1,k,i,t}} Y^{D}_{1,k,i,t}, \dots, \frac{1}{a_{j,k,i,t}} Y^{D}_{k,k,i,t}, \dots, \frac{1}{a_{J,k,i,t}} Y^{D}_{J,k,i,t}, A_{k,i,t} L_{k,i,t}\right) \quad (10)$$

The level of production of firm i in sector k is defined as a share $z_{k,i,t}$ of sector k's demand:

$$Y_{k,i,t} = z_{k,i,t} Y_{k,t} \quad (11)$$

The level of demand from firm i for sector j products is therefore defined as follows:

$$Y^{D}_{j,k,i,t} = a_{j,k,i,t} Y_{k,i,t} \quad (12)$$

The demand for labor expressed by firm i is defined as follows:

$$L_{k,i,t} = \frac{Y_{k,i,t}}{A_{k,i,t}} \tag{13}$$

$A_{k,i,t}$ represents the labor productivity of firm i.

Technical change at the level of the firm consists of changes in labor productivity (Eq. 14), and by changes in the coefficient of intermediate demand ($a_{j,k,i,t}$).

Labor productivity dynamics are represented as follows:

$$\frac{\Delta A_{k,i,t}}{A_{k,i,t-1}} = \beta_k + \lambda_k \frac{\Delta Y_{k,i,t}}{Y_{k,i,t-1}} \tag{14}$$

The changes in intermediate demand coefficients are assumed to be stochastic. Changes in intermediate coefficients are formally represented by the following algorithm:

1.Firms draw a number from a Uniform distribution on [0 ; 1].

2.If this number is contained in the interval [0 ; σ], a technological shock occurs. σ is the fixed probability of a technological shock occurring.

3.If a technological shock occurs, every coefficient changes according to the following procedure:

$$a'_{j,k,i,t} = a_{j,k,i,t-1} + \epsilon_{j,k,i,t} \tag{15}$$

$$\epsilon_{j,k,i,t} \sim N(0; \rho) \tag{16}$$

where ρ is a given.

The new set of coefficients $(a'_{1,k,i,t}, \ldots, a'_{j,k,i,t}, \ldots, a'_{J,k,i,t})$ is introduced in the production function if the potential unitary cost is lower then the actual unitary cost ($\kappa_{k,i,t}$):

$$(a_{1,k,i,t+1}, \ldots, a_{J,k,i,t+1}) = \begin{cases} (a'_{1,k,i,t}, \ldots, a'_{j,k,i,t}, \ldots, a'_{J,k,i,t}) & \text{If } \sum_{j=1}^{J} a'_{j,k,i,t} p_{j,t} < \kappa_{k,i,t} \\ (a_{1,k,i,t}, \ldots, a_{j,k,i,t}, \ldots, a_{J,k,i,t}) & \text{Otherwise} \end{cases} \tag{17}$$

The market share of firm i is defined by a replicator dynamic, as follows:

$$z_{k,i,t} = z_{k,i,t-1}\left(1 + \phi\left(\frac{E_{k,i,t}}{E_{k,t}} - 1\right)\right) \tag{18}$$

where $E_{k,i,t}$ and $E_{k,t}$ respectively, represent the level of competitiveness of firm i and the average competitiveness in sector k. Each firm's competitiveness level is defined as the inverse of the firm's price level:

$$E_{k,i,t} = \frac{1}{p_{k,i,t}} \tag{19}$$

Firms set prices, applying a mark-up ($\mu_{k,i}$) on their unitary production costs ($\kappa_{k,i,t}$). These latter are defined as:

$$\kappa_{k,i,t} = \sum_{j=1}^{J} a_{j,k,i,t}\, p_{j,t} + \frac{w_{k,t}}{A_{k,i,t}} \tag{20}$$

where $p_{j,t}$ represents the average price in sector j :

$$p_{j,t} = \sum_{i} z_{j,i,t}\, p_{j,i,t}$$

and $w_{k,t}$ is the wage rate applied in sector k at time t. Firms set prices as follows:

$$p_{k,i,t} = 1 + \mu_{k,i}\left(\sum_{j=1}^{J} a_{j,k,i,t}\, p_{j,t} + \frac{w_{k,t}}{A_{k,i,t}}\right) \tag{21}$$

Wages are set at sectoral level. For a given sector k, the wage dynamic is correlated with sector k productivity[6] growth rate $\left(\frac{\Delta A_{k,t}}{A_{k,t-1}}\right)$ right)\) as well as with the aggregate productivity growth rate $\left(\frac{\Delta A_{t}}{A_{t-1}}\right)$ The effect of these two variables on wage dynamics is weighted by the parameter $\nu \in [0;1]$, such that :

- When $\nu = 1$, the wage dynamics in each sector depend on the macro-level productivity growth rate (i.e. as a centralized wage negotiation system);

- When $v = 0$, the wage dynamics in each sector depend on the sector–level productivity growth rate (i.e. as a sectoral wage negotiation system);
- The wage dynamic of sector k is defined as:

$$\frac{\Delta w_{k,t}}{w_{k,t-1}} = v\frac{\Delta A_t}{A_{t-1}} + (1-v)\frac{\Delta A_{k,t}}{A_{k,t-1}} \tag{22}$$

Note that wage negotiations occur during the period t and the resulting wage level is applied by firms at period $t + 1$. Wage dynamics in our model act as a second macro-constraint on firms, as they directly affect firm competitiveness. Firms lose competitiveness if their productivity growth rates are slower than the average.

Moreover, $v \neq 0$, wage dynamics generate a selection process among sectors. If the sectoral average productivity grows at a slower rate than the average aggregate productivity growth rate, this sector loses competitiveness, due to the wage dynamics mechanism. The amplitude of this effect is a function of the value of the parameter v.

A firm exits the market if its market share is below \(\bar{z}\). In this case, it is immediately replaced by a firm whose characteristics correspond to the average value of the sectoral characteristics.

The dynamic functioning of the model is based on the following mechanisms, across different levels of analysis:

1. An (exogenous) technological shock translates, at the firm level, into lower costs and prices. These latter increase firms' market shares. An increase in market shares leads to a growth in firms' output. In turn, the Kaldor-Verdoorn mechanism ensures that output growth translates into positive labor productivity dynamics, further lowering costs and prices and further increasing market shares.

2. At the sectoral level, the micro-dynamics affect the structure of intermediate demand. This in turn feeds back into the growth of firms (and their potential productivity growth), by constraining sectoral demand growth. This ensures the presence of meso-to-micro feedback mechanisms.

3. At the macro-level, growth is a function of (i) the single firm's adoption of technological shocks; (ii) the meso–level diffusion of these shocks and changes in intermediate demand; (iii) changes in the structure of final consumption, in relative prices, and in the employment structure induced by the diffusion of these shocks at the macro-level. In turn, aggregate growth constrains sectoral

growth and, consequently, firms' growth potential and labor productivity. Respectively, these changes exemplify macro-to-meso and macro-to-micro feedback mechanisms.

Structural change is the outcome of the co–evolution of these three levels of dynamic mechanisms and the feedback occurring between them.

3 SIMULATION RESULTS

3.1 Simulation procedure

We conducted numerical simulations on the model developed in Section 2. The simulation setting is summarized as follows:

- the country specification contains 13 sectors, corresponding to the 13 sectors in the I–O SDA carried out in Savona and Lorentz (2005) and reported for convenience in Table 1 in the Appendix;
- each of the sectors includes 20 firms;
- the results presented are the average outcome of a minimum of 50 replications of the simulation setting;
- each simulation runs over 500 steps.

In order to reduce the spectrum of parameters to be analyzed, we set the initial structure of the economy on the basis of the data used in Savona and Lorentz (2005), focusing on the German case. The simulations are carried out on the basis of the actual OECD I–O tables (1978–1995) and OECD STAN (1970–1999), at the first time–step, for the following variables and parameters:

- Sectoral intermediate I–O coefficients ($a_{j,k,t}$). The intermediate coefficients are drawn from the German I–O table for 1978 (Table 2 in the Appendix).
- Sectoral exports ($X_{j,t}$). These figures are drawn from the I–O table for Germany 1978 (Table 3 in the Appendix).
- Sectoral shares of final consumption ($c_{j,t}$). These are computed as the ratio of sector consumption and total consumption using the 1978 German I–O table (Table 3 in the Appendix).
- Sectoral shares of import ($m_{j,t}$). These are computed as the ratio of sectoral foreign demand and total demand (final and intermediate), once again using the 1978 German I–O table (Table 3 in the Appendix).

- Sectoral Kaldor–Verdoorn parameters (β_j and λ_j). These figures are estimated using the OECD STAN (1970–1999) data (Table 3[7]).

We identify three stylized scenarios based on different parameter settings, and analyze the occurrence of structural change on the basis of each of these scenarios in the case of the simulation specification illustrated above. The scenarios are detailed in Section 3.2. It is useful to bear in mind that the objective is not to carry out a proper calibration exercise, as we do not aim to reproduce the trend observed in the data. Rather, we want to investigate whether the results that emerge from the various simulation scenarios are plausible with respect to the empirical evidence in Section 1.

We quantify the occurrence of structural change in terms of two different dimensions:

1. the degree of concentration, in income (nominal product), real output and employment, measured using an inverse Herfindahl index. This index is intended to measure the unevenness of labor and resource allocations among sectors, as well as changes in the latter;
2. the sectoral composition of the economy, in terms of real output and employment. This dimension allows us to analyze the nature of the changes in the structure of the economy generated by the various scenarios.

3.2 Simulation scenarios

Three main scenarios driving structural change are identified, based on changes in intermediate demand. Each of these scenarios corresponds to a specific setting for a number of key parameters. They are described as follows.

1. The *"Baumol's disease"* scenario: The structural changes in both the em ployment and output composition of the economy are driven by the pro ductivity growth differentials among sectors. This scenario emerges as a result of cross-sector differences in the Kaldor–Verdoorn parameters, holding final and intermediate demand constant. These differences lead to higher shares of employment in the sectors with lowest productivity growth, and affect the structure of the economy through wage and price dynamics. Structural change based on this scenario emerges if productivity growth differences are not perfectly absorbed by wages, i.e. when the wage setting is centralized. The parameters are set as follows:

(a)the changes in intermediate coefficients are neutralized ($\sigma = 0$);

(b)wages are centralized ($\nu = 1$);

(c)the selection mechanism occurs ($\phi = 1$);

(d)the structure of final demand remains constant (All $c_{j,t} = c_j$).

2. The *"Schumpeterian"* scenario:[8] Structural change is exclusively driven by firms' reactions to technological shocks. The differences in productivity growth rates are neutralized by decentralized wages. The diffusion of the shocks to the economy relies only on the selection mechanism occurring at sectoral level. Structural change is therefore due only to the characteristics of the stochastic processes underlying the changes in the intermediate coefficients and the selection mechanism. The parameters are set as follows:

a) the changes in intermediate coefficient occur ($\sigma \neq 0$);

b) wages neutralize the differences in sectoral productivity growth rate ($\nu = 0$);

c) the selection mechanism occurs ($\phi = 1$);

d) the structure of final demand remains constant (All $c_{j,t} = c_j$);

3.The *"Cost reduction"* scenario: Structural change is triggered by both the reaction to technological shocks by firms and the differences in productivity growth rates among sectors. Centralized wage–setting allows these differences to affect both wages and prices and, therefore, production costs. Technological shocks are adopted when they affect production costs. Adoption is therefore biased towards the most productive sectors. In combination with the selection mechanisms, this bias should amplify the effects on structural change as emerge in the "Baumol's disease" scenario. In this case the parameters are set as follows:

a) the changes in intermediate coefficient occur ($\sigma \neq 0$);

b) wages are centralized ($\nu = 1$);

c) the selection mechanisms occur ($\phi = 1$);

d) the structure of final demand remains constant (All $c_{j,t} = c_j$).

The scenarios rely on a limited number of parameter changes. Modifying the values for σ and ν allows us to consider three different sets of causalities leading to changes in the structure of intermediate demand, i.e. supply– and intermediate demand–led structural changes.

3.3 The case of Germany

The empirical evidence for Germany, as per Savona and Lorentz (2005), shows an increase in the degree of concentration of output between 1978 and 1995. In other words, aggregate output has been growing, but in a small number of sectors.

Figures 1 to 3, respectively, present the degree of concentration for income, employment and real output. The figures were obtained for various specifications of the parameters σ and v, in such a way that they emerge as the effects of the dynamics consequent on the three different scenarios. In particular:

- keeping σ null and moving along the y-axis corresponds to the emergence of a "Baumol's disease" type of dynamics;
- keeping v null and moving along the x-axis corresponds to a "Schumpeterian" type of structural change dynamics;
- modifying simultaneously v and σ generates a "Cost reduction" type of structural change.

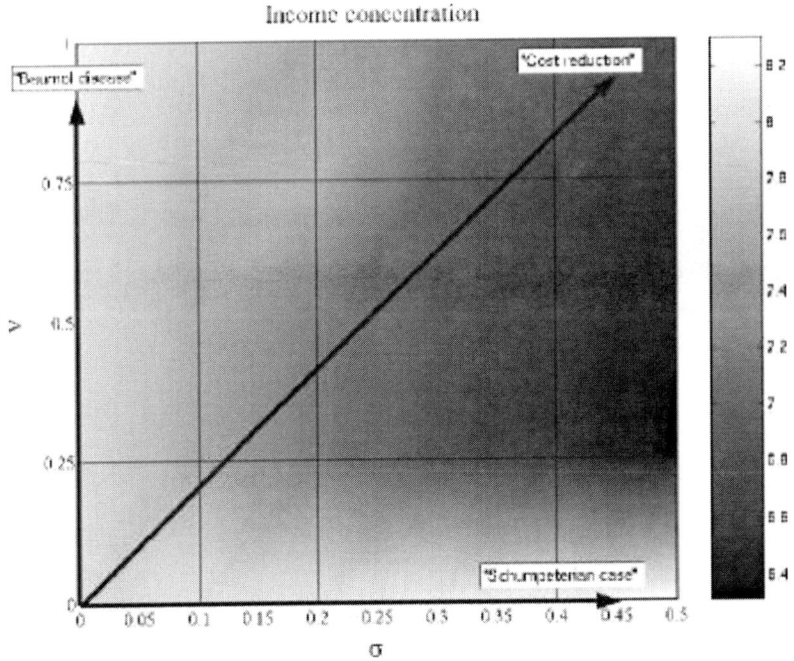

Figure 1. Income sectoral concentration (Inverse Herfindahl index)

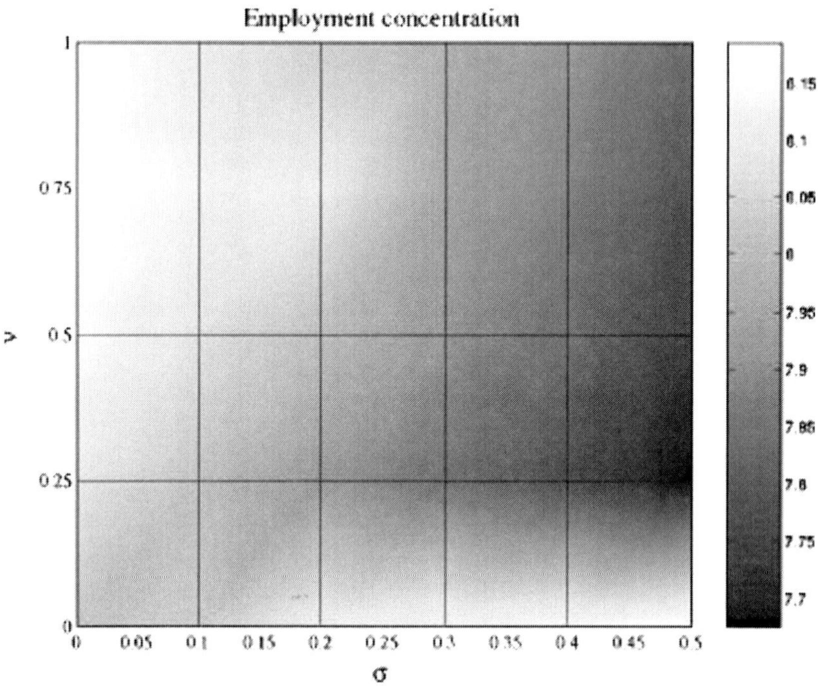

Figure 2. Employment concentration (Inverse Herfindahl index)

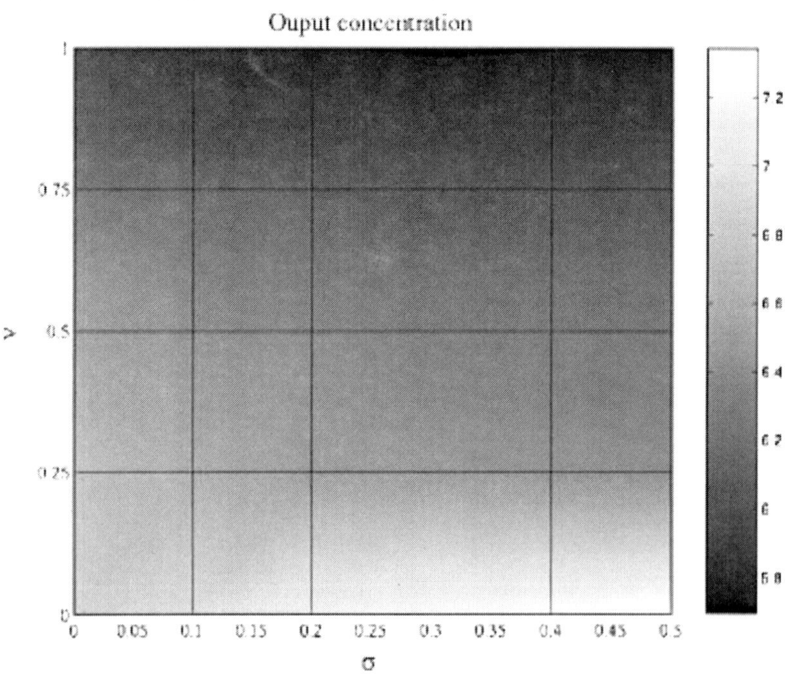

Figure 3. Real output concentration (Inverse Herfindahl index)

As illustrated by Fig. 1, in the two extreme cases, the "Baumol's disease" and the "Schumpeterian", the dynamics lead to lower degrees of concentration in income with respect to the "Cost Reduction" or intermediate cases. A similar pattern emerges when considering the concentration in employment (see Fig. 2).

Figure 3 presents the concentration levels in terms of output, measured for the various specifications of parameters ν and σ. A dramatic difference is evident with respect to income and employment. As the wage dynamics tend to be more centralized, when keeping the probability of technological shocks to zero, the output concentration becomes higher. Economic activity is therefore more concentrated in the "Baumol's disease" and the "Cost reduction" scenarios, while the dynamics considered in the "Schumpeterian" scenario lead to a lower level of concentration (higher dispersion).

In the course of the simulations of the "Baumol's disease" case, the output tends, on average, to be concentrated in a small number of sectors. This tendency is amplified as wages tend to be more centralized. Similar patterns emerge for the "Cost reduction" case. In the "Schumpeterian" scenario, however, the structural changes generated by the simulations lead to lower concentration, or higher value of the inverse Herfindahl index.

The differences in the outcomes of the three scenarios are less obvious for employment. In all cases, in the course of the simulations, employment is concentrated in a smaller number of sectors. The employment dynamics are mainly driven by the productivity dynamics, which explains the similarities in these patterns. Small differences can, however, be observed: in the "Schumpeterian" case, the more frequent technological shocks slightly slow down the employment concentration. In the case of the "Baumol's disease" scenario, and the "Cost reduction" scenario, a higher degree of wage centralization seems to slow down slightly the concentration process.

These findings can be explained as follows. In the "Baumol's disease" case, structural change is driven only by the differences in productivity dynamics across sectors. As wages are centralized, these productivity differences directly affect the demand structure, *via* the relative prices and the employment structure. Sectors with higher (than average) productivity growth experience a decrease in prices over time and, therefore, an increase in market shares. This explains the growth in the degree of concentration of real output. The high productivity growth sectors increase their levels and shares of output, reducing their costs and prices. The low productivity growth sectors reduce their levels of output as they experience an increase in costs and prices. These two effects compensate for one another, explaining the low degree of concentration in the income structure. Similarly the losses/gains, in output are partially compensated for by the higher/lower, gains in labor productivity, implying a reduction/increase, in the sectoral shares of total employment. This would also account for the lower degree of concentration in the employment structure.

In the "Schumpeterian" case, wages are decentralized and therefore absorb completely the differences in productivity dynamics. The only source of structural change are the technological shocks occurring at the micro-level, which change the technological coefficients. The more frequent the shocks, the more frequent the changes in the structure of intermediate demand. However, the shocks follow similar patterns among sectors. As a consequence, technological shocks tend to reduce the sectoral differences in intermediate demand. Therefore, the more frequent the shocks, the lower the degree of concentration in output. As wages absorb the changes in labor productivity, price dynamics follow the changes in the technological coefficients. At the meso-level, this implies less concentration in output and in the income structure. The employment structure of the economy is a direct consequence of the differences in productivity dynamics among sectors, though this effect is slowed by the technological shocks.

In the "Cost reduction" scenario, structural change is simultaneously due to the differences in the productivity dynamics among sectors and to the technological shocks. In this case, as technological shocks diffuse among the sectors and in the economy, they tend to amplify the sectoral heterogeneity in intermediate demand due to the differences in productivity growth rates. The shocks are absorbed at the micro and meso levels through selection mechanisms, only if these reduce the production costs. The absorbed shocks are those favoring the most productive sectors. Hence, the productivity growth differences affect demand, *via* relative prices, but also through the cost reduction linked to the adoption of technological shocks. In line with the Kaldor–Verdoorn law, the sectors with higher demand growth experience higher productivity growth. The combination of these two mechanisms, therefore, reinforces the concentration dynamics in a small number of highly productive sectors.

Figures 4 to 9 present the evolution of the sectoral composition of the economy for each of the scenarios. This allows us to consider in more detail the nature of the structural changes occurring through the various scenarios.

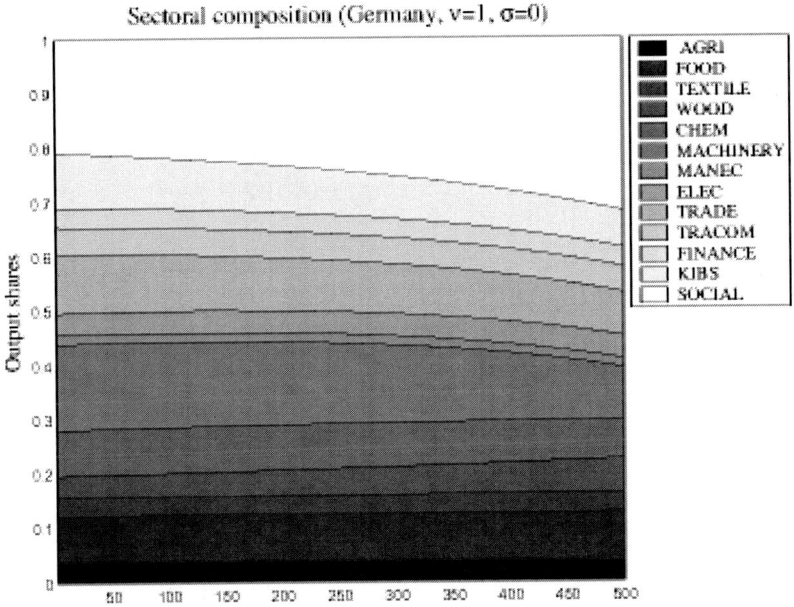

Figure 4. Sectoral composition in real output ("Baumol disease")

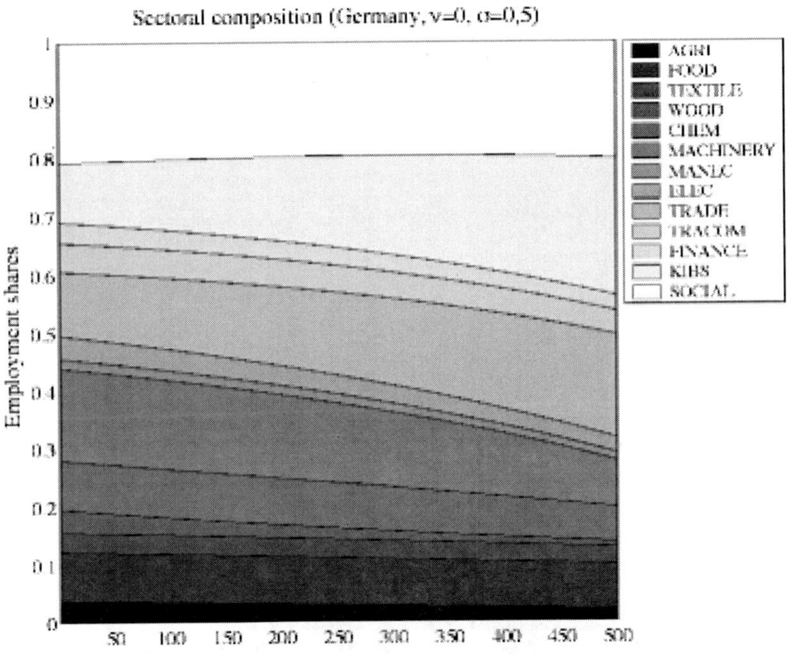

Figure 5. Employment sectoral composition ("Baumol disease")

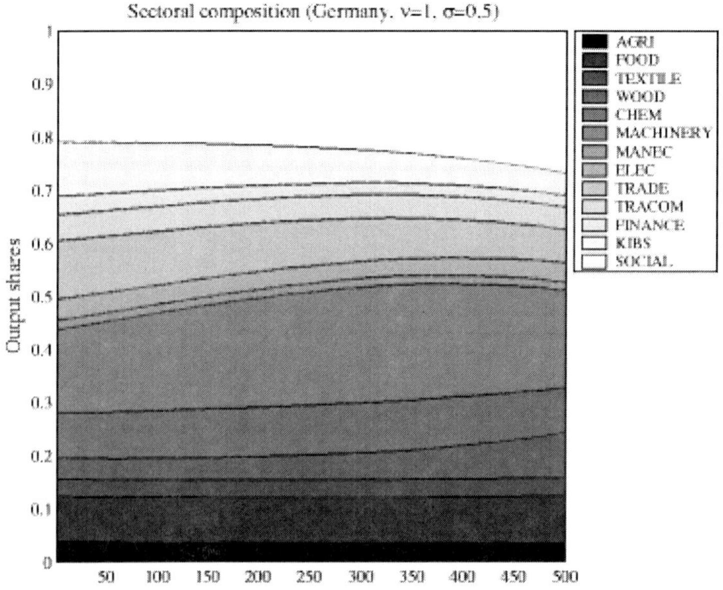

Figure 6. Sectoral composition in real output ("Cost reduction")

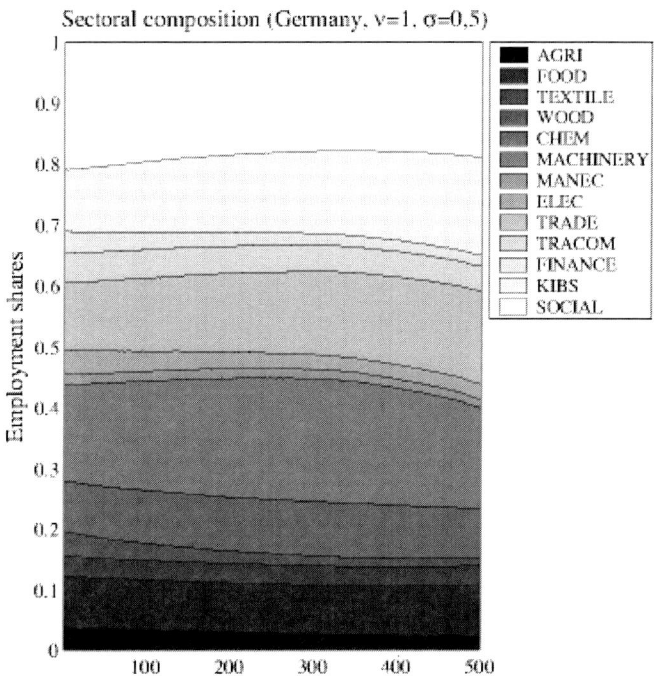

Figure 7. Employment sectoral composition ("Cost reduction")

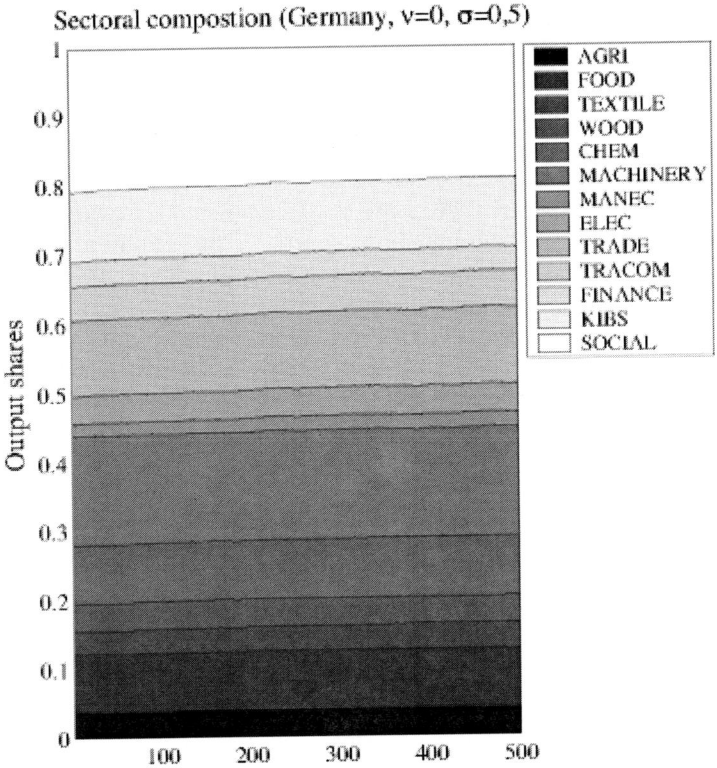

Figure 8. Sectoral composition in real output ("Schumpeterian case")

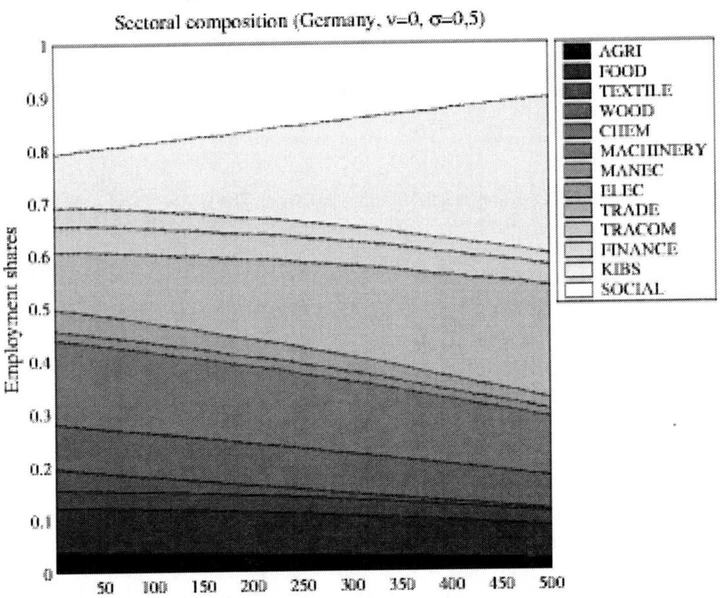

Figure 9. Employment sectoral composition ("Schumpeterian case")

In the "Baumol's disease" case (Fig. 4), except for the SOCIAL sector, all the service sectors, and especially KIBS and TRADE, decline. Manufacturing activities, on the other hand, have an increased role in the economy. The manufacturing sectors (especially MACHINERY), together with the SOCIAL sector, experience the highest productivity growth while, as expected, these sectors experience a drastic drop in employment shares (Fig. 5). KIBS and TRADE are the two sectors that experience the highest increase in employment shares. The "Baumol's disease" mechanism certainly explains the growth of employment in services. However, structural changes as generated in this scenario lead to a re-industrialization and a de-tertiarization of the economy in terms of output created. The mechanisms behind the "Baumol's disease" scenario favor high productivity manufacturing activities, yet they are unable to account for the empirical evidence for the case of KIBS.

Similarly, structural changes in the "Cost reduction" scenario favor manufacturing activities (Fig. 6). The changes in the output structure are amplified with respect to the "Baumol's disease" case. Again, the manufacturing branches benefit from the mechanisms underlying this scenario, due to the fact that these sectors are characterized by higher productivity growth rates. This result is directly linked to the fact that the dynamics implied in this scenario accelerate and amplify the effects triggered by productivity differences (as in the "Baumol disease" case) or by technological shocks.

In terms of employment, however, slight differences occur. For certain manufacturing activities (especially MACHINERY), the share of employment slightly increases (Fig. 7). The growth of output, therefore, over-compensates for the loss of employment potentially induced by the productivity dynamics.

In the "Schumpeterian" case, structural changes lead to a convergence in the output share of each sector (Fig. 8). This result is directly linked to the symmetry of the technological shocks among sectors. These latter follow the same distribution patterns across sectors.

The structure of employment shows the same trend as that in the "Baumol's disease" case (Fig. 9). Employment is structured by the productivity differences, as in the above case. As wages are decentralized, the effect of the productivity differences is confined to the employment structure.

Figure 10 presents the evolution of the sectoral structure in Germany for the period 1978–1995. There is a clear tendency toward tertiarization with the rise of KIBS and SOCIAL shares and, more generally, a gain in importance of all the service sectors, accompanied by a relative decline in manufacturing activities.

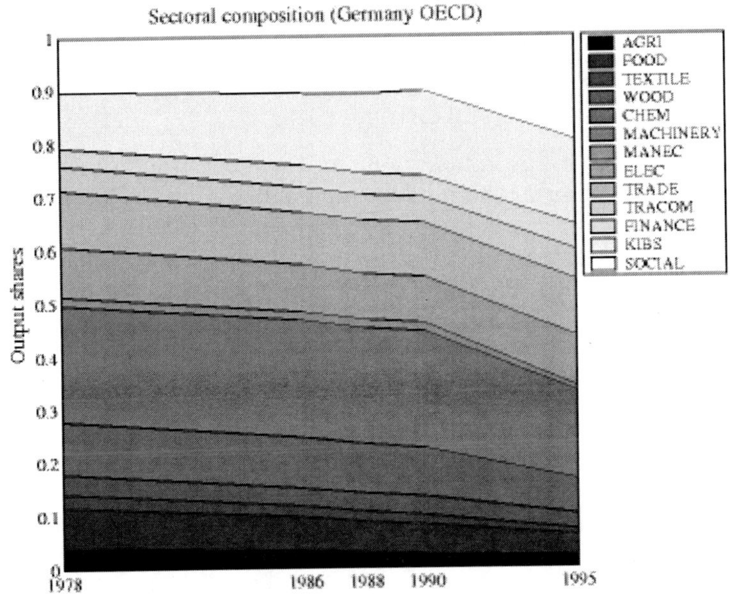

Figure 10. Sectorial composition in real output (Germany 1978–1995)

This structure is the opposite to the one generated by the "Baumol's disease" and the "Cost reduction" scenarios, which rely on the existence of productivity differences among sectors. The growth of services in Germany can hardly be completely imputed to productivity growth rate differentials. The simulated results for the various scenarios allow us to question seriously the "Baumol's disease" explanation, at least for the period considered.

Moreover, the growth of services in Germany seems to have been complementary rather than detrimental to the growth in manufacturing sectors. Tertiarization processes in Germany have been driven by the combination of highly productive manufacturing sectors and asymmetric technological shocks. These shocks have favored the expansion of services following an increase in the inter–sectoral division of labor and an increase in intermediate demand for service activities.

4 FINAL REMARKS

The paper aimed to add to the on-going debate on the determinants of structural changes to the economy, particularly those leading to the growth of services. In the present work, we have built upon the empirical evidence found in Savona and Lorentz (2005) and summarized in Section 1. Our conjecture is that the determinants of structural change, and particularly the growth of services in the advanced countries over the last few decades, imply the co-presence of (and most likely a virtuous circle between) a sustained growth in patterns of final demand and radical changes in the sectoral division of labor.

A growth model with evolutionary micro-founded structural change was developed in Section 2. The model was simulated on the basis of three different scenarios, accounting for both intermediate demand and technological determinants of structural change. The scenarios were identified both along the main lines around which the debate over tertiarization has revolved over time, and on the empirical evidence found in previous work and recalled in Section 1.

The simulation results based on the actual German data allow us to conclude that the structural changes that occurred in the case of Germany cannot only be due to inter-sectoral differences in productivity growth. In other words, and in line with the empirical evidence, the "Baumol's disease" case is not able to account for the actual (and most recent) patterns of tertiarization that have occurred in Germany. Rather, it is the intertwined effect of changes in the intermediate demand and technological shocks that has been operating.

However, more a refined account of the nature and effects of technological shocks at the micro-level should be considered. The model is based on the hypothesis of symmetrical technological shocks. We plan to abandon this simplified hypothesis in future work in order to account for asymmetrical technological shocks across firms and sectors. In line with the methodological approach adopted in this work, we intend to do this by relying on empirical evidence based on micro-level data, in line with the findings in Cainelli et al. (2006).

Overall, this work aimed at healing the fracture between Keynesian and neo-Schumpeterian 'lines of thought' (Verspagen 2002) in the belief that more effort should be devoted to integrating – especially in the domain of services – these two main theoretical streams. As part of our future research agenda, we intend to explore in more depth growth and changes in the composition of final demand, which, along with the dramatic changes in cross-sectoral intermediate linkages accounted for in the present work, are the ultimate shapers of changes in the structural composition of advanced economies.

FOOTNOTES

[1] For an exhaustive review see Rose and Casler (1996).

[2] The term KIBS was first coined by Miles (1994) and variously reprised by among others Miles et al. (1995), Gallouj (2002). For a detailed list of the sectors considered as KIBS, see Table 1 in the Appendix.

[3]The importance of technical change for growth and competitiveness of firms, sectors and countries, emphasized by Schumpeter (1934) has been reprised within the neo-Schumpeterian stream of literature, starting from the seminal contribution by Nelson and Winter (1982) (See also, among others, Dosi et al. 1988; Chiaromonte and Dosi 1993; Silverberg and Verspagen 2005). This stream of literature is characterized by an almost exclusive focus on the nature and economic effects of technology adoption and diffusion, and neglects both the role of the demand-side determinants of firms' strategic behavior and the consequences of macro-level demand constraints.

[4]Interestingly, both Verspagen (1993), on the one hand, and Llerena and Lorentz (2004), on the other, re-consider Kaldor's Cumulative Causation mechanism. The former does so by introducing explicit 'evolutionary' selection processes within a cumulative causation framework, the latter by providing a micro-foundation of the process of emergence and diffusion of technologies. We refer the reader to both these contributions for a more detailed discussion of the use of the Kaldorian Cumulative Causation within the neo–Schumpeterian models.

[5]The price index is computed as:

$$\bar{p}_t = \sum_{k=1}^{J} p_{k,t} \frac{p_{k,t} Y_{k,t}}{\sum p_{k,t} Y_{k,t}}.$$

[6] With

$$A_t = \frac{Y_t}{L_t} \text{ and } A_{k,t} = \frac{Y_{k,t}}{L_{k,t}}.$$

[7]The Kaldor–Verdoorn elasticities are estimated over the same time–span (1970–1999) covered by the OECD I–O Tables. We chose to gain in coherence rather than in the actuality of the data with respect to the hypotheses formulated in Section 1, which refer to the time-span in the I–O tables of 1978–1995.

[8]We refer here to the Neo-Schumpeterian models considered in Section 1, which consider the technological changes occurring at the firm level as being driven by stochastic processes.

REFERENCES

1. Appelbaum E, Schettkat R (1999) Are prices unimportant? The changing structure of industrialised economies. J Post Keynes Econ 21:387–398
2. Baumol W (1967) Macroeconomics of unbalanced growth: the anatomy of an urban crisis. Am Econ Rev 57:415–426
3. Baumol W (2001) The growth of service industries. The paradox of exploding costs and persistent demand. In: ten Raa T, Schettkat R (eds) Paradox of the services: exploding costs and persistent demand. Edward Elgar, Aldershot
4. Baumol W (2008) The two-sided cost disease and its frightening consequences. In: Gallouj F, Djellal F, Gallouj C (eds) Handbook of innovation and services. Edward Elgar, Aldershot (forthcoming)
5. Baumol W, Bowen W (1966) Performing arts: the economic dilemma. Twentieth Century Found, New York
6. Cainelli G, Evangelista R, Savona M (2006) Innovation and economic performance in services. A firm-level analysis. Camb J Econ 30:435–458
7. Chiaromonte F, Dosi G (1993) Heterogeneity, competition, and macroeconomics dynamics. Struct Change Econ Dyn 4(1):39–63
8. Clark C (1940) The conditions of economic progress. MacMillan, London
9. Dosi G, Freeman C, Nelson R, Silverberg G, Soete L (1988) Technical change and economic theory. Pinter, London
10. Fagerberg J (1994) Technology and international differences in growth rates. J Econ Lit 32:1147–1175
11. Fisher A (1935) The clash of progress and security. MacMillan, London
12. Fisher A (1945) Economic progress and social security. MacMillan, London
13. Fourastié J (1949) Le Grand Espoir du XX Siècle. PUF, Paris
14. Fuchs V (1968) The service economy. National Bureau of Economic Research, New York
15. Gallouj F (2002) Knowledge intensive business services: processing knowledge and producing innovation. In: Gadrey J, Gallouj F (eds) Productivity, innovation and knowledge in services. Edward Elgar, Aldershot

16. Kaldor N (1957) A model of economic growth. Econ J 70:65–94, December

17. Kaldor N (1966) Causes of the slow rate of growth in the United Kingdom. Cambridge University Press, Cambridge

18. Kox H, Rubalcaba L (2007) Analysing the contribution of business services to european economic growth. Discussion Paper, Bruges European Economics Research Papers (BEER Paper n. 9)

19. Leontief W (1951) The structure of American economy 1919–1939, 2nd edn. Oxford University Press, New York

20. Leontief W (1953) Studies in the structure of the American economy. Oxford University Press, New York

21. Llerena P, Lorentz A (2004) Cumulative causation and evolutionary micro-founded technical change: on the determinants of growth rates differences. Rev Econ 55(6):1191–1214

22. Miles I (1994) Innovation in services. In: Dodgson M, Rothwell R (eds) Handbook of industrial innovation. Edward Elgar, Cheltenham

23. Miles I, Kastrinos N, Bilderbeek P, den Hertog P (1995) Knowledge intensive business services – users, carriers and sources of innovation. Discussion paper, EIMS – European Innovation Monitoring System

24. Montobbio F (2002) An evolutionary model of industrial growth and structural change. Struct Change Econ Dyn 13:387–414

25. Nelson R, Winter S (1982) An evolutionary theory of economic change. Harvard University Press, Cambridge

26. Parrinello S (2004) The service economy revisited. Struct Change Econ Dyn 15:381–400

27. Pasinetti L (1973) The notion of vertical integration in economic analysis. Metroeconomica 25:1–29

28. Pasinetti L (1981) Structural change and economic growth: a theoretical essay on the dynamics of the wealth of the nations. Cambridge University Press, Cambridge

29. Peneder M, Kaniovsky S, Dachs B (2003) What follows tertiarisation? Structural change and the role of knowledge-based services. Serv Ind J 23:47–66

30. Pugno M (2006) The service paradox and endogenous economic growth. Struct Change Econ Dyn 17:99–115

31. Rose A, Casler S (1996) Input-output structural decomposition analysis: a critical reappraisal. Econ Syst Res 8(1):33–62

32. Savona M, Lorentz A (2005) Demand and technology contribution to structural change and tertiarisation: an input-output structural decomposition analysis. Working papers, LEM, Pisa

33. Schettkat R, Yocarini L (2006) The shift to services employment: a review of the literature. Struct Change Econ Dyn 17:127–147

34. Schumpeter J (1934) The theory of economic development. An inquiry into profits, capital, credit, interest and the business cycle. Harvard University Press, Cambridge

35. Silverberg G, Verspagen B (2005) Evolutionary theorizing on economic growth. In: Dopfer K (ed) The evolutionary foundations of economics. Cambridge University Press, Cambridge, pp 506–539

36. ten Raa T, Schettkat R (2001) The growth of service industries. The paradox of exploding costs and persistent demand. Edward Elgar, Cheltenham

37. van Ark B, Inklaar R, McGuckin R (2002) Changing gear'. Productivity, ICT and service industries. Europe and the US. In: Paper for the ZEW Conference on Economics of Information and Communication Technology, Mannheim, June 2002

38. Verdoorn P (1949) Fattori che regolano lo sviluppo della produttivitá del lavoro. L'Industria 1:45–53

39. Verspagen B (1993) Uneven growth between interdependent economies: evolutionary views on technology gaps, trade and growth. Aldershot, Avenbury

40. Verspagen B (2002) Evolutionary macroeconomics: a synthesis between neo-schumpeterian and post-keynesian line of thought. Elec J Evol Model Econ Dyn 1007 (http://www.e-jemed.org/1007/index.php)

41. Verspagen B (2004) Structural change and technology. A long view. Rev Econ 55(6):1099–1126

4

OPTIMAL MODULARITY: A DEMONSTRATION OF THE EVOLUTIONARY ADVANTAGE OF MODULAR ARCHITECTURES

Koen Frenken · Stefan Mendritzki

Eindhoven Centre for Innovation Studies (ECIS), School of Innovation Sciences, Eindhoven University of Technology, Eindhoven, The Netherlands

ABSTRACT

Modularity is an important concept in evolutionary theorizing but lack of a consistent definition renders study difficult. Using the generalized NK-model of fitness landscapes, we differentiate modularity from decomposability. Modular and decomposable systems are both composed of subsystems, but in the former, these subsystems are connected via interface standards, while in the latter, subsystems are completely isolated. We derive the *optimal level of modularity*, which minimizes the time required to globally optimize a system, both for the case of two-layered systems and for the general case of multi-layered hierarchical systems containing modules within modules. This derivation supports the hypothesis of modularity as a mechanism to increase the speed of evolution. Our formal definition clarifies the concept of modularity and provides a framework and an analytical baseline for further research.

Keywords: Modularity, Decomposability, Near-decomposability, Complexity, NK-model, Search, Hierarchy

1 INTRODUCTION

Simon's (1962) seminal work on complex systems emphasized the modular and hierarchical structure of most complex systems, both natural and artificial. The modular nature of complex systems refers to the nearly decomposable architecture of the interaction between elements. In modular systems, the great majority of interactions occur within modules and only a few interactions occur between modules.

Modular architectures offer evolutionary advantages because, in most instances, the effect of a change in a given module is confined to that module. Due to this localization of the effects of changes, the probability of a successful change is greatly enhanced. Each module can be improved more or less independently of other modules. For example, modular technologies allow for innovation in each module without the risk of creating malfunctions in other modules. Similarly, modular organizational designs allow different departments to change their operating routines without creating problematic side effects in other departments. More generally, the typical feature of modular systems holds that they can more easily be improved by random mutation and natural selection than other complex systems.

The NK-model, originally developed by Kauffman (1993) and generalized by Altenberg (1994), is a common tool to analyze the evolutionary dynamics of complex systems, including organizations and technologies (Levinthal 1997). In the economics and management literatures, several simulation studies have been carried out to analyze the conditions under which modular systems favor adaptation compared to other complex systems (Frenken et al. 1999, Marengo et al. 2000; Ethiraj and Levinthal 2004; Dosi and Marengo 2005; Brusoni et al. 2007; Rivkin and Siggelkow 2007; Ciarli et al. 2008; Geisendorf 2010; McNerney et al. 2011; cf Bradshaw 1992; Baldwin and Clark 2000). These studies tend to confirm the central idea that modular systems are improved by random mutation and natural selection at a faster rate than other complex systems. Yet, the exact results of the simulation exercises differ across these studies, as they utilize different assumptions regarding search behaviour and memory constraints, as well as differing definitions of modularity.

In the following, we propose a formal definition of modularity that distinguishes it from decomposability. Though many use the terms decomposability and modularity interchangeably, we argue that modular systems differ from decomposable systems; while decomposability requires a full decomposition of a complex system into subsystems, modularity requires a system architecture in which subsystems are still connected via interface standards. Conceptually, the problem of the decomposability concept is that a decomposable system is no longer one system, but simply a collection of several smaller systems. As a representation of a technology, or an organization, it falls short in conceptualizing the fact that elements in a technology or organization always act together and are collectively subject to selection. The idea of a decomposable system is thus better understood as an analytical construct or as an approximation of reality rather than a precise representation of a real-world system. The concept of modularity overcomes these conceptual issues. A modular system cannot be partitioned into completely independent subsystems, but rather contains nearly independent subsystems (modules) which are connected via interfaces. These interfaces are elements of a system that connect subsystems such that the only interdependencies between the subsystems are via the interface standards. This definition corresponds quite closely to the concept of near decomposability introduced by Simon (1962, 1969, 2002), as well the more recent notion of modularity in complex networks (Newman 2006).

The applied literature on modularity has drawn similar distinctions between modularity and decomposability. For example, Baldwin (2008) compares perfect modularity (similar to our definition of decomposability) with near decomposability (similar to our definition of modularity). Langlois and Garzarelli (2008, p.128) differentiate between decomposable systems and modular systems which are "nearly decomposable system that preserves the possibility of cooperation by adopting a common interface". This paper, then, is best seen not as creating a novel distinction, but as adopting an existing distinction and expressing it formally.

We will argue below, using a generalized NK framework developed by Altenberg (1994), that modular systems, defined in this way, can be optimized globally given the right sequence of problem-solving. Though a decomposition strategy is not feasible, modules can be optimized independently as long as interface standards between modules are left unchanged. This means that, contrary to decomposable systems, optimization of modular systems requires *hierarchical* problem-solving, where interface standards are defined first, followed by module design within the constraints of the standards.

Following this definition, we will proceed to derive the optimal level of modularity for systems of a given size, where the optimum is defined by the search time required for global optimization. This result is shown to be extendable to multi-layered hierarchical complex systems, where modules are defined recursively. We find this extension important since hierarchical complex systems are ubiquitous in technological artefacts and organizational design, yet have not been analyzed thus far in the NK-modelling framework.

The reader will note that the model we propose is quite simple. For example, it adopts a global search strategy. This is done purposively for the purpose of creating a framework and a baseline. The framework offers the possibility of comparability of results derived from different assumptions. The baseline of a simple model provides an anchor for comparison with more complex models. This approach of using a simplified model as a baseline is common in NK modelling. It should be noted, then, that the purpose of this model is not to make the empirical claim that it reflects actual behaviour. It rather should be interpreted as a tool to be useful in integrating and reconciling various models on modularity. The importance of creating common frameworks is discussed in terms of the ongoing debate as to whether over-modularity has evolutionary advantages.

2 DECOMPOSABILITY AND MODULARITY IN A GENERALIZED NK-MODEL

We define a system as consisting of N elements (n = 1,...,N). For each element, n, there exist A_n possible states. The number of possible system designs that make up the system's *design space* (Bradshaw 1992) is given by the product of the number of possible states for each element:

$$S = \prod_{n}^{N} A_n \qquad (1)$$

In the following, we will assume that $A_n = A$ for all n, which implies that the size of the design space equals A^N.

We assume that each pair of elements is either interdependent or not. Interdependence between a pair of elements means that, if a mutation is carried out in one element, the functioning of the other element is also affected. Decomposability means that a system can be partitioned into non-overlapping subsystems such that no interdependencies exist between subsystems. This implies that subsystems can be optimized independently and in parallel. The time required to globally optimize a system is then bounded by the size of the largest subsystem.

For example, consider a system with $N = 5$ and a binary design space (A = 2). The number of possible designs is $2^5 = 32$. If the functioning of all elements is dependent on the state of all other elements, global optimization requires exhaustive search: one has to evaluate the fitness of all 32 possible designs to determine which design has the highest fitness. Assuming one evaluation per time period, the search time is 32 periods. Now, consider the case in which the functioning of the first and second elements are interdependent, and the functioning of the third, fourth and fifth elements are interdependent. In this case, the subsystem containing the first and second elements can be optimized independently from the subsystem containing the third, fourth and fifth elements. Since search can proceed in parallel, the search time required to globally optimize the system is bounded by the size of the largest subsystem, in this case $2^3 = 8$ periods. The computational complexity of a system, as defined by the search time required to globally optimize a system, can then be expressed as a function of the number of elements of this largest subsystem (three in this example), also known as the cover size of a system (Page 1996).

2.1 Altenberg's generalized NK-model

To formally model modular systems, the original NK-model as developed by Kauffman (1993) has to be generalized to allow for interface standards. The distinguishing feature of modular systems is that some elements of the system (the interface standards) have no direct contribution to the system's fitness, but solely mediate the interdependencies between modules. However, in the original formulation of the NK-model by Kauffman, elements in a complex system by definition have a fitness value. As such, the Kauffman-type of NK-model is ill suited to deal with modular systems. The generalized NK-model developed by Altenberg (1994) allows a more general treatment in which elements are not required to have inherent fitness values, which allows the inclusion of mediating elements.

Altenberg's generalized NK-model describes a system by N elements ($n = 1,...,N$) and F fitness elements ($f = 1,...,F$). In biological systems, for which this generalized NK-model was conceived, an organism's N genes are the system's elements and an organism's F traits are the selection criteria. The string of genes is collectively referred to as an organism's genotype, while the set of traits is collectively referred to as an organism's phenotype. A single gene affects one or several traits in the phenotype, and a single trait is affected by one or several genes in the genotype. The vector of genes affecting a trait is called a polygeny vector, while the vector of traits affected by a gene is called a pleiotropy vector. The structure of epistatic relations between genes and traits is represented in a "genotype-phenotype map", which is represented by a matrix of size $F \cdot N$ with:

$$M = [m_{fn}] \ , \ f = 1, ..., F \ , \ n = 1, ..., N \qquad (2)$$

Analogously, a technology can be described in terms of its N elements and the F functions it performs *i.e.* the quality attributes taken into account by users (Frenken and Nuvolari 2004). The string of alleles of elements describes the "genotype" of a product, and the list of functions describes the "phenotype" of the product (e.g., speed, weight, efficiency, comfort, safety, etc). The genotype–phenotype map of a product is generally called a product's architecture (cf. Henderson and Clark 1990).

The original NK-model can now be understood as a special case of the generalized genotype–phenotype matrices. Three restrictive assumptions are operative in the original NK-model, namely N-F symmetry, N-F reflexivity, and polygeny symmetry. N-F symmetry is the condition that the number of functions *F* equals the number of elements *N*. This assumption is necessary in order to enforce N-F reflexivity, which is that each element (n_x) affects its counterpart function (f_x); in terms of the genotype–phenotype matrix, this implies that the diagonal is always characterized by presence of a relation between element and function. Polygeny symmetry is the requirement that each function is affected by the same number of elements. In the NK-model the polygeny of each function is assumed to be exactly $K + 1$, with pleiotropy of each element being determined randomly (with pleiotropy being on average equal to $K + 1$). Dropping these restrictions (i.e. allowing N ≠≠ F, not enforcing $n_x \rightarrow f_x$ interdependencies, and allowing polygeny to differ from $K + 1$ for individual functions) provides a generalized NK-model of complex systems.

In Altenberg's generalized NK-model, the fitness landscapes are constructed in the same way as in the original formulation by Kauffman (1993). An example of a genotype–phenotype map is given in Fig. 1(a). In this example, the fitness of the first function \emphw1\emphw1 is affected by the first and second elements, and the fitness of the second function \emphw2\emphw2 is affected by second and third elements.

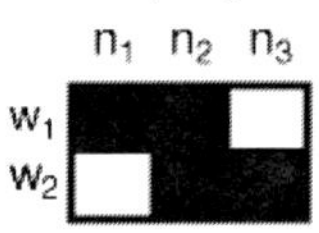

(a) Example of a genotype-phenotype map

	w_1	w_2	W
000:	0.8	0.9	0.85
001:	0.8	0.6	0.70
010:	0.4	0.3	0.35
011:	0.4	0.2	0.30
100:	0.2	0.9	0.55
101:	0.2	0.6	0.40
110:	0.9	0.3	0.60
111:	0.9	0.2	0.55

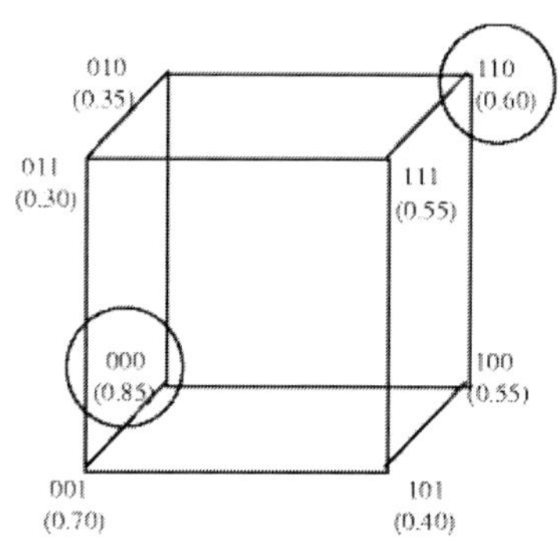

(b) A simulation of the genotype-phenotype matrix in (a)

Figure 1. Altenberg's generalized NK-model (**a, b**)

In this example, we assume, without loss of generality, that $A = 2$. Given the matrix specifying the system's architecture and the design space of all possible designs, the fitness landscape of a system can be simulated as in Fig. 1(b). A fitness landscape is a mapping of fitness values onto all possible designs. As with Kauffman's original NK-model, the fitness landscape is generated by randomly drawing a fitness value from a uniform distribution between 0 and 1 for each possible setting of alleles of the elements affecting a function *f*. Total fitness is then derived as the normalized sum of the fitness values of all functions:

$$W = \frac{1}{F} \cdot \sum_{f=1}^{F} w_f \tag{3}$$

2.2 Non-decomposable, decomposable and modular systems

Using Altenberg's generalized NK approach, one can conceptualize interface standards as elements that do not have an intrinsic function, but solely affect functions that are associated with other elements (Frenken 2006). Figure 1 provides an example of a modular system, albeit the most elementary one. The second element affects both functions, each of which is associated with one of the other two elements. Once the choice of the second element is made (i.e. the interface standard), each function can be optimized independently by tuning the element affecting it. Depending on whether the standard is 0 or 1, the designer ends up in either 000 or 110 (circled in the figure).

In Fig. 2, an example is given of three types of systems that can now be distinguished. System (a) is an NK-system in the sense of Kauffman's Kauffman (1993) original NK-model. For this system, $N = 9$ and $K = 8$ (maximum polygeny). Since the system is not decomposable, the time required to globally optimize the system equals the size of the design space. Assuming again that A = 2, the size of the design space is $2^9 = 512$. System (b) is a decomposable $N = 9$ system that can be decomposed into three, equally sized with a polygeny of three ($K = 2$). The time required to globally optimize the system equals the size of the design space of each subsystem ($2^3 = 8$), because search can proceed in parallel (Frenken et al. 1999). Of course, a decomposable system with subsystems of size one, which corresponds to minimum polygeny ($K = 0$), would only require two periods to globally optimize (in fact, there are no local optima is such systems). The optimal level of decomposability with regard to the search time required to globally optimize the system, is a fully decomposable system with subsystems of size one.

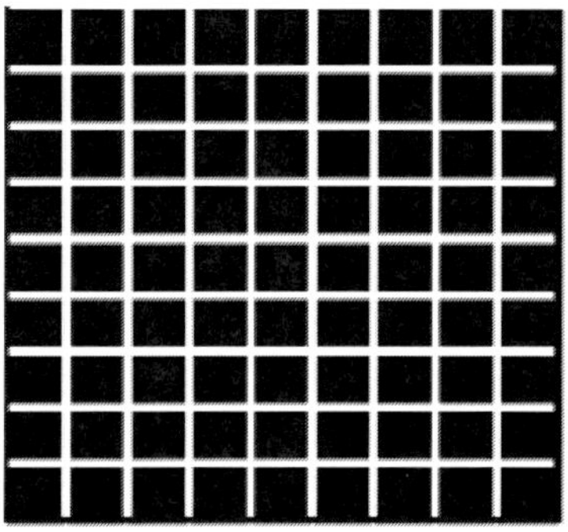

(a) Non-decomposable system, polygeny = 9

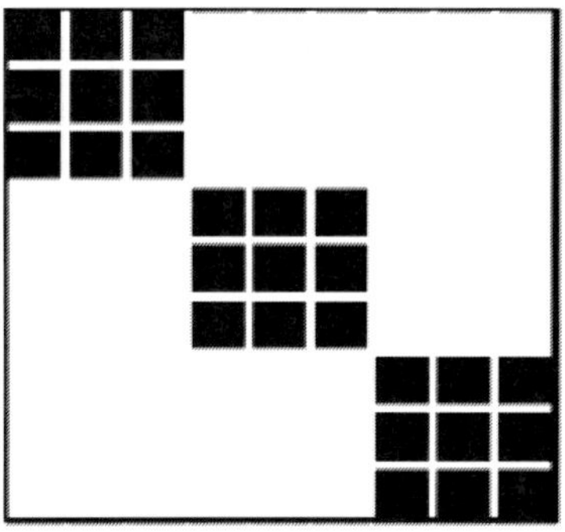

(b) Decomposable system, polygeny = 3

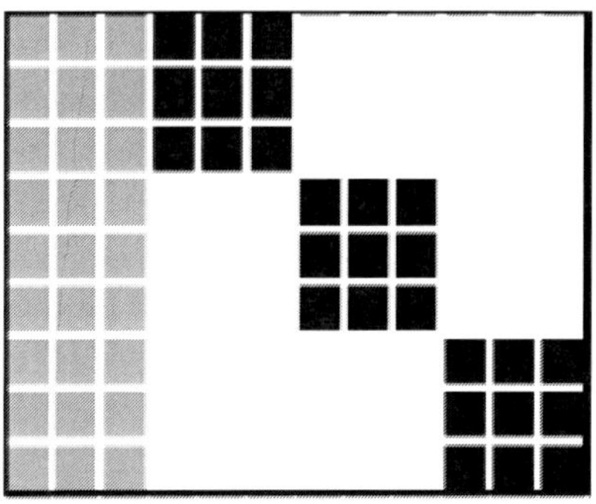

(c) Modular system, polygeny = 6
(interface standards indicated in gray)

Figure 2. Three complex systems (*rows* polygeny vectors; *columns* pleiotropy vectors) (**a**–**c**)

System (c) is a modular system according to our previous definition with three subsystems of size three, which are mediated by three interface standards yielding a polygeny of six (each function is affected by three elements in the subsystem and the three interface standards). The total number of elements in the new system, denoted by N', is 12. Though the number of elements has been increased from nine to 12, the number of trials required to globally optimize the system *hierarchically* is much less that in case (a). For each set of interface standards, there exists an optimal setting of subsystems that can be found in $2^3 = 8$ periods (as for system b). As there are three standards, and thus $2^3 = 8$ settings of interface standards, the total time required adds up $8 \cdot 8 = 64$ periods. Thus, comparing system (a) with system (c), an increase in the number of design dimensions in a system actually simplifies the search for its optimal solution. A modular system can thus be constructed by *increasing* the number of elements in the system such that the elements become organized in modules, thereby *decreasing* the complexity of a system in terms of the search time required for global optimization. Contrary to decomposable systems, the optimal level of modularity with regard to the search time required to globally optimize the system is non-trivial.

3 OPTIMAL MODULARITY IN TWO-LAYERED HIERARCHIES

We first investigate the case of two-layered hierarchies (precluding modules within modules) before proceeding with the generalized case of multi-layered hierarchies (allowing modules within modules) in the next section. The number of modules in which a system can be modularized varies between a single module (absence of modularity) and N modules (maximum modularity). The question becomes how many modules should be created as a function of the original size N of a non-decomposable system. Following our example of Fig. 2(c), we make three assumptions.

Assumption 1

The number of interface standards in a modular system equals the number of modules in a modular system (given that modular systems contain two or more modules).

Assumption 2

An interface standard affects all functions, i.e., the pleiotropy of a standard equals F.

Assumption 3

All modules are of equal size, the possible sizes ranging from one module of size N (absence of modularity) to N modules of size one (maximum modularity).

The first assumption is not crucial to our argument, and can be relaxed. The reasoning behind this assumption is that more modules require more interface standards. The second assumption defines a standard as an interface between all elements. As an interface standard affects all functions, all the fitness values of the non-modular system are redrawn to obtain the fitness values of the modular system. Note that this implies that the fitness values of a modular system are uncorrelated with the fitness values of the original non-modular system. The third assumption follows from the principle of cover size (Page 1996), which states that the search time to globally optimize a system is bounded by the size of the largest subsystem. Thus, optimal modularity requires the partitioning the system in equally sized modules.

To minimize the number of trials required to solve the system, one needs to compute the optimal level of modularity. Let N stand for the size of original non-decomposable system, as in the original NK-model. Let N' stand for the size of original non-decomposable system plus the number of interface standards. Let M stand for the number of interface standards. Finally, let S stand for module size. It follows from assumption 1 that $N' = N + M$ and from assumption 3 that $S = N/M$.

Within this framework, it can be shown that maximum modularity, unlike maximum decomposability, can never be optimal in terms of minimizing the time required to find the global optimum. Consider the case of modifying the example in Fig. 2(a) to be of maximum modularity as in Fig. 3, by adding nine interface standards to the system (of nine elements). Assuming $A = 2$, there are 512 unique options for interfaces and two unique options for each module. Thus, optimization requires 512 × 2 = 1024 periods, compared to the 512 periods to optimize the original NK-system as depicted in Fig. 2(a). It holds that, for any N, polygeny in a maximally modular system is N + 1 (N interface standards plus the function itself), compared to a polygeny of N for non-decomposable systems. So maximum modularity can never be the optimal solution. It will be shown that optimal modularity is determined by minimization of polygeny, which stands in a nonlinear relationship with level of modularity.

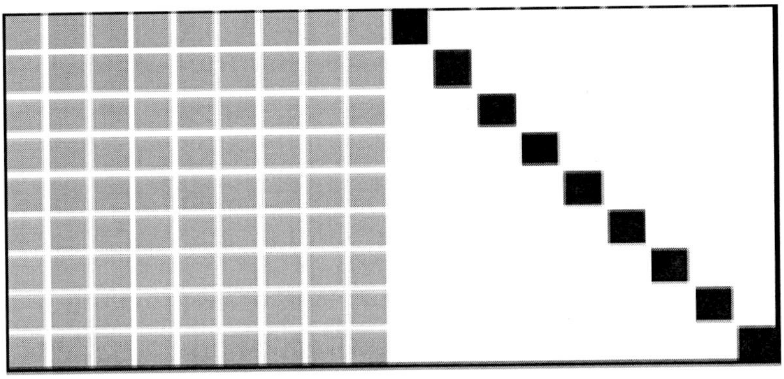

Maximum modularity, N'=18, F=9, S=1, polygeny = 10
(interface standards indicated in gray)

Figure 3. Maximum modularity

Global optimization of a module requires exhaustive search, that is, the testing of all possible combinations. Optimizing a module, given a set of standards, thus equals $A^{N/M}$ periods. As modules can be searched in parallel, the time required to optimize all modules is equal to the time required to optimize a single module. The number of possible sets of standards equals A^{M}. Optimal modularity, i.e. the optimal number of modules, can now be derived as the number of modules that minimizes search time required to globally optimize the system. The time required to globally optimize a modular system, C_{time}, is given by the product of time required to solve a module ($A^{N/M}$) and the time required to design all possible architectures (A^{M}):

$$C_{time} = A^{N/M} \cdot A^{M} = A^{(N/M)+M} \tag{4}$$

This process is guaranteed to find the global optimum as it optimizes each module for all possible architectures. Note that the exponent of Eq. 4 represents the polygeny of the elements. The optimal number of modules can be derived by minimizing (4) with respect to M, which yields:

$$M = N^{1/2} \tag{5}$$

Thus, the optimal number of modules to be created in a non-decomposable system that originally has N elements equals the square root of N (a result independent of A). Given $S = N/M$ it follows that the optimal module size also equals the square root of N. The resulting time required to globally optimize the optimal modular system, equals:

$$C_{optimal} = A^{2(N)^{1/2}} \tag{6}$$

4 OPTIMAL MODULARITY IN MULTI-LAYERED HIERARCHIES

The analysis has thus far only considered modular systems with two layers: a layer of interface standards and a layer of modules. Our reasoning can be generalized for modular systems with more than two layers by considering an iterated modularization process. Iterated modularization allows for the formation of more than two levels (*i.e.* for the creation of a hierarchy of modules within modules). In order to derive the optimal modularity for a hierarchy of modules, we introduce variable L, which stands for number of levels of modularization. Under this notation, $L = 1$ stands for no modularization and $L = 2$ describes the single level of interfaces considered in the previous section. We now consider the general case of $L \geq 2$.

A module is defined recursively within a perfect n-ary tree structure. This structure is a simple, analytically tractable construct from computer science for representations of hierarchical systems. Formally, it is a tree in which every internal node has exactly n children. (See Fig. 4 for an example of n = 3 represented as genotype–phenotype matrix and Fig. 5 for the same example represented as a perfect 3-ary tree.) Within this structure, modules are defined recursively as being formed of a set of interface standards and a set of child modules. In the limit of the bottom of the hierarchy, we reach the leaf modules (those modules which have intrinsic functions). If we take functional (leaf) modules to be Func, the size of the leaf modules to be S (i.e. | {Func} | = S), a module at level n to be mod_n, the set of modules at level n to be Mod_n, and interface standards at level n to be IS_n, a hierarchical modular system can be formally written as:

$$\begin{aligned} \text{mod}_n &= \{\{IS_n\}, \{Mod_{n+1}\} : n \neq L\} \\ \text{mod}_n &= \{\{Func\} : n = L\} \end{aligned}$$

Where:

$$Mod_n = \{\{\text{mod}_{n+1}\}, \{\text{mod}_{n+1}\}, \ldots\}$$

The system in Fig. 4 graphically represents the following N = 27, L = 3 system:

$$
\begin{aligned}
\text{mod}_1 &= \{\{IS_1\},\{Mod_2\}\} = \{\{IS_1\},\{\{\text{mod}_2\},\{\text{mod}_2\},\{\text{mod}_2\}\}\} \\
\text{mod}_2 &= \{\{IS_2\},\{Mod_3\}\} = \{\{IS_2\},\{\{\text{mod}_3\},\{\text{mod}_3\},\{\text{mod}_3\}\}\} \\
\text{mod}_3 &= \{Func\}
\end{aligned}
$$

Note that Fig. 4 represents a projection of the hierarchical structure shown in Fig. 5 onto the NK structure. Within this projection, the following assumptions are implicit:

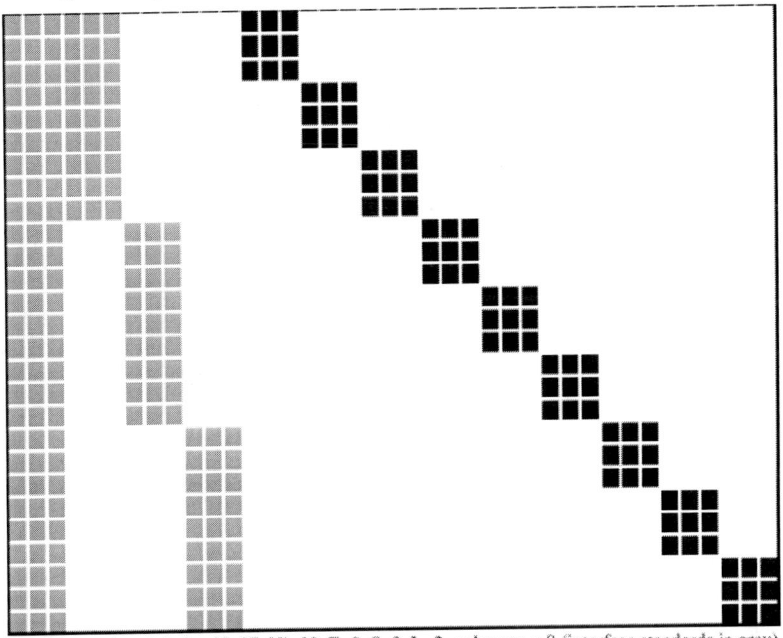

Three-layered modularity, N=27, N'=39, F=9, S=3, L=3, polygeny = 9 (interface standards in gray)

Figure 4. Multi-level modularity

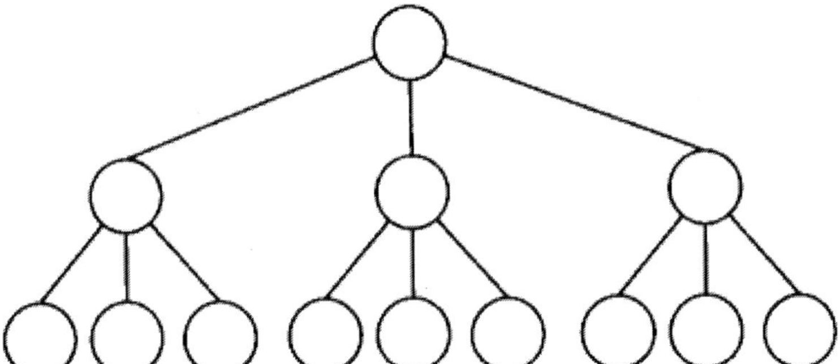

Figure 5. Perfect 3-ary Tree, Height = 3

Assumption 4

The number of interface standards at any level of the hierarchy equals the size of the leaf modules (i.e. $|\{IS_n\}| = S$*).*

Assumption 5

A standard affects all functions in the level at and below the standard in the hierarchy (i.e. top level standards affect all functions).

Assumption 6

Division into modules is symmetrical across levels (i.e. $|\{Mod_n\}| = S$*).*

All functions are thus affected by at least one standard in the multi-layered case. As for the single-layered case, this implies that the fitness values of a multi-layered modular system are uncorrelated with the fitness values of the original non-modular system.

To globally optimize this multi-layered modular system, one has to search *hierarchically* via multiple cycles fixing the standards at the top level, then fixing the standards at the middle level, and then optimize each leaf module. Since the top level interface consists of three interfaces, there are 2^3 possible standard settings at the first layer requiring 2^3 cycles of exploration. For each of the settings at the first layer, testing the middle layer interfaces also involves 2^3 cycles because each subsystem can be searched in parallel. Finally, optimizing each individual module takes 2^3 periods. Thus, total search time is $2^3 \cdot 2^3 \cdot 2^3 = 2^9 = 512$ periods, which is a small fraction of the time required to globally optimize a system of $N = 27$ (which requires 2^{27} periods).

Again, we look to minimize the time to globally optimize the system. Since, by Assumption 4, the number of interface standards equals the number of elements in the leaf modules, each level of the hierarchy takes the same amount of time to optimize. Thus, the time to global optimization is simply the product of the time required to optimize each level. We have, for modular systems:

$$C_{time} = (A^S)^L = A^{SL} \tag{7}$$

Due to symmetry, we may replace the size of the leaf modules (S) with an equivalent term utilising N and L. This relationship is (as shown by detailed proof in Appendix A):

$$S = N^{1/L} \tag{8}$$

Combining (7) and (8) gives:

$$C_{time} = A^{LN^{1/L}} \tag{9}$$

The previous, non-iterated optimization result may thus be seen as a specific case of this result with $L = 2$. Minimizing (9) with respect to L gives:

$$\begin{aligned} N^{1/L} + L(-L^{-2})N^{1/L}\ln(N) &= 0 \\ L &= \ln(N) \end{aligned} \tag{10}$$

Then the time that is required to globally optimize the optimal modular system is:

$$C_{optimal} = A^{(\ln N)N^{1/\ln N}} \tag{11}$$

Note again that optimal level of modularity is independent of A.

Given (8) and (10), one can derive the optimal module size:

$$\begin{aligned} S &= N^{1/\ln N} \\ \ln S &= 1 \\ S &= e \end{aligned} \tag{12}$$

Given optimal module size, one can now derive the values of N at which optimal modularity requires the introduction of a new layer. One should introduce a new layer of modules moving from $L = x$ to $L = x + 1$ if:

$$N = e^{x+1} \tag{13}$$

At this size, the system can be symmetrically divided into $x + 1$ layers with modules of optimal size.

It follows from Eq. 13 that, as N increases exponentially, L increases linearly; a corollary is that, as N increases linearly, L increases logarithmically. Modularity thus represents a mechanism for coping with exponential system growth. It also suggests a hypothesis that early in linear growth processes of a complex system, modularity structure will change regularly, while later in the process, changes in modularity structure will be increasingly rarer. Introduction of a modular structure slows the growth of polygeny relative to system size.

In order to understand the consequences of deviating from optimal modularity, we examined whether under- or over-modularization is more costly in terms of the additional search time required. Using Eq. 9, we plot computational complexity as $log_A(C_{time})$ for different values of L and N in Fig. 6. Note that we express the search time required for global optimization in terms of the logarithm of A, which render values of search time to be independent of A. The figure shows that computational complexity sharply decreases with addition of layers of modules, reaches the minimum, and then slowly increases. This suggests that it is a more robust strategy to over-modularize than under-modularize.

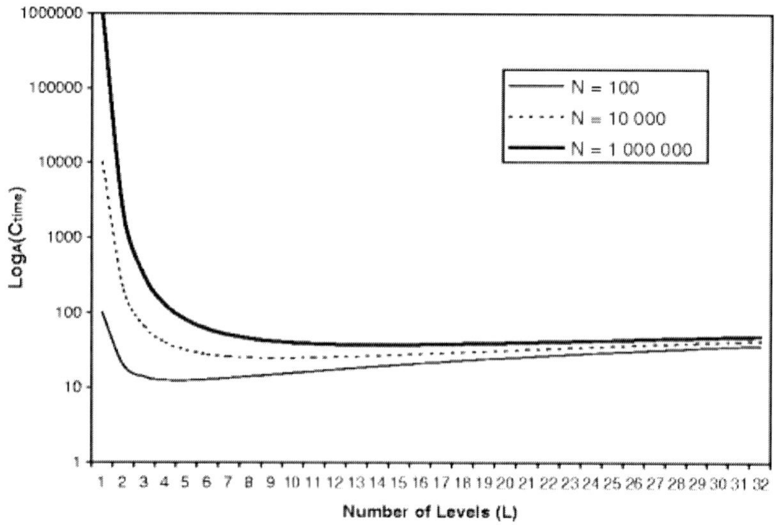

Figure 6. Search time required to find the global optimum

The question of whether under- or over-modularity is to be preferred has important general implications. They suggest, for example, heuristic strategies for product design under conditions of uncertainty. However, different models within the NK tradition exhibit conflicting results on this question. Geisendorf (2010) summarizes the debate as between those (Dosi and Marengo 2005; Brusoni et al. 2007) who find speed of evolution advantages to over-modularization and those (Levinthal 1997; Ethiraj and Levinthal 2004; Geisendorf 2010) who do not. There are also other papers which address the question which do not explicitly frame their results in terms of over-modularization (e.g. Frenken et al. 1999). These many papers vary significantly in their assumptions. These differences in assumptions (or model specifications) are important in explaining these divergent results. As an example of the understanding which can be gained from detailed comparison of specifications, we compare our model to the model by Ethiraj and Levinthal (2004) which did not find benefits to over-modularization. Here we present only the conclusions of this comparison, the full comparison being available in Appendix B. Our model focuses only on search time and thus only looks at the theorized advantages of modularity through reduced polygeny. The Ethiraj–Levinthal model features parallel search with no co-ordination regarding mutations in interface standards, meaning that increasing modularity leads to increasingly chaotic fitness dynamics. Given the many differences between the models, it is difficult to decide which model is likely to exhibit the more robust results.[1] It highlights the value of developing common frameworks in which differences between specifications can be tested more explicitly.

5 DISCUSSION

This paper has focused on the implications of modular structure from an evolutionary time savings perspective. The question has been what kind of modular architecture is optimal with respect to the speed at which trial-and-error search can find the global optimum. In line with recent ideas on evolvability (Ethiraj and Levinthal 2004; Rivkin and Siggelkow 2007), creating an architecture which allows efficient search may be as important as the search strategy applied to a given problem.[2] The interaction between the processes of architectural search and search within the current architecture is an interesting, though non-trivial, problem. Our analysis indeed shows that the choice of the right modular architecture creates strong advantages in the subsequent evolutionary search process towards the global optimum. If a designer is able to create a modular design with modules of optimal size, she realizes huge savings in the time required to find the global optimum by trial-and-error.

Our approach has been based on two important simplifications. First, we assumed that the creation of modular architectures did not itself involve time. The time devoted to creating a modular architecture will generally increase with the degree of modularity of that architecture (as more interface standards need to be introduced to separate elements into distinct modules). Once the problem of minimizing search time is translated into a cost minimization problem using a monetary value of time, the minimization problem can be extended to include the cost of the construction of an architecture, with such construction costs increasing with the degree of modularity as indicated previously by M. The cost perspective may have an impact on the desirability of over-modularization, as it would tend to attenuate the benefits of modularization.

A second simplification in our analysis is that our derivation of optimal modularity only takes into account the search time required to globally optimize the system and ignores the effects of modularization on the fitness value of the global optimum obtained. In our model, optimal modularity is achieved by minimizing the search time required for global optimization. Put differently, in designing a system with optimal modularity, one aims at minimizing the number of times the fitness values are redrawn. In the case of a non-modular system, for example, fitness values are redrawn A^N times, while for a system with optimal modularity, fitness values for each module are redrawn only $A^{(S+M)}$ times. Since fitness values are redrawn less often for a system with optimal modularity compared to other systems, this implies that the global optimum of a non-modular system has a higher fitness than the global optimum of a system with optimal modularity, since N is greater that S+M (Kaul and Jacobson 2006). Thus, the advantage of modular systems in terms of search time may be offset by lower fitness, depending on how much weight is given to fitness obtained compared to search time required.

Note that the fitness of the global optimum of a non-modular system and the fitness of the global optimum a system with optimal modularity approach 1 asymptotically as system size N goes to infinity. Thus, the difference in their fitness values will start decreasing at some point as system size N increases. For sufficiently large systems, the negative effect of modularization on the fitness of the global optimum is only marginal and can be neglected. This conclusion is tied to the global search strategy, which is employed here. Whether fitness effects can similarly be taken as minimal when alternative search strategies are employed is an open question.

A final area for future research is to consider different search strategies within the framework we have discussed. Similar to our argument about the status of decomposable systems, a global optimization strategy is an analytical construct rarely seen in reality. In reality, shifts in the underlying landscape, cognitive and power limitations of agents, and opportunity costs (i.e. the tension between exploration and exploitation) mean that search processes are in reality satisficing as opposed to optimizing (Simon 1969). This then poses the question as to what hierarchical search might look like in a satisficing context. Two possibilities are discussed which suggest the utility of this framework in terms of future research potential.

Gavetti et al. (2005) explore the idea of analogy as a search strategy within an NK context. Their conceptualization of search is the resolution of "high level" choices through analogical knowledge flowing from experience followed by resolution of "low level" choices through local search. In this case, analogy is a tool that leverages past experience in order to suggest promising segments of the landscape within which to search using local search. In the original paper, the idea was to explore knowledge derived from different regions of the fitness landscape. In the case of the modular structure proposed here, it would be interesting to explore experiential knowledge of architectures. This would mean setting the interfaces on the basis of analogy, followed by local search within these interfaces. A first step in this setup might be to set standards randomly and proceed with low-level search. This would provide a baseline for assessing the impact of architectural knowledge.

A second possibility is to model recursive problem solving (a concept inspired by Arthur 2007). The departure point of this is to frame invention as a recursive problem solving process, in which work on a solution proceeds between levels and focuses on the most problematic component. This could be abstracted as a hierarchical extremal search wherein the lowest functioning module is the focus of search. If a satisfactory solution can be found at the level of the module, then it is resolved at that level. If this is not the case, search proceeds down the hierarchy in a recursive manner. After sufficient exploration of sub-modules, if a satisfactory solution is still not found, then the problem is elevated to the level of the hierarchy above which the problem occurred. In our terms, search begins at level N, moves down the hierarchy to level L, and then is elevated to exploration of the interfaces at level N + 1.

These discussion points indicate that, though the model we have presented is rather restrictive in the assumptions it utilized, it offers interesting possibilities for further research, which relaxes these assumptions. It represents the crucial first step of offering a formally consistent framework wherein an analytical baseline can be defined. Further, it confirms the primary hypothesis of the modularity literature: that modularity increases speed of evolution (Simon 2002). It does so by formally linking modular structure to a decrease in interdependencies between elements.

6 CONCLUDING REMARKS

We had aimed to define modularity formally and explore the hypothesis that it represents a mechanism for increasing the speed of evolution. We have derived the optimal level of modularity with respect to the time required to globally optimize a system, both for two-layered hierarchies and multi-layered hierarchies. Our approach has taken advantage of rather restrictive assumptions in order to generate analytically tractable results. We have discussed several logical routes to relax these assumptions in future work.

A second line of research is to conduct empirical research on the levels of modularity of systems varying in size, so as to provide an empirical basis for the formal theory. For example, further work might be conducted into the suggestions that modularity of problem decomposition is observable in entrepreneurs who are involved in rapidly expanding enterprises (Sarasvathy and Simon 2000).

In the longer run, we hope our approach to modular systems contributes to a consistent formal approach to modularity in the fields of economics, innovation studies and organization science in a way that renders the results from different modelling exercises mutually comparable.

FOOTNOTES

[1] Robustness refers to a result that survives changes in specification.

[2] A similar argument has been made by Wagner and Altenberg (1996) in the context of biology.

[3] In fact, under one variant of the Ethiraj and Levinthal specification (2004, p.170), over-modularity is in fact preferable. Thus, even within the confines of a particular approach, small variances in specification can be important.

REFERENCES

1. Altenberg L (1994) Evolving better representations through selective genome growth. In: Proceedings of the IEEE world congress on computational intelligence, pp 182–187
2. Arthur WB (2007) The structure of invention. Res Policy 36(2):274–287
3. Baldwin CY (2008) Where do transactions come from? Modularity, transactions, and the boundaries of firms. Ind Corp Change 17(1):155–195
4. Baldwin CY, Clark KB (2000) Design rules, vol 1: the power of modularity. Cambridge: MIT Press
5. Bradshaw G (1992) The airplane and the logic of invention. In: RN Giere (ed) Cognitive models of science. The University of Minnesota Press, Minneapolis, pp 239–250
6. Brusoni S, Marengo L, Prencipe A, Valente M (2007) The value and costs of modularity: a problem-solving perspective. Eur Manage Rev 4:121–132
7. Ciarli T, Leoncini R, Montresor S, Valente M (2008) Technological change and the vertical organization of industries. J Evol Econ 18:367–387
8. Dosi G, Marengo L (2005) Division of labor, organizational coordination and market mechanisms in collective problem-solving. J Econ Behav Organ 58:303–326
9. Ethiraj SK, Levinthal DA (2004) Modularity and innovation in complex systems. Manage Sci 50:159–173

10. Frenken K (2006) A fitness landscape approach to technological complexity, modularity, and vertical disintegration. Struct Change Econ Dynam 17(3):288–305

11. Frenken K, Nuvolari A (2004). The early development of the steam engine: an evolutionary interpretation using complexity theory. Ind Corp Change 13(2):419–450

12. Frenken K, Marengo L, Valente M (1999) Interdependencies, near-decomposability and adaptation. In: Brenner T (ed) Computational techniques for modelling learning in economics. Kluwer, Boston, pp 145–165

13. Gavetti G, Levinthal DA, Rivkin JW (2005) Strategy making in novel and complex worlds: the power of analogy. Strateg Manage J 26(8):691–712

14. Geisendorf S (2010) Searching NK fitness landscapes: on the trade off between speed and quality in complex problem solving. Comput Econ 35:395–406

15. Henderson RM, Clark KB (1990) Architectural innovation. Admin Sci Q 35:9–30

16. Kauffman SA (1993) The origins of order. Self-organization and selection in evolution. Oxford University Press, New York

17. Kaul H, Jacobson SH (2006) Global optima results for the Kauffman NK model. Math Program 106(2):319–338

18. Langlois R, Garzarelli G (2008) Of hackers and hairdressers: modularity and the organizational economics of open-source collaboration. Ind Innov 15(2):125–143

19. Levinthal DA (1997) Adaptation on rugged landscapes. Manage Sci 43:934–950

20. Marengo L, Dosi G, Legrenzi P, Pasquali C (2000) The structure of problem-solving knowledge and the structure of organizations. Ind Corp Change 9:757–788

21. McNerney J, Farmer JD, Rdener S, Trancik JE (2011) The role of design complexity in technology improvement. Proc Natl Acad Sci USA 108(22):9008–9013

22. Newman MEJ (2006) Modularity and community structure in networks. Proc Natl Acad Sci USA 103:8577–8582

23. Page SE (1996) Two measures of difficulty. Econ Theory 8:321–346

24. Rivkin JW, Siggelkow N (2007) Patterned interactions in complex systems: Implications for exploration. Manage Sci 53:1068–1085

25. Sarasvathy S, Simon HA (2000) Effectuation, near-decomposability, and the creation and growth of entrepreneurial firms. In: Presented at the first research policy technology entrepreneurship conference, University of Maryland. Available online at http://www.effectuation.org/ftp/Neardeco.doc., accessed on 18 September 2009

26. Simon HA (1962) The architecture of complexity: hierarchic systems. Proc Amer Phil Soc 106:467–482

27. Simon HA (1969) The sciences of the artificial, third edition. MIT Press, Cambridge, 1996

28. Simon HA (2002) Near decomposability and the speed of evolution. Ind Corp Change 11:587–599

29. Wagner GP, Altenberg L (1996) Complex adaptations and the evolution of evolvability. Evol 50:967–976

5

WHAT TURNS KNOWLEDGE INTO INNOVATIVE PRODUCTS? THE ROLE OF ENTREPRENEURSHIP AND KNOWLEDGE SPILLOVERS

Joern H. Block[1,2,3,] · Roy Thurik1,2,4,5 · Haibo Zhou[6]

[1]Centre for Advanced Small Business Economics, Erasmus School of Economics, Erasmus University Rotterdam, P.O. Box 1738, 3000 DR Rotterdam, The Netherlands

[2]Erasmus Research Institute of Management (ERIM), Erasmus University Rotterdam, Rotterdam, The Netherlands

[3]Schöller Chair in Technology and Innovation Management, Technische Universität München, München, Germany

[4]Panteia/EIM, P.O. Box 7001, 2701 AA Zoetermeer, The Netherlands

[5]GSCM-Montpellier Business School, Montpellier, France

[6]Department of Innovation Management and Strategy, University of Groningen, P.O. Box 800, 9700 AV Groningen, The Netherlands

ABSTRACT

The knowledge spillover theory of entrepreneurship seeks to explain the fundamentals and consequences of entrepreneurship with respect to economic performance. This paper uses the knowledge spillover theory to explain different innovation outcomes. We hypothesize that a high rate of entrepreneurship facilitates the process of turning knowledge into new-to-the-market innovation but has no effect on the relationship between knowledge and new-to-the-firm innovation. Our results using European country-level and pooled OLS, fixed- and random-effects regressions show that a high rate of entrepreneurship increases the chances that knowledge will become new-to-the-market innovation. The findings highlight the importance of Schumpeterian entrepreneurship in the process of the commercialization of knowledge. We discuss the implications for entrepreneurship and innovation policy.

Keywords: Innovation, Entrepreneurship, Knowledge spillovers, Patents, Commercialization of knowledge, Community innovation survey

1 INTRODUCTION

Endogenous growth theory assumes that an economy automatically benefits from its investments in new knowledge (Lucas 1988; Romer 1990) because knowledge is a public good that can be used by an entire economy, leading to innovation and economic growth (Cantner et al. 2008). In the empirical world of the R&D capital approach (Mansfield 1965; Griliches 1998, 2000), the development of total factor productivity (TFP) is explained using an R&D stock variable.[1] Although a great deal of evidence shows that knowledge (R&D stock) leads to growth (TFP growth), some countries seem to benefit more from investments in new knowledge than others. The US, for example, is thought to commercialize new knowledge better than Europe, giving rise to what is referred to as the Swedish paradox (Ejermo and Kander 2006) or the European paradox (Audretsch 2007). Investment in new knowledge is only one necessary condition; new knowledge must be exploited and put to commercial use so that it can translate into stronger competitiveness and subsequent economic growth (Braunerhjelm and Svensson 2010; Carlsson et al. 2009) This barrier between knowledge and its commercialization is referred to as the knowledge filter (Acs et al. 2009; Braunerhjelm et al. 2010).[2]

The contribution of Acs et al. (2009) extends the microeconomic foundations of endogenous growth models (Lucas 1988; Romer 1990) through the knowledge spillover theory of entrepreneurship, which holds that knowledge creation can lead to knowledge spillovers, creating technological opportunities. Entrepreneurs then exploit these opportunities, leading to economic growth and development. New product innovations may come from both incumbent firms and start-ups. Incumbent firms mainly produce incremental innovations from the flow of knowledge, whereas start-ups tend to exploit knowledge spillovers to produce radical innovations.

Braunerhjelm et al. (2010) use the knowledge spillover theory of entrepreneurship to explain the European or Swedish paradox (Ejermo and Kander 2006; Audretsch 2007). They develop a theoretical model in which the transformation of knowledge into economic growth depends on how knowledge diffuses through both incumbent and entrepreneurial activity. The entrepreneur is the "missing link in converting knowledge into economically relevant knowledge" (Braunerhjelm et al. 2010, p. 105). Based on OECD data from 1981 to 2002, they show that entrepreneurship Granger-causes economic growth and that this effect increased in the 1990s, as the knowledge economy began to grow.

Our paper links the knowledge spillover theory of entrepreneurship (Acs et al. 2009) to empirical innovation research using different types of innovation as outcome variables. Whereas the empirical model of Braunerhjelm et al. (2010) tests the effects of entrepreneurship on economic growth when the link to innovation is indirect, we seek to explain the effect of entrepreneurship on the transformation of knowledge into innovation. A research gap exists in the link between the knowledge spillover theory of entrepreneurship and empirical research about innovation and the commercialization of knowledge (Carlsson et al. 2009; Braunerhjelm and Svensson 2010). In our paper, we will discriminate between innovations that are *new to the market* and those that are *new to the firm*. Based upon the knowledge spillover theory, we hypothesize that a high rate of entrepreneurship facilitates the process of turning knowledge into new-to-the-market innovation but has no important effect on the relationship between knowledge and new-to-the-firm innovation.

Our focus, and, therefore, our unit of observation, is at the country level rather than at the individual-firm level. We use a panel dataset that covers the innovation activity of 21 European countries in four waves, corresponding to the period from 1996 to 2006. The results clearly show that entrepreneurship, measured as the business ownership rate, is an important driver for turning knowledge into new-to-the-market innovation but has no impact on new-to-the-firm innovation. This finding is precisely what the knowledge spillover theory of entrepreneurship and prior entrepreneurship research predicts. Entrepreneurs as individuals are considered risk takers (Kihlstrom and Laffont 1979) who are tolerant of ambiguity (Schere 1982). Thus, they play an important role when risk and uncertainty are involved, such as new-to-the-market innovations, but less so for new-to-the-firm innovations, for which product uncertainty and risk are much lower. Our paper contributes to our understanding of the knowledge spillover theory, particularly why and under what conditions entrepreneurship leads to innovation and economic growth.

This paper also enhances understanding of the types of innovation that are most closely related to entrepreneurship.

Following this introduction, Section 2 introduces the literature on economic growth, knowledge spillovers and types of innovation. Section 3 develops our hypotheses using the knowledge spillover theory of entrepreneurship and links this theory to different innovation outcomes. Section 4 summarizes our data and the empirical model. Section 5 reports our regression results, which are discussed in Section 6. Section 7 concludes.

2 RELATED LITERATURE

2.1 Entrepreneurship and economic growth

A small part of the literature on the economics of entrepreneurship focuses on the role of entrepreneurship as it impacts economic growth. In this literature, entrepreneurship is often presented as an additional production factor, called entrepreneurship capital (Audretsch 2007). In this sense, however, it does not contribute to our understanding of the exact mechanism of the transformation of knowledge into economic growth. The main question is *why* entrepreneurship leads to growth. Literature surveys of the influence of entrepreneurship on economic growth (Van Praag and Versloot 2007; Braunerhjelm 2008; Parker 2009; Carree and Thurik 2010) are relatively vague, except to say that entrepreneurship is expected to lead to diversity, innovation, competition, employment, and learning, at which point economic growth occurs. Among the studies of entrepreneurship and economic growth, Baumol (2002) is the clearest in stating that innovation is the essence of economic growth. The knowledge spillover theory of entrepreneurship (Acs et al. 2009; Braunerhjelm et al. 2010) is an important step in understanding the microeconomic foundations of how entrepreneurship leads to economic growth. In the three succeeding subsections, we briefly summarize the literature on knowledge spillovers and the knowledge spillover theory of entrepreneurship, and then we turn to the main focus of this study: the different types of innovation and their relation to knowledge.

2.2 Knowledge spillovers and geographical boundaries

The production of knowledge can lead to spillovers when individuals or organizations other than the creators of knowledge benefit from the knowledge that the creator has produced. Thus, by investing in knowledge, a firm not only increases its own level of knowledge but also contributes to the aggregate stock of knowledge (Romer 1986; Lucas 1993; Griliches 1998). For example, when securing a patent, a firm produces new knowledge, and the information included in the patent becomes accessible to the general public and to competitors. A competitor may use the information from the patent for its own research and invest in related knowledge, and this related knowledge may lead to new patents or innovative products. In other words, knowledge may spill over from one firm to another. There is extensive research on knowledge spillovers in multiple contexts, such as technology transfer (e.g., Anselin et al. 1997; Carlsson and Fridh 2002), innovation networks (e.g., Breschi and Lissoni 2001), technology clusters (e.g., Werker and Athreye 2004), and the evolution of industries (e.g., Malerba 2006). This research has shown that geographical proximity matters if knowledge spillovers are to occur. Although knowledge may spill over to firms or individuals far from the creator of knowledge, the literature has shown that spillovers are more likely to occur on a local level (Jaffe et al. 1993; Anselin et al. 1997; Varga 2000; Keller 2002; Bottazzi and Peri 2003). Anselin et al. (1997) show that university research and regional innovative activities are positively related, and there is evidence that university research impacts business R&D both directly and indirectly. Using a dataset that covers most of the world's innovative activity between 1970 and 1995, Keller (2002) shows that the benefits of knowledge spillovers decline with distance. However, there is evidence of an autonomous time trend towards more global knowledge diffusion.

2.3 The knowledge spillover theory of entrepreneurship

Entrepreneurship is identified by its role in the recognition, discovery, and creation of opportunities (Shane and Venkataraman 2000). Little is known, however, about the source of these opportunities. The knowledge spillover theory of entrepreneurship (Acs et al. 2009; Braunerhjelm et al. 2010, for a collection of recent papers, see Acs 2010) has helped to close this gap in understanding, and knowledge spillovers are now regarded as a possible source of entrepreneurial opportunities, called endogenous entrepreneurship.[3] Due to the noncompetitive nature of knowledge as an asset, it may spill over so that the producers of knowledge are not able to appropriate the entire value of their knowledge for themselves. These spillovers may then serve as a source of opportunities for other firms and for individuals who want to start their own businesses (Acs et al. 2009; Braunerhjelm et al. 2010). The knowledge spillover theory of entrepreneurship holds that entrepreneurial activity is greater when there is greater investment in knowledge. This argument is supported by Audretsch and Lehmann (2005), among others, who show that regions with greater investments in new knowledge also have higher start-up rates. Another facet of the theory holds that opportunities for entrepreneurship are superior when the ability to access knowledge spillovers from geographically proximate sources is greater, based on the assumption that knowledge spillovers increase economic performance (Lucas 1988; Romer 1990; Glaeser et al. 1992; Acs and Armington 2004) and that this relationship is moderated by geographical proximity (Jaffe et al. 1993; Anselin et al. 1997; Varga 2000; Keller 2002; Bottazzi and Peri 2003). This is especially likely when the entrepreneur is located in close proximity to universities, large high-tech firms or other research-intensive institutions that produce knowledge (Anselin et al. 1997; Carlsson and Fridh 2002).

In short, the knowledge spillover theory shows how entrepreneurship can contribute to growth by helping knowledge to spill over or to permeate the filter that impedes knowledge spillover. The knowledge spillover theory attributes importance not only to the role of persons but also to regional agglomerations of knowledge activities (entrepreneurship capital) that become the breeding ground for growth.

2.4 Knowledge and types of innovation

The literature discusses the following types of innovation and innovation indicators: (1) R&D efforts, (2) patent measures, and (3) product-related indicators (Hauser and Zettelmeyer 1997; Kleinknecht et al. 2002). R&D efforts comprise R&D as a percentage of sales or assets and measure a firm's input in the innovation process. R&D efforts also serve to measure a firm's absorptive capacity (Cohen and Levinthal 1989) and knowledge potential. Patent measures, which comprise patent counts and patent issuances, may be interpreted as output-based measures of technological knowledge (Park and Park 2006). Product-related innovation indicators refer to measures of new product introduction. New product introductions can be differentiated into *new-to-the-firm* and *new-to-the-market* product introductions. The former category is sometimes interpreted as imitative behavior, and the latter category is interpreted as 'true' innovation (Kleinknecht et al. 2002). Due to their high degree of novelty, new-to-the-market innovations are characterized by high levels of technological and market uncertainty (Scherer et al. 2000), whereas this may not be true of new-to-the-firm innovation. The risk of customer acceptance can be reduced with a strategy of imitation because the product is already known to the market and to its customers (Bolton 1993). In conjunction with differences in the degree of uncertainty, new-to-the-market innovation should show a stronger association with patents than new-to-the-firm innovation because novelty is a central requirement for the patentability of an invention.

Our paper aggregates firm-level innovation data to the country level and then distinguishes between a country's level of *new-to-the-firm* and *new-to-the-market* innovations as outcome variables.

3 ENTREPRENEURSHIP AS A FACTOR THAT TURNS KNOWLEDGE INTO INNOVATION

The purpose of this paper is to apply the knowledge spillover theory of entrepreneurship (Acs et al. 2009; Braunerhjelm et al. 2010) to analyze the effect of entrepreneurship in turning knowledge into different innovation outcomes. As summarized in the preceding section, existing literature using the knowledge spillover theory of entrepreneurship examines the sources of entrepreneurship and their effects on economic growth. The link between entrepreneurship and innovation is indirect. For example, the literature suggests that entrepreneurship increases economic output by facilitating the commercialization of knowledge, but this link has not been analyzed in detail, and no distinction has been made between different types of innovation (Hauser and Zettelmeyer 1997; Kleinknecht et al. 2002). This paper attempts to take the first steps in these directions by arguing that entrepreneurship is more likely to influence the process that leads knowledge to be converted into *new-to-the-market* innovations as opposed to *new-to-the-firm* innovations.

Innovation relates to two interrelated processes, the production of knowledge[4] and the exploitation of knowledge. We focus on the exploitation phase, particularly on the mechanism that turns knowledge into innovative products. The commercialization of knowledge, especially new knowledge, includes efforts such as financing product development or market research. The outcome of this process is often uncertain and requires a risk-taking attitude among the managers of the process, making the entrepreneurial attitude important at this stage. Entrepreneurs are considered different from other individuals because, for example, they are believed to have an above-average level of willingness to take risks (Block et al. 2010a; Kihlstrom and Laffont 1979; Brockhaus 1980), a tolerance for ambiguity (Timmons 1976; Schere 1982), a need for achievement (McClelland 1961), and a preference for autonomy (Benz and Frey 2008; Block and Köllinger 2009). In particular, risk-taking and a tolerance for ambiguity are crucial for managing the process of commercializing new knowledge. A high rate of entrepreneurship and exposure to an entrepreneurial climate thus facilitates the process of turning knowledge into innovative products (Beugelsdijk 2007). Thus, we propose the following hypothesis:

Entrepreneurship moderates the relationship between knowledge and new-to-the-market innovation.

We hypothesize that entrepreneurship has little or no effect on turning knowledge into new-to-the-firm innovation because this type of innovation requires less risk taking and uncertainty. New-to-the-firm innovation is 'imitative' innovation and is associated with little market and/or technology uncertainty. It requires different skills and capabilities than new-to-the-market innovation, and places more importance on a firm's learning and imitation capabilities (Cohen and Levinthal 1989; Schewe 1996) than on entrepreneurship. Hence, we propose the following hypothesis:

Entrepreneurship does not moderate the relationship between knowledge and new-to-the-firm innovation.

4 DATA AND EMPIRICAL MODEL

4.1 Data sources

Our study combines data from the Community Innovation Survey (CIS),[5] the COMPENDIA database,[6] and the OECD Economic Outlook Database.[7]

The CIS is commissioned by the European Commission and records the innovation activity of firms in the EU member states, in EU candidate countries, and in Iceland and Norway. The first CIS was conducted in 1993 using a pilot version (CIS1). Since then, four additional surveys have been conducted: CIS2 (1996–1998), CIS3 (1998–2000), CIS4 (2002–2004), and CIS2006 (2004–2006). The survey unit of the CIS is the enterprise, and the target population is the total population of enterprises in a particular country. Because sampling rates may differ across countries, the CIS uses a stratified sampling procedure and weighting procedures to ensure that the samples are representative of the total population of enterprises in each country. The results of the firm-level CIS are aggregated and transmitted to Eurostat on a compulsory basis. CIS data are accepted in the research community and have been widely used in innovation research (Arundel 2001; Mairesse and Mohnen 2002, 2005; Hoelzl 2009).

COMPENDIA (COMParative ENtrepreneurship Data for International Analysis) is developed and maintained by EIM Business and Policy Research (a Panteia company) in the Netherlands. The database summarizes and harmonizes information about the number of business owners and the size of the labor force from the OECD databases, the ILO Yearbook of Labour Statistics and the European Observatory for SMEs. The quotient of these two variables is called the business ownership rate (Van Stel 2005). Business ownership includes all unincorporated self-employed persons and owner-managers of incorporated businesses (OMIBs) (Van Stel 2005). Although it has been argued that business ownership is not synonymous with entrepreneurship, Carree et al. (2002) acknowledge that the level of business ownership is a fair reflection of the level of entrepreneurship in a particular country. The main advantage of this harmonized dataset is that it makes entrepreneurship activity comparable across countries and over time. The latest version of the COMPENDIA consists of 23 OECD countries for the period of 1972–2007.

The OECD Economic Outlook Database indicates historical trends and future projections for a wide range of macro indicators that describe the demographic, social, economic and environmental developments of a country, including the gross domestic product, rate of unemployment and deflators and prices. The dataset encompasses longitudinal information on macro indicators from the 30 OECD member countries and 6 selected non-OECD countries. We rely on this database to build our country-specific control variables.

Our final assembled dataset includes aggregated information on innovation activity from manufacturing firms (NACE 15–37),[8] business ownership rates, and macro indicators for 21 European countries[9] in four waves during the period from 1996 to 2006. We restrict our sample to the manufacturing sector to ensure that our results are not driven by differences in industry structure between countries. Because not all countries are included in each wave, our final dataset takes the form of an unbalanced panel dataset.

4.2 Dependent variables

The measurement of innovation includes various dimensions and varies according to firms and their life-cycle phases. Innovation and its performance can be measured in many ways: by the turnover of new products, increases in productivity or decreases in production cost as a result of introducing new processes, or customer satisfaction with new products or services (for overviews, see Hauser and Zettelmeyer 1997; Kleinknecht et al. 2002). The CIS measures innovation performance in two ways: (1) shares of turnover attributable to new or significantly improved products that are new to the firm (variable *new-to-the-firm innovation*) and (2) shares of turnover attributable to new or significantly improved products that are new to the market (variable *new-to-the-market innovation*). With respect to *new-to-the-firm innovation*, the CIS asks respondents to state the share of "goods and service innovations introduced during the last three years that were only new to your firm (your enterprise introduced a new or significantly improved good or service that was already available from your competitors in your market)". With respect to *new-to-the-market innovation*, the CIS asks the respondents to report the share of "goods and service innovations introduced during the last three years that were new to your market (your enterprise introduced a new or significantly improved good or service onto your market before your competitors) [...]".

As noted in our theory section, we argue that entrepreneurship and an entrepreneurial attitude are particularly important with regard to *new-to-the-market innovation* and are less important for *new-to-the-firm innovation*.

4.3 Independent variables

Rate of knowledge-intensive firms

As discussed above, the production of new knowledge is a crucial factor that leads to innovation. We measure a country's level of knowledge as the share of firms that applied for at least one patent in the survey year. We consider this measure a good proxy for knowledge in the context of this study because patents are property rights granted by a patent authority, such as the European Patent Office (EPO). For a patent to be granted, the invention must be non-trivial and must have potential commercial value. Patents have been used in a number of studies as a proxy for knowledge and knowledge spillover (Jaffe et al. 1993, 2000; Acs et al. 2002; Furman et al. 2002). We use data obtained from the CIS. As a robustness check, as proxies for knowledge production, we use alternative measures, such as a country's gross expenditure on R&D or its level of business R&D. We believe, however, that patent-based measures are more appropriate than R&D-based measures for our particular research question because our paper examines the role of entrepreneurship in turning 'commercializable' knowledge into innovation. Patents constitute an intermediate output of knowledge production (Kleinknecht et al. 2002) and are proxies for knowledge that can be commercialized. Not surprisingly, we find that our patent-based knowledge measure correlates strongly with a country's gross expenditure on R&D ($r = 0.68$, $p < 0.01$) and/or its level of business R&D ($r = 0.69$, $p < 0.01$).

Entrepreneurship rate

Because of the heterogeneous context of entrepreneurship, there is no unique variable that measures entrepreneurship or entrepreneurial climate. Commonly used measures are self-employment rates, business ownership rates, and numbers of new firm start-ups. We use the business ownership rate to measure entrepreneurship. Our results also hold when we use the rate of self-employment as a proxy for entrepreneurship. The business ownership rate is calculated as the share of business owners in the total labor force. Business owners are defined as individuals whose main occupation is self-employment, including owner-managers of incorporated businesses. The data are obtained from COMPENDIA. As an alternative entrepreneurship measure, we could have used data from the Global Entrepreneurship Monitor (GEM) (Acs and Varga 2005; Reynolds et al. 2005). However, there is little overlap between the CIS data, which we used to construct our two dependent variables, *new-to-the-firm innovation* and *new-to-the-market innovation*, and the GEM data. In particular, we would not be able to run panel data regressions and control for unobserved heterogeneity.

Control variables

To control for macro-economic influences, two macro-economic variables are included in the regression models, *GDP* and *GDP per capita*. These variables are taken from the OECD Economic Outlook Database. To achieve comparability over time, the values of *GDP* and *GDP per capita* are adjusted to 1995 prices. Both variables are represented as logged values and refer to a country's size or level of wealth. As robustness checks, we also include the variables *share of small firms* and *share of venture capital investments in GDP* as additional controls.

4.4 Empirical model

The following two pooled OLS equations are used for the empirical analysis:

$$I_{i,t} = \alpha + \beta_1 (K_{i,t}) + \beta_2 (E_{i,t}) + \beta_3 (K_{it} E_{it}) + \beta_4 (Controls_{i,t}) + \beta_5 (Years_t) + \varepsilon_{i,t},$$

where *I* is either *new-to-the-market innovation* (the share of turnover attributable to new or significantly improved products that are new to the market) or *new-to-the-firm innovation* (the share of turnover attributable to new or significantly improved products that are new to the firm); *K* denotes the rate of knowledge-intensive firms measured by the share of firms that applied for at least one patent in the last three years; *E* denotes the business ownership rate as a proxy for the entrepreneurship rate; *Controls* denotes the control variables, which are the natural logarithm of *GDP* and the natural logarithm of *GDP per capita*; *Years* corresponds to year dummies for the years 1998, 2000, 2004, and 2006; and *i* and *t* are country and year indices, respectively. Table 1 describes the construction of the variables in more detail. To conduct a robustness check, we estimated random- and fixed-effects regressions (Wooldridge 2002) using the same variables.

Table 1. Description of variables

Variable	Description	Data source
New-to-the-market innovation (in %)	CIS question: "What is the percentage of total turnover from goods and service innovations introduced during the last three years that were new to the market?" The question was included in CIS2 (1996–1998), CIS3 (1998–2000), CIS4 (2002–2004), and CIS2006 (2004–2006)	Community Innovation Survey: CIS2, CIS3, CIS4, and CIS2006 (only answers from manufacturing firms)
New-to-the-firm innovation (in %)	CIS question: "What is the percentage of total turnover from goods and service innovations introduced during the last three years that were new to the firm?" The question was included in CIS2 (1996–1998), CIS3 (1998–2000), CIS4 (2002–2004), and CIS2006 (2004–2006)	Community Innovation Survey: CIS2, CIS3, CIS4, and CIS2006 (only answers from manufacturing firms)
Ln (GDP)	Natural logarithm of Gross Domestic Product in million US $; in purchasing power parities adjusted to prices from 1995	OECD Economic Outlook Database 2009
Ln (GDP per capita)	Natural logarithm of Gross Domestic Product divided by total population; US dollars; in purchasing power parities adjusted to prices from 1995	OECD Economic Outlook Database 2009
Entrepreneurship rate (in %)	The number of business owners (excluding the agricultural sector) as a percent of the total labor force	COMPENDIA (version of 2007)
Rate of knowledge-intensive firms (in %)	CIS question: "During the last three years, did your enterprise apply for a patent?" The question was included in CIS2 (1996–1998), CIS3 (1998–2000), CIS4 (2002–2004), and CIS2006 (2004–2006). The variable is calculated as the number of firms that answered 'yes' as a percentage of the total number of firms	Community Innovation Survey: CIS2, CIS3, CIS4, and CIS2006 (only answers from manufacturing firms)

5 RESULTS

5.1 Descriptive statistics

Descriptive statistics for the variables are presented in Table 2. The mean percentage of turnover for new-to-the-market innovations is 8%, with a variation of 1% to 24%. The mean percentage of turnover for new-to-the-firm innovations is 13%, with a variation of 4% to 41%. The mean rate of entrepreneurship is 11%, with a variation of 5% to 21%, and the mean proportion of firms that applied for a patent is 10%, with a range of 2% to 27%. Table 3 shows a correlation table. The variables *new-to-the-market innovation* and *new-to-the-firm* *innovation* are *not* correlated ($r = 0.05$, $p > 0.1$), indicating that they relate to different characteristics of new products (and countries). Except for the correlations between *knowledge* and the natural logarithm of *GDP per capita* as well as *knowledge* and *new-to-the-firm innovation*, all correlations are below 0.5. With innovation and imitation performance as the dependent variables, the variance inflation factors (VIFs) do not exceed 3. Although we conclude that multicollinearity is not likely to be an issue, we use step-wise regressions to learn about the interrelationships among the independent variables.

Table 2. Descriptive statistics

Variables	Mean	Median	Std. dev.	Min.	Max.
New-to-the-market innovation (in %)	8.12	7.30	3.96	1.00	23.90
New-to-the-firm innovation (in %)	12.84	10.40	7.71	3.70	41.10
Ln(GDP)	12.47	12.25	1.17	8.97	14.55
GDP (in million US $)	486,722	208,854	565,727	7,867	2,076,601
Ln(GDP per capita)	10.03	10.08	0.31	9.30	10.96
GDP per capita (in US $)	23,734	23,820	7,985	10,985	57,282
Entrepreneurship rate (in %)	10.78	9.80	3.90	5.20	21.00
Rate of knowledge-intensive firms (in %)	10.14	9.70	6.38	1.60	27.20

N = 57 observations from 21 countries
Data sources: CIS, COMPENDIA, and OECD Economic Outlook Database

Table 3. Correlations and variance inflation factors

	Variables	1	2	3	4	5	VIFs
1	New-to-the-market innovation						
2	New-to-the-firm innovation	0.05					
3	Enterepreneurship rate	0.01	−0.20				1.69
4	Rate of knowledge-intensive firms	0.02	0.51*	−0.48*			2.97
5	ln (GDP per captia)	−0.26*	0.09	−0.34*	0.56*		1.83
6	ln (GDP)	0.10	0.32*	0.24*	0.27*	−0.15	1.59

* $p < 0.10$, two-tailed tests
N = 57 observation from 21 countries; VIF = variance inflation factor
Year dummies are included in the calculation of the VIFs
The VIF values are all below 3 in the regressions
Data sources: CIS, COMPENDIA, and OECD Economic Outlook Database

5.2 Pooled OLS regressions of new-to-the-market innovation

Table 4 shows the results of pooled OLS regressions with respect to new-to-the-market innovation (standard errors are clustered). The empirical analysis is conducted in four steps with four representative models.

Model I is the baseline model, which includes the macro-economic control variables and the year dummies. This model explains 13% of the variation in *new-to-the-market innovation* (our dependent variable). In Model II, the knowledge variable is added to the baseline model to test the effect of *knowledge* on *new-to-the-market innovation*. As expected, a higher share of knowledge-intensive firms leads to a higher share of new-to-the-market innovations ($\beta = 0.27, p < 0.1$). The positive relationship of *knowledge* and *new-to-the-market innovation* increases the explanatory power of the model by 9% and confirms that the stock of knowledge is an important determinant of innovation performance. Model III includes the entrepreneurship variable in the model and shows that the rate of entrepreneurship itself does not seem to affect new-to-the-market innovation ($\beta = 0.09, p = 0.67$). The effect of the knowledge variable hardly increases, from $\beta = 0.27$ ($p < 0.10$) in Model II to $\beta = 0.31$ ($p < 0.05$) in Model III. Model IV tests the moderation effect of entrepreneurship, and the interaction term shows a positive effect ($\beta = 0.07, p < 0.05$). The explanatory power increases by 7%, from $R^2 = 22\%$ in Model III to $R^2 = 29\%$ in Model IV. A higher rate of entrepreneurship seems to increase the rate by which knowledge leads to new-to-the-market innovations, indicating that a higher rate of entrepreneurship facilitates the commercialization of knowledge. Entrepreneurship is found to moderate the relationship between knowledge and new-to-the-market innovation. To determine whether the OLS model produces consistent results, we perform a Breusch-Pagan test for random effects (Breusch and Pagan 1980). The test shows significant results for Models I–II and insignificant results for Models III–IV. Thus, we conclude that the OLS coefficients are consistent in Models III–IV and inconsistent in Models I–II.

5.3 Pooled OLS regressions of new-to-the-firm innovation

As a further test of the role of entrepreneurship, we investigate whether entrepreneurship does *not* moderate the relationship between knowledge and new-to-the-firm innovation. Table 5presents the results of the regressions with respect to new-to-the-firm innovation and shows that knowledge clearly leads to a higher share of new-to-the-firm innovations. A higher rate of knowledge-intensive firms increases turnover with new-to-the-firm products ($\beta = 0.51, p < 0.05$, Model II). However, Table 5 also shows that entrepreneurship does *not* have an effect with regard to new-to-the-firm products. Neither the entrepreneurship variable included directly ($\beta = -0.29, p = 0.13$, Model III) nor the interaction term ($\beta = -0.02, p = 0.65$, Model IV) shows significant results. Thus, a higher rate of entrepreneurship does not lead to more new-to-the-firm products. This

Table 4. Pooled OLS regressions on *new-to-the-market innovation*

Independent variables	Model I Coeff. (SE)	Model II Coeff. (SE)	Model III Coeff. (SE)	Model IV Coeff. (SE)
Macro-economic variables				
ln(GDP)	0.28 (0.49)	−0.21 (0.67)	−0.34 (0.61)	−0.70 (0.66)
ln(GDP per capita)	−3.17 (1.57)†	−6.54 (2.29)**	−6.69 (2.19)**	−7.38 (2.25)**
Rate of knowledge-intensive firms		0.27 (0.14)†	0.31 (0.12)*	−0.33 (0.24)
Entrepreneurship rate			0.09 (0.20)	−0.38 (0.19)†
Rate of knowledge-intensive firms X entrepreneurship rate				0.07 (0.03)**
Year dummies (reference year: 1998)				
Year 2000	1.94 (1.45)	2.94 (1.76)	3.01 (1.78)	3.25 (1.70)†
Year 2004	1.70 (1.08)	2.81 (1.50)†	2.91 (1.39)*	3.13 (1.29)*
Year 2006	2.64 (0.79)**	3.98 (1.33)**	4.16 (1.12)**	3.13 (1.29)*
Constant	34.83 (17.98)†	71.11 (27.33)*	72.77 (26.97)*	88.43 (26.70)**
F-value	5.31**	4.67**	4.60**	6.53**
p-value Breusch-Pagan test for random effects	0.01	0.05	0.10	0.14
R^2	0.13	0.22	0.22	0.29
R^2 (without year dummies)	0.07	0.11	0.11	0.17
Adjusted R^2	0.04	0.12	0.11	0.18
N observations (countries)	57 (21)	57 (21)	57 (21)	57 (21)

SE = robust and clustered standard errors; Coeff. = regression coefficient
Data sources: CIS, COMPENDIA, and OECD Economic Outlook Database
†: at 0.1 significance level; *: at 0.05 significance level; **: at 0.01 significance level; two-tailed tests
We also calculated the effect of a time trend variable with year 1998=1, year 2000=2, year 2004=3, and year 2006=4. The coefficients (SE) are as follows: Model I: $\beta = 0.759$ (0.31)*; Model II: $\beta = 1.13$ (0.42) *; Model III: $\beta = 1.18$ (0.33)**; Model IV: $\beta = 1.22$ (0.32)**

result confirms our proposition that entrepreneurship moderates the relationship between knowledge and new-to-the-market innovation but does *not* impact the relationship between knowledge and new-to-the-firm innovation. The results should be interpreted with caution because the Breusch-Pagan test for random effects (Breusch and Pagan 1980) yields significant results. OLS coefficients may be inconsistent; therefore, we also estimate random- and fixed-effects regressions (see below for robustness checks).

5.4 Further results from the regressions

Our analysis yields several other interesting findings. First, there seems to be a positive time trend for new-to-the-market innovations ($\beta = 1.18, p < 0.01$, Table 4, Model III) and a negative time trend for new-to-the-firm innovations ($\beta = -3.57, p < 0.01$, Table 5, Model III). The ratio of 'true' innovation versus imitative innovation has increased over time in the 21 European countries. This phenomenon is one of the many indicators of the switch from a 'managed' to an 'entrepreneurial' economy

Table 5. Pooled OLS regressions on *new-to-the-firm innovation*

Independent variables	Model I Coeff. (SE)	Model II Coeff. (SE)	Model III Coeff. (SE)	Model IV Coeff. (SE)
Macro-economic variables				
ln(GDP)	1.91 (1.29)	0.98 (0.94)	1.40 (1.20)	1.52 (1.42)
ln(GDP per capita)	2.50 (2.12)	−3.89 (2.34)	−3.41 (2.04)	−3.19 (2.10)
Rate of knowledge-intensive firms		0.51 (0.18)*	0.39 (0.13)**	0.59 (0.48)
Entrepreneurship rate			−0.29 (0.19)	−0.14 (0.23)
Rate of knowledge-intensive firms X entrepreneurship rate				−0.02 (0.05)
Year dummies (reference year: 1998)				
Year 2000	−0.95 (1.92)	0.96 (2.02)	0.73 (1.86)	0.65 (1.90)
Year 2004	−9.53 (2.04)**	−7.44 (1.71)**	−7.78 (1.71)**	−7.85 (1.75)**
Year 2006	−10.43 (2.28)**	−7.88 (2.14)**	−8.48 (1.91)**	−8.53 (1.95)**
Constant	−30.58 (32.95)	38.23 (24.64)	32.81 (23.74)	27.82 (29.92)
F-value	6.51**	6.93**	6.13**	6.84**
p-value Breusch-Pagan test for random effects	0.01	0.11	0.05	0.04
R^2	0.50	0.59	0.60	0.61
R^2 (without year dummies)	0.15	0.33	0.33	0.33
Adjusted R^2	0.45	0.54	0.55	0.54
N observations (countries)	57 (21)	57 (21)	57 (21)	57 (21)

SE = robust and clustered standard errors; Coeff. = regression coefficient
Data sources: CIS, COMPENDIA, and OECD Economic Outlook Database
†: at 0.1 significance level; *: at 0.05 significance level; **: at 0.01 significance level; two-tailed tests
We also calculated the effect of a time trend variable with year 1998=1, year 2000=2, year 2004=3, and year 2006=4. The coefficients (SE) are as follows: Model I: $\beta = -4.07$ (0.77)**; Model II: $\beta = -3.37$ (0.66)**; Model III: $\beta = -3.57$ (0.66)**; Model IV: $\beta = -3.71$ (0.71)**

(Audretsch and Thurik 2000, 2001). Second, the regressions for new-to-the-firm innovation have higher R^2 values than the regressions for new-to-the-market innovation (R^2 = 61% vs. 29% in Model IV) because of the effect of the year dummies. The inclusion of year dummies explains 42% of the variation in new-to-the-firm innovation but explains only 5% of the variation in new-to-the-market innovation. The autonomous decline in new-to-the-firm innovation seems to override the autonomous increase in new-to-the-market innovation. This phenomenon is one of many indicators of a decline in the competitiveness of European countries. Finally, the finding that knowledge plays a role in both new-to-the-market innovation ($\beta = 0.27, p < 0.1$, Table 4, Model II) and new-to-the-firm innovation ($\beta = 0.51, p < 0.05$, Table 5, Model II) supports our expectations and shows that investments in knowledge increase a country's level of absorptive capacity (Cohen and Levinthal 1989), which has an effect on both types of innovation.

5.5 Robustness checks

To check the robustness of our results, we estimate random- and fixed-effects models (see Tables 6 and 7). Both models confirm our main finding that entrepreneurship moderates the relationship between knowledge and new-to-the-market innovation (Table 6: Model II: $\beta = 0.07, p = 0.03$; Model IV: $\beta = 0.12, p = 0.01$), but the models indicate no relationship between knowledge and new-to-the-firm innovation (Table 7: Model II: $\beta = -0.04, p = 0.46$). A Hausman specification test is used to compare the coefficients of the random-and fixed-effects regressions (Hausman 1978). In all estimations, the test shows an insignificant result ($p > 0.10$) because the coefficients of the random-effects model do not differ systematically from the coefficients of the fixed-effects model. Nevertheless, the fact that our results also hold for a fixed-effects specification is important. We conclude that our main findings hold irrespective of country-specific variables such as openness to trade or geographic location.

Table 6. Random and fixed-effects regressions on *new-to-the-market innovation*

Independent variables	Random-effects regressions		Fixed-effects regressions	
	Model I Coeff. (SE)	Model II Coeff. (SE)	Model III Coeff. (SE)	Model IV Coeff. (SE)
Macro-economic variables				
ln(GDP)	−0.02 (0.60)	−0.40 (0.67)	−23.30 (36.00)	−9.26 (37.28)
ln(GDP per capita)	−5.78 (2.26)**	−6.32 (2.16)**	31.30 (49.04)	21.22 (50.93)
Rate of knowledge-intensive firms	0.22 (0.10)*	−0.42 (0.30)	0.06 (0.10)	−0.91 (0.34)*
Entrepreneurship rate	−0.001 (0.21)	−0.46 (0.27)†	−0.19 (0.36)	−0.99 (0.63)
Rate of knowledge-intensive firms X entrepreneurship rate		0.07 (0.03)*		0.12 (0.04)*
Year dummies (reference year: 1998)				
Year 2000	3.09 (1.65)†	3.16 (1.57)*	2.73 (1.77)	2.04 (1.65)
Year 2004	2.69 (1.11)*	2.82 (0.99)**	1.84 (2.01)	0.69 (1.61)
Year 2006	4.06 (1.00)**	4.18 (0.94)**	2.92 (2.09)	1.39 (1.79)
Constant	61.64 (26.65)*	75.97 (26.13)**	−15.57 (89.36)	−81.48 (80.17)
Wald chi^2	26.83**	34.89**		
Hausman specification test[a]	$p > 0.10$	$p > 0.10$	$p > 0.10$	$p > 0.10$
F-value			2.04†	3.63**
Rho	0.22	0.20	0.99	0.97
R^2 within; between; overall	0.15; 0.30; 0.21	0.20; 0.36; 0.29	0.21; 0.11; 0.03	0.28; 0.12; 0.03
N observations (countries)	57 (21)	57 (21)	57 (21)	57 (21)
Obs. per group (min., avg., max.)	1; 2.7; 4	1; 2.7; 4	1; 2.7; 4	1, 2.7, 4

SE = robust standard errors; Coeff. = regression coefficient
Data sources: CIS, COMPENDIA, and OECD Economic Outlook Database
†: at 0.1 significance level; *: at 0.05 significance level; **: at 0.01 significance level; two-tailed tests
[a]Model I is tested against Model III and Model II is tested against Model IV

Table 7. Random and fixed-effects regressions on *new-to-the-firm innovation*

Independent variables	Random-effects regressions		Fixed-effects regressions	
	Model I	Model II	Model III	Model IV
	Coeff. (SE)	Coeff. (SE)	Coeff. (SE)	Coeff. (SE)
Macro-economic variables				
ln(GDP)	1.60 (0.99)	1.87 (1.14)	−27.12 (75.15)	−48.92 (69.13)
ln(GDP per capita)	−3.07 (2.64)	−2.67 (2.79)	32.17 (91.98)	47.84 (84.95)
Rate of knowledge-intensive firms	0.34 (0.19)[†]	0.68 (0.52)	0.12 (0.19)	1.63 (0.76)*
Entrepreneurship rate	−0.36 (0.23)	−0.13 (0.42)	−2.05 (0.92)*	−0.81 (1.13)
Rate of knowledge-intensive firms X entrepreneurship rate		−0.04 (0.06)		−0.18 (0.09)[†]
Year dummies (reference year: 1998)				
Year 2000	0.63 (2.44)	0.54 (2.42)	−0.27 (2.70)	0.80 (2.26)
Year 2004	−8.07 (1.88)**	−8.25 (1.89)**	−8.84 (3.69)*	−7.06 (2.81)*
Year 2006	−8.65 (2.21)**	−8.79 (2.19)**	−8.88 (4.44)[†]	−6.51 (3.25)[†]
Constant	28.39 (30.79)	19.26 (35.75)	54.19 (240.37)	156.61 (196.99)
Wald chi^2	55.76**	56.74**		
Hausman specification test[a]	$p > 0.10$	$p > 0.10$	$p > 0.10$	$p > 0.10$
F-value			8.03**	10.78**
Rho	0.14	0.20	0.98	1.00
R^2 within; between; overall	0.57; 0.68; 0.60	0.59; 0.67; 0.60	0.62; 0.11; 0.01	0.65; 0.17; 0.04
N observations (countries)	57 (21)	57 (21)	57 (21)	57 (21)
Obs. per group (min., avg., max.)	1; 2.7; 4	1; 2.7; 4	1; 2.7; 4	1, 2.7, 4

SE = robust standard errors; Coeff. = regression coefficient
Data sources: CIS, COMPENDIA, and OECD Economic Outlook Database
[†]: at 0.1 significance level; *: at 0.05 significance level; **: at 0.01 significance level; two-tailed tests
[a]Model I is tested against Model III and Model II is tested against Model IV

As a further robustness check, we include the share of small firms (calculated from CIS data) as a control in our regression models. Because entrepreneurship is often related to small firms, our findings could also suggest that small firms face relatively lower costs of experimentation than do large firms. Potential losses from innovation at small firms have a lower limit than at larger firms (Jovanovic 1982). In addition, small firms may have an advantage because it is easier for them to reward their employees for high-value innovation (Wiggins 1995). As another robustness check, we include the share of venture capital investment in GDP (calculated from the annual yearbook of the European Venture Capital Association, EVCA) in our regressions because research by Kortum and Lerner (2000) shows that venture capital firms have a strong influence on innovation. After including these additional controls, our primary results remain unchanged, and the explanatory power of the respective regressions increases slightly. As a further robustness check, we experiment with alternative knowledge variables. To this end, we first regress the two alternative OECD knowledge measures (gross domestic expenditure on R&D and business expenditure on R&D) on our knowledge variable. We include the residuals of these regressions into the new-to-the-market and new-to-the-firm innovation regressions. This not only avoids the dangers of multicollinearity but also includes the additional effect of the two alternative OECD measures. The interaction term between entrepreneurship and knowledge remains significant and has a similar magnitude (new-to-the-market innovation regression) when compared to the analyses without the newly introduced variables (i.e., the residuals of a regression of the alternative OECD measures on our knowledge variable). The newly included residual variables have non-significant effects.

Finally, we estimate seemingly unrelated regression models (SUR) and two-stage simultaneous equation models in which the entrepreneurship variable is treated as endogenous. The moderation effect of entrepreneurship on the relationship between knowledge and innovation performance is similar to the effects in the other models. The estimation results relating to the robustness checks are available from the authors upon request.

6 DISCUSSION

6.1 Innovation in the knowledge spillover theory of entrepreneurship

Both the endogenous growth theory and the R&D capital approach point to knowledge as a major driver of economic growth. Less is known about the exact mechanism *how* knowledge affects growth. Thus, it is difficult for policymakers to identify policy instruments to promote growth. Glaeser et al. (1992) have established that knowledge and ideas do not spill over automatically; in the context of cities, at least, competition and diversity are required to generate growth (Audretsch 1995; Audretsch and Feldman 1996; Acs and Armington 2004). The finding that knowledge does not automatically spill over has given rise to the concept of the knowledge filter, the group of impediments that prevent knowledge from spilling over from the site where it is created to the site where it can be commercialized. Independently of the investigation of the role of knowledge, a different strand of literature emphasizes the role of entrepreneurship in economic growth. The development of this literature culminates in the view that the older 'managed' economy has been replaced by a newer 'entrepreneurial' economy (Audretsch and Thurik 2000, 2001). The view that entrepreneurship is an independent production factor like human, physical and knowledge capital has led to the introduction of entrepreneurship capital into the production function (Audretsch and Keilbach 2004). Various studies have shown that entrepreneurship influences economic growth (Parker 2009; Erken et al. 2009). Although there are many indications in the knowledge literature that the (spatial) organization of business has an effect (Audretsch and Feldman 1996; Anselin et al. 1997; Keller 2002) and indications in the entrepreneurship literature that knowledge and its diffusion are important (Audretsch and Thurik 2001), only the knowledge spillover theory of entrepreneurship unites these strains of thought (Acs et al. 2009; Braunerhjelm et al. 2010), giving rise to its description as a "missing link" (Acs et al. 2004). Our paper uses the knowledge spillover theory of entrepreneurship to analyze the effect of entrepreneurship on the commercialization of knowledge leading to different innovation outcomes. Knowledge and entrepreneurial activity may ultimately lead to economic growth, but only by first producing innovative products. This link is addressed in the present paper using a panel dataset for the aggregate innovation activity of 21 European countries collected in four time waves. Our results clearly show that entrepreneurship moderates the relationship between knowledge and new-to-the-market innovation but has *no* impact on the relationship between knowledge and new-to-the-firm innovation. In other words, our results show that countries with a high rate of entrepreneurship perform better in terms of what is sometimes referred to as 'true' innovation (Kleinknecht et al. 2002).

Figure 1 illustrates our conceptual model. The production of knowledge increases the aggregate stock of knowledge (arrow 1). Both existing firms and new firms can draw from this aggregate stock and develop both new-to-the-firm (arrow 2) and new-to-the-market products (arrow 3).[10]Entrepreneurship moderates the relationship between the aggregate stock of knowledge and the number of new-to-the-market products ('true' innovation performance) (arrow 4), but it has *no* impact on the relationship between the aggregate stock of knowledge and the number of imitative products.[11] Both new-to-the-firm, imitative products and new-to-the-market products may lead to economic growth. However, the mechanisms involved differ and may depend on the country's level of development (Vandenbussche et al. 2006). We will not expand upon this discussion because it is beyond the scope of our paper.

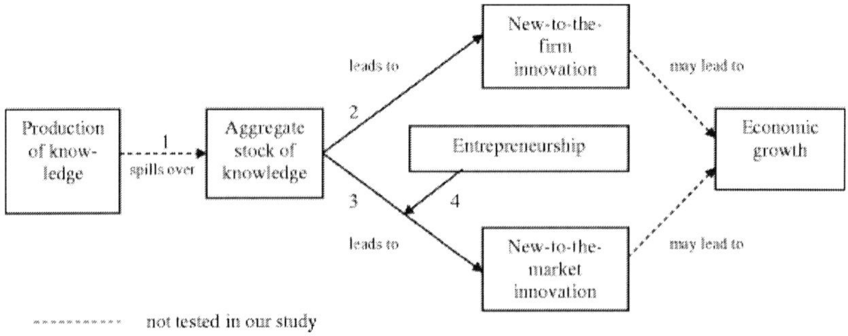

Figure 1. The moderating role of entrepreneurship in the relationship between knowledge and innovation

6.2 Schumpeterian explanation for the moderating role of entrepreneurship

Our findings concerning the role of entrepreneurship are consistent with a Schumpeterian view of entrepreneurship and innovation. Schumpeter divided the creative process of economic development into three stages: invention, innovation (commercialization) and imitation. In his early works, Schumpeter argued that entrepreneurs are not necessarily inventors or knowledge creators (Schumpeter 1934); instead, they transform knowledge into products (Brouwer 2002). That is, entrepreneurs are innovators who introduce new products, create new production methods and open new markets. Schumpeter saw the entrepreneur as an agent who can cope with uncertainty, thereby inducing technological change and progress (Brouwer 2002). Therefore, entrepreneurs should be more effective than other agents at successfully commercializing inventions. Braunerhjelm and Svensson (2010) show that the likelihood of the commercial success of an invention increases significantly when the invention is commercialized by an entrepreneur rather than by an inventor. Our findings regarding the role of entrepreneurship clearly support a Schumpeterian view of entrepreneurship and innovation. Entrepreneurship moderates the relationship between a country's level of knowledge and new-to-the-market innovation but has no impact on the relationship between knowledge and new-to-the-firm innovation. The former relationship is characterized by a high degree of uncertainty, whereas the latter may not be. The entrepreneur's capacity for risk taking and absorbing uncertainty is more important with new-to-the-market innovation than with new-to-the-firm innovation. The moderating role of entrepreneurship in new-to-the-market innovation is related to the level of product complexity in the manufacturing sector. With increasingly complex products and production processes, imitation is hardly a feasible way for new firms to enter the manufacturing sector (Hobday 1998). A firm's chances of survival increase when it has 'true' innovations. Successful market entry by entrepreneurs requires the ability to turn knowledge into innovation.

6.3 Implications for innovation and entrepreneurship policy

Our main finding, that entrepreneurship moderates the relationship between knowledge and 'true' innovation performance, has important policy implications. From an innovation policy perspective, promoting the production of new knowledge (e.g., by means of R&D subsidies or university education) is not sufficient; it is equally important for entrepreneurs to turn this new knowledge into innovative products to fuel economic growth. If there are only a few entrepreneurs in a knowledge-intensive region, the so-called Swedish or European paradox (Ejermo and Kander 2006; Audretsch 2007) may emerge, with the implication that commercial opportunities will remain under-exploited or will only be exploited outside the region. In any case, profits will not flow back to the region in which the knowledge was produced. To prevent this situation, policymakers may want to promote entrepreneurship in their own country or region through subsidized loans to high-tech entrepreneurs, regulatory exemptions for innovative new start-ups, or tax benefits. However, we believe that simply encouraging more people to become entrepreneurs is not an effective policy. The government should support those entrepreneurs who take the risk of transforming new knowledge into innovative products and focus less on those entrepreneurs who merely start another shop around the corner.[12] Many start-ups do not fall into the first category but belong to the latter group (Block et al. 2010a; Koellinger 2008). In fact, prior research shows that many entrepreneurs start their venture out of economic necessity (Block and Sandner 2009; Block and Wagner 2010). An alternative long-term strategy for policymakers would be to promote (entrepreneurship) education to increase the number of qualified and risk-taking entrepreneurs (Block et al. 2012b).

6.4 Limitations and further research

Our paper has limitations in the scope of the dataset and the measurement of innovation. These limitations suggest opportunities for further research.

Regarding the first limitation, our dataset is limited to the countries participating in the CIS. An extension of the dataset to emerging countries in Asia or Latin America would be interesting. Given prior research about the role of entrepreneurship in emerging economies (Naudé 2011), we would expect the positive effects of entrepreneurship in the commercialization of knowledge into innovations to be even greater. As noted above, the dataset of the GEM (Reynolds et al. 2005) and the recently developed Global and Entrepreneurship Development Index (GEDI, Acs and Szerb 2011) could be used as a source of entrepreneurship data. The difficulty is in finding comparable country-level data about innovation activities that goes beyond information about aggregated levels of R&D spending.

In terms of measuring innovation, our paper is limited to two specific types of innovation, *new-to-the-market* and *new-to-the-firm* innovation. However, the concept of innovation has many different facets and dimensions (Kleinknecht et al. 2002). For example, we would expect entrepreneurship to have a greater effect with regard to radical versus incremental innovation (Arrow 1962). Research by Henderson (1993) suggests that established firms are more likely than entrants to invest in incremental innovation. In addition, incumbent firms seeking to exploit radical innovation are significantly less productive in their research efforts than new firms entering the market.

In addition to the differences between incremental and radical innovation, there may be industry-specific and technology-specific patterns in the role of entrepreneurship with respect to the transformation of knowledge into commercial products. Prior research on the distinction between Schumpeter Mark I and Schumpeter Mark II industries, for example, suggests that the determinants of innovation may be industry- and technology-specific (Breschi et al. 2000; Malerba and Orsenigo 1995).

7 CONCLUDING REMARKS

Additional research is needed to determine how to identify, attract, and support those entrepreneurs who transform knowledge into 'truly' innovative products and thereby increase the competiveness of their particular region. Some questions worth investigating include the following: What types of entrepreneurs turn knowledge into new products (inexperienced versus experienced entrepreneurs)? How should these entrepreneurs be funded (equity versus debt)? What role do VCs and their specific social capital play in the commercialization process?[13] How does the path to entrepreneurship (e.g., business takeover versus new venture start?[14]) influence the entrepreneur's ability to turn knowledge into innovation? What is the role of technology clusters and government-sponsored technology parks with respect to the relationship between entrepreneurship and innovation?

The stagnation of competitiveness in European economies is often attributed to their inability to transform new knowledge into commercially viable products. Policymakers have persistently believed that entrepreneurs play a larger role in this transformation than do large corporations. A wave of policies focusing on the promotion of entrepreneurship has ensued, and the present analysis shows that this policy trend is justified.

FOOTNOTES

[1] The R&D capital approach also takes into account international effects, such as those of foreign R&D, import shares, openness and catch-up mechanisms. See Erken et al. (2009).

[2]This concept was first presented in two CEPR discussion papers (Acs et al. 2004, 2005).

[3]The theory starts from the assumption that, given constant individual characteristics, entrepreneurial decisions are driven by context, particularly by the knowledge intensity of the context. Hence, entrepreneurship is not only driven exogenously by individual characteristics, behaviors and traits but also by the endogenous response to opportunities created by the context (Audretsch 2007).

[4]The production of knowledge is emphasized by Baumol (2002), who represents the Schumpeterian 1934 view that an environment in which most of the breakthrough innovation occurs in small firms and most of the improvement on those innovations and wide-scale dissemination occurs in large firms is an efficient one. See Ortega-Argilés (2009) for a survey of the various roles of small firms in the process of technological change.

[5]Extended information is available at http://epp.eurostat. ec.europa.eu/ portal/page/portal/science_technology_innovation/data/database (acces sed September 7, 2009).

[6]Extended information is available at http://data.ondernemerschap .nl (accessed September 7, 2009).

[7]For detailed information on the CIS data set, we refer to http:// epp.eurostat.ec.europa.eu/portal/page/portal/microdata/cis/publication s (accessed September 7, 2009) and http://stats.oecd.org/ wbos/index.aspx?r=582080 (accessed September 7, 2009).

[8]For the NACE codes, see http://stats.oecd.org/glossary/ detail.asp?ID=1713 (accessed September 7, 2009).

[9]The countries are Austria, Belgium, Czech Republic, Denmark, Finland, France, Germany, Greece, Hungary, Iceland, Ireland, Italy, Luxembourg, Netherlands, Norway, Poland, Portugal, Slovakia, Spain, Sweden, and the United Kingdom.

[10]Consider the following example: firm A discloses new knowledge (e.g., by filing a patent). Firm B applies this new knowledge to create a product that is similar to the product idea of firm A (which leads to an imitative product). Firm C, however, uses this new knowledge to create a product that is new to both firm A and firm B (which leads to an innovative product).

[11]A different mechanism is suggested by Audretsch et al. (2008), where innovation efforts are assumed to generate technical knowledge and entrepreneurship capital, and the latter two are assumed to lead to economic growth.

12See also Shane (2009), who discusses at length why simply encouraging more people to become entrepreneurs is a bad public policy.

13 See Alexy et al. (2012) for a discussion of the social capital of VCs.

14 See Block et al. (2010b) for a discussion of business takeover versus new venture start.

ACKNOWLEDGEMENTS

Comments by David Audretsch, Werner Boente, Marcus Dejardin, Hugo Erken, Michael Fritsch, Philipp Koellinger, Eva Lutz, Sandra Phlippen, Christian Roessler, Lorraine Uhlaner, Andre van Stel, and the participants of the DIME workshop in Jena (October 15–17, 2009) and the Entrepreneurship and Innovation Brown Bag Seminar of Erasmus University Rotterdam are gratefully acknowledged. This paper has been written in cooperation with the research program SCALES, carried out by EIM and financed by the Dutch Ministry of Economic Affairs.

Open Access

REFERENCES

1. Acs ZJ (ed) (2010) The knowledge spillover theory of entrepreneurship. Edward Elgar, Cheltenham
2. Acs ZJ, Armington C (2004) Employment growth and entrepreneurial activity in cities. J Evol Econ 38(8):911–927
3. Acs ZJ, Szerb L (2011) The global entrepreneurship and development index 2012. Edward Elgar Publishers
4. Acs ZJ, Varga A (2005) Entrepreneurship, agglomeration and technological change. Small Bus Econ 24(3):323–334
5. Acs ZJ, Anselin L, Varga A (2002) Patents and innovation counts as measures of regional production of new knowledge. Res Policy 31(7):1069–1085
6. Acs ZJ, Audretsch DB, Braunerhjelm P, Carlsson B (2004) The missing link: the knowledge filter and entrepreneurship in endogenous growth. CEPR discussion paper no. 4783

7. Acs ZJ, Braunerhjelm P, Audretsch DB, Carlsson B (2005) The knowledge spillover theory of entrepreneurship. CEPR discussion paper no. 5326

8. Acs ZJ, Braunerhjelm P, Audretsch DB, Carlsson B (2009) The knowledge spillover theory of entrepreneurship. Small Bus Econ 32(1):15–30

9. Alexy O, Block J, Sandner P, Ter Wal A (2012) Social capital of venture capitalists and start-up funding. Small Bus Econ.:

10. Anselin L, Varga A, Acs ZJ (1997) Local geographic spillovers between university research and high technology innovations. J Urban Econ 42(3):422–448

11. Arrow K (1962) Economic welfare and the allocation of resources for invention. In: Welson RR (ed) The rate and direction of economic activity. Princeton University Press, Princeton, pp 609–625

12. Arundel A (2001) The relative effectiveness of patents and secrecy for appropriation. Res Policy 30(4):611–624

13. Audretsch DB (1995) Innovation and industry evolution. MIT Press, Cambridge

14. Audretsch DB (2007) Entrepreneurship capital and economic growth. Oxf Rev Econ Policy 23(1):63–78

15. Audretsch DB, Feldman MP (1996) R&D spillovers and the geography of innovation and production. Am Econ Rev 86(3):630–640

16. Audretsch DB, Keilbach MC (2004) Entrepreneurship capital and economic performance. Region Stud 38(8):949–959

17. Audretsch DB, Lehmann EE (2005) Does the knowledge spillover theory hold for regions? Res Policy 34(8):1191–1202

18. Audretsch DB, Thurik AR (2000) Capitalism and democracy in the 21st century: from the managed to the entrepreneurial economy. J Evol Econ 10(1–2):17–34

19. Audretsch DB, Thurik AR (2001) What is new about the new economy: sources of growth in the managed and entrepreneurial economies. Ind Corp Change 10(1):267–315

20. Audretsch DB, Boente W, Keilbach MC (2008) Entrepreneurship capital and its impact on knowledge diffusion and economic performance. J Bus Venturing 23(6):687–698

21. Baumol WJ (2002) The free market innovation machine: analyzing the growth miracle of capitalism. Princeton University Press, Princeto

22. Benz M, Frey B (2008) Being independent is a great thing: subjective evaluations of self-employment and hierarchy. Economica 75(298):362–383

23. Beugelsdijk S (2007) Entrepreneurial culture, regional innovativeness and economic growth. J Evol Econ 17(2):187–210

24. Block J, Köllinger P (2009) I can't get no satisfaction—necessity entrepreneurship and procedural utility. Kyklos 62(1):191–209

25. Block J, Sandner P (2009) Necessity and opportunity entrepreneurs and their duration in self-employment: evidence from German micro data. J Ind Compet Trade 9(2):117–137

26. Block J, Wagner M (2010) Necessity and opportunity entrepreneurs in Germany: characteristics and earnings differentials. Schmalenbach Business Review 62(2):154–174

27. Block J, Sandner P, Spiegel F (2010a) How do risk attitudes differ within the group of entrepreneurs? The role of motivation and procedural utility. SSRN working paper

28. Block JH, Thurik, AR, Van der Zwan, PW, Walter S (2010b) Business takeover or new venture? Individual and environmental determinants from a cross-country study. ERIM research paper ERS-2010-042-ORG. http://hdl.handle.net/1765/21239

29. Block J, Hoogerheide L, Thurik R (2011) Education and entrepreneurial choice: an instrumental variables analysis. Int Small Bus J.

30. Braunerhjelm P (2008) Entrepreneurship, knowledge and economic growth. Foundations and Trends in Entrepreneurship 4(5):451–533

31. Bolton MK (1993) Imitation versus innovation: lessons to be learned from the Japanese. Organ Dyn 21(3):30–45

32. Bottazzi L, Peri G (2003) Innovation and spillovers in regions: evidence from European patent data. Eur Econ Rev 47(4):687–710

33. Braunerhjelm P, Svensson P (2010) The inventor's role: was Schumpeter right? J Evol Econ 20(3):413–444

34. Braunerhjelm P, Acs ZJ, Audretsch DB, Carlsson B (2010) The missing link: knowledge diffusion and entrepreneurship in endogenous growth. Small Bus Econ 34(2):104–125

35. Breschi S, Lissoni F (2001) Knowledge spillovers and local innovation systems: a critical survey. Ind Corp Change 10(4):975–1005

36. Breschi S, Malerba F, Orsenigo L (2000) Technological regimes and Schumpeterian patterns of innovation. Econ J 110(463):388–410

37. Breusch TS, Pagan AR (1980) The Lagrange multiplier test and its application to model specification in econometrics. Rev Econ Stud 47(1):239–253

38. Brockhaus RH (1980) Risk taking propensity of entrepreneurs. Acad Manage J 23(3):509–520

39. Brouwer MT (2002) Weber, Schumpeter and Knight on entrepreneurship and economic development. J Evol Econ 12(1):83–105

40. Cantner U, Gaffard J, Nesta L (2008) Schumpeterian perspectives on innovation, competition and growth. J Evol Econ 18(3):291–293

41. Carlsson B, Fridh A (2002) Technology transfer in United States universities. J Evol Econ 12(1):199–232

42. Carlsson B, Acs ZJ, Audretsch DB, Braunerhhjem P (2009) Knowledge creation, entrepreneurship and economic growth: a historical review. Ind Corp Change 18(6):1193–1229

43. Carree MA, Thurik AR (2010) The impact of entrepreneurship on economic growth. In: Acs ZJ, Audretsch DB (eds) Handbook of entrepreneurship research, international handbook series on entrepreneuship, vol 5. Springer, New York, pp 557–594

44. Carree MA, van Stel A, Thurik AR, Wennekers S (2002) Economic development and business ownership: an analysis using data of 23 OECD countries in the period 1976–1996. Small Bus Econ 19(3):271–290

45. Cohen WM, Levinthal DA (1989) Innovation and learning: the two faces of R&D. Econ J 99(397):569–596

46. Ejermo O, Kander A (2006) The Swedish paradox. CIRCLE Electronic Working Paper Series 2006/01, CIRCLE, Lund

47. Erken H, Donselaar P, Thurik AR (2009) Total factor productivity and the role of entrepreneurship. Tinbergen Institute discussion papers TI09-034/3, Rotterdam, Netherlands

48. Furman JL, Porter ME, Stern S (2002) The determinants of national innovative capacity. Res Policy 31(6):899–933

49. Glaeser EL, Kallal HD, Scheinkman JA, Shleifer A (1992) Growth in cities. J Polit Econ 100(6):1126–1152

50. Griliches Z (1998) R&D and productivity: the econometric evidence. University of Chicago Press, Chicago

51. Griliches Z (2000) R&D, education, and productivity. A retrospective. Harvard University Press, Cambridge

52. Hauser J, Zettelmeyer F (1997) Metrics to evaluate R, D & E. Res Technol Manag 40(4):32–38

53. Hausman JA (1978) Specification tests in econometrics. Econometrica 46(6):1251–1271

54. Henderson R (1993) Underinvestment and incompetence as responses to radical innovation: evidence from the photolithographic alignment equipment industry. Rand J Econ 24(2): 248–271

55. Hobday M (1998) Product complexity, innovation and industrial organization. Res Policy 26(6):689–710

56. Hoelzl W (2009) Is the R&D behaviour of fast-growing SMEs different? Evidence from CIS III data for 16 countries. Small Bus Econ 33(1):59–75

57. Jaffe AB, Trajtenberg M, Henderson R (1993) Geographic localization of knowledge spillovers as evidenced by patent citations. Q J Econ 108(3):577–598

58. Jaffe AB, Trajtenberg M, Fogarty MS (2000) Knowledge spillovers and patent citations: evidence from a survey of inventors. Am Econ Rev 90(2):215–218

59. Jovanovic B (1982) Selection and the evolution of industry. Econometrica 50(3):649–670

60. Keller W (2002) Geographic localization of international technology diffusion. Am Econ Rev 92(1):120–142

61. Kihlstrom RE, Laffont JJ (1979) A general equilibrium entrepreneurial theory of firm formation based on risk aversion. J Polit Econ 1(4):719–748

62. Kleinknecht A, Van Montfort K, Brouwer E (2002) The non-rival choice between innovation indicators. Econ Innov New Technol 11(2):109–121

63. Koellinger P (2008) Why are some entrepreneurs more innovative than others? Small Bus Econ 31(1):21–37

64. Kortum SS, Lerner J (2000) Assessing the contribution of venture capital to innovation. RAND J Econ 31(4):674–692

65. Lucas RE (1988) On the mechanics of economic development. J Monet Econ 22(1):3–42

66. Lucas RE (1993) Making a miracle. Econometrica 61(2):251–272

67. Mairesse J, Mohnen P (2002) Accounting for innovation and measuring innovativeness: an illustrative framework and an application. Am Econ Rev 92(2):226–231

68. Mairesse J, Mohnen P (2005) The importance of R&D for innovation: a reassessment using French survey data. J Technol Transf 30(1–2):193–197

69. Malerba F (2006) Innovation and the evolution of industries. J Evol Econ 16(1–2):3–23

70. Malerba F, Orsenigo F (1995) Schumpeterian patterns of innovation. Camb J Econ 19(1):47–65

71. Mansfield E (1965) Rates of return from industrial research and development. Am Econ Rev 55(1/2):310–322

72. McClelland DC (1961) The achieving society. Van Nostrandt, Princeton

73. Naudé W (2011) Entrepreneurship and economic development. Palgrave McMillan, Houndmills, Basingstoke

74. Ortega-Argilés R, Vivarelli M, Voigt P (2009) R&D in SMEs: a paradox? Small Bus Econ 33(1):3–11

75. Park G, Park Y (2006) On the measurement of patent stock as knowledge indicators. Technol Forecast Soc Change 73(7):793–812

76. Parker S (2009) The economics of entrepreneurship. Cambridge University Press, Cambridge

77. Reynolds PD, Bosma N, Autio E, Hunt S, De Bono N, Servais I, Lopez-Garcia P, Chin N (2005) Global entrepreneurship monitor: data collection design and implementation 1998–2003. Small Bus Econ 24(3):205–231

78. Romer PM (1986) Increasing returns and long-run growth. J Polit Econ 94(5):1002–1037

79. Romer PM (1990) Endogenous technical change. J Polit Econ 98(5):S71–S102

80. Schere JC (1982) Tolerance of ambiguity as a discriminating variable between entrepreneurs and managers. In: Academy of management proceedings, pp 404–408

81. Scherer FM, Harhoff D, Kukies J (2000) Uncertainty and the size distribution of rewards from innovation. J Evol Econ 10(1–2):175–200

82. Schewe G (1996) Imitation as a strategic option for external acquisition of technology. J Eng Technol Manag 13(1):55–82

83. Schumpeter JA (1934) The theory of economic development. Harvard University Press, Cambridge

84. Shane S (2009) Why encouraging more people to become entrepreneurs is a bad public policy. Small Bus Econ 33(2):141–149

85. Shane S, Venkataraman S (2000) The promise of entrepreneurship as a field of research. Acad Manag Rev 25(1):217–226

86. Timmons JA (1976) Characteristics and role demands of entrepreneurship. Am J Small Bus 3(1):5–17

87. Van Praag CM, Versloot PH (2007) What is the value of entrepreneurship? A review of recent research. Small Bus Econ 29(4):351–382

88. Van Stel A (2005) COMPENDIA: harmonizing business ownership data across countries and over time. Int Entrep Manag J 1(1):105–123

89. Vandenbussche J, Aghion P, Meghir C (2006) Growth, distance to frontier and composition of human capital. J Econ Growth 11(2):97–127

90. Varga A (2000) Local academic knowledge spillovers and the concentration of economic activity. J Reg Sci 40(2):289–309

91. Werker C, Athreye S (2004) Marshall's disciples: knowledge and innovation driving regional economic development and growth. J Evol Econ 14(5):505–523

92. Wiggins S (1995) Entrepreneurial enterprises, endogenous ownership, and the limits to firm size. Econ Inq 33(1):54–69

93. Wooldridge JM (2002) Econometric analysis of cross section and panel data. The MIT Press, Cambridge

6

TRADE POLICY AND LONG-TERM ECONOMIC DEVELOPMENT: HISTORICAL EVIDENCE FROM AUSTRALIA'S COLONIES IN 19TH CENTURY

Kris Li * and Veicheng Yu

Faculty of Business, City University of Macau, Macau, China

ABSTRACT

In our studies, historical data on neighboring colonies of New South Wales and Victoria in 19th century are used to shed new light on an issue which has intrigued economic historians and economists: How is trade policy linked to long-term economic growth? It is found that Victoria's higher protection restricted productivity growth directly, but stimulated it indirectly through the revenue effects of promoting greater infrastructure and a consequentially-larger population base.

Keywords: Colonial Australia; Trade policy; Aggregate productivity; Time-series analysis

INTRODUCTION

The Setting and our Approach

Why did more-protectionist Victoria (abbreviated as Vic thereafter) develop faster in the later nineteenth century than freer-trade New South Wales (abbreviated as NSW thereafter)? Historians have mused over this question; and many economists have been reluctant to accept higher trade protection as a growth-creating agent. Economic theories of this issue tell us little: protection (or increased protection) can either retard or accelerate long-term economic development, when allowance is made for its effects on factor supply (including foreign factors acquired by the protecting country) and productivity growth, through research and development. But contemporary statistical techniques used widely in economics today enable us to shed new light on an old puzzle after some detailed assembly of data.

We focus on economic growth and especially `productivity growth'. Seminal economic-history studies associated with Rostow, Madison, and Denison all emphasize productivity growth, as did Australia's comprehensive Vernon report released in 1965. Trade policy theories are not directed to giving any insights into economic growth. And the economic growth literature makes few if any links to trade protection. But the growth literature does contain the Schumpeterian notion that, by limiting rivalry, productivity growth can and predictably will be enhanced [1].[1]

The importance of the above notion is that restrictions on freemarket competition, like Victoria practiced in the later nineteenth century, can foster long-term higher growth rates. Indeed, we have historical affirmation from other countries showing that market intervention can limit competitive rivalry and enhance economic development. For instance,

`Germany and the United States, engaging in government-subsidized internal improvements, in particular, increasingly began to overtake Britain in the production of basic commodities like steel and pig iron' [2].

Moreover, the few empirical studies which examine this link using time-series data may not have sufficiently resolved such historical precedents. For example, a long-series empirical study by Clemens et al. tested a number of common hypotheses for explaining the lack of persistent correlation between tariffs and growth, without statistically conclusive results. Similar, a recent contribution by Greasley et al. [3] finds no clear relationship between primary-sector intensity and output growth, using multi-country data for many decades. The scene is thus set for a fresh look at this epoch and this issue that has fascinated economic historians and been largely ignored by economists. We use tools of statistical research designed to find linkages relating to long spans of data that are familiar to economic historians.

Colonial Australia lacked the skills, capital, and natural endowments for agriculture beyond self-sustenance, and even that was a struggle. But there was a stream of visiting sea vessels from 1820s to 1840s that needed supplies. As such, small-scale and inefficient land grants were given to migrants and ex-convicts to take advantage of this momentary comparative advantage. Like protection as applied by Victoria especially, purposive interference with free-market forces characterized the approach to economic policy.

Manufacturing developed rapidly in the South-Eastern colonies of NSW and Vic after 1850s gold rushes. Vic adopted significant and widespread protection against imports from 1860s, under the prominent advocacy of newspaper baron David Syme. In 1890s the different approaches to protection between these two colonies became a debating issue delaying Federation. The faster growth of Vic compared with NSW has encouraged many casual inferences that protection fostered faster development of industry: debates that rage today and form history can reveal genuinely relevant insights. This case study is a good natural experiment: few real differences then existed as between the two colonies considered, other than the protectionist policy stance of Vic.

This paper revisits this intriguing issue, using reconstructions of long series of data [4] and modern time-series econometrics. During this time, the Australian colonies shared a dominant economic policy objective of producing manufactures themselves [5]. An overview of the adjacent colonies is given in **Table 1**, followed by a comparison of protective tariff rates in the period considered **Table 1**.

Table 1: Comparison of NSW and Vic 1861-1900: average statistics.

Factors	NSW	Vic
Population	825446	909021
City density (persons/km^2)	4.3376	4.5247
Output ($'000)	13800	13000
Manufacturing workers	32862	35060
Factory numbers	2396	2313
Private capital ($'000)	5915	5272
Public capital ($'000)	17600	16300

Average values across the years 1861-1900 inclusive. Monetary units converted to 1890 equivalent values. Table figures are primarily sourced from Butlin (1964), supported by a collection of other records as stated in the Appendix, unless explained otherwise.

We notice from **Table 1** that the mean tariff rate in NSW in was 8.9%; it was higher at 11.4% in Vic, using our definition of revenue-based tariff rates. This is not a massive difference, compared with inferences made by economic historians. We thus question the simplicity of this case comparison as presented by more contemporary academic observers, notably Sinclair [6]. That literature focuses on large and rapid changes in the tariffs applying to specific products that had strong political ties to lobby groups. But these product types constituted a small part of manufacturing, itself a small part of the economy. More narrowlydefined tariff rates are given in **Table 2**, which highlights some of the more pronounced tariff-rate differences **Table 2**.

Table 2: Sample of major tariffs during colonial Australia.

Durable Items	NSW		Vic	
	1876	1893	1876	1893
Boots and shoes	Nil	10%	3-25d†/doz	4-60d†/doz
Gloves	Nil	10%	10%	20%
Hats and caps	Nil	10%	20%	36d/doz
Millinery	Nil	10%	10-20%	25%
Apparel and slops	Nil	10%	20%	35%
Blankets	Nil	10%	10%	35%
Fancy goods	Nil	10%	10%	10-15%
Floorcloth and oilcloth	Nil	10%	10%	20%
Furniture	Nil	10%	20%	40%
Carriages	Nil	15%	20%	$50
Carts	Nil	15%	20%	20%
Harness and saddlery	Nil	10%	20%	45%

Selected tariff schedule of major imports NSW and Vic during the years 1876 and 1893.

Source: Selections of tariff schedule derived from Butlin (1964).

†240d = 1£

This paper is organized into five further sections. Section 4 provides a brief overview of existing literature on this topic, including reflections from economic historians and any available insights from economists linking trade policy and long-term development. Section 6 describes the meaning and sources of the statistics we used in our research, emphasizing data properties and limitations. Section 5 describes the research methods we have used. Section 7 contains our analysis and results. Section 8 provides some discussion, our findings and some areas of potential further investigation by both historians and economists.

A Survey of Relevant Literature

The first significant research on the Vic-NSW development comparison arose in the nineteenth century itself [7]. This study used limited descriptive statistics. The purpose was to demonstrate that the 'freer-trade' policy of NSW was more beneficial than Vic's protectionist regime. While Powers did not define his measure of 'beneficial', he did define 'free trade' to mean 'tariffs for revenue only' [8].[2] This assumption differs greatly from the modern definition of free trade, meaning the absence of all trade barriers: it shows the need for care when examining historical data.

This practice has not always been followed. For example, the authoritative W.A. Sinclair, made his own evaluation of the effects Vic tariffs [9], considering only the changes that would have occurred had there been no tariffs, wrongly representing the moderate protection reality in NSW. Sinclair was, however, careful to frame his comments in terms of cause-and-effect relationships that tariffs had on production levels. Sinclair was not able to examine the interaction between tariffs, tariff revenue, public works expenditure, and productivity effects, which is our central objective here. He did not, moreover, use an econometric approach capable of filtering out other influences on economic development as we have sought to do.

Historians, Patterson and Butlin et al. [5,10] were antecedents to whom Sinclair often referred. Patterson recognized that most of the differences in tariff income between NSW and Vic were explained by the differences in land sales, which constituted another major source of revenue. The overriding consideration was still the immediate developmental needs of a new land rather than with long-term considerations such as productivity growth.

Butlin's extensive work [10], emphasizes data interpretation in an historical context. Butlin provide a large and varied set of results to be used in many studies as primary data, including this one. Butlin posited a relationship between the availability of investment capital and economic cycles the colonies faced at this time [11]. He found that reduced financial support from England required alternative sources of revenue. Hence, the change in productivity caused by a change in tariff rates may be more accurately described as a strong side-effect of that motive.

Later accounts of the development of industry in Victoria imply a protection-development linkage that became the accepted version of this period of history. As an example, the Centenary Edition of The Victorian Year Book, published in 1973, gives this account:

'At first the (Victorian general industry protective) tariff was low: 10 per cent on certain manufactured goods. In 1871, the tariff was raised to 20 per cent for finished manufactures, including boots, clothing, textiles, leather goods and iron and steel goods. Six years later the tariff was raised again and duties of 30 and 40 per cent measures were imposed on some commodities' (p.323).

The authors then infer that high and increased protection was associated with the fuller development and evolution of industry, compared with NSW:

'...by 1891 nearly 25 per cent more people were employed in secondary industry in Victoria than in the more populous New South Wales' (p.323).

The authors then document the firms, industries and towns that experienced this nineteenth century Victorian manufacturing development. But there is no attempt to link this development to protection specifically (pp.323-6). In another place, the writers state:

"Victoria did in fact lead other states in the development of (textiles, clothing, footwear and carriage building, against British and other overseas competition) and in the replacement of consumer goods by raw materials and capital goods as its major overseas imports. However, it is an open case whether these developments would have occurred in any case, since the population attracted by the gold discoveries already provided a sizeable local market and a readily available workforce." ... "Perhaps the most that can be said is that industrial development in Victoria was somewhat accelerated by protection."

In the four decades since these accounts were written, little solid statistical or other analysis has been made to check these cursory inferences and strong assertions. A recent study on the links between trade-openness, foreign direct investment, and long-term economic growth, Pradhan et al. [12] struggles to find any theory-based foundations for their work, while citing several empirical papers upon which they advance in a ten-country comprehensive study of recent data. As neither trade policy theory nor economic development gives any rigorous specification for the study we are making, the inspiration for our study must therefore come from less fully-specified theory, from observations and inferences at the time and since, and from empirical studies, by economists and economic historians and observers of the day.

Since 1960s there has been a resurgence of interest in analyzing tariff history, using more advanced econometric techniques. For example, an ambitious attempt to evaluate of overall social and economic welfare effects of iron and steel tariffs in nineteenth-century United States by Irwin [13] involved estimating linking coefficients. However, without sufficient information to deal with the interplay between import quantity, import price and the price-sensitivity of the supply of the foreign good(s), Irwin concedes that his approach remains a static comparative exercise [14]. A more relevant study was also conducted by Tena, who compared the effects of tariffs on the growth of Gross Domestic Product (GDP) in many nations [15] using a specification to separate tariff effects from other influences. Tena attributes the lack of statistically-significant results to the sparseness of his dataset, but this might not be the main problem.

Another contemporaneous paper [16] measures the change in Australian GDP from 1870 to 2002, amazingly with data available through all thirteen decades. The authors find a weak but statisticallysignificant negative relationship between tariffs and growth of around 0.28%. Concurrently, they noticed many qualitative disruptions throughout the period, inevitably these are caused by historical changes, which the authors handle by adding dummy variables that have no economic interpretation.

Our approach in this study captures multiple influences on productivity growth, which are consistent with the enumeration of explanatory factors found in the more-applied economics literature. Our choice of explanatory variables is supported by the Denison method embraced in Matthews [17] and more recently by Australia's National Office for the Information Economy [18].

Our Method

The simplest approach in econometric analysis is to begin with a testing equation. By convention, the measure for productivity is placed at the left and the candidate factors explaining it are place at the right. We selected variables that are causally linked to economic development according to the likelihood that the factor will influence the statistical estimates for tariff rate effects, the main independent variable, as well as being important to manufacturing in the colonies.

We start with a conceptual relationship between production rates and our cited dependent variables, for each colony in turn. Denote t as the time index of each variable. We write:

$$Y_t = f\,(trate_t;\ pub_t;\ fac_t;\ work_t;\ pri_t;\ city_t) \tag{1}$$

Where,

Y_t stands for output

$trate_t$ stands for tariff rates

pub_t stands for public capital

fact stands for establishments

$work_t$ stands for workers

pri_t stands for private capital and

$city_t$ stands for city density

We now state the derivation of each variable. Detailed empirical reasons for variable definitions are included in Appendix 1 for the interested reader.

Subject variable: production per worker

Our subject variable is total manufacturing output in 1890-adjusted dollars, divided by the total number of workers.

Main explanatory variable: Tariff rates

We define tariff rates as total customs revenues divided by the monetary value of imports.

Public capital expenditure

Public capital investment is assumed to be an externality: rather than measuring it on a per-worker or per-person basis, we compute capital investment using public capital expenditure data. The view of Sinclair is taken, that the primary incentive was to foster railroads, judging by the large share they consume. We estimate the accumulated stock of public capital investments in railroads in each year t, defined as follows:

$$Pub_t = pub_{t-1} + (New\ capital - Replacement\ Outlays_t)$$

(2)

Additionally, we know that the obvious revenue motive for imposing high tariff rates was to finance public works. The most important government initiative of this sort was railroad construction, lead to indirect benefits for manufacturing. Therefore, we attempt to estimate the hypothetical level of capital stock if income from tariffs were removed. We denote this value as , computed as follows:

$$\widehat{pub}_t = \widehat{pub}_{t-1} + MAX(total\ public\ capital\ investments, 0) * percentage\ of\ public\ capital\ investments\ in\ railroads - average\ maintenance\ cost * 2.5\% * \widehat{pub}_{t-1} \quad (3)$$

The 2.5% is the average maintenance cost, derived as follows:

$$\frac{\sum_1^T pub_t}{Replacement\ Outlays_t} * \frac{1}{T} \quad \textbf{(4)}$$

Economies of scope: number of factories

The total number of factories captures both scale economies effect at the firm level and scope between firms. If the infant-industries argument holds, productivity should increase when the sector is shared amongst fewer, larger firms.

Economies of scope: number of workers

Total number of workers in manufacturing, directly taken from sources.

Economies of scope: private capital accumulation

Private capital accumulation is defined as the total capital accumulated, in dollar amounts, during each year for each factory. This requires the assumption that the benchmark value of factory capital was close to zero before the 1860s, when growth really began to take off.

External factor: city density

City density is a measure of urban population. Most manufacturing activity occurs in urbanized areas of the colonies so this measure makes more sense than overall population levels of the entire colony. A higher population creates a price support for manufacturers due to consequential demand-side externalities; the price support created by increased tariff rates was thought to translate to factories being able to hire more workers.

The production function

As the number of data points in our study is limited, we use a modified Cobb-Douglas production relationship, which is commonly used for studies where prior information does not indicate any specific functional form for the function.

$$Y_t = (1 + trate_t)^{\beta_1} (pub_t)^{\beta_2} (fac_t)^{\beta_3} (work_t)^{\beta_4} (pri_t)^{\beta_5} (city_t)^{\beta_6} \quad (5)$$

The main properties and limitations are documented in Hoover [19].

By specifying tariff rates as ($1+trate_t$), our working assumption is that tariffs provide a price effect, and that small price changes are associated with an approximately constant own-price elasticity of demand, leading to the convenience of the log-log specification. If the tariff rate is applied directly, low tariff percentages will drive the log value to a large negative number. That would then imply that, at very low tariff rates, marginal changes would have a very large impact, when in reality small percentages from near zero should not have a very high percentage effect.

We now divide both sides of the equation by the number of workers to obtain the subject variable as production per worker, we can get a log-log model in the following form,[3]

$$Y_t = \beta_0 + \beta_1 ln(1 + trate_t) + \beta_2 ln(pub_t) + \beta_3 ln(fac_t) + (\beta_4 - 1) ln(work_t) + \beta_5 ln(pri_t) + \beta_6 ln(city_t) + \varepsilon_t \quad (6)$$

Where,

y_t denotes the log of output per worker

ε_t denotes $N(0,\Sigma^{-1})$ iid errors.

Econometric modifications

In addition to the basic model, we will introduce three modifications. The first refinement relates to data integrity issues raised by Butlin [9]. One of his objections was that data during the early years of the Statistical Registers could be inaccurate. This limitation is potentially most serious in relation to the first two years of this study [9]. Outliers do not always invalidate results and they can never be excluded arbitrarily. For this study, the years 1861 and 1862 are excluded as outliers because Vic was still at her early stages, and the underlying phenomenon would have been uncharacteristic.

The second modification, which closely related to the first one is the treatment of the final years of the data, during the recession of the 1890s. Global recessions are external shocks that affect small-scaled economies such as Australia during the colonial-era. This study will add a dummy variable for the years 1893-1900 to prevent shocks in the underlying economic parameters of the respective colonies from distorting estimates for the other years.

Our third and final refinement we introduce is a statistical justification of the variables included in the model. This means sifting through the list of variables to select those that best explain productivity growth, striking a middle-ground between excluding important variables and over-fitting the model. This study will do so by estimating the above regression model using all possible combinations of the listed variables we have specified above. At the next stage, the Akaike Information Criterion (AIC) and Bayesian Information Criterion (BIC) scores are computed. These scores are a measure of information lost when each variable is excluded. The five variables being tested are: worker count, factory count, total private capital, city density and the recession dummy variable. They are included and excluded in turn for a total of 2^5=32 total combinations, presented in **Table 3**. AIC and BIC scores for all combinations of dependent variables are included in Appendix 2 **Table 3**.

Table 3: Variables included for the best model based on AIC/BIC exogeneity tests.

		Variables in best model				
Statistic	Dataset	Workers	Factory	Private capital	City density	Recession
AIC	NSW		Y	Y	Y	Y
BIC	NSW			Y	Y	Y
AIC	Vic	Y	Y	Y	Y	Y
BIC	Vic	Y	Y			Y
AIC	dummy	Y	Y			Y
BIC	dummy		Y			Y
AIC	pooled	Y	Y	Y	Y	Y
BIC	pooled	Y	Y	Y	Y	Y

Variables included in the `best' specification as defined by scores of the AIC and BIC exogeneity tests. A total of 32 combinations were estimated by ordinary least-squares; tariff rates are the primary variable and always included. `Y' indicates that the specification includes that variable. Information scores for each combination of dependent variables are included in Appendix 2.

Production per worker is the dependent variable, while tariff rates and public capital are always included because both are central to this study. Factory count and the recession dummy appear almost everywhere and are also included. The number of workers variable is excluded because it is not a significant factor for NSW. Only factors relevant for both colonies are included for comparison. As for the private capital and city density variables, both of them appear in the same specifications. The decision is to include private capital and omit city density because the latter depended a lot more on interpolation to fill the gaps. The need to exclude one is due to their high correlation with each other and with population in general. Estimation results using all available variables are included for reference as a robustness check.

Data and Variables

Manufacturing output, workers

Output in sterling terms is taken from Butlin [10], who estimated output as five times the value of total wages. Total workers in manufacturing data are taken from the source above except NSW workers in 1861/62. Those two years were not available so it is assumed that the percentage growth of workers is the same as during the years 1863/64, extrapolated backwards. The same is done for Victoria in 1861 using 1862/63; Butlin stated that the figure of 3830 was `clearly incomplete'. NSW during 1891 is taken from government statistics. **Figure 1**.

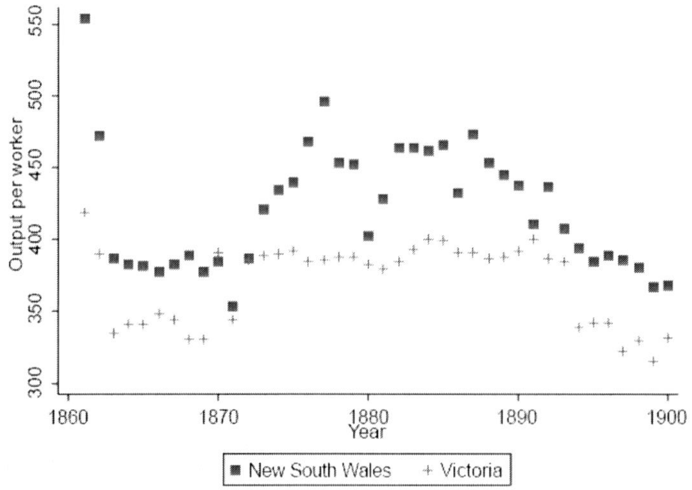

Figure 1: Output per worker, 1861-1900.

Figure 1: Output per worker, 1861-1900.

The movement of production per worker in the two colonies, summarized in **Figure 1**, seems to have mirrored each other. This may well reflect common external factors that impinged on both these colonies. This is particularly evident during 1872/83 in NSW, when indices of production per worker increased from 387 to 421, closely coinciding with the increase enjoyed by Vic the year before, when production per worker rise from 344 to 386. Again, in the recession two decades later, NSW production per worker fell from 436 to 408 during 1892/93, with Vic following similarly a year later, dropping from 385 to 339. Alternatively, NSW simply have converted less of its primary sector into manufacturing, hiring only the best workers. It would be difficult for a regression estimate to distinguish between these effects.

Private capital, public capital, tariffs

Private capital formation is taken from p.282 of Butlin [10]. For NSW 1861-85, Butlin found that no data are available and hence he extrapolated backwards using techniques based on `three-year recursive running averages'. Public capital figures are taken from Butlin [10] at pp.348-67. Tariff rates on an ad-valorem basis are unavailable so they were computed.

Total imports were taken directly from Statistical Registers, as well as customs & duties collected from 1891-1900 for NSW and for 1865-1900 for Victoria. Those for NSW during 1861-90 were taken from Patterson [5]; Victorian data 1861-64 were manually tallied from the `interchange' section of the Statistical Registers by aggregating the `duty collected' at the foot of each page **Figure 2**.

Figure 2: Annual average tariff rates, 1861-1900.

Figure 2: Annual average tariff rates, 1861-1900.

Movements in tariff rates, as shown in **Figure 2**, tended to coincide inversely with large apparent reductions in production per worker, in both colonies. In NSW, the tariff rates increased from 9.89% to 14.20% during 1891/92, a year before the colony saw a drop in production per worker. Similarly, in Vic there was a surge from 14.65% to 16.91% in the same year. Paradoxically, the temporal closeness between the movements of these two variables actually reduces the strength of the anti-tariff arguments made in earlier comparative studies, which state that protectionist measures do not pay in the long run. A more probable explanation is that recessions fuel populist sentiment for higher protection; but this does not establish how tariffs affect manufacturing output **Figures 3 and 4**.

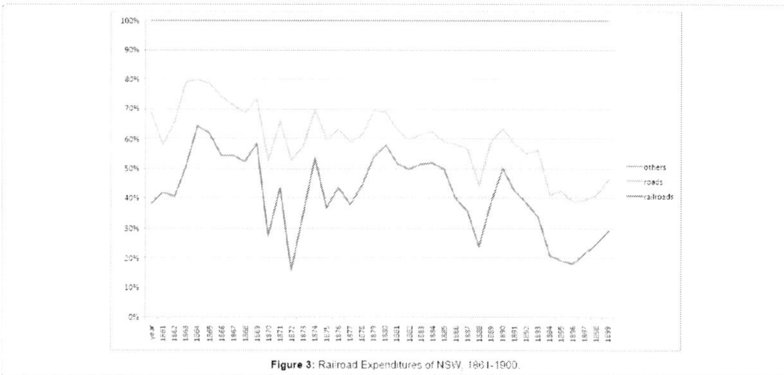

Figure 3: Railroad Expenditures of NSW, 1861-1900.

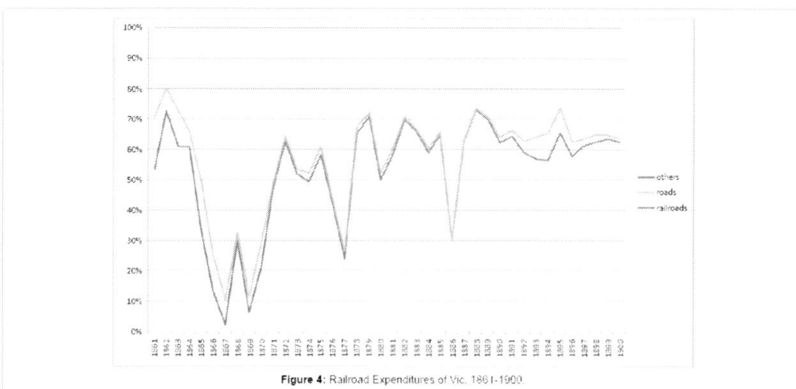

Figure 4: Railroad Expenditures of Vic, 1861-1900.

Establishments (factories)

A Number of establishments for the years 1861-64 are taken from their respective Statistics Registers, shown in **Figures 3 and 4**. The bases between the colonies were not exactly the same. For NSW the 1861/62 figures only include `old settled districts' and for 1863/64 excluded machines `Connected with or dependent upon agriculture'. 1861/62 figures from Victoria include `breweries' and `Mills for Grinding and Dressing Grain'. Establishment figures 1891-1900 uses 1895 Statistical Registers as they are in line with Butlin's figures. Numbers from 1865-90 are taken from Patterson [5]. Both the 1861-64 numbers and Patterson's sources exclude isolated machines as establishments.

Population

Census dates did not coincide with the beginning of the year so linear extrapolation was performed according to the actual day of the year between the gaps. Before 1896, the numbers were taken from Keltie et al. [20]. The 1883 figure for NSW does not have a date so it is assumed to be mid-year, as consistent with other Victoria estimates. The 1891 census taken in NSW also does not have a date, so the customary date of 1 April is assumed. After 1896 the figures are taken from Coghlan [21].

City density

City density is highly incomplete and only a few points were available, hence the collinearity problem with population when used for regression analysis. First, city population censuses were taken during the years 1861/71/81/91 in the two colonies as well as `percentage of the total colonial population' figures. They are available in McCarty et al. [22]. Percentages between census dates were first filled in by linear interpolation, and then multiplied by colony population data. We use colony population instead of interpolated city population as a check: we found estimated city populations were all monotone around the census `nodes', confirming that the basis for counting population in both sources was consistent. Land area in hectares was available from Spearritt [23] for the years 1901/21/31 and extrapolated backwards; it also estimated for the year 1821 in Phillips [24].

Analysis and Results

We present out results in two parts. The first half will present our main findings. The second half contains variations in estimation strategy that serve as robustness checks for the interested reader. Tables of exact sources by year and a complete listing of variable values are listed in Appendix 3 for readers interested in replication.

Main estimation results

Parameter estimates of the colonial production function and their corresponding t-values are listed in **Table 4**. Four sets of regression estimates are presented: NSW only, Vic only, colony dummy variable, and pooled regression **Table 4**.

Table 4: Parameter estimates of log-log regressions on output per worker 1863-1900.

Variable	NSW only	Vic only	Colony dummy	Pooled
log(tariff rate)	-0.0342	0.5259	-0.1063	*-1.7161
	(0.1097)	(1.2543)	(0.4161)	(5.6703)
log(public capital)	-0.0803	0.0081	0.0083	-0.0109
	(1.6632)	(0.3706)	(0.6261)	(0.5681)
log(factory)	0.0605	*0.2038	*0.1997	0.0623
	(0.6647)	(2.6785)	(3.8553)	(0.6839)
log(private capital)	0.1346	-0.0418	-0.0303	0.0500
	(1.6478)	(1.6857)	(1.8442)	(1.4860)
Recession dummy	*-0.1340	*-0.1425	*-0.1309	*-0.1269
	(6.3724)	(5.1640)	(7.0812)	(3.9979)
Colony dummy			*-0.1187	
			8.2790	
(Constant)	*4.8321	*4.8052	*4.8462	*5.0953
	(30.1593)	(22.5390)	(42.4383)	(27.1627)
R^2	0.6894	0.7243	0.7886	0.5991
Adj R^2	0.6409	0.6812	0.7702	0.5705
Durbin-Watson	1.2860	2.0701		

Parameter estimates and standard errors of the log-production-function regression estimate, between the total output per work and the explanatory variables as listed here.

The figure on top is the parameter estimate and the value below is the t-value.

For the colony dummy, NSW=0 and Vic=1.

Recession dummy equals 1 for the years 1893-1900 inclusive, 0 otherwise.

*indicates 95\% significance level.

Both Patterson and Butlin believed, with some significant justification, that the income motive was more important than traderelated concerns such as prices and competition. The results here are consistent with their hypothesis, as tariff rates do not have much direct effect on manufacturing productivity at all. Parameter values for tariff rates for the first three specifications are close to zero and are not statistically significant. The fourth specification, the pooled regression, displays a large and statistically significant negative value of -1.7161 but this is probably a misspecification because the effect reduces to -0.1063 once a colony dummy variable is added. Historically Vic did have higher tariff rates and lower productivity. However, in order to claim that tariff rates are detrimental to productivity, the same effect must be observed within each colony itself. Neither the parameter values of -0.0342 for NSW and 0.5259 for Vic are statistically significant and both are much smaller than the pooled-regression estimate.

The two variables that do have significant effects are total factory count and the Australian recession of the 1890s. Recessions are global historical events beyond the control of the colonies and are simply external factors to control for. For the number of factories parameter, the Vic-only regression specification obtained an estimate of 0.2038 while the dummy model had a significant value 0.1997. The factory number coefficient for the other two regressions is smaller but is still positive. These results are consistent with the presence of external economies of scale, a benefit that a protective tariff is meant to foster.

The actual effectiveness of protective tariffs in fostering economies of scale will be discussed further shortly.

Another claim propounded by both Vic and NSW is that tariffs were needed for infrastructure development. Specifically, tariffs will raise money for railroads for supporting the manufacturing sector. A preliminary way to test this effect is to construct a hypothetical scenario where tariff income, as computed by tariff rate times manufacturing output. This amount is removed from public capital investment values and the model is estimated again in **Table 5**.

There is little evidence that public capital, even at the reduced level, promotes manufacturing productivity. Parameter values are not significant for the colony-only specifications and even negative at -0.0314 for the dummy specification. These results do not support the notion that tariff-supported infrastructure development accelerates manufacturing development.

Robustness check 1: correlation between explanatory variables

Co-relationship between explanatory variables is a common concern in time-series regression analysis. Admittedly, with fragmented historical data, the possibilities for measuring and correcting for this problem are limited. Causality may be a close analogue, tested by running a vector-autoregression (VAR) model followed by a Granger causality test. This is done separately for the two colonies: NSW in **Table 6** and Vic in **Table 7**. The pooled version does not seem relevant to most of this study **Table 6**.

Table 5: Change in marginal effects after hypothetical reductions in public capital expenditures.

Variable	NSW only	Vic only	colony dummy	pooled
log(tariff rate)	-0.2416	0.5094	-0.0658	*-1.6221
	(0.1097)	(1.2543)	(0.4161)	(5.6703)
log(public capital)	-0.0099	-0.0007	0.0074	0.0137
	(1.6632)	(0.3706)	(0.6261)	(0.5681)
log(factory)	0.1186	*0.2197	*0.2031	0.0337
	(0.6647)	(2.6785)	(3.8553)	(0.6839)
log(private capital)	0.0369	-0.0427	*-0.0316	0.0415
	(1.6478)	(1.6857)	(1.8442)	(1.4860)
Recession dummy	*-0.1435	*-0.1344	*-0.1321	*-0.1495
	(6.3724)	(5.1640)	(7.0812)	(3.9979)
Colony dummy			*-0.1159	
			(8.2790)	
(Constant)	*4.745	*4.8385	*4.8586	*5.0596
	(30.1593)	(22.5390)	(42.4383)	(27.1627)
R^2	0.6622	0.7230	0.7903	0.6065
Adj R^2	0.6094	0.6797	0.7721	0.5784
Durbin-Watson	1.1314	2.0347		

Parameter estimates and standard errors of the log-production-function regression estimate using hypothetically reduced levels of public capital investments as a result of a reduction in tariff income. See the methods section for computational details.

The first significant causal relationship we found is the correlation between the recession dummies and tariff rates specifically for NSW. The significance levels are 1.3% for tariffs to recession and 3.2% for recession to tariffs; the lower the significance level, the stronger the relation. Importantly, a similar causal relationship is not observed in Vic, even though the Vic reaction of raising tariff rates in the face of recession is well documented **Table 7**.

A cursory glance at the results in the tables might suggest that it was in fact NSW that responded to populist sentiments by raising tariffs. It is possible that because Vic already started with higher tariff rates, they may not have had much scope to raise them further. The significance here is that estimated marginal effect of tariff rates reinforces the observation that the colonies in fact had similar ideas about tariff policy.

Table 6: Robustness: Vector-Autoregression and Granger causality, NSW.

Subject Variable	Excluded variable	X^2 statistic	Deg. Freedom	(Prob)
log(output per worker)	log(tariff rate)	0.171	1	0.679
log(output per worker)	log(public capital)	1.980	1	0.159
log(output per worker)	log(factory)	4.861	1	*0.027
log(output per worker)	log(private capital)	0.016	1	0.899
log(output per worker)	Recession dummy	2.390	1	0.122
log(output per worker)	(constant only)	18.642	5	*0.002
log(tariff rate)	log(output per worker)	1.135	1	0.287
log(tariff rate)	log(public capital)	1.558	1	0.212
log(tariff rate)	log(factory)	0.680	1	0.410
log(tariff rate)	log(private capital)	0.004	1	0.953
log(tariff rate)	Recession dummy	6.224	1	*0.013
log(tariff rate)	(constant only)	8.473	5	0.132
log(public capital)	log(output per worker)	2.682	1	0.101
log(public capital)	log(tariff rate)	10.892	1	*0.001
log(public capital)	log(factory)	2.219	1	0.136
log(public capital)	log(private capital)	0.264	1	0.608
log(public capital)	Recession dummy	0.129	1	0.719
log(public capital)	(constant only)	17.722	5	*0.003
log(factory)	log(output per worker)	0.903	1	0.342
log(factory)	log(tariff rate)	0.103	1	0.749
log(factory)	log(public capital)	2.031	1	0.154
log(factory)	log(private capital)	2.428	1	0.119
log(factory)	Recession dummy	0.587	1	0.444
log(factory)	(constant only)	5.218	5	0.390
log(private capital)	log(output per worker)	3.929	1	*0.047
log(private capital)	log(tariff rate)	0.108	1	0.743
log(private capital)	log(public capital)	5.236	1	*0.022
log(private capital)	log(factory)	6.060	1	*0.014
log(private capital)	Recession dummy	4.106	1	*0.043
log(private capital)	(constant only)	11.843	5	*0.037
Recession dummy	log(output per worker)	0.002	1	0.963
Recession dummy	log(tariff rate)	4.624	1	*0.032
Recession dummy	log(public capital)	0.470	1	0.493
Recession dummy	log(factory)	10.674	1	*0.001
Recession dummy	log(private capital)	6.036	1	*0.014
Recession dummy	(constant only)	23.250	5	*0.000

Vector-auto-correlation (VAR) estimate of log-production function with lag of 1, followed by Granger causality test between each variable, for NSW.

Table 7: Robustness: Vector-Autoregression and Granger causality, Vic.

Subject Variable	Excluded variable	X^2 statistic	Deg. Freedom	(Prob)
log(output per worker)	log(tariff rate)	0.954	1	0.329
log(output per worker)	log(public capital)	1.215	1	0.270
log(output per worker)	log(factory)	16.309	1	*0.000
log(output per worker)	log(private capital)	6.178	1	*0.013
log(output per worker)	Recession dummy	23.268	1	*0.000
log(output per worker)	(constant only)	60.333	5	*0.000
log(tariff rate)	log(output per worker)	3.693	1	0.055
log(tariff rate)	log(public capital)	1.601	1	0.206
log(tariff rate)	log(factory)	1.048	1	0.306
log(tariff rate)	log(private capital)	0.330	1	0.566
log(tariff rate)	Recession dummy	2.240	1	0.134
log(tariff rate)	(constant only)	9.620	5	0.087
log(public capital)	log(output per worker)	0.730	1	0.393
log(public capital)	log(tariff rate)	1.658	1	0.198
log(public capital)	log(factory)	7.259	1	*0.007
log(public capital)	log(private capital)	2.744	1	0.098
log(public capital)	Recession dummy	0.501	1	0.479
log(public capital)	(constant only)	29.538	5	*0.000
log(factory)	log(output per worker)	0.073	1	0.786
log(factory)	log(tariff rate)	1.283	1	0.257
log(factory)	log(public capital)	0.259	1	0.611
log(factory)	log(private capital)	2.659	1	0.103
log(factory)	Recession dummy	0.044	1	0.834
log(factory)	(constant only)	3.320	5	0.651
log(private capital)	log(output per worker)	0.003	1	0.954
log(private capital)	log(tariff rate)	5.941	1	*0.015
log(private capital)	log(public capital)	1.334	1	0.248
log(private capital)	log(factory)	6.740	1	*0.009
log(private capital)	Recession dummy	0.053	1	0.819
log(private capital)	(constant only)	18.842	5	*0.002
Recession dummy	log(output per worker)	0.213	1	0.644
Recession dummy	log(tariff rate)	2.954	1	0.086
Recession dummy	log(public capital)	7.069	1	*0.008
Recession dummy	log(factory)	2.201	1	0.138
Recession dummy	log(private capital)	0.514	1	0.474
Recession dummy	(constant only)	11.781	5	*0.038

Vector-auto-correlation (VAR) estimate of log-production function with lag of 1, followed by Granger causality test between each variable, for Vic.

Robustness check 2: unobserved determinants of number of factories

The parameter estimate for the number of factories, as shown in **Table 4**, stands out in importance and deserves a second check for correlation with other variables. In particular, the driving force of private capital in increasing the number of factories may be important. According to results in **Table 4**, this relationship exists for both NSW (1.4%) and Vic (0.9%). On the surface this is unsurprising because more factories obviously require more capital. However, the fact that there is a positive relationship between private capital and factory count then naturally leads to question of why private capital is not dropped altogether as an explanatory variable. An obvious concern is that including two endogenous parameters causes inflated parameter estimates.

A simple way to assess this is to set the number of factories as the dependent variable. The results are listed in **Table 8**. The most notable finding here is actually the non-result between tariff rates and number of factories. All the parameter values are negative but not significant. In **table 4** above it was shown that there are significant positive relationships between total factory count and productivity, supporting the notion that external economies of scale should be fostered. But despite the relationship between factory count and productivity, there is no evidence suggesting that a protective tariff is an effective means to foster external economies of scale: benefits of size that accrue to others. Indeed, the slightly negative parameters suggest that it may even be detrimental **Table 8**.

We include both private capital and number of factories for two reasons. First, there is no obvious sign that the inflation in parameter estimates is serious. The estimate for private capital is not significant anyway. The second reason is that available capital per factory can vary, so the variables are measuring different things. Inflation-adjusted capital per factory increased during this time period, while factories in NSW also had more capital available than the ones in Vic.

Robustness check 3: autocorrelation of dependent variables

The next issue we need to address is autocorrelation. The Durbin- Watson statistics in **Tables 4 and 6** do not suggest a strong presence of autocorrelation, but an additional check can be conducted by running the same model using an autoregressive specification of order 1, presented in **Table 9**.

Table 8: Robustness: Number of factories as the subject variable.

Variable	NSW only	Vic only	Colony dummy	Pooled
log(output per worker)	0.1399	0.7198	*0.5978	0.1194
	(0.6113)	(1.8379)	(2.8063)	(0.6930)
log(tariff rate)	-0.6229	-1.1697	-1.1382	-0.3571
	(0.7241)	(1.0840)	(1.8444)	(0.6004)
log(public capital)	-0.1465	0.0894	0.0564	0.0865
	(1.9275)	(1.8354)	(1.2405)	(1.7473)
log(private capital)	*0.5788	*0.2882	*0.3154	*0.3102
	(6.1087)	(6.2032)	(6.1687)	(5.6779)
Recession dummy	*-0.1306	-0.0529	-0.0821	*-0.1818
	(2.1267)	(0.6075)	(1.6364)	(5.0591)
Colony dummy			*0.1255	
			(3.3524)	
(Constant)	0.4981	-2.2145	-1.4904	0.9610
	(0.4474)	(1.0426)	(1.3166)	(0.9780)
R^2	0.9593	0.9679	0.9573	0.9482
Adj R^2	0.9529	0.9629	0.9536	0.9445
Durbin-Watson	1.6396	1.4504		

Parameter estimates of the log-production function, with the subject variable switched from output-per-worker to total number of factories.

Parameter estimates for the explanatory variables did decrease in magnitude and are no longer significant, which may seem to suggest that the majority of significant results are actually autocorrelation. However this is not the case because the autocorrelation parameter is not significant for the colonies either. The autocorrelation score is positive but not significant for NSW; it is close to zero for Vic. Hence, there is little evidence of misattribution for previously observed effects in the explanatory variables. A time-series specification does not bring any tangible gains and can be safely ruled out.

Time lags between certain explanatory variables and productivity may also exist. This could be driven by differences in accounting dates between the variables or actual time gaps for changes in explanatory variables to take effect. This can be measured by estimating the model using first differences **Table 10**.

Table 9: Robustness: Estimate using autoregressive specification of order 1.

Variable	NSW only	Vic only
log(tariff rate)	0.0111	0.6440
	(0.0101)	(0.5993)
log(public capital)	-0.0449	0.0094
	(0.4840)	(0.2579)
log(factory)	0.0696	0.2081
	(0.3470)	(1.9219)
log(private capital)	0.0818	-0.0448
	(0.7386)	(0.8578)
Recession dummy	*-0.1246	*-0.1465
	(2.0311)	(3.0738)
(Constant)	4.9887	4.7848
	(7.4528)	(15.7768)
AR(1)	0.4285	-0.0645
	(1.5373)	(0.2995)

Parameter estimates of log-production function with autocorrelation model of order 1.

Table 10: Robustness: Estimate using first-differences specifications.

Variable	NSW only	Vic only
log(tariff rate)	2.5389	1.4621
	(1.5423)	(0.5752)
log(public capital)	0.0308	0.1612
	(0.1993)	(1.8045)
log(factory)	*1.6957	*1.3234
	(5.6772)	(4.6501)
log(private capital)	-0.5110	*-0.4670
	(1.9520)	(3.9400)
Recession dummy	-0.0206	-0.1685
	(0.1961)	(1.2988)

Parameter estimates of log-production function using the first-differences specification.

Overall results for the first-differences model as listed in **Table 10** are more difficult to evaluate because the standard errors are much higher, reducing significance levels. The good news is that number of factories consistently remains a statistically significant factor for productivity in both the NSW (1.6957) and Vic (1.3234) data points. On the other hand, the large positive relationship between tariff rates and productivity in the first differences model is very different than that of **Table 4**. We recall that the only difference is a slight change of specification using the same set of variables. What this means is that, once again, there may be insufficient evidence to link high tariff rates to any perceived reduction in trade and development.

Robustness check 4: validity of excluding variables

The decision to include a recession-years dummy variable is based on historical knowledge, not any statistical deduction or tests for structural breaks. To justify the validity of doing this, the same model as **Table 4** is estimated again by removing this dummy variable. The important results as shown in **Table 11** remain the same. Tariff rates still do not have significant effects on productivity, while the number of factories still do, with parameters for the latter ranging from around 0.25 to 0.45 in all four specifications. The new anomaly here is the compounded negative relationship between public capital and productivity. There is no clear reason for why this effect should exist or that it was hidden by including a recession year dummy. The more likely scenarios would be that public capital projects were initiated during the recession years. Hence including the recession dummy variable is the better specification decision **Table 11**.

Table 11: Robustness: Estimates removing recession-years dummy.

Variable	NSW only	Vic only	Colony dummy	Pooled
log(tariff rate)	0.2035	-0.4327	-0.2339	*-1.8112
	(0.3617)	(0.7554)	(0.5677)	(4.6329)
log(public capital)	*-0.1090	*-0.0560	*-0.0397	*-0.0570
	(2.1848)	(2.2687)	(2.9132)	(3.4687)
log(factory)	*0.3118	*0.4202	*0.4191	*0.2775
	(3.0445)	(4.6617)	(6.9758)	(3.5381)
log(private capital)	0.0427	*-0.0834	*-0.0890	-0.0084
	(0.5144)	(2.6813)	(4.2699)	(0.3275)
Colony dummy			*-0.1165	
			(6.3982)	
(Constant)	4.7109	4.8876	4.8097	5.0554
	(23.7915)	(19.161)	(36.4959)	(26.9897)
R^2	0.5275	0.5311	0.6752	0.4925
Adj R^2	0.4702	0.4743	0.6520	0.4639
Durbin-Watson	0.9600	1.0572		

Parameter estimates of log-production function using ordinary least-squares (OLS) estimates, without recession dummy variable.

The exclusion of a number of available variables from the analysis also demands support. The choice of variables in the main model depended entirely on comparisons using AIC/BIC likelihood statistics. The statistical justification is sufficient, but regression results estimated from including all available variables is included in **Table 12** for completeness anyway **Table 12**.

Table 12: Robustness: Regression results including all variables.

Variable	NSW only	Vic only	Colony dummy	Pooled
log(tariff rate)	0.4473	0.1659	-0.1942	*-1.4302
	(1.2487)	(0.3766)	(0.8133)	(5.1668)
log(public capital)	*-0.2601	0.0535	0.0219	*0.0892
	(2.2844)	(0.7995)	(0.8831)	(2.2492)
log(factory)	0.1533	*0.4167	*0.2552	*0.2365
	(1.5738)	(2.5551)	(3.8820)	(2.2720)
log(workers)	*1.1038	*0.8172	*0.9242	*0.7375
	(7.8118)	(7.4357)	(14.5538)	(10.7828)
log(private capital)	0.1468	-0.0417	-0.0240	0.0691
	(1.8202)	(1.6967)	(1.1569)	(1.8052)
log(city density)	*0.4221	-0.0514	0.0303	-0.1081
	(2.1391)	(0.3384)	(0.4015)	(1.0420)
Recession dummy	*-0.1323	*-0.1319	*-0.1333	*-0.1371
	(5.5167)	(3.9149)	(7.4156)	(4.8838)
Colony dummy			*-0.1097	
			(7.3735)	
(Constant)	*5.1280	*4.4299	*4.8429	*4.6716
	(25.3477)	(6.6710)	(32.1512)	(20.3583)
R^2	0.7382	0.7629	0.7940	0.6774
Adj R^2	0.6771	0.7076	0.7694	0.6442
Durbin-Watson	1.7199	2.3654		

Parameter estimates of log-production function using OLS estimates with all variables, including the total number of workers and city density that were excluded previously from the AIC/BIC criteria.

We preserve the core findings from **Tables 4 and 5**; namely, the weak results from tariff rates and the stronger result from external economies of scale. The difference here is that the total number of workers and an estimated city density are also included. The significant effects of the number of workers are not surprising as it is very closely related to the number of factories. Accurate estimates of city density are not available, making this a tenuous addition in the first place. More importantly, it is credible to infer that they are very highly correlated with population, workers and number of factories. Adding them all will cause major endogeneity problems.

Discussion and Conclusion

It is often asked why the two colonies of NSW and Vic performed so similarly while practicing such different trade policies between 1860 and 1900. Part of the paradox stems from placing the labels `free trade' and `protectionist' on these two colonies. Both colonies actually had reasonably similar tariff levels; the main difference was that Vic made demonstrable duty-rate increases on many prominent items to appease protectionist sentiments. While Vic exhibited a large and impressive list of dutiable imported products, covering many pages in the records, collectively they did not generate much additional tariff revenue. The chief imports to Vic remained alcohol, sugar and agricultural products, all of which had strong externality effects on manufacturing. On analysis, the tariff policies for those products were very similar in both colonies.

We have shown that the effect of tariff rates on productivity was statistically insignificant. This finding advances beyond existing economic theory, which is simply silent on this important matter. Of great importance is our proof of the presence of the external economies of scale in the manufacturing sector. In relation to Vic, we have found a proven benefit in fostering larger external economies of scale for the manufacturing sector. However, there is insufficient evidence to conclude that protective tariffs have any significant effect towards development. Proponents of protection in Victoria at the time have clearly, in terms of our findings, exaggerated the pro-productivity and pro-development benefits of Vic's protectionist policies over four decades. Again, NSW's freer-trade proponents cannot in retrospect and on our analysis lay claim to have fostered longer-term development with their more libertarian trade policy. Our central finding is that forces other than international trade policy seem to have been central in the evolution of spectacularly productivity growth and very rapid economic development in the major Australian colonies, especially for the later nineteenth century.

NOTES

[1]As in the massive literature contained in and associated with Kamien and Schwartz(1982)

[2]"We must have revenue," they often said, "and the duties we propose will provide the sums we require. Incidentally, they may be of use to some of our industries." '. (Mills 1925)

[3]This is possible because $Var(\beta_4-1)=Var(\beta_4)$; all tables will display estimates of β_4.

REFERENCES

1. Kamien M, Schwartz NL (1982) Market Structure and Innovation.
2. Palen MW (2010) Protection, Federation and Union: The Global Impact of the McKinley Tariff upon the British Empire, 1890-94. The Journal of Imperial and Commonwealth History 38:395-418.
3. Greasley D, Madsen JB (2010) Curse and Boon: Natural Resources and Long-Run Growth in Currently Rich Economies. Economic Record 274: 311-328.
4. Williamson JG (2003) Was It Stolper-Samuelson, Infant Industry or Something Else? World Trade Tariffs 1789-1938. NBER Working Papers.
5. Patterson GD (1968) The tariff in the Australian colonies 1856-1900.
6. Sinclair WA (1976) The process of economics development in Australia.
7. Mills S (1925) Taxation in Australia.
8. Powers P, Fred (1888) The Australian Tariff Experiment. The Quarterly Journal of Economics 3:87-98.
9. Sinclair WA (1971) The Tariff and Economic Growth in Pre-Federation Vic. The Economic Record117:77-92.
10. Butlin NG (1962) Australian Domestic Product, Investment and Foreign Borrowing 1861-1938/39.
11. Butlin NG (1964) Investment in Australian Economic Growth.
12. Pradhan RP, Bagchi TP, Chowdhury K, Norman NR (2012) Growth, Foreign Investment and Trade-Openness Interactions in Ten OECD Countries: A Panel-VAR Approach. *International Journal of Banking, Accounting and Finance* 4:273-293.
13. Irwin DA (2000) Did Late-Nineteenth-Century U.S. Tariffs Promote Infant Industries? Evidence from the Tinplate Industry. Journal of Economic History 60:335-360.
14. Irwin DA (1998) Higher Tariffs, Lower Revenues? Analyzing the Fiscal Aspects of The Great Tariff Debate of 1888. Journal of Economic History 58:59-72.

15. Tena A (2007) Tariff Structure and Institutions in the Late 19th Century. New Perspectives on the Tariff Growth Paradox.

16. Athukorala PC, Chand S (2007) *Tariff-Growth Nexus in the Australian Economy, 1870-2002: Is there a Paradox?*

17. Matthews RCO (1969) Why Growth Rates Differ. Economic Journal 79:261-268.

18. National Office for the Information Economy (2004) Productivity Growth in Australian Manufacturing.

19. Hoover KD (2001) The Methodology of Empirical Macroeconomics.

20. Keltie JS, Martin F (1861-1900) The Statesman's Year-Book 1861-1900.

21. Coghlan TA (1902) A statistical account of the seven colonies of Australasia.

22. McCarty JW, Schedvin CB (1978) Australian Capital Cities: Historical Essays.

23. Spearritt P (1999) Sydney's century: a history. UNSW Press, Sydney.

24. Phillips M (1909) A colonial autocracy: NSW under Governor Macquarie, 1810-1821 (King, London).

25. Eilon S, Gold B, Soesan J (1976) Applied productivity analysis for industry.

7

LABOR MARKET INTERMEDIARIES MAKE THE WORLD SMALLER

Carlo Gianelle

European Commission, Joint Research Centre (JRC), Institute for Prospective Technological Studies (IPTS), C/ Inca Garcilaso, 3, 41092 Seville, Spain

ABSTRACT

This paper uses network analysis to study how employment intermediaries have influenced inter-firm worker mobility in a region of Italy, in response to a 1997 reform that introduced temporary employment agencies. Worker reallocations from a matched employer-employee dataset are mapped onto a directed graph where the vertices are firms and the links denote transfers of workers between firms. Temporary employment agencies significantly improve network integration and practicability, while rapidly increasing the control over mobility channels. The trade off inherent in intermediation activity is captured and discussed. The potential of network analysis as a tool for monitoring regional labor markets is highlighted.

Keywords: Labor market intermediaries, Information brokerage Inter-firm networks, Matched employer-employee data

1 INTRODUCTION

This paper provides an empirical contribution on how to capture the effects of employment intermediation by exploiting complex network analysis applied to worker mobility data. Network models are operationalized in the attempt to provide a novel understanding of two central issues of labor intermediation: (1) how and to what extent the arrival of labor intermediaries following enactment of a reform affects market integration and accessibility of different employers by people who reallocate within the market, and (2) whether and how the power of intermediaries in controlling and directing worker flows grows over time, and the fundamental dynamics of this process.

These questions are derived directly from the fundamental trade-off characterizing brokerage activity, according to which, on the one side, intermediation increases matching opportunities by reducing both parties' information costs, and on the other side, it produces monopolistic rents for the intermediary, due to the information asymmetries inherent in information brokerage which also favor concentration of the market in the hands of a few intermediaries.

To explore these issues, we apply for the first time a complex network approach to employer-employee matched data covering the universe of private employment in Veneto, a highly industrialized region in the North–East of Italy. A network representation is used to organize individual mobility events over a ten-year period, and network models are used to capture the effects of labor intermediaries on the structure of inter-firm reallocations.

We focus on a special category of intermediaries, temporary employment agencies (TEAs), that was introduced in Italy by the 1997 "Treu" reform of the labor market as a response to the persistently high level of unemployment especially in the southern regions of the country and among young people. Prior to the Treu reform, employment services were a public monopoly operated through a network of provincial agencies, which generally were inefficient and of little help to unemployed people (Barbieri et al. 2001). TEAs are, thus, the very first example of a private employment intermediary in contemporary Italy (detailed information about the novelties introduced by the Treu reform are provided in Appendix I).

The main object of the analysis is a directed graph where the vertices indicate employers, private firms or TEAs, and the links denote transfers of workers between employers. The data track all worker reallocations involving TEAs as either origin or destination, which captures all labor mobility involving intermediaries.

The first analytical focus is on the degree to which the network of labor mobility works as an integrated and easily practicable system for workers reallocating from one job to another, measured by the small-world characteristics of the network. The impact of TEAs on the network architecture is assessed by interpreting the tendency of the "world" of worker mobility to become smaller as a sign that the labor market is more accessible and more pervious to reallocation flows, and vice versa.

The second main focus is on the position of TEAs in the reallocation market or, more specifically, on their power in controlling hiring channels, as revealed by the number of incoming links pointing to intermediaries in the labor mobility network. To this purpose, the evolution of the statistical distribution of connections over vertices is tracked, highlighting the way in which global labor flows adjust to the presence of labor market intermediaries (LMIs). This is followed by a discussion of the predictions of several models of network formation describing evolution of the link distribution in the presence of information costs.

Exploratory in its nature, the approach developed in this work allows for quantitative analysis of the effects of employment intermediation on the labor market system as a whole, while also identifying the possible mechanisms governing the evolution of intermediaries' market power. Ultimately, the paper provides a novel set of tools for monitoring labor market functioning and supporting policy actions aimed, for instance, at improving the efficiency of job matching through intermediation or formulating better regulations for intermediated markets.

The paper is organized as follows. Section 2 discusses the theoretical foundations of economic intermediation, with a special focus on the labor market; Section 3 introduces the network framework and the empirical strategy; Section 4 describes the data. Sections 5 and 6 present the results; Section 7 discusses the empirical evidence on the evolution of TEAs market power in the light of network formation models; Section 8 concludes.

2 THEORETICAL BACKGROUND

The conceptual foundations of labor intermediation are rooted in the existence of market imperfections that hamper an efficient matching of demand and supply. A major feature of real, imperfect labor markets is the difficulty encountered by both individuals and firms to locate matches/partners and/or to negotiate successfully the terms of matching agreements. Third parties –intermediaries – may exploit these circumstances and attempt to realize profits by selling information or ad hoc matching services to workers and firms.

The economic literature has long recognized that information in real markets is costly and asymmetrically distributed between prospective parties in a transaction. It has been demonstrated that the existence of private information can have substantial implications in terms of market functioning and deviation from perfect competition benchmark.

Akerlof (1970) highlighted in a seminal paper the potential magnitude of market failure under asymmetric information. When the quality of a good is uncertain or difficult to determine for prospective buyers, there is an incentive for sellers to offer goods of poor quality. Buyers who are aware of such behavior may refrain from buying, generating a reduction in the size of the market, up to the emergence of no-transaction equilibria, that is, the disappearance of the market while demand and supply remain unsatisfied and resources unemployed. In these cases, public or private institutions may come into play to solve information asymmetries to everyone's advantage and, in the case of private organizations, make a profit out of such activity. Interestingly, Akerlof warned of the possible concentration of power in the hands of intermediary institutions that control information.

Transaction cost economics, rooted in the work of Coase (1937) and Williamson (1975), describe how incomplete and costly information result in transaction costs that are at the foundation of decisions between markets and hierarchies. Spulber (1996) extended the same argument to the organization of market institutions, identifying four main activities of intermediary organizations: setting prices, providing liquidity to markets, coordinating transactions between buyers and sellers, and generating market information about the quality of goods. Dixit (2003) explored a model of private intermediation as a mode of governance that helps enforcing contracts by means of collecting and conveying costly information about individual behaviors. In all these cases, the role of intermediaries is to facilitate transactions, putting their skills at the service of market clearing.

The central problem of information being asymmetrically distributed and costly to obtain has been assumed in macroeconomic models of search and matching in the labor market. Decentralized search for information has been demonstrated to generate non-market-clearing equilibria characterized by frictional unemployment. This is because jobs and workers are heterogeneous and thus a degree of mismatch is possible between the parties on different sides of the market. While people may be willing to accept some of the risk associated with imperfect matching, they can reduce the risk by engaging in costly search for potential matching opportunities. The important element here is the trade off individuals face between the option value of keeping on searching and the increasing cost of delaying matching. In equilibrium, frictional unemployment would be a direct consequence of search activity and represent a departure from the market-clearing hypothesis.

Search and matching theory integrates these elements in a consistent framework that describes the formation of new relationships between parties as a function of workers' search decisions and firms' decisions about disclosures of job vacancies. Mortensen and Pissarides (1994) provided a comprehensive formalization of search and matching in the labor market, building on previous individual work. Diamond (1982) probably presented the first model of a search economy where traders' expectations about the level of aggregate activity determine the actual level of activity, resulting in multiple, non-market-clearing equilibria. Again, this framework opens up the potential for intermediaries to come into play offering market-clearing support services.

One of the most harmful consequences of asymmetric information prior to a contractual agreement is adverse selection of prospective matching counterparts. To mitigate the effects of adverse selection in the labor market, workers and firms can typically engage in screening (Stiglitz 1975) and signalling (Spence 1973) activities. Screening is the activity of collecting and processing information about the qualities or characteristics of individuals, firms and jobs. Signalling is the activity of reporting own characteristics to prospective counterparts in a credible way. Both such activities are costly and require specialized skills, thus offering the possibility for third parties to specialize in these activities and perform them on behalf of clients. This is precisely one of the roles of intermediaries in the labor market, or LMIs.

Workers bear the direct costs of exploring the employers' side of the market, applying for jobs and attending interviews, as well as the indirect costs of lost working or leisure time. Employers bear the direct costs of advertising vacancies and screening applicants, and the indirect costs of reduced output until a vacancy is filled. LMIs reduce search costs for both parties by collecting information on players on one side of the market and then selling it to the players on the other side, at a price that is lower than the cost to the buyers of searching on their own.

Workers may hide or distort some of the information provided in their CVs or credentials, in order to make them more attractive to potential employers. Similarly, firms might exploit asymmetric information to the detriment of workers, for instance, by under-promoting deserving workers in order to save on wages (Garcia-Pérez and Muñoz-Bullón 2005), or by misrepresenting job conditions in order to attract workers (Lee 2009). LMIs can mitigate the problem of adverse selection due to asymmetric information by performing accurate screening of both job seekers and employers, and assuming direct responsibility for selection through special contractual provisions.

The literature highlights an additional aspect of information asymmetry that is specific to intermediation activity, namely, the asymmetry between the LMI and its clients. LMIs, which are in the business of selling information, are inherently better informed about the information they sell than are their customers. The informational advantage of LMIs over participants in a labor market transaction represents a potentially strong incentive for the intermediary to use its information to extract rents from its service. The analyses in Lee (2009) and Kleiner and Todd (2009) provide examples of how intermediaries can use their advantage to the detriment of customers.

The potentially harmful consequences of this sort of informational asymmetry anticipated by Akerlof (1970) highlight the compelling trade off in any information brokerage/concentration process, between the benefits of increased accessibility to information, in our case, represented by the availability of huge chunks of information at low prices, and the costs in the form of the monopolistic and/or monopsonistic position of the mass information provider. In our cases, these costs are translated into the non-competitive mark ups charged by LMIs for their intermediation services, or the promotion of high mark-up matches, rather than matches that would be optimal for the parties.

In markets with imperfect information, the amount of information available to the parties through a broker depends positively on the broker's access to information through its clientele, hence on its actual market share. A self-reinforcing incentive mechanism is therefore at play, according to which the bigger the broker the larger the number of people who will be tempted to use its services, which further increases the broker's influence in the market. The informational advantage of the intermediary over its clients and the resulting monopolistic/monopsonistic behavior also increase with market share, up to the point where they may neutralize the benefits of information brokerage and produce net damages and the market reaches a level of major concentration.

According to standard arguments related to the effects of competition, rivalry between private LMIs, and/or between private LMIs and public employment agencies, can favor workers and firms by keeping the price of intermediation services low (competitive) and preventing the emergence of dominant positions, while guaranteeing quality matching. In this respect, the role of policy makers in market design and regulation is of fundamental importance in order to have intermediated labor markets that encourage innovation and performance through mechanisms of labor reallocation (Kılıçaslan and Taymaz 2008); in turn, economic research should feed policy decisions with new evidence and thorough explanation of the evolutionary dynamics of labor markets.

The present paper focuses on a particular category of LMIs, namely temporary employment agencies. People apply to TEAs to access short-term employment opportunities through negligible investment in job search, and as an entry stage to more long-term positions (Autor 2001;

Autor and Houseman 2002). Firms rely on TEAs in order to reduce the fixed costs of searching for temporary workers, and they also often outsource to TEAs the recruitment of critical worker categories or even whole workforces. In the latter case, workers seeking employment in these firms are forced to work through TEAs (Houseman 2001; Ichino et al. 2005).

Garcia-Perez and Muñoz-Bullón (2005: 1) advance a strong argument that TEAs 'in fact offer a unique screening device that matches the individual with the most appropriate skill-level to the job in question'. Using TEAs in order to screen their workers and offering permanent positions to the most suitable ones is becoming a common strategy for firms. Autor (2001) shows that, in several sectors of the US economy, TEA services represent the most important channel for recruiting permanent workers.

In Italy, in the period analyzed in this study, TEAs were the only intermediaries in the market; therefore, using TEAs is a unique means available to firms and workers to access search and screening services. This context extends the scope of TEAs to the whole range of typical LMI functions and provides an ideal setting within which to appreciate the effect of intermediaries on labor market flows.

3 NETWORK SETUP AND EMPIRICAL STRATEGY

Analysis of labor mobility at the individual level using network concepts dates back to the seminal work of Granovetter (1973), which illustrates the importance of different types of social connections for successful job search. Since then, joint research on labor mobility and network analysis has attracted attention from scholars in economics and economic geography on aspects related to innovation mechanisms, knowledge spillovers and the spatial diffusion of economic activities.[1]

The properties and structure of the global architecture of firm to firm labor flows, their evolution and determinants remain today largely unexplored and unknown.[2] At the firm level, worker reallocation appears to be a gradual process that can be likened to percolation through a porous material, the microscopic architecture of which ultimately determines the direction and timing of flows usually observed at some higher level of aggregation. This study assumes a network representation of inter-firm worker mobility – where the vertices are firms and the links are worker flows occurring in the space of one year – which is used to support an original investigation of the role of labor intermediaries in shaping the web of inter-firm worker flows. The precise graph-theoretic definitions used in the paper are provided in Appendix II.

The extent to which one type of vertex with the function of intermediary (TEA) affects the degree of integration and practicability of the web of inter-firm flows is the first focus. The goal is to see whether and how TEAs contribute to linking different parts of the labor market in a robust and reliable way, while shortening the network distance between firms and making the reallocation market potentially more accessible for mobile workers.

Network theory relates the notion of integration and practicability directly to a specific network model known as the "small world" (Watts and Strogatz 1998; Newman 2000; Goyal et al. 2006), the functional significance of which is precisely that vertices are easily reachable from one to another via a minimum assembly of links. The small-world model has been shown to be highly efficient for enabling reliable communication and flows between vertices (Latora and Marchiori 2001).

We use measurable small-world properties of the inter-firm network as indicators of the effects of TEA on labor market integration and permeability to reallocation flows: the closer the network to a small world model, the more integrated and permeable the system will be to reallocation flows.

A network is said to be a small world if the following four conditions simultaneously apply:

(i)A large number of vertices are reachable from/can reach many other vertices in the network, that is, there are uninterrupted sequences of links connecting a relevant fraction of possible pairs of vertices.

(i)Vertices are reachable with little effort, that is, interconnected vertices on average are just a few steps/links apart (going along a link is assumed to be costly).

(iii)The system is parsimonious overall, that is, the actual number of links is much smaller than the maximum possible if there is a link between every possible pair of vertices (and providing additional links is assumed to be costly).

(iv)Vertices form cohesive groups, that is, vertex neighbors or vertices directly connected to the given one tend also to be interconnected with each other, resulting in alternative ways of reaching a former neighbor vertex should the direct connection be lost.

Reframing these conditions in economic terms, we can consider a network to be a small world when, whichever vertex is considered, the number of vertices potentially reachable is high (condition 1), the cost of actually reaching these vertices, on average, is low (conditions 2 and 3), and the system is robust to local disconnections (condition 4). In real world situations, there is often a positive relationship between the actual number and variety of alternatives for moves or choices, and the average cost of exploiting these opportunities for achieving targets. The small world has been shown to be an extremely effective configuration in the context of problematic relationships of this kind because it guarantees maximum reachability while minimizing the costs to both the system designer (i.e. the cost of providing links) and the system user (i.e. the cost of moving through sequences of links in order to reach a given target).[3]

For workers reallocating between firms, the cost of linking is given by several components, for instance, the cost of performing direct job search or the price paid to an intermediary in order to screen the market and identify suitable vacancies, the loss of salary during possible periods of inactivity between subsequent job spells, the cost of adapting to a new job environment or the effort of learning new tasks and procedures, or the short-term cost of lower wages in the new job, because information about the real value of the match, and hence of the worker, is not completely disclosed to the employer at the very beginning of the employment relationship.

The costly move of a worker from one firm to another is not neutral with respect to other workers employed in the origin or destination firms. The reallocation of an individual from firm A to firm B links the social network of employees of company A to the social network of employees of company B. As demonstrated in Granovetter (1974) and more recently in Cingano and Rosolia (2012), this is likely to produce positive externalities for other employees in A, because personal relationships act as preferential channels for transmitting information about employment opportunities in B and mitigate the asymmetric information problem associated with job changes, possibly leading to other employees from firm A to later follow the same reallocation path, should firm B be recognized as a good employer. A small-world network is therefore parsimonious with respect to reallocation costs, for so long as workers move along established paths they bear lower costs.

A small-world network appears to be an integrated system dominated by local clustering, with a relatively small number of long-range links acting as shortcuts between different clusters of vertices that otherwise would be much farther from one another. A giant strongly connected component guarantees the existence of connecting paths between all possible vertices within its boundaries, while short distance indicates that vertices can be reached with little effort. Clustering or redundancy of local level links promotes robustness to disconnection and reliable connectivity based on multiple independent pathways (White and Houseman 2002).

The four defining properties of the small-world model can be formulated, for a directed network, in exact graph-theoretical terms, to obtain the four propositions presented in Table 1, column 2; the evaluation rules in Table 1, column 3, identify a range of network parameter values within which a network exhibits small-world characteristics (Watts 1999; Newman 2003). Based on these rules, Section 5 describes how far the empirical labor mobility network resembles a small world, and how TEAs push the network architecture farther from or closer to a small world.

Table 1. The four defining properties of a small-world network

	Properties		Evaluation criteria
	Description	Network-theoretic definition	
1.	A large number of vertices are reachable from or can reach many other vertices	Network exhibits a giant weakly connected component (WCC) and a giant strongly connected component (SCC) in the network	The SCC and the WCC cover a minimum of 25 % and 50 % of vertices, respectively; the other components are small (typically of the order ln(n), where n is the total number of vertices)
2.	Vertices are reachable with little effort	Average path length (APL) in the SCC is appreciably small	The APL in the SCC is of the same or lower order as the APL of a similar sized random network
3.	The system is parsimonious	The density of links is low	The link density is several orders of magnitude lower than the maximum possible value
4.	Vertices form cohesive groups	Average clustering coefficient (ACC) is appreciably high	The ACC is one or more orders of magnitude larger than the ACC of a similar sized random network with the same in-degree and out-degree distributions

The second research question is how TEAs affect the distribution of labor flows, namely, whether and how reallocation flows crowd into TEAs resulting in appreciable concentration of the market in the hands of intermediaries. In the labor mobility network, this can be addressed by considering the degree centrality, i.e. the number of incident links, of TEA vertices and comparing this indicator across firms and time.

In networked systems, the presence of pivotal actors with high degree centrality, called hubs, is signalled by a right-skewed degree distribution, with a long or fat tail that contains vertices with many more connections than average and which appear more frequently than in a standard Gaussian distribution. The literature on complex networks shows that the tail of the degree distribution of a network with hubs can often be approximated by a Pareto distribution or a negative power law (Barabási and Albert 1999; Albert and Barabási 2002; Newman 2003).

Building on this ground, in the present study we verify whether TEAs form a hub tail, searching for Paretian behaviors in the in-degree distribution of labor flows and using the power law as a benchmark for evaluation. This is accomplished in two steps. First, we calculate the total-degree distribution of the network, i.e. the distribution of both incoming and outgoing links, and we determine the TEAs ranking within the distribution. Second, we focus on hiring channels, as given by the in-degree of the network vertices, or the number of incoming labor flows, representing the capacity of firms to attract applicant workers from other source firms in the network. The in-degree provides a measure of firm shares of new hires, and therefore the evolution of TEAs market power can be appreciated by determining the TEAs position within the in-degree distribution while assessing how the distribution overall evolves over time before and after TEAs arrival.

4 DATA

The empirical investigation is based upon the Veneto Worker History panel (VWH), a matched employer-employee dataset derived from the Italian Social Security Institute (Inps) administrative records and covering the entire population of workers and employers in Veneto in the period 1991–2001.[4]

Veneto is a dynamic regional economy centered on manufacturing. The industrial system is represented by a large population of small and medium sized firms, often organized in industrial districts, the specializations of which are garment manufacture, textiles, leather and shoes, goldsmithing, mechanical products, furniture, and plastics. The average firm size in 2001 was three employees for the whole economy and nine for manufacturing, according to census data from Istat.

In the late 1980s and the second half of the 1990s, the Veneto labor market was characterized by a positive rate of job creation in almost every economic sector and decreasing unemployment to almost frictional levels.[5] The employment stock in the private sector was 968,149 in 1991 and 1,120,278 in 2001, according to census data. The manufacturing sector represented 55.7 % and 50.7 % of total private sector employment in 1991 and 2001, respectively.

The VWH data cover all individual workers employed in the private sector, and every establishment with at least one employee. The available information allows to build a monthly history of the working lives of all employees hired for at least one day during the period of observation by firms based in Veneto, including TEAs. VWH covers only employment spells, while no direct observations are available for transitions to/from unemployment status. Individual inactivity between job spells cannot be distinguished between unemployment and exit from the labor force on the basis of the registered information.

The labor mobility network is obtained by counting the individual hires occurring within a 12-month window that give rise to reallocations, where a reallocation is defined as a pair of events constituted by a separation (i.e. conclusion of a job relationship with a given employer) and a subsequent engagement of the same individual in a job relationship with another employer. Reallocations are mapped onto a binary directed graph the vertices of which are firms and TEAs, and the links between them the flows of workers between firms or between TEAs and firms.

The structure of provisional contracts is triangular; TEAs are formal employers of temporary workers. We do not know which client firms the temporary employees work for when contracted through a TEA, but we can track all reallocations the origins or destinations of which are a TEA. Most important, it is possible to track the network of mobility episodes related to people – especially young people – who enter the labor market via a TEA, and subsequently become direct employees of a private firm.

Eleven networks are constructed for the period 1991–2001; the analytical focus is restricted to reallocations of workers, of either sex, aged between 15 and 65 years, whose engagement occurred between 1st January and 31st December each year, and where the time between the separation and subsequent engagement did not exceed six months.[6] Reallocations are tracked cutting across the administrative boundaries of Veneto, meaning that firms located outside the region can enter the network sample if they transfer/receive workers to/from firms located in Veneto. No restrictions are made for job spell duration or type of occupation; reallocations to the same firm are excluded.

Table 2 reports the total number of individual reallocations occurred in the period 1997–2001 originating from TEA and non-TEA firms, by worker and firm characteristics. In the five-years period, an average of 171,000 individual reallocations per year are reported. TEAs constitute the destination of 34,215 reallocations and the origin of 40,088 reallocations; 7.1 % of total reallocations registered in the Veneto labor market in the 1997–2001 period has TEAs either as origin or destination, increasing from just 1 % in 1998 to more than 14 % in 2001.

Table 2. Reallocations originating from TEA and non-TEA firms, by worker and firm characteristics

Variable	Categories	Non-TEA (column %)	TEA (column %)
Gender:	Female	376,806 (37.5)	14,344 (35.8)
	Male	629,067 (62.5)	25,744 (64.2)
Age:	15–24	287,100 (28.6)	11,706 (29.2)
	25–34	422,558 (42.0)	19,443 (48.5)
	35–49	246,454 (24.5)	8,114 (20.2)
	50–65	49,761 (4.9)	825 (2.1)
Firm size:	0–9	333,064 (33.1)	7,837 (19.6)
	10–19	157,617 (15.7)	5,098 (12.7)
	20–49	164,851 (16.4)	7,076 (17.7)
	50–249	189,346 (18.8)	10,476 (26.1)
	≥ 250	160,995 (16.0)	9,601 (23.9)
Sector:	Manufacturing	446,396 (44.4)	22,420 (55.8)
	Construction	64,757 (6.4)	661 (1.7)
	Transport	69,050 (6.9)	2,028 (5.1)
	Trade	144,435 (14.3)	5,225 (13.0)
	Hotel trades	88,612 (8.8)	1,822 (4.6)
	Professional and financial services	127,377 (12.7)	6,634 (16.5)
	Education, social, health services	56,084 (5.6)	1,182 (3.0)
	Others	9,162 (0.9)	116 (0.3)

TEA and non-TEA flows are substantially aligned in terms of gender composition, with only a slightly higher percentage of men in TEAs. Intermediated employment flows are on average younger than non-TEA ones, with the age group 25–34 overrepresented by 6.5 percentage points, and the age group 35–49 underrepresented by 4.3 points. TEA reallocations are directed towards larger firms, especially those sized 50 and above that represent one of the more dynamic components of the Italian manufacturing system (Caprio 2002). Finally, TEA flows target manufacturing and professional services comparatively more than non-TEA flows, and less than the construction and hotel trades.

5 RESULTS I: NETWORK INTEGRATION AND PRACTICABILITY

For each year network, the following indicators are calculated: number of vertices and links, density, size of the WCC and SCC, APL, and ACC. The structural properties of the actual networks for the 1997–2001 period are compared to the corresponding properties of two series of randomized networks taken as null models:

- Null model (1): all TEA vertices and incident links are removed from the actual network to obtain a new network with the same architecture, but no TEA vertices and no reallocation flows involving TEAs.
- Null model (2): for each TEA vertex j in the actual network, the non-TEA vertex i is removed which satisfies k_i=min(k) subject to the condition $k \geq k_j$, where k is the total-degree; in this way a network is obtained that excludes the non-TEA firms most equivalent to TEAs in terms of number of connections.

The difference between the actual networks and null model (1) provides an estimate of the impact of the TEAs conditional on TEA mobility (i.e. labor mobility involving TEAs as the origin or destination) having no substitute in the labor market; this yields an upper bound to the real TEA effect. The difference between the actual network and null model (2) provides an estimate of the mobility effect of those firms that are most similar to TEAs in terms of the number of labor flows involved. On the assumption that this effect can proxy for the substitution of TEA mobility by other non-TEA firms, the difference between null model (1) and null model (2) provides a more reliable approximation of the TEA effect. In practice, if TEAs play a substantial role in shaping the network architecture, null model (1) will exhibit different structural properties from the actual network, and null model (2) will be more similar to the actual network.

Figure 1 depicts the evolution of network size. The system exhibits a minimum extension in 1993, with 67,578 vertices and 86,602 links, and a maximum extension in 2001, with 104,439 vertices and 207,504 links. Link density is always very low at around 2.0e-05, with a minimum of 1.84e-05 in 1992, and a maximum of 2.23e-05 in 1995. Over the whole period considered, the network is extremely sparse, which complies with the small-world model.

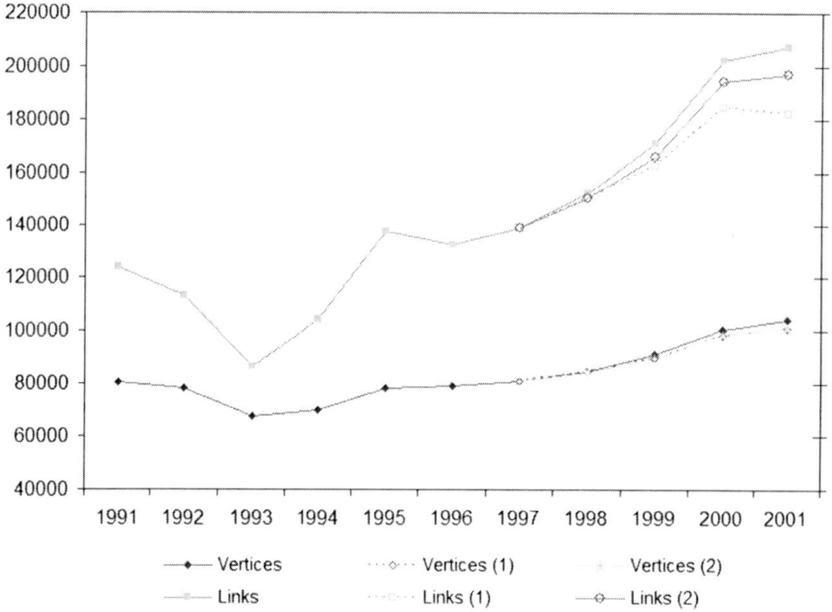

Figure 1. Vertices and links

Time series of labor mobility networks of the type considered in the present analyses are affected by the business cycle, since worker turnover tends to be markedly pro-cyclical, and job-to-job mobility constitutes the most dynamic component of this trend.[7] The business cycle thus affects the size and the density of the reallocation network; when the level of economic activity is low – as was the case in Italy during the 1992-93 recession – the network appears comparatively much sparser and less interconnected than in high performing business cycle periods (as occurred in 1994-95 in Veneto).

In Fig. 1, the number of links exhibit a clear pro-cyclical pattern during the period 1991-1997. There is a pronounced downward spike corresponding to the 1992-93 recession (–25 % links), followed by rapid growth in 1994-95 (+ 47 % links), as the economy recovered due to a Lira devaluation that boosted export competitiveness which, in turn, especially favored the largely export-oriented economy of Veneto. After 1997, the impact of the business cycle is less clear: across the whole period 1997-2001, in the presence of moderate economic growth, the network exhibits an intense, sustained increase in the number of vertices and links (respectively + 29 % and + 49 %), with a slight slowdown in 2001 corresponding to the downturn induced by the burst of the new-economy bubble and increasing uncertainty about the international geopolitical scenario.

Comparing the actual trend with null model (1), it can be seen that TEA links contribute significantly to explaining the observed growth in connections, increasing the null model base by 1 % in 1998, 5 % in 1999, 10 % in 2000, and 14 % in 2001. Notably, null model (1) exhibits a reduction in the number of links in 2001 compared to 2000 so that, in the last year of observation, the activity of labor market intermediaries appears to be the sole driver of the increase in the actual number of reallocation channels between firms. Null model (2) has 8 % more links in 2001 than null model (1); this figure represents our prudent estimate of the impact of TEA at the end of the period of observation, which reveals that the 1997 reform, through the establishment of private intermediaries, was able effectively to unlock new mobility opportunities.

Figure 2 shows the extent of the largest strongly/weakly connected components in terms of the percentage of vertices covered, allowing a first inspection of network interconnection or integration. A pro-cyclical pattern is clearly identifiable. The SCC shows a minimum in 1993 at 13 % and a maximum in 2000 at 30 %; for the WCC the figures are 77 % and 90 %, respectively. Starting in 1995, the SCC remains above 25 %, and the WCC remains above 85 %; in the same period, the second largest strongly connected component never covers more than six vertices, while the second largest weakly connected component has just 14 vertices. So, from 1995, the system exhibits the inter-connectivity structure distinctive of a small world.

In 1997, the giant components embark on a steady growth path leading to a cumulative increase of 13 % for the SCC, and 4 % for the WCC for the period 1997–2001. In 2001, the SCC of null model (2) essentially superimposes the actual SCC, and both are 6 % larger than the null model (1) SCC, revealing that mutual connectivity appears to be positively affected by TEAs, but insensitive to the exclusion of non-TEA firms. TEAs seem to favor integration of the system.

Figure 3 shows the APL and ACC; the first (left axis) is expressed by the number of links between vertices, the second (right axis) is an index number that varies between 0 (no clustering) and 1 (complete clustering). Across the whole period, the ACC of the actual network is at least one order of magnitude higher than the ACC of a comparable network with the

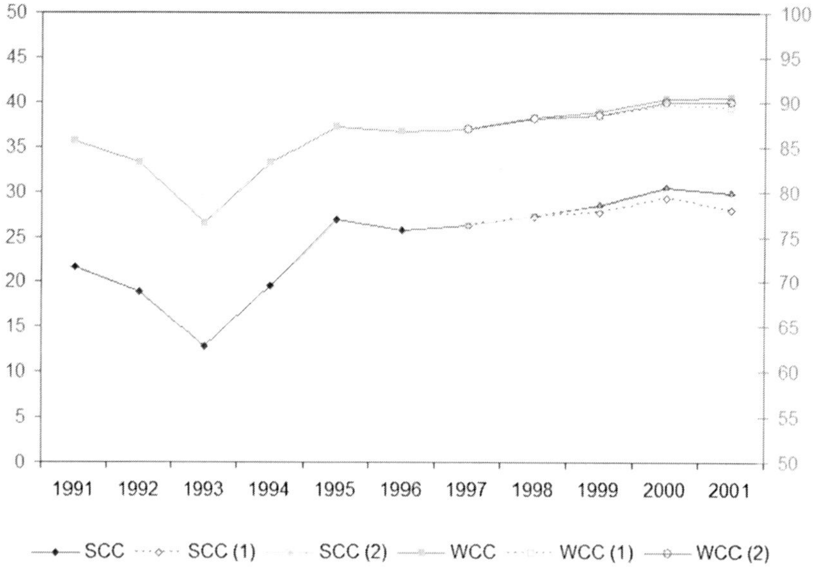

Figure 2. SCC *(left axis)* and WCC *(right axis)*, % coverage of the entire network

same joint distribution of in-degree and out-degree, but with links positioned randomly. This clustering pattern is typical of a small world network. Up to 1998, the ACC fluctuates between 0.007 and 0.010, with a very slight tendency to increase over time; from 1999 to 2001, it shows a phase of intense growth to reach 0.015 by the end of the period, 57 % higher than the 1997 level.

The ACC of null model (1) remains substantially flat, at the pre-reform level; the ACC of null model (2) closely follows the actual path. In 2001, the actual ACC is 63 % higher than the null model (1) ACC, while the ACC of null model (2) is 46 % above null model (1), pointing to a strong, positive effect of TEAs on clustering.

The APL reaches a maximum in 1993 of 8.5, and a minimum in 2001 of 5, and across the whole period it is strictly lower than the APL of a random network of equivalent size, which fits the requirements for a small world network. After the 1997 reform, mutually interconnected vertices are much closer to each other: between 1997 and 2001, the average distance reduces by 24 %.

The APL of null model (1) exhibits an almost flat behavior, while the APL of null model (2) is just one percentage point above the actual APL. In 2001, the actual APL is 20 % less than the null model (1) APL which indicates that TEAs provide effective shortcuts within the network by substantially reducing the distances between firms.

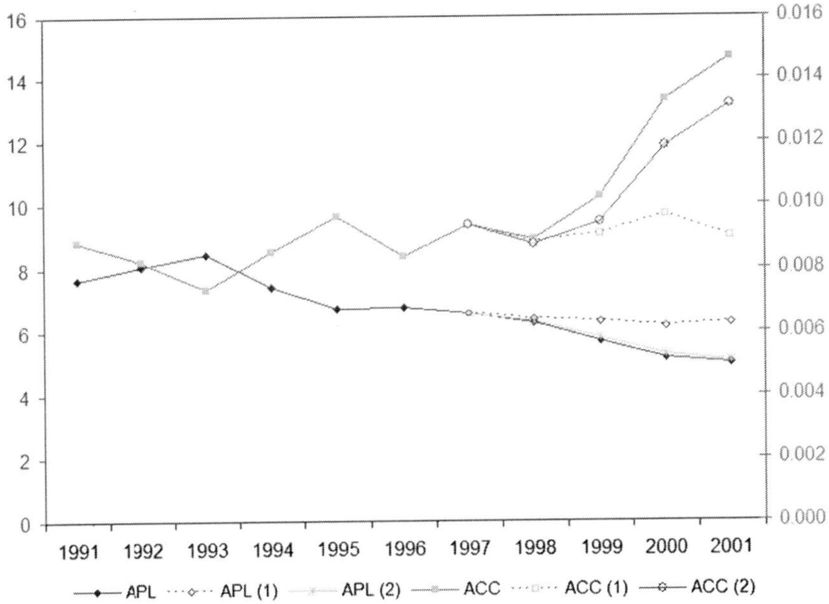

Figure 3. APL and ACC

Comparing the null model (1) in Figs. 1 and 3, it can be seen that the number of links increases over time, but this expansion is not accompanied by an appreciable change in the link arrangement, as revealed by the ACC and the APL. On the contrary, the increase in network size due to labor intermediation modifies the network structure in the direction of higher cohesion and lower distances.

The results of the analysis suggest that TEAs act to make the small-world network of labor mobility significantly smaller and, therefore, more integrated and more permeable to reallocation flows, through the establishment of shortcut paths that span the economy, interweaving distant vertices into more cohesive communities, and reducing average distances.

6 RESULTS II: DISTRIBUTION OF LABOR FLOWS

The total-degree distributions for each year network are derived and some descriptive statistics are presented in Table 3, including: average degree (k_G), median degree (k_{50}), degree of the 99 th percentile (k_{99}), and maximum degree (k_{max}).

Table 3. Total-degree distributions: main descriptive statistics

year	n	k_G	k_{50}	k_{99}	k_{max}
1991	80,680	3.1	1	23	429
1992	78,300	2.9	1	21	315
1993	67,578	2.6	1	17	507
1994	69,816	3.0	1	22	527
1995	78,450	3.5	2	28	467
1996	78,966	3.4	2	27	358
1997	80,820	3.4	2	29	480
1998	84,823	3.6	2	30	731
1999	91,136	3.8	2	32	2,100
2000	100,671	4.0	2	35	4,635
2001	104,439	4.0	2	33	6,524

The total-degree sequences exhibit a broad range of values that tends to increase over time. Despite the relatively high maxima (315 in 1992, increasing to 6,524 in 2001), the average degree is always very low, ranging from 2.6 in 1993 to 4 in 2000 and 2001. This is due to the extreme concentration of the distribution around the minimum degree, revealed by the median values which are 1 up to 1994, and 2 thereafter. Two features are striking: the degree value of the largest fraction of vertices is smaller than the average, with the majority of vertices having just the minimum degree; a small fraction of vertices has a degree value that is many times larger than the average, e.g. the scores for the 99 th percentile are six to nine times larger than average.

Across the whole period, the total-degree distribution exhibits a markedly right-skewed pattern, with a heavy or fat tail. This applies also if we consider in-degree and out-degree distributions separately. Therefore, network architecture of labor mobility appears to be dominated by a few vertices, referred to as hubs, which have many more connections than average. Moreover, the maximum degrees increase steeply just after 1997, with average annual growth of around 100 %, suggesting that the 1997 reform favored the formation of large hubs.

Table 4 reports the overall ranking based on total degree, of the ten biggest TEAs, labelled *a* to *k*. In 1997, only two TEAs were operating with very limited activity, as revealed by their low ranking. By 1998, one TEA was at the extreme tail of the connectivity distribution, and ranked 4 th overall; four TEAs were positioned within the first hundred positions, and all the first ten ranked TEAs were within the 99 th percentile of the distribution. In 1999, TEAs dominated the degree distribution, with four intermediaries in the first four positions. Soon after their appearance in the system, TEAs showed high levels of attractiveness and a strong capacity to redirect labor flows, and quickly became the most important hubs in the mobility network.

Table 4. Ranking of the ten biggest TEA according to total-degree

TEAs	ranking (1=highest total-degree)				
	1997	1998	1999	2000	2001
a	162	4	1	1	1
b	162	16	2	2	2
c	–	37	3	3	3
d	–	56	4	4	4
e	–	103	7	6	6
f	–	135	22	8	7
g	–	137	27	10	9
h	–	138	30	13	11
i	–	150	36	22	13
k	–	156	55	23	14
Total n. of positions	163	189	204	215	220

Following the 1997 labor market reform, the system became progressively more dependent on TEAs, and on a few in particular. This situation is critical because collapse or malfunction of even a small number of TEA hubs could compromise connectivity (Albert et al. 2000); policy makers might be concerned about growing monopolistic/monopsonistic power of a few TEAs in the labor reallocation market.

The distribution of hiring channels, the in-degree distribution, is of particular relevance for capturing the evolution of TEA market power. Figure 4 shows the complementary cumulative in-degree distributions (CCDD), plotted on a double logarithmic scale, together with the corresponding power-law fits. Power law-like degree distributions have been extensively investigated in network analysis and are widely acknowledged to represent a benchmark model for many real-world phenomena (Barabási and Albert 1999; Newman 2005). Most relevant for the present study, power-law models support the existence of hubs.

1991

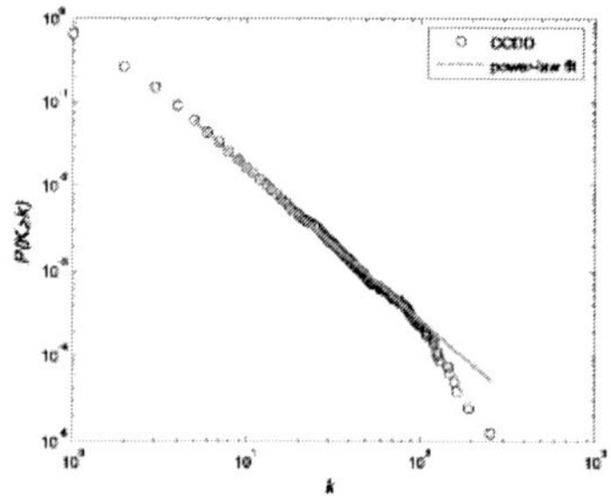

1992

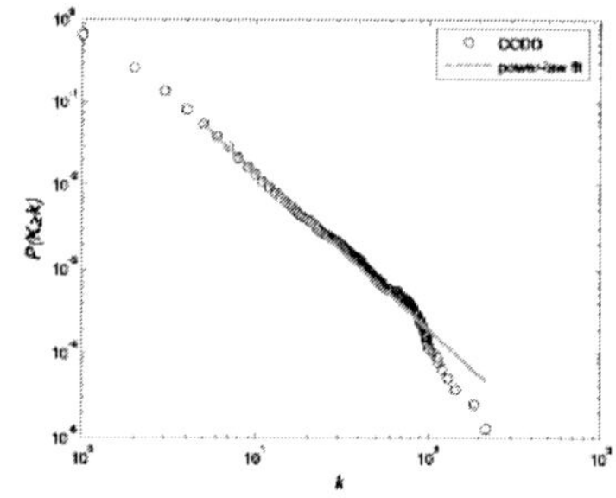

1993

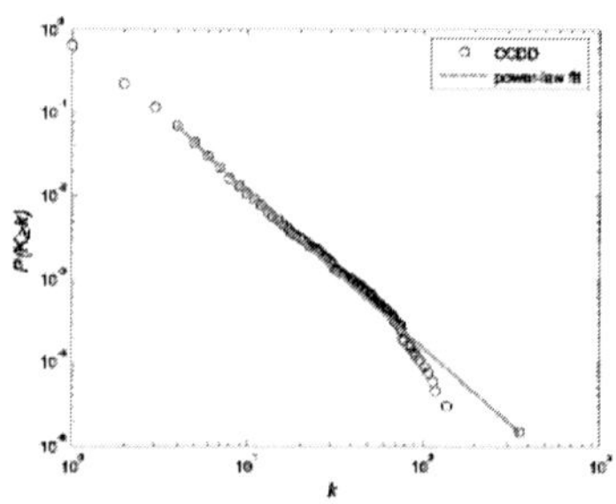

1994

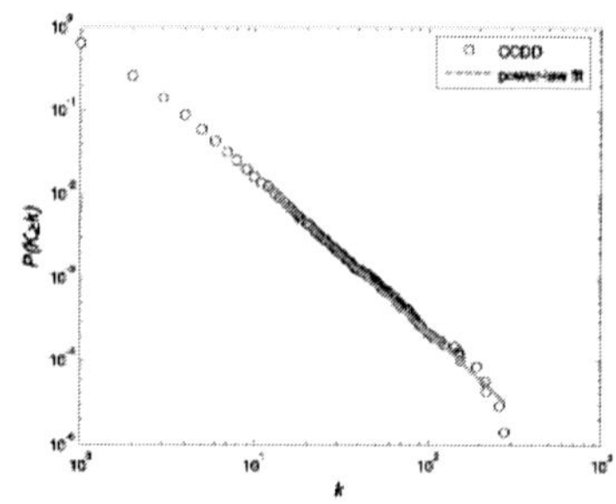

1995

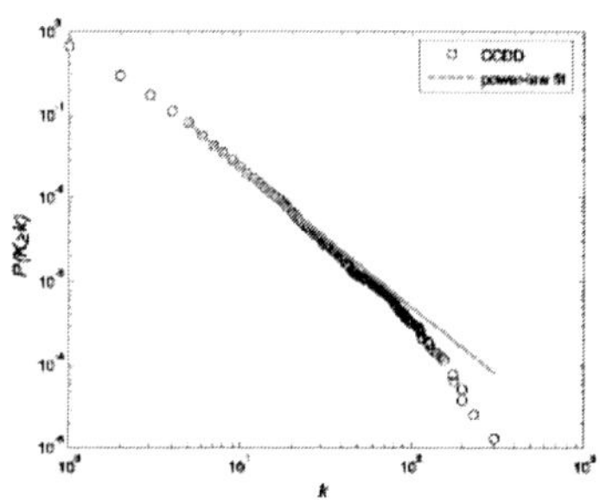

1996

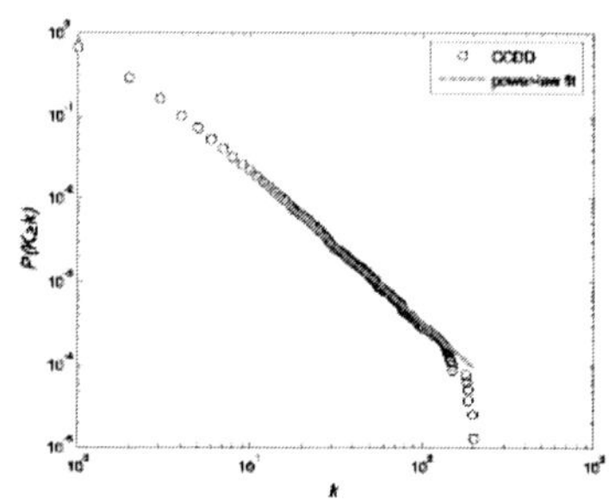

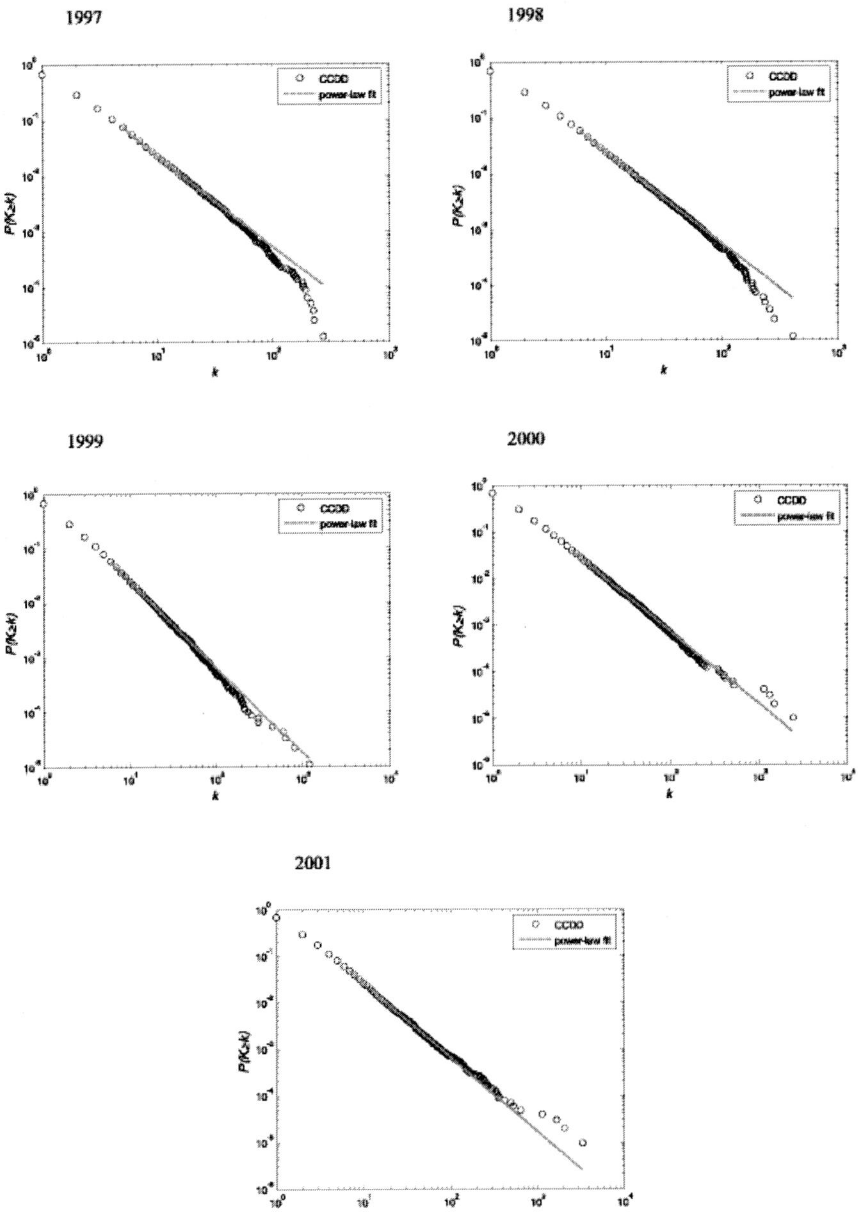

Figure 4. In-degree distributions and power-law fits

Each year plot in Fig. 4 follows a negative and almost linear trend; at the extreme tail of the distribution, a downward departure from the power-law fit is evident for the years 1991, 1992, 1995, 1996, 1997, and 1998, but is less pronounced for 1993 and 1994. In 1999, the empirical data almost exactly overlap the power-law fit, while in 2000 and 2001, the distribution tail drifts progressively upwards, concentrating greater weight than predicted by a pure power law.

Visual inspection of the plots suggests several things. First, a necessary condition for data to be power-law distributed is that they align along a straight line, on a double logarithmic plot; the empirical distributions would seem to match this condition. Second, the rapid decay of the tail or the truncation observed up to the year 1998 means that extreme, massive events are less likely in reality than predicted by pure power law. Third, after 1998 and coincident with the materialization of TEA effects on the connectivity structure, the in-degree distribution shows a transition from an upper truncated to a much more unequal pattern with a much heavier tail.

In 1999, 2000, and 2001 the four biggest hubs are TEAs, and several other TEAs occupy the extreme percentiles of the degree distribution, concentrating shares of hiring channels which increase constantly over time, and being ultimately responsible for the transitions observed in the distribution tail. Intermediaries produce a sharp polarization of the degree distribution which consistently deviates from both a pure and a truncated power law distribution.

This evidence is explored more deeply by statistically comparing the empirical distributions with pure power-law models, and with power law with exponential cut off that allows for tail decay. The general form of a power-law distribution for the quantity k is $p(k)=ck^{-\alpha}$ for $k>k_{min}$, c being a constant of proportionality; the general form of a power-law distribution with exponential cut off is $p(k)=ck^{-\alpha}e^{\beta k}$. Following the procedure developed in Clauset et al. (2009):

- We fit the complementary cumulative in-degree distribution using maximum likelihood, simultaneously estimating the scaling parameter, α, and the minimum threshold above which power law behavior holds, k_{min}.
- We evaluate the goodness of the power-law fit by calculating an appropriate p-value.
- We conduct a likelihood-ratio test to contrast the pure power law with a power law with exponential cut off.[8]

Table 5 presents the key parameters of the fitted power laws and the p-values of the related goodness-of-fit tests; the likelihood-ratio tests comparing the pure power law and a power law with exponential cut off, and the related p-values, are reported in the last two columns.[9] With the exception of 1992 and 1995, in all years the power-law model provides good fits, with excellent performance in 1991, 1994, and in the period 1998-2001; in 1993, 1996 and 1997 there is only moderate evidence in support of the model, but, overall, the power law performs quite well, which means it is a reasonable theoretical benchmark for the data.

Table 5. Distribution fit

	Power-law fits			Comparison with power law with cutoff	
year	a	k_{min}	p-value	LR test	p-value
1991	2.752	5	0.520	−2.354	0.030
1992	2.822	5	0.000	−0.552	0.293
1993	2.827	4	0.060	−0.262	0.469
1994	2.857	12	0.780	−0.268	0.464
1995	2.630	5	0.000	−11.176	0.000
1996	2.787	10	0.140	−2.749	0.019
1997	2.595	5	0.080	−7.779	0.000
1998	2.609	6	0.500	−4.958	0.002
1999	2.554	6	0.540	−1.604	0.073
2000	2.556	8	0.560	−0.065	0.716
2001	2.576	7	0.880	0.000	1.000

For 1991, 1996, 1997 and 1998 the power law with exponential cut off is strictly preferred to a pure power law, but for 1999, 2000, and especially 2001, the models are not statistically different based on the likelihood-ratio test. However, the plots in Fig. 4 show that, in the last three years of observation, the pure power law is unquestionably favored over the cut-off version.

Overall, the analyses reveal the following: up to 1998, the data are well fitted to a power law with upper truncation; in 1999, as TEAs reach the tail of the distribution, pure power-law sets in; in 2000–2001 the tail of the distribution, led by the biggest TEAs, drifts upward away from power law prediction and pushes the system towards an increasingly polarized configuration in which a few of the biggest TEA hubs control major hiring channel shares.

7 DISCUSSION ON THE EVOLUTION OF TEA MARKET POWER

Consideration of the functional shape of the degree distribution, rather than just the number of links incident to the TEAs, helps us to understand how the system adjusts to the presence of TEAs and allows us to relate observed behaviors to the vast literature on models of network formation, which should increase understanding of the dynamics of intermediation activity.

Several network formation models have been proposed, which can produce degree distributions with similar functional forms to those observed in the labor mobility network, and account for transition paths comparable to the one triggered by the arrival of intermediaries. There are two classes of models that build on an information cost argument and provide insights for understanding the possible dynamics of intermediation in the labor reallocation market.

In the literature on complex networks, right-skewed degree distributions with heavy tails are usually associated with link formation mechanisms based on preferential attachment rules, where the probability that one vertex connects to another is assumed proportional to the degree of the recipient vertex (Barabási and Albert 1999). Based on this simple framework, scholars have built models that account for upper truncation to power-law behavior, by introducing constraints on the attachment mechanism that limit the addition of new vertex links. Varying the intensity or bindingness of constraints provides a range of distributions with more or less pronounced cut offs, where the pure power law is a special case, and extremely concentrated distributions are obtained when attachment constraints are sufficiently weak.

In Mossa et al. (2000), the constraint on link formation is modelled explicitly as an information cost. Agents/vertices are assumed to bear some costs for gathering and analyzing information about the other vertices. This assumption is especially realistic if the system is large, because it is unlikely that agents know in advance the state of the entire network. The decision about which vertex to connect to is most likely taken based only on the information about a subset – a fraction or a fixed number – of possible vertices; within such a subset, some form of preferential attachment then comes into play. The link distribution resulting from these rules is a power law with an upper exponential cut off the strength of which depends on the incidence of information costs.

Other studies propose a network formation paradigm in which preferential attachment is not assumed, but arises naturally from the simultaneous optimization of multiple competing objectives. This approach is of particular interest from an economic perspective because it explicitly models the trade off between the typical costs and benefits for agents making decisions in a context of scarce resources, which is characteristic of job search problems.

The fundamentals of this sort of model are described and discussed in Fabrikant et al. (2002) and developed further in D'Souza et al. (2007). Agents/vertices are randomly arranged in a given space; they are assumed to benefit from linking with vertices that are centrally located in the system, that is, high degree vertices, but carry attachment costs that are proportional to the Euclidean distance between the current and target location. Linking decisions will then involve targets that are both close to the actual position in the space and centrally located in the network.

In other words, networking activity tries to optimize on a trade off between the search and attachment costs represented by distance, and the benefits or option values represented by network centrality. As search costs fall relative to centrality benefits, the resulting degree distribution will shift from a power law with cut off to a pure power law and even beyond, ultimately resulting in a winner-take-all distribution, corresponding to a star configuration network in which one vertex receives all incoming connections.

The behavior of these trade-off models can be likened to the introduction of intermediation in a system in which link formation is subject to information costs. Also, the empirical evidence provided in Section 6 would seem to match the theoretical predictions (taking account of the models' abstractness). In the real world, intermediaries exactly concentrate information and provide low-cost shortcuts to employment opportunities. Their value as gateways to future employment makes them attractive for workers.

In the Veneto mobility network, a few years after their entry, a small group of TEAs overtakes the power law distribution of labor flows, triggering an evident polarization of the system, which likely will deepen over time. This tendency, identified and evidenced through the network approach in this study, is extremely relevant for policy. The theory hints that the polarization process is self sustaining and eventually will produce strong concentration of the market in a few TEAs. The presence of intermediaries will likely increase the systemic risks inherent in the labor reallocation system and result in eventual monopolistic/monopsonistic power.

8 CONCLUSIONS

This paper investigated the role of labor market intermediaries in shaping the inter-firm network of worker mobility in a highly industrialized regional economy. The proposed methodology attempts to assess and quantify in an original way the effects that constitute the major trade-off in intermediation activity. We show that TEAs significantly enhance integration and perviousness of the reallocation market, while leading to a process of market concentration which is identifiable at an early stage and the determinants of which are embedded in the activity of intermediation.

In relation to the dynamics involved, on the one side, TEAs are very effective at fostering labor market inter-connection; on the other side, the largest TEA firms threat to corner the labor market, exacerbating the effects of information asymmetries which have a negative impact on their clients.

In future research, it would be desirable to produce causal evidence of the effects of TEAs on the probability to transit from unemployment to employment. However, to assess how much of the unemployment reduction observed in Veneto in 1997-2001 is due to the introduction of TEAs goes beyond the scope of the present paper. This work is a first and exploratory attempt of showing how network analysis can be used as tool for monitoring intermediated labor markets and the activities of single intermediaries.

An efficient reallocation of labor is essential in order for the economy to be productive, to allocate the available resources effectively, and to absorb local and transitory shocks that affect sectors and industries selectively. An easy and smooth reallocation process is fundamental for guaranteeing more rapid and less costly job market transitions for workers, with immediate and long-lasting benefits for individual incomes. A decrease in the dimensions of the small world of labor mobility favors the good functioning of a reallocation market.

When intermediation is allowed, policy interventions might be needed to ensure that the sector remains competitive. Certain regulatory mechanisms should be devised to prevent the market from becoming concentrated in a few intermediaries.

The trend we observed in the empirical distribution of hiring channels indicate that TEA market shares might increase over time, leaving the market for hiring services controlled by a few large intermediaries. Their dominant positions could be used to exploit their informational advantage, to the detriment of their customers. This would be harmful because of the high rents that the dominant TEAs could extract from their activity, and because of the poor matching services firms and workers would likely receive in a non-competitive intermediation market.

Theoretical insights from network formation provide compelling evidence for the need for well-timed policy interventions. Once self-sustaining linkage mechanisms, for example, preferential attachments, are set in motion, it is more difficult to intervene in order to modify the underlying individual-level incentive structure. It is better to rectify budding adverse market trends rather than to wait until they are fully developed and widespread. Good market monitoring is essential to enable this.

Network-based methodologies for mapping labor markets, of the type we proposed in this paper, could help policy makers in detecting early signs of market concentration, and therefore could provide useful evidence-based input about whether and how to control the activities of intermediaries through appropriate regulatory measures or to foster competition through the setting up of efficient public intermediaries.

As for the Italian case, currently debated, influential proposals of labor market reform suggest a profound revision of employment protection mechanisms that would imply a wider and more critical role for private intermediaries.[10] In this light, policy makers can, and perhaps should, be interested in having a better knowledge of the way in which intermediated labor markets actually work and how to effectively monitor their functioning.

The set of methodologies presented in this paper nonetheless requires further development. In particular, the trade off between the economic efficiency gained from centralized brokerage, and the opportunity for monopolistic behavior of the top TEAs deserves a separate and more sophisticated analysis that yields finer indications about market evolution.

For instance, the time span after TEAs establishment should be expanded and labor network evolution tracked beyond 2001, in order to demonstrate the existence/persistency/evolution of the observed trends. Moreover, complementary information about the quality of matching through TEAs (e.g. duration of the new job, wage progression, changes of occupation between old and new jobs, etc.) and the mark ups charged by labor market intermediaries, in particular the biggest ones, should be collected and analyzed in order to give further evidence of the monopolistic/monopsonistic behavior of intermediaries.

Unfortunately, the VWH dataset alone does not provide the necessary information to carry out such analyses and hence the answer should be based on other sources or on merging several sources into one dataset. The present limitations would be valuable topics for an exciting, future research on possible applications of network methodologies to labor mobility, based on matched employer-employee data.

FOOTNOTES

[1]The phenomenon of knowledge spillovers enabled by worker mobility between organizations is addressed in Almeida and Kogut (1999), Owen-Smith and Powell (2004), Audretsch and Keilbach (2005) among other works. Insightful analyses of the role of worker mobility in sustaining firm dynamics and cluster formation are provided by Fallick et al. (2006), who discuss the relationship between innovation performance and mobility of skilled personnel in the Silicon Valley cluster, and Casper (2007), who focuses on the mobility of managers as a cohesive force in the San Diego biotechnology cluster. Agrawal et al. (2006) highlight the role of

interpersonal relationships or social embeddedness in sustaining knowledge flows beyond workers' physical mobility, and some more recent studies address the territorial localization of spillovers due to worker mobility (Breschi and Lissoni 2009), also making use of matched employer-employee data (Eriksson and Lindgren 2009; Boschma et al. 2009). Comprehensive reviews of network analysis and its application in many fields of science can be found in Albert and Barabási (2002) and Newman (2003).

[2] A first attempt of describing firm-to-firm worker mobility using complex networks can be found in Gianelle (2012).

[3] The efficiency of small-world networks has been studied empirically with reference mostly to transport networks, such as railway systems (for instance, Latora and Marchiori 2002), or airport connections (for instance, Li and Cai 2004).

[4] On the Inps dataset used in the present paper, see Tattara and Volpe (2001); Tattara and Valentini (2010); Gianelle (2012).

[5] According to Istat data, the unemployment rate increased from around 5 % at the beginning of the 1990s to 7.5 % in 1994, immediately after the economic downturn of 1992–1993; then it decreased progressively to 4.5 % in 2001.

[6] Since long periods of apparent inactivity might be hiding voluntary exits from the labor force, we made the relatively conservative choice of excluding from the analysis people who remain inactive for more than six consecutive months.

[7] For the US labor market, see e.g. Davis et al. (1996) and Fallick and Fleischman (2004). For the Italian labor market, see Tattara and Valentini (2010) and Leombruni and Quaranta (2005).

[8] Power law and power law with exponential cut off are nested distributions; as Clauset et al. (2009) point out, it is always the case that the larger family of distributions, the power law with exponential cut off, provides at least as good a fit as the smaller family, since every member of the smaller family is also member of the larger one. The p-value associated with the likelihood-ratio test is meant to indicate whether the fit improvement of the pure power law over a power law with cut off is substantial or not.

[9] In the goodness of fit test for a pure power law, p-values are used to rule out the pure power-law hypothesis. Therefore, if the pure power law is to be a plausible model, p-values must be high, and vice versa. We make the standard choice of rejecting the pure power law for p-values less than 0.05. Whereas in the likelihood-ratio test, a small p-value and a positive (negative) likelihood ratio indicate that the pure power law wins (loses)

over the alternative, when the *p*-value is sufficiently high (>0.05), the test does not favor one model over the other.

[10]See, for instance, the legislative bills d.d.l. n. 1873 of 11 November 2009 and d.d.l. n. 555 of 18 April 2013, both signed first by Senator Pietro Ichino.

[11]The precise normative references is Legge 196/1997 (artt. 1-11), integrated by Decreto Ministero del Lavoro 381/97 and 382/97, Circolare esplicativa Ministero del Lavoro 141/97, Decreto Ministero del Lavoro 31/05/1999 and 29/11/1999, and modified by Legge 488/1999 and 388/2000. See also CCNL "Imprese fornitrici di lavoro temporaneo" (National Labor Contract for the temporary employment sector) of 1998.

[12]The relevant normative was modified in 2003 by D.lgs. 276/03, the so called Biagi reform, enlarging the scope of labor market intermediation.

[13]According to the Italian Statistical Institute (Istat), the overall unemployment rate at the national level was 8.6 % in 1991, 11.2 % in 1995 and 11.2 in 1997; among people aged 15-24, these figures were, respectively, 26.9 %, 29.9 % and 29.6 %. In the southern regions of Italy the overall unemployment rate was 14.1 % in 1991, 18.2 % in 1995 and 19 % in 1997.

[14]The normative references are: codice civile (Civil Code) art. 2127; Legge 264/49, and Legge 1369/60.

[15]Towards the end of the 1990s, the Italian labor market was still governed by very strict employment protection legislation for standard employment. In 1999, the OECD (1999) ranked Italy 23rd out of 27 countries for "overall strictness of protection against dismissals" (the lower the ranking the stricter the regulation).

[16]Brandt et al. (2005) report that Italy achieved the largest reduction in the OECD Employment Protection Legislation sub-index for temporary employment since the mid-1990s, due to the Treu reform.

ACKNOWLEDGMENTS

The main ideas of this paper have been developed while the author was visiting the CLE - Center for Labor Economics of the University of California at Berkeley, whose hospitality is gratefully acknowledged. Special thanks go to Francesca Bettio, Giuseppe Tattara, David Card, Massimo Riccaboni, David Avra Lane, Francesco Devicienti, Stefano Schiavo and Sandro Montresor for valuable suggestions and constant support, and also to Aaron Clauset, Cosma Rohilla Shalizi and Mark Newmanfor making available the software used for the estimations.

Disclaimer

The views expressed are purely those of the author and may not in any circumstances be regarded as stating an official position of the European Commission.

REFERENCES

1. Agrawal A, Cockburn I, McHale J (2006) Gone but not forgotten: knowledge flows, labour mobility, and enduring social relationships. J Econ Geogr 6(5):571–591
2. Akerlof GA (1970) The market for "lemons": quality uncertainty and the market mechanism. Q J Econ 84(3):488–500
3. Albert R, Barabási A-L (2002) Statistical mechanics of complex networks. Rev Mod Phys 74:47–97
4. Albert R, Jeong H, Barabási A-L (2000) Error and attack tolerance in complex networks. Nature 406:378–382
5. Almeida P, Kogut B (1999) Localization of knowledge and the mobility of engineers in regional networks. Manage Sci 45:905–917
6. Audretsch DB, Keilbach M (2005) The mobility of economic agents as conduits of knowledge Spillovers. In: Fornahl D, Zellner C, Audretsch DB (eds) The role of labour mobility and informal networks for knowledge transfer. Springer, Boston, pp 8–29
7. Autor DH (2001) Why do temporary help firms provide free general skills training? Q J Econ 116(4):1409–1448
8. Autor DH (2009) Studies of Labor Market Intermediation: Introduction. In: Autor D H (ed) Studies of labor market intermediation. University of Chicago Press, Chicago, pp 1–27
9. Barabási A-L, Albert R (1999) Emerging of scaling in random networks. Science 286:509–512
10. Barbieri P, Scherer S (2009) Labour Market Flexibilization and its Consequences in Italy. Eur Sociol Rev 25(6):677–692
11. Barbieri G, Gennari P, Sestito P (2001) Do public employment services help people in finding a job? An evaluation of the Italian case. Rivista di statistica ufficiale 3:177–216
12. Boccaletti S, Latora V, Moreno Y, Chávez M, Hwang D (2006) Complex networks: structure and dynamics. Phys Rep 424:175–308

13. Boschma RA, Eriksson R, Lindgren U (2009) How does labour mobility affect the performance of plants? The importance of relatedness and geographical proximity. J Econ Geogr 9(2):169–190

14. Brandt N, Burniaux J-M, Duval R (2005) Assessing the OECD Jobs Strategy: Past Developments and Reforms. OECD Economics Department Working Papers no. 429

15. Breschi S, Lissoni F (2009) Mobility of skilled workers and co-invention networks: an anatomy of localized knowledge flows. J Econ Geogr 9(4):439–468

16. Caprio L (2002) I gruppi di medie imprese industriali del Nord Est, Mediobanca-Unioncamere, Le medie imprese industriali del Nord Est (1996–2000). Mediobanca-Unioncamere, Milano-Roma, pp 125– 172

17. Casper S (2007) How do technology clusters emerge and become sustainable?: social network formation and inter-firm mobility within the San Diego biotechnology cluster. Res Policy 36(4):438–455

18. Cingano F, Rosolia A (2012) People i know: job search and social networks. J Labor Econ 30(2):291– 332

19. Clauset A, Shalizi CR, Newman MEJ (2009) Power-law distributions in empirical data. SIAM Rev 51:661–703

20. Coase RH (1937) The nature of the firm. Economica 4(16):386–405

21. D'Souza RM, Berger N, Borgs C, Chayes JT, Kleinberg RD (2007) Emergence of tempered preferential attachment from optimization. PNAS 104(15):6112–6117

22. Davis SJ, Haltiwanger J, Schuh S (1996) Job creation and destruction. MIT Press, Cambridge

23. Diamond PA (1982) Aggregate demand management in search equilibrium. J Polit Econ 90(5):881–894

24. Dixit A (2003) On modes of economic governance. Econometrica 71(2):449–481

25. Eriksson R, Lindgren U (2009) Localized mobility clusters: impacts of labour market externalities on firm performance. J Econ Geogr 9(1):33–53

26. Fabrikant A, Koutsoupias E, Papadimitriou CH (2002) Heuristically optimized trade-offs: a new paradigm for power laws in the internet. Proceedings of the 29th International Colloquium on Automata, Languages, and Programming. Lect Notes Comput Sci 2380:110–122

27. Fallick B, Fleischman CA (2004) Employer to employer flows in the U.S. labor market: the complete picture of gross worker flows. FEDS Working Paper no. 2004–34. Federal Reserve Board, Washington

28. Fallick B, Fleischman CA, Rebitzer JB (2006) Job-hopping in silicon valley: some evidence concerning the microfoundations of a high-technology cluster. Rev Econ Stat 88(3):472–481

29. Garcia-Pérez JI, Muñoz-Bullón F (2005) Temporary help agencies and occupational mobility. Oxford Bull Econ Stat 67(2):163–180

30. Gianelle C (2012) Discovering the regional small world of labour mobility: evidence from linked employer-employee data. Reg Stud iFirst:1–16

31. Goyal S, van der Leij MJ, Moraga-Gonzales JL (2006) Economics: an emerging small world. J Political Econ 114(2):403–412

32. Granovetter MS (1973) The strength of weak ties. Am J Sociol 78:1360–1380

33. Granovetter MS (1974) Getting a job: a study of contacts and careers. Harward University Press, Cambridge

34. Houseman SN (2001) Why employers use flexible staffing arrangements: evidence from an establishment survey. Ind Labor Relations Rev 55 (1):149–170

35. Iacus SM, Porro G (2002) Il lavoro interinale in Italia: uno sguardo all'offerta. Università di Milano Working paper no. 26.2002

36. Ichino A, Mealli F, Nannicini T (2005) Temporary Work Agencies in Italy: A Springboard Toward Permanent Employment? Giornale degli Economisti e Annali di Economia 64(1):1–27

37. Kılıçaslan Y, Taymaz E (2008) Labor market institutions and industrial performance: an evolutionary study. J Evol Econ 18:477–492

38. Kleiner MM, Todd RM (2009) Mortgage Broker Regulations That Matter: Analyzing Earnings, Employment, and Outcomes for Consumers. In: Autor D H (ed) Studies of labor market intermediation. University of Chicago Press, Chicago, pp 183–234

39. Latora V, Marchiori M (2001) Efficient behavior of small-world networks. Phys Rev Lett 198701:87

40. Latora V, Marchiori M (2002) Is the Boston subway a small-world network? Phys Stat Mech Appl 314(1–4):109–113

41. Veneto Lavoro V (2008a) L'erosione mancata. Il lavoro a tempo determinato cresce... come quello a tempo indeterminato. Misure, Working paper no. 14

42. Veneto Lavoro V (2008b) Il mercato del lavoro nel Veneto. Tendenze e politiche. Rapporto 2007. Franco Angeli, Milano

43. Lee W (2009) Private deception and the rise of public employment offices in the United States, 1890–1930. In: Autor D H (ed) Studies of labor market intermediation. University of Chicago Press, Chicago, pp 155–182

44. Leombruni R, Quaranta R (2005) Eppure si muoveva già. Una breve storia della mobilità dei lavoratori in Italia. In: Contini B, Trivellato U (eds) Eppur si muove. Dinamiche e persistenze nel mercato del lavoro italiano. Il Mulino, Bologna

45. Li W, Cai X (2004) Statistical analysis of airport network of China. Phys Rev E 69:046106

46. Ministero del Lavoro e delle Politiche Sociali (2001) Rapporto di Monitoraggio sulle politiche occupazionali e del lavoro. Ministero del Lavoro e delle Politiche Sociali, Roma

47. Mortensen DT, Pissarides CA (1994) Job creation and job destruction in the theory of unemployment. Rev Econ Stud 61(3):397–415

48. Mossa S, Barthélémy M, Stanley HE, Nunes Amaral LA (2000) Truncation of power law behavior in "Scale-Free" network models due to information filtering. Phys Rev Lett 88(13):138701

49. Newman MEJ (2000) Models of the small world. J Stat Phys 101:819–841

50. Newman MEJ (2003) The structure and function of complex networks. SIAM Rev 45:167–256

51. Newman MEJ (2005) Power laws, Pareto distributions and Zipf's law. Contemp Phys 46:323–351

52. OECD (1999) Employment outlook. OECD, Paris

53. Owen-Smith J, Powell W (2004) Knowledge networks as channels and conduits: the effects of spillovers in the Boston biotechnology community. Organ Sci 15(1):5–21

54. Porro G, Vezzulli A, Iacus SM (2004) Temporary agency workers in Italy: alternative techniques of classification. Labour 18(4):699–725

55. Sciulli D (2006) Making the Italian labour market more flexible: an evaluation of the Treu Reform. Economics Working Papers n. 06-34-08. Universidad Carlos III, Departamento de Economia, Madrid

56. Spence M (1973) Job market signaling. Q J Econ 87(3):355–374

57. Spulber DF (1996) Market microstructure and intermediation. J Econ Perspect 10(3):135–152

58. Stiglitz JE (1975) The theory of "Screening", education, and the distribution of income. Am Econ Rev 65(3):283–300

59. Tattara G, Valentini M (2010) Turnover and excess worker reallocation. The Veneto labour market between 1982 and 1996. Labour 24(4):474–500

60. Tattara G, Volpe M (2001) I distretti industriali: definizioni e storia. In: Tattara G (ed) Il piccolo che nasce dal grande. Le molteplici facce dei distretti industriali veneti. Franco Angeli, Milano, pp 9–77

61. Watts DJ (1999) Small worlds: the dynamics of networks between order and randomness. Princeton University Press, Princeton

62. Watts DJ, Strogatz SH (1998) Collective dynamics of 'small-world' networks. Nature 393:440–442

63. Williamson OE (1975) Markets and hierarchies: analysis and antitrust implications. Free Press, New York

64. White DR, Houseman M (2002) The navigability of strong ties: small worlds, tie strength and network topology. Complexity 8(1):72–81

8

FIRMS NAVIGATING THROUGH INNOVATION SPACES: A CONCEPTUALIZATION OF HOW FIRMS SEARCH AND PERCEIVE TECHNOLOGICAL, MARKET AND PRODUCTIVE OPPORTUNITIES GLOBALLY

Maureen McKelvey[1]

[1] Department of Economy and Society, IIE, Institute for Innovation and Entrepreneurship, University of Gothenburg, Gothenburg, Sweden

ABSTRACT

The main contribution of this paper is a theory-based conceptual framework of innovation spaces, and how firms must navigate through them to innovate. The concept of innovation systems - at the regional, sectoral and national levels - have been highly influential. Previous literature developing the concept of innovation systems has stressed the importance of institutions, networks and knowledge bases at the regional, sectoral and national levels. This paper primarily draws upon an evolutionary and Schumpeterian economics perspective, in the following three senses. The conceptualization of 'innnovation spaces' focuses upon how and why firm search for innovations is influenced the opportunities within certain geographical contexts. This means that the firm create opportunities and can span different context, but they are influence by the context in term of the access, flow and co-evolution of ideas, resources, technology, people and knowledge, which help stimulate business innovation in terms of products, process and services. The paper concludes with an agenda for future research and especially the need to focus on globalization as a process of intensifying linkages across the globe.

Keywords: Innovation and Invention, Technology Management, Opportunities, Global R&D Management, Innovation Systems

1 INTRODUCTION

An area of important contribution – but also a key conceptual problem - for evolutionary approaches to social science is how and why to link micro-level data with macro-level theorizing. [1] van den Bergh and Gowdy (2003) outline the promises and problems of developing the micro-foundations of macroeconomics, from an evolutionary perspective. They address a range of approaches, from multi-agent models including complexity and hierarchy to group selection as well as the need to recognize heterogeneity of firms in analyzing macro processes. More specifically in this line of reasoning, Dosi et al. (2008:601) stress that four basic notions are: 1) innovation is a key driver of economic growth; 2) the heterogeneity of firms; 3) markets are selection devices that affect decentralized decisions like entry and exit; and 4) the above three Schumpeterian micro-foundations are complementary with a Kuznetsian perspective on industrial dynamics. Within management literature inspired by evolutionary economics and organizational learning, a key concept has been 'firm search', often related to the creation of economic opportunities (Laursen 2012). This paper focuses upon how to help explain how and why firms differential abilities to 'navigate' through three dimensions of innovation spaces influence their ability to recognize opportunities, and therefore, in longer run, be able to compete and generate aggregate economic growth. This paper is an initial step in developing this understanding. This paper therefore uses elements of existing theoretical and empirical understanding in a new combination, in order to propose a new synthetic conceptualisation of the innovation process in firms as the navigation of a complex space involving different types of opportunities.

Empirically, these topics are increasingly important to both firms and economies, due to the globalization of all types of business activities – from research and development through production, service and customers. Archibugi and Iammarino (2002:99) define globalization as 'a high (and increasing) degree of interdependency and interrelatedness among different and geographically dispersed actors." Similarly, the authors provide empirical evidence of globalization, and why this shift matters for invention and innovation. Taking this proposition of globalization seriously also means that firms increasingly have to search and develop opportunities globally. Globalization thus also requires a more complex theoretical understanding of how such interdependencies and interrelatedness affect firms, and the observation that firms struggle with search and opportunities on a global scale prompted this line of research to better conceptualize the processes.

A key concept used in this paper is opportunities. Opportunities are most often discussed in recent years within entrepreneurship literature, although also inherent in Schumpeter's (1934, 1942) conceptualization of the dynamics of the economy. Within entrepreneurship literature, there has been a debate about whether opportunities are created or discovered (Alvarez and Barney 2007; Alvarez et al. 2013). In the creation theory within entrepreneurship literature, the nature of opportunities means that the actions of the entrepreneurs create opportunities, as compared to the situation where opportunities exist and are simply uncovered. *Ex ante*, the persons who become entrepreneurs may not be significant different from those who do not become entrepreneurs – but the process of having been and becoming entrepreneurs probably does change them, *ex post*. Given that firms develop innovations in relation to the creation of opportunities, their knowledge about the future is limited yet as they act, they also create new knowledge (Holmèn and McKelvey 2013). Accordingly, some work has stressed that the firms' innovative search occurs in an environment of co-evolution with market, technologies and institutions, as widely acknowledge in the innovation system literature (Nelson 1993; Lundvall et al. 2002) and related literature (McKelvey 1996, 2004; McKelvey and Holmèn 2006).

This paper therefore starts from the viewpoint that opportunities are created over time, which is also in line with an evolutionary epistemology (Buenstorf 2007; McKelvey et al. 201). In order to conceptualize whether, how and why firms do, or do not, move through complex space, it is necessary to start from two insights from evolutionary economics: a) that firms search for opportunities under conditions of selection and b) that the ability to identify and exploit that knowledge is related to firm internal capabilities (see review in Salter and McKelvey 2016). The implication is that firm search is necessary because this ability to innovate – and to create opportunities – is not randomly spread over the population of firms in an industry, but is concentrated in firms with certain capabilities and routines. Moreover, in the existing literature addressing evolutionary economics, there are different approaches, methodologies and theories, which this paper makes no claim to address all of them.

This paper only focuses on three core questions of an evolutionary approach to the development of knowledge and innovations in the economy– namely from where do different types of opportunities emerge? Why do we assume that firm search is necessary for innovation? And how does the innovation system help define the industrial, regional and national context, within which firms search? The answers to these questions are used to develop a conceptualization, which includes the microfoundations of firm search with the macro processes involving technology, markets and institutions.

2 FROM WHERE DO DIFFERENT TYPES OF OPPORTUNITIES EMERGE?

The first question is, From where do different types of opportunities arise? This question is explicitly addressed within evolutionary economics, in that capitalism is restless (Nelson 1996; Metcalfe 2002). Evolutionary economics focus upon dynamics and emergent systems as well as the peculiar role of knowledge and the appropriation of value of innovation. Industrial dynamics is driven through innovation in large companies and through entrepreneurship through new companies (Schumpeter 1934, 1942). Recent literature has both examined to what extent that Schumpeter was evolutionary and dynamic in his theorizing, as well as strived to define principles for evolutionary economics (Andersen 2011; Witt 2010; McKelvey and Holmén 2006; Foster and Metcalfe 2001). Metcalfe (2002 and 2008) argues that the restless nature of capitalism has to do with knowledge as the pre-eminent source of variation, but that there is a difference between knowledge and information which helps explain why heterogeneity of firms also matters. Here as well, markets are the primary arenas of selection for micro-processes.

From this literature, a key insight for this paper is thus that the creation of opportunities is a process of knowledge accumulation (Metcalfe 2002; McKelvey et al. 2015), and therefore one must understand firm search in relation to the innovation spaces within which they navigate. Moreover, opportunities are generated endogenously through the dynamics of the economic system and not through exogenous shocks. In other words, the phenomena of innovation and entrepreneurship exist because the actors create different types of opportunities, which involve engaging in decisions and actions under conditions of uncertainty and risk-taking.

Existing literature defines innovative opportunities as “the possibility to realize a potential economic value inherent in a new combination of resources and market needs, emerging from changes in the scientific or technological knowledge base, customer preferences, or the interrelationships between economic actors” (Holmén et al. 2007, p. 37).

As such, an innovative opportunity consists of the following three components: a) an economic value for someone; b) mobilization of resources; and c) the ability of the actor pursuing the opportunity to appropriate some of the economic value.

Three types of opportunities can be identified in the literature, and the issue is from where each type of opportunity emerges – which leads to the follow-on question for this paper, namely where should the firm be searching?

The first type that firms monitor is technological opportunities, which arise from scientific and technological knowledge (Scherer 1965; Nelson and Winter 1982; Breschi et al. 2000; Oltra and Flor 2003; Palmberg 2004). Note that there appears to be a relatively uneven distribution of 'technical opportunities' at different times and in different technologies and industries (Nelson and Winter 1982; Dosi 1982). Breschi et al. (2000) further develop the 'technological regime' proposed by Nelson and Winter (1982). They argue that '*Technological opportunities* reflect the likelihood of innovating for any given amount of money invested in search' (ibid). Differences between industry help explain where the generation of these types of opportunities occur. Breschi et al. (2000: 390–391) state that 'observed sectoral patterns of innovative activities are related to the nature of the relevant technological regime....defined by the specific combination of technological opportunities, appropriability of innovations, cumulativeness of technical advances and the properties of the knowledge base underlying firms' innovative activities.' This research implies that sectoral differences impact the ability to find new opportunities and to appropriate the value to the firm.

Technological knowledge is also related to how technology develops more generally in society, usually though a combination of public and private investment into new knowledge (McKelvey 2014; Archibugi and Filippetti 2015). Technological opportunities are thus created through the development of related areas of knowledge, including a range of relevant scientific and technological knowledge bases, techniques, and instrumentation.[2] Technologies can be seen as general bodies of human knowledge, which are often created and further developed within specific application areas, such as within firms, industries or other societal contexts of use; one must distinguish the stock of 'useful human knowledge as well as the continuous addition of new knowledge' (Moykr 2002).[3] Literature within the history of science and technology and in economic history suggests that such knowledge development is an on-going process, usually driven forward by specific individuals and acting within specific societal institutions (Rosenberg 1982, 1994). Some technologies develop quickly and general purpose technology, whereas other technologies develop slowly.

Technological knowledge is useful because it helps to solving problems, and so there are evolutionary dynamics in the underlying system of innovation whereby solving one technological problem often opens up new technical opportunities and new technical problems of relevance for developing complex engineering products. Solving one technical problem often focuses the attention of decision-makers on the need to improve related complementary technologies, which are known as 'focusing devices' for bottlenecks and as 'reverse salients' in a large technical system (Rosenberg 1982; Hughes 1983). These technical problems often require search activities in a variety of technological areas, and these search activities and problem-solving activities involve technological and market learning by diverse actors. Relatedly, Stankiewicz (2002) calls the opening up of new areas of 'cognitive space' and 'design space' as the exploration of new search space, to develop new technological opportunities. This helps explain why the science and university system are potent drivers of economic change. However, the science and business system need to have interdependencies and be interconnected because there are feedback loops between practical application of knowledge within an industry and the broader scientific and technological knowledge (Kline and Rosenberg 1986).[4] Biotechnology is one example, where scientific progress has stimulated extensive economic development, regeneration of existing firms, and knowledge intensive entrepreneurship (Audretsch and Feldman 1996; Senker 1999; McKelvey 1996; Faulkner and Senker 1995).

The second type of opportunity that firms must monitor is market opportunities. Entrepreneurship literature originally focused upon market imperfections and arbitrage profits, and therefore had a particular focus on how the entrepreneur could use that knowledge to engage in purposeful action (see discussion in Holmèn et al. 2007). Shane (2000) demonstrated how the individual entrepreneurs' prior knowledge affected cognition and the interpretation of opportunities. This is one type of the market opportunities of interest here, whereby information asymmetries may exist due to the differences in individual cognition, thereby opening up market opportunities.

More broadly, in the economics of innovation literature, however, a debate was originally formulated about the driving forces for the development of new knowledge, which is useful in the economy. A dichotomy was proposed between 'technology' and 'market' in a dynamic sense, as one classical distinction is between 'technology push' and 'market pull' (Mowery and Rosenberg 1991). Technology push means that the investments into research and technology lead to the development of new ideas that can be tested and introduced to the market. The technology 'pushes' out new ideas. The notion of market pull means that the inventor or innovating firm comes up with an idea, because they are responding to the perceived wants and preferences of customers. In other words, the market 'pulls' out creativity and new ideas. In more recent years, the discussion focuses not on markets in general but on the role that lead users often significantly impact the direction of technology development in an early phase (von Hippel 1988; Franke and von Hippel 2003). As the technology matures and diffuses, new types of user groups may express quite different needs than the early ones, thereby influencing both the technology per se as well as the range of potential future uses.

Innovations require both, and because business innovations must ultimately be sold, recent innovation literature stresses that customers, and relevant knowledge about customers and societal links, needs to be integrated into business innovation theory (Dodgson et al. 2014). New business models is one tool to integrate ideas, technology, markets and so forth into what the firm offers to different types of customers and how the firm appropriates value.

The third type of opportunity that firms must monitor is the productive opportunity. This relates to how the firm should organize its resources internally. Penrose (1959) argued that the firm has the possibility to combine its internal resources in many new ways. The 'productive opportunity' limits the number of combinations, especially as perceived by managers in the firm. A key issue involves the managers' capacity to envision alternative modes of using the resources at hand (Penrose 1959: 31–42, 111). In more recent literature, one can argue that the notion of productive opportunities relates to internal firm issues, and what is known as capabilities. By capabilities, we mean the knowledge, experience and skills that firms have which are appropriate for carrying out specific activities (Richardson 1972). Capability building is seen as a major source of sustained competitive advantages for the firm (Barney 1991). Combinative capability can be defined as the ability to integrate and synthesize internal resources and external learning and deploy them in a competitive environment (Kogut & Zander, 1993). Recent literature includes many contributions about capabilities, dynamic capabilities and capabilities as specifically related to innovation (Helfat and Lieberman 2002; Bingham et al. 2007; Teece 2007; Hine et al. 2013). Helfat and Lieberman (2002:725) distinguish between resources 'as stocks of available factors that are owned or controlled by the firm, and capabilities as the firm's capacity to deploy resources for a desired end result'. The literature on dynamics capabilities stresses that the firm must adapt to demands in the external environment, and reconfigure resources (Teece et al. 1997). Firms with high levels of motivation and the capacity to learn should be more open to gaining experience from different situations; this makes them more likely to seize pre-emptive opportunities than more defensive firms which employ static resource-exploitation strategies (Teece et al. 1997). Hine et al. (2013:17) distinguish between different types of capabilities, across the dimensions of predominate resources, routine patterning, learning focus and strategic intent. The three levels of capabilities are 'higher-order dynamic learning capabilities' which involve creative ability; 'lower-order dynamic functional capabilities' which involve dynamic ability; and 'first-order ordinary capabilities' which involve static ability. The latter category involves general resources, rigid routine patterning, exploitative focus of learning tasks and subsistent strategic intent. Search processes involve higher-order and lower-order ones.

In summary, this section has addressed evolutionary literature that helps to answer the question, From where do different types of opportunities emerge? These theories help to conceptualize how and why firms are searching for new opportunities, and especially in relation to technological, market, and productive opportunities. Given the evolutionary epistemology, this paper also follows the conceptualization that the firm involved in innovation processes must also be engaged in, and help to create, these three types of opportunities. An active firm – with high levels of motivation and the capacity to learn – is more likely to search and be able to create opportunities across all these three dimensions. Moreover, the literature specifies that firms can be analyzed as engaging in specific, identifiable processes, specifically to identify economic value; mobilize resources; and appropriate at least some of the economic value.

In terms of the conceptualization of firms navigating innovation spaces, a first constituent element is:

> Firm help to seize and create opportunities in their innovation space, over time. The innovation space can be thought of – and analyzed – through three axes. The first axis is of creation of technological opportunities through scientific and technological knowledge. The second axis is the creation of market opportunities related to new market and customer knowledge. The third axis is the creation of productive opportunities, dependent upon using business knowledge of how to operate innovation in the firm locally and globally and leading to a reconfiguration of capabilities.

3 WHY DO WE ASSUME THAT FIRM SEARCH IS NECESSARY FOR INNOVATIONS?

The second question to address, is what does the literature say about, Why do we assume that firm search is necessary for innovation? Search is core to evolutionary thinking, because, a key notion is that firms are heterogeneous in a way that matters to economic change. Selection takes place at the population level, and therefore differences at the unit level matter for determining which organization disappears, or else continues to exist. If the firm does not search – or does not find opportunities – they are likely to disappear, due to market selection.

In relation to firms search for technical innovations, McKelvey (1996) specifies three key points in a conceptualization based upon evolutionary economic theories. Firstly, there is an assumption of intentionality, and that humans generate novelty and diversity, which are intended to satisfy environment conditions. Secondly, because of intentionality in relation to perceived environmental conditions, firms explore certain 'search spaces which can be presented as a three-dimensional space, full of hills, valleys and plains'. Because the search for innovation does not occur randomly in time and space, this means that certain parts of search space are more explored than other. Thirdly, there is an expectation of diversity at the micro level of firms, which will in turn impact future performance of firms and also of their ability to search for, and learn about, innovations. The reason is that the firm needs to access ideas and information in order to take advantage of different types of opportunities and to innovate in different geographic contexts and cognitive frameworks. A key insight is also that due to heterogeneity, firms will have explored different parts of the innovation space.

Hence, search is not just a question of identifying 'the right information' which exists out there. Focusing on search means that the firm's internal combinations of routines, resources, capabilities, and learning must be taken into consideration, and will also change over time, in response to internal and external conditions (Nelson 1996; Penrose 1959; Teece et al. 1997; Teece 2007). Theories in innovation management explicates how the internal capabilities of the firm is linked to opportunities arising in the environment, thereby stressing the role of relationships and networks for the firm to search, identify and seize relevant business opportunities (Brusoni et al. 2001; Dodgson et al. 2014). The proposition here is thus that firms will have different capabilities to search for information related to opportunities, as well as different abilities to process and use that information to create new opportunities. Moreover, because the focus here is on search activities related to invention and innovation, this means that the firm is searching under conditions of uncertainty and also in an increasingly globalized context.

From an evolutionary perspective, the argument has been put forth that firms have difficulties in developing innovation relevant to new situations, whether these arise from changes in the industry or in the country. Nelson and Winter (2002:29) call it the competence puzzle:

> "How can the same organizations be so impressively competent from one perspective and yet so strikingly "bounded" in their rationality? ... In the evolutionary view, the key to the puzzle lies in the contrasting demands of different types of situations. High

> competence is often achievable where skills and routines can be learned and perfected through practice. For individuals and organizations (not to speak of animals), learning guided by clear short-term feedback can be remarkably powerful, even in addressing complex challenges. But that sort of learning does little to enable sophisticated foresight, logically structured deliberation and/or the improvisation of novel action patterns and situations that demand these are rarely handled well."

This quote suggests that firm have difficulties dealing with the future – and explicitly states that decisions that must rely upon foresight, logically structured deliberation and novel action patterns. This suggests that search is difficult.

Still, a key aspect of understanding innovation spaces is the role of firms, and explicitly that firms must search for new innovative opportunities, and search for solutions to their technical and market problems (Holmén et al. 2007; Laursen 2012). So, one answer as to why firms must search is related to the types of knowledge involved in invention and innovation as well as the particular role of learning. Existing literature outlines that there is an imperative for firms to learn, develop routines, and access new types of inputs as sources of competitive advantage (Nelson and Winter 1982; Fleming and Sorenson 2001; Rosenkopf and Nerkar 2001; Katila and Ahuja 2002). Another way to understand what firms do is that they need to find new knowledge, which helps them solve different types of problems. According to the problem-solving perspective as developed within the knowledge-based theory of the firm, the key task of the manager is to 'not how to organize to exploit already developed knowledge or capability, but rather how to organize to efficiently generate knowledge and capability' (Nickerson and Zenger 2004:617). Firms are recognized as the actors, which play the key role in the development of incremental changes in existing technologies and products along a trajectory (Pavitt 1991; Dosi 1982).

Uncertainty is, by definition, a characteristic of the firm search activities, because novelty is involved in invention and innovation. Business innovation in a broad sense can be defined as 'novelty of economic value'.[5] Because innovations require novelty, this implies that the processes leading to innovation will occur under conditions of limited knowledge about the future. Therefore, the decision-making context is uncertain, in the meaning proposed by Knight (1921) of not being able to predict or assess the probability of potential outcomes. Firms face uncertainty rather than risk in that uncertainty cannot be measured nor calculated. In contrast, risk refers to situations where the odds can be predicted, even if we do not predict the outcomes.

But what does it mean that innovation processes involve uncertainty and risk-taking? This paper proposes that: 1) innovation by definition includes an element of novelty for the future, and the novel idea may or may not work; 2) decision-makers are unable to access or process all relevant information; 3) often the future is uncertain in the sense of unknown-able rather than risky in the sense of calculate possible alternatives and 4) multiple possible paths of scientific and technological alternatives can exist to solve any identifiable user needs.

From the firm's perspective, they are investing in search activities about innovations of which they cannot predict future outcomes. In order to innovate, the firm must make complex decisions under conditions of uncertainty about future technologies and future market preferences. In the Campbell (1960) sense, blind-variation helps explain that the development of knowledge cannot necessarily be predicted, but once new knowledge is developed, there is a change in the later direction of search for new knowledge. In relation to innovations and technical development, these blind-search paths whereby later search is affected should lead to path dependency. In that sense, failures are an inherent part of testing and selection among a variety of alternatives to solve any one problem (Basalla 1988; Vincenti 1990; Dosi 1982, 1988). The literature on radical versus incremental innovations suggests that the degree of uncertainty and the degree of risk may, however, be different in different industries and types of innovations.

In summary, this part of the literature motivates the focus here upon firm search, under conditions of uncertainty about the future as well as making decisions involving risk. An evolutionary perspective of creation of opportunities suggests that the firms (actors) must be understood as heterogeneous actors, with diverse sets of knowledge and capabilities. That is a given, if selection is to occur over time on the population level. Moreover, firms have difficulties in searching for areas further away from their existing resources and capabilities and focus on knowledge that is useful for problem-solving.

In terms of the conceptualization of firms navigating innovation spaces, a second constituent element is:

> Firms must navigate through an innovation space, in an evolutionary process, as they search and develop different types of business innovations. By definition, an innovation entails the unknown, as the concept focuses upon novelty of economic value.

4 How does the innovation system help define the industrial, regional and national context, within which firms search?

This section addresses the question, How does the innovation system help define the industrial, regional and national context, within which firms search?

Previous literature developing the concept of innovation systems has stressed the importance of institutions, networks and knowledge bases at the regional, sectoral and national levels, known as innovation systems (Malerba 2002, 2009; Edquist 2006; Lundvall et al. 2002; Cooke et al. 1997; Nelson 1993; Edquist and McKelvey 2000). This provides an understanding of the context for innovation processes. Perhaps because economic geographers develop notions of space and proximity, it makes sense to help define the context from their discussions first (Boschma and Frenken 2006; Boschma and Martin 2010; Boschma 2012). In Boschma and Martin (2010: 6–7), an ambitious range of scholarship for an evolutionary economic geography approach is staked out:

> The processes by which the economic landscape – the spatial organisation of economic production, circulation, exchange, distribution and consumption - is transformed over time....spatialities of economic novelty (innovations, new firms, new industries, new networks), with how the spatial structure of the economy emerge from the micro-behaviours of economic agents (individuals, firms, organisations); with how, in the absence of central coordination or direction, the economic landscape exhibits self-organisation, and with how the processes of both path creation and path dependence interact to shape geography of economic development and transformation, and why and how such processes may themselves be place dependent.

The current paper shares an intellectual heritage and interest in these types of questions; although the purpose here is much more narrow than their agenda. Still this quote identifies many of the core issues about self-organization, path dependency and microfoundations that are also found in evolutionary economics.

That leaves us with the task of exploring how theoretical insights can be applied to understand the micro-behavior of firms, as agents navigating through complex spatial and industrial dimensions, and in ways this will impact their future development of innovations.

This brings us back to how microfoundations are linked to macro processes. In this conceptualization, it is useful to define an innovation space, because there is a relationship between the development of firm capabilities and the innovation system. The innovation system provides many elements, such as access to networks, institutions, as well as technology and science. Firms do not search randomly, nor does it only occur inside the firm. Innovation processes rely upon search outside the firm, and innovation is distributed in the sense that actors are distributed across countries, industries and different types of firms and organizations (Metcalfe 2008).

Thus, the proposal here is to draw upon these insights from innovation systems, to express that firm search activities must span industries as well as regions/countries. This is visualized in Fig. 1 below.

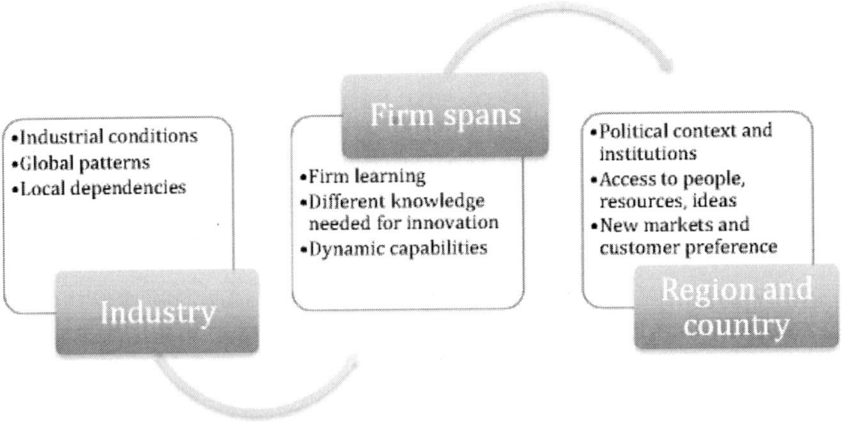

Figure 1. Interactions as the firm spans between industry and region/country

The firm is conceptualized as spanning the industry and the region/country level, in the sense that they must search this external environment in order to find relevant new knowledge and create opportunities. The visualization in Fig. 1 suggests that there are interdependencies, or co-evolution, between the firm and contexts in which the firm is active, as explained below.

At the industry level, the innovation space takes it specific form (expression) through a combination of industrial conditions, global patterns, and local dependencies. The industrial sector, or sectoral system of innovation is likely the basis of firm search and learning, rather than the nation (Malerba 2001). The industry life cycle literature claims that rapidly changing technologies lead to the development of new industries (see Abernathy and Utterback 1975; Utterback 1994; Klepper 1996). In the early phase, many competing firms exist, and they compete on alternative product designs; in the later phase, a dominant design emerges; competition is based on economies of scale; and the firms tend to become larger in order to reap scale economies while managing such processes. Hence, the stage in the industry life cycle will also affect the ability and direction of the firm's search for innovations.

At the region and country level, the innovation space takes it specific form (expression) through a combination of political context, agglomeration effects such as access to people, resources and ideas, and the development of new markets and customer preferences, the national innovation system, including societal structures and institutions. Some literature links this national level of technological and market learning to institutions and social structure, which are simultaneously embedded in the firm, sector and/or region (Fransman 2001; Harvey et al. 2003). Much of economic geography suggests that regions and nations are key geographical spaces, and scales include the regional and national. Therefore, even though this literature is vast and different arguments about the importance of local, regional, national, international levels have been put forward: the concepts of geographical scales or level of analysis are useful here.[6] This line of research provides the insight that a) geographical contexts can differ in important ways at different scales; and 2) firm networks can help link different innovation spaces to each other through the operations of the firm.

In summary, the firm is said to be searching in space, which links different actors, and the definition of that space consists of innovation systems, where the context may be industrial regional and national, or all three at the same time. From the perspective of the firm, they need to use their networks and organizational structure in order to explore the different opportunities possible in different geographical scales. What is key to the conceptualization here is that firms are the actors, which are spanning between the industry and the regional/national institutional setting. The proposition is: the notion of distributed innovation processes implies that geographic space, context and scale may matter, but that the international knowledge flows as well as firm actions mean that innovation is not restricted to specific places or contexts.

In terms of the conceptualization of firms navigating innovation spaces, a third constituent element is:

> An innovation space constitutes a geographical context, which affects innovation through a process of interaction of firms spanning industry as well as the regional/national institutional setting. Because innovation space can be analyzed as this interplay, the innovation space is not bounded by geography per se. Geography matters in that certain regions and countries tend to have a concentration of potential opportunities. However, firms can span across several spaces through networks and through activities in multiple countries and thereby the firm can configure its capabilities to link innovation spaces through the operations and capabilities of the firm.

5 CONCLUSIONS: A CONCEPTUALIZATION AND FUTURE RESEARCH AGENDA

The contribution of this paper is intentionally at a high level of abstraction in conceptualization, given the early stage of this line of research, although a few comments related to research design are included below. This paper has focused on three core questions of an evolutionary approach to the development of knowledge and innovations in the economy– namely from where do different types of opportunities emerge? Why do we assume that firm search is necessary for innovation? And how does the innovation system help define the industrial, regional and national context, within which firms search? The answers to these questions have been used to develop a conceptualization, which includes the microfoundations of firm search with the macro processes involving technology, markets and institutions.

The proposed concept of 'innovation spaces' developed in previous sections - and synthesized below - can thus be understood as a systematic manner in which to organise the various models of the nature and function of what firms do as they search through the space of opportunities, under conditions of uncertainty, seeking to discovery new source of value.

5.1 Conceptualization

Putting together the three constituent elements, the conceptualization of firms navigating innovation spaces, as proposed in this paper is:

> Firm help to seize and create opportunities in their innovation space, over time. The innovation space can be thought of - and analyzed - through three axes. The first axis is of creation of technological opportunities through scientific and technological knowledge. The second axis is the creation of market opportunities related to new market and customer knowledge. The third axis is the creation of productive opportunities, dependent upon using business knowledge of how to operate innovation in the firm locally and globally and leading to a reconfiguration of capabilities.
>
> Firms must navigate through an innovation space, in an evolutionary process, as they search and develop different types of business innovations. By definition, an innovation entails the unknown, as the concept focuses upon novelty of economic value.

An innovation space constitutes a geographical context, which affects innovation through a process of interaction of firms spanning industry as well as the regional/national institutional setting. Because innovation space can be analyzed as this interplay, the innovation space is not bounded by geography per se. Geography matters in that certain regions and countries tend to concentrate opportunities. However, firms can span across several spaces through networks and through activities in multiple countries and thereby the firm can configure its capabilities to link innovation spaces through the operations and capabilities of the firm.

The perspective taken here is that of the economist, using tools from an evolutionary analysis of knowledge for invention and innovation, in order to understand why and how the microfoundations matter. The focus is put upon the firm searching and creating opportunities, of which three types have been identified. The three types of opportunities that are created are proposed to entail technological, market, and productive opportunities. Given the focus on invention and innovation, the business managers are making decisions in a dynamic context with Knightian uncertainty. The metaphor of firms navigating innovation spaces suggests the importance of directionality, spatial, and context.

5.2 Future research agenda

Researchers interested in the future research agenda should tackle key theoretical issues, including develop testable hypotheses as well as tackle empirical issues related to research design and especially, how to use data to capture what firms are doing and why it differs.

In order to help structure a future research agenda, Table 1 provides a synthesis of the conceptualization, as divided into the three constituent parts. The left hand column summarizes the main points, when answering the three questions relevant to evolutionary approaches. The middle column states the main theoretical challenges, which should be further developed, including proposing hypothesis. The right column identifies some of the empirical challenges, which are naturally aligned with the theoretical challenges as well

In terms of empirical strategy for the research design, the following provides some initial comments about how to tackle the issues. A key scientific challenge is that given the theoretical propositions about the heterogeneity of firms in terms of both capabilities and search, this implies that the research design must take into consideration how the firm interprets its environment, and cannot just assume 'objective data' will be processed the same way by all firms.

For the first constituent element in developing a research design to study opportunities, the existing innovation and management literature provides multiple tools that have already been operationalized and validated. In order to study technological opportunities, there are a range of refined indicators of publications and patents as being indicators, respectively, of science and technology as well as many measures of 'impact' through citations, referencing, authorship/ownership and so forth. In order to study market opportunities, the data often used includes

Table 1. Conceptualization of firms navigating innovation spaces: Constituent elements, theoretical and empirical challenges

	Theoretical challenges	Empirical challenges
Part I: Opportunities are created in process These represent different types of innovative opportunities	Explain the creation of opportunities Delineate the three types of opportunities – technological, market and productive	Propose how the search for certain types of innovations involve different degrees of uncertainty vs risk Describe firm search and problem-solving in the context of uncertainty and knowledge accumulation
Part II: Firms navigate and search for innovation, under conditions of uncertainty	Discuss uncertainty vs risk Define innovations Describe firm search and problem-solving	Propose how heterogeneous firms can span the context of sectoral, regional and national innovation systems in ways which affect the direction and rate of innovations introduced Explain in detail how the firm can use networks and organizational/operational capabilities to access multiple innovation spaces
Part III: Firms span the industrial, regional and national institutional context	Define context of sectoral, regional and national innovation systems Discuss how the firm can use networks and organizational/operational capabilities to access multiple innovation spaces	Explore how the firm engages in the creation of opportunities while spanning the industry and regional/national context Delineate whether the three types of opportunities – technological, market and productive – are visible to firm managers

both quantitative numbers of the size of markets, usually on the vector of increase, as well as more qualitative input on the role of users within innovation processes. In order to study productive opportunities, quantitative tools that relate to internal management control as well as to more qualitative concepts like dynamic capabilities are needed, in a longer time frame. Interesting questions about opportunity creation, for example, is whether, how and why entrepreneurial firms transit from being focused upon technological opportunities primarily, to also take into consideration market and productive opportunities?

For the second constituent element of firms navigating, the research design should take into consideration that innovation spaces are multi-dimensional. Moreover, the word 'navigating' indicates the active and heterogeneous nature of firms. Firms may not always be moving and navigating – but search suggests the firms are engaged in exploring new areas and thereby must develop maps and navigate their ways towards new goals. Thus, a detailed empirical strategy combined with an historical methodology could be a useful approach. Search could be made more specific, relative to existing literature, such as existing taxonomies of different kinds of innovations as related to a specification of the degree of uncertainty and/or risk-taking. For example, firm search activities can be mapped in terms of high/low uncertainty and in terms of whether the search pertains to technological, market or productive opportunities. Finally, especially in industries in crises, such as the pharmaceutical industry in recent years, firms at time congregate around the same innovation spaces and use the same search strategies, while at other times, much diversity can be observed. One interesting question is then, How firm who change their strategy to more globalized networks also change their global networks? This could also be done comparative, between firms initially having similar technological knowledge (as signaled by patents and publications for example).

For the third constituent element, developing a research design should draw extensively on concepts and variables found in economic geography and innovation systems. This literature can be used to operationalize and validate the importance of variables such as institutions, networks, flows, etc. For example, literature could further develop the analysis of firms in emerging markets, which try to catch up with developing countries, as a dynamic process of co-evolution, between firms and countries (Malerba and Nelson 2012; Bell and Pavitt 1993). Finally, given that co-evolution over time is expected to occur, then theoretical as well as empirically grounded propositions can be developed. These propositions may help explain different trajectories of development, when firms search in different geographical contexts.

In terms of theoretically interesting issues, there are many to tackle. This paper started by focusing upon the challenges of research based upon microfoundations, and the four basic notions, as outlined by Dosi et al. (2008:601) are: 1) innovation is a key driver of economic growth; 2) the heterogeneity of firms; 3) markets are selection devices that affect decentralized decisions like entry and exit; and 4) the above three Schumpeterian micro-foundations are complementary with a Kuznetsian perspective on industrial dynamics. Each of these notions could be further developed, specifically in relation to innovation spaces and firm search. For example, because search and innovation processes generally occur before, as well as concurrently with, market processes, this means that market selection is not the only selection mechanism. Thus, from an evolutionary and Schumpeterian economics perspective, future research should return to fundamental theoretical issues, such as which mechanisms and processes tend to generate novelty, retain capabilities and attributes, and select amongst alternatives.

Finally, an important topic for future research is to develop the conceptualization, in order to more deeply understand the globalization of invention and innovation. Indeed, this paper was inspired by earlier empirical work to try to understand the rise of Asia – both as economies and as companies located in those countries (McKelvey and Bagchi-Sen 2015). The resulting book examined ongoing process of global interdependencies and interrelatedness, by looking within Asia as well as Asian firms moving to Western countries and at Western firms moving into Asia. In other words, the book provides some empirical evidence and some conceptualization of what Asia means to global invention and innovation. The book argues that four myths are debunked: a) There is a lot of talk about Asia, but it is only talk. Government policy and national institutions are not supportive of technological development and innovation b) Firms from Asia tend not to be entrepreneurial c) Large firms from Asia tend not to be innovative. They focus on low cost, and not on investing in resources to compete through technology and innovation d) Western firms can easily move to outsource customer development, technological development and research and development to Asia. Hence, much more work should be done on issues of globalizaton in general and of Asia in particular, because Asia is quickly becoming a key innovation space where technological, market and productive opportunities are being created. The complexities of globalization of invention and innovation involving firms and countries is an area where theoretical developments are needed, and aligned with empirical studies.

FOOTNOTES

[1]Acknowledgements to the financiers, specifically the Sten A Olsson Foundation for Research and Culture; Getinge; Volvo AB; and SKF. I would also like to acknowledge my co-author Sharmistha Bagchi-Sen, especially our co-edited book on related topics.

[2]The rate and distribution of change across technological areas can be measured empirically in many different ways, including studies of technical aspects, such as performance of new materials, as well as studies of more interrelated economic-technological aspects, such as the ratio of price to performance, or second-order effects on demand.

[3]Moykr (2002) also proposes a conceptualization of two types of useful knowledge, namely 'propositional' (what) and 'prescriptive' (how). He argues that much of technology is about 'prescriptive' knowledge but is based upon much 'propositional' knowledge.

[4]The use of techniques and instrumentation as well as the use of machines and capital equipment in factories were initially studied, as places where users impacted technical development.

[5]Note that the concept of business innovation as economic phenomena includes a notion of 'economic value'. Thereby innovation must be linked to a conceptualization of customer and markets, and not just remain at the stage of an idea. That is why the innovation literature generally distinguishes invention – such as an idea or technical item – from innovation – such as a new product introduced to the market.

[6]Economic geography and human geography have extensive work on related concepts, including a recent special issue of *Regional Studies* (Boschma 2012; Healy and Morgan 2012; Shearmur 2012).

REFERENCES

1. Abernathy W, Utterback J (1975) A dynamic model of process and product innovation'. Omega 7:379–394
2. Alvarez SA, Barney JB (2007) Discovery and creation: alternative theories of entrepreneurial action. Strateg Entrep J 1:11–26
3. Alvarez SA, Barney JB, Anderson P (2013) Forming and exploiting opportunities: the implications of discovery and creation processes for entrepreneurial and organizational research. Organ Sci 24:301–317
4. Andersen ES (2011) Joseph A Schumpeter A theory of social and economic evolution. Palgrave Macmillan, UK
5. Archibugi D, Filippetti A (2015) The handbook of global science, technology and innovation. Wiley publishers, Oxford
6. Archibugi D, Iammarino S (2002) The globalization of technological innovation: definition and evidence. Rev Int Polit Econ 9(1):98–122
7. Audretsch D, Feldman M (1996) R&D spillovers and the geography of innovation and Production'. Am Econ Rev 86:630–640
8. Basalla G (1988) The evolution of technology. Cambridge University Press, Cambridge
9. Bell M, Pavitt K (1993) Technological accumulation and industrial growth: contrasts between developed and developing countries'. Ind Corp Chang 2(2):157–210
10. Bingham C, Eisenhardt K, Furr N (2007) What makes a process a capability? heuristics, strategy, and effective capture of opportunities. Strateg Entrep J 1(1–2):24–47
11. Boschma R (2012) Proximity and innovation: a critical assessment. Reg Stud 34(3):213–229
12. Boschma R, Frenken K (2006) Why is economic geography not an evolutionary science? towards an evolutionary economics geography. J Econ Geogr 6(3):273–302
13. Boschma, R. and Martin, R. (2010). The Handbook of Evolutionary Economic Geography. Edward Elgar

14. Breschi S, Malerba F, Orsenigo L (2000) Technological regimes and schumpeterian patterns of innovation. Econ J 110:388–410

15. Brusoni S, Prencipe A, Pavitt K (2001) Knowledge specialisation, organizational coupling, and the boundaries of the firm: why firms know more than they make. Adm Sci Q 46(4):597–621

16. Buenstorf G (2007) Creation and pursuit of entrepreneurial opportunities: an evolutionary economics perspective. Small Bus Econ 28:323–337

17. Campbell DT (1960) Blind variation and selective retentions in creative thought as in other knowledge processes. Psychol Rev 67:380–400

18. Cooke P, Gomez UM, Etxebaria G (1997) Regional innovation systems institutional and organizational dimensions. Res Policy 26(4–5):475–491

19. Dodgson M, Gann D, Phelps N (2014) The handbook of innovation management. Oxford University Press, Oxford

20. Dosi G (1982) Technological paradigms and technological Trajectories'. Res Policy 11(3):147–162

21. Dosi, G. (1988). 'Sources, Procedures and Microeconomic Effects of Innovation' Journal of Economic Literature XXVI:3 (Sept), pp. 1120–1171.

22. Dosi G, Gaffard J-L, Nesta L (2008) Schumpeterian themes on industrial evolution, structural change and their microfoundations: an introduction. Ind Corp Chang 17(4):601–609

23. Edquist C (2006) Systems of innovation. Perspectives and Challenges. In: Fagerberg J, Mowery DC, Nelson RR (eds) The oxford handbook of innovation. Oxford University Press, Oxford

24. Edquist C, McKelvey M (eds) (2000) Systems of innovation. A reference collection. Edward Elgar, Cheltenham

25. Faulkner W, Senker J (1995) Knowledge frontiers: public sector research and industrial innovation in biotechnology, engineering ceramics and parallel computing. Clarendon, Oxford

26. Fleming L, Sorenson O (2001) Technology as a complex adaptive system: evidence from patent data. Res Policy 30(7):1019–1039

27. Foster J, Metcalfe JS (2001) Frontiers of evolutionary economics: competition, self-organization and innovation policy. Edward Elgar Publishers, Cheltenhamn

28. Franke N, von Hippel E (2003) Satisfying heterogeneous user needs via innovation toolkits: the case of apache security software'. Res Policy 32:1199–1215

29. Fransman M (2001) Designing dolly: interactions between economics, technology and science and the evolution of hybrid institutions'. Res Policy 30(2):263–273

30. Harvey M, Quilley S, Beynon H (2003) Exploring the tomato: transformations of nature, society and economy. Edward Elgar, Cheltenham

31. Healy A, Morgan K (2012) Spaces of innovation: learning, proximity and the ecological turn. Reg Stud 46(8):1041–1053

32. Helfat C, Lieberman M (2002) The birth of capabilities: marke entry and the importance of pre-history. Ind Corp Chang 11(4):725–760

33. Hine D, Parker R, Pregelj L, Verreynne M-L (2013) Deconstructing and reconstructing the capabilities hierarchy. Ind Corp Chang. Holmèn M, McKelvey M (2013) Restless capitalism and the economizing entrepreneur'. Econ Innov New Technol 22(7):684–701

34. Holmén M, Magnusson M, McKelvey M (2007) What are innovative opportunities? Ind Innov 14:27–45

35. Hughes T (1983) The networks of power: electrification in western society, 1880–1930. John Hopkins Press, Baltimore

36. Katila R, Ahuja G (2002) Something old, something new: a longitudinal study of search behavior and New product introduction. Acad Manag J 45(8):1183–1194

37. Klepper S (1996) Entry, exit, growth, and innovation over the product life cycle'. Am Econ Rev 83(3):562–583

38. Kline, S. and Rosenberg, N. (1986), 'An Overview of Innovation'. In Lanau, R. and Rosenberg, N., The Positive Sum Strategy: Harnessing Technology for Economic Growth, Washinton D.C., National Academy Press

39. Knight F (1921) Risk, uncertainty and profit. Houghton Mifflin, Boston

40. Laursen K (2012) Keep searching and you'll find: what do we know about variety creation through firms' search activities for innovation?'. Ind Corp Chang 21(5):1181–1220

41. Lundvall BÅ, Johnson B, Andersen ES, Dalum B (2002) National systems of production, innovation and competence building. Res Policy 31(2):213–231

42. Malerba, F (2002). Sectoral Systems of Innovation. Research Policy

43. Malerba, F. (2009). Sectoral Systems of Innovation: Concepts, Issues and Analyses of Six Major Sectors. Cambridge, U.K.: Cambridge University Press

44. Malerba, F and Nelson, R.R. (2012).Economic Development as a Learning Process: Variation Across Sectoral Systems. Edward Elgar Publishers, Cheltenham U.K. and Northampton MA. USA.

45. McKelvey M (1996) Evolutionary innovations: the business of biotechnology. Oxford University Press, Oxford

46. McKelvey, M. (2004). 'How and why dynamic selection regimes affect the firm's innovative activities'. Innovation: Management, Policy & Practice. Issue 6, vol 1. Pp.

47. McKelvey M (2014) Science, technology and business innovation. In: Dodgson M, Gann D, Phelps N (eds) The handbook of innovation management. Oxford University Press, Oxford

48. McKelvey M, Holmèn M (2006) Flexibility and stability in the innovating economy. Oxford University Press, Oxford

49. McKelvey, M., Zaring, O. and Ljungberg, D. (2015). 'Creating innovative opportunities through collaborative research: an evolutionary framework and empirical illustration from engineering'. Technovation. 10.1016/j.technovation.2014.05.008i. Volume 39–40, Pages 26–36

50. Metcalfe S (2002) Knowledge of growth and growth of knowledge. J Evol Econ 12(1):3–13

51. Metcalfe S (2008) Restless capitalism – the evolutionary nature of capitalism. Princeton University Press, Princeton

52. Mowery D, Rosenberg N (1991) Technology and the pursuit of economic growth. Cambridge University Press, Cambridge

53. Moykr J (2002) The gifts of athena: historical origins of the knowledge society. Oxford University Press, Oxford

54. Nelson RR (1993) National systems of innovation: a comparative analysis. Oxford University Press, Oxford

55. Nelson RR (1996) The sources of economic growth. Harvard University Press, Cambridge

56. Nelson, R. and Winter, S. (1982). An Evolutionary Theory of Economic Change. Cambridge, MA.: Belknap Press of Harvard University Press

57. Nickerson JA, Zenger TR (2004) A knowledge-based theory of the firm-the problem-solving Perspective'. Organ Sci 15(6):617–632

58. Oltra MJ, Flor M (2003) The impact of technological opportunities and innovative capabilities on firms' output innovation'. Creat Innov Manag 12(3):137–144

59. Palmberg C (2004) The sources of innovation looking beyond technological opportunities. Econ Innov New Technol 13(2):183–197

60. Pavitt K (1991) 'What makes basic research economically useful?'. Res Policy 20:109–119

61. Penrose ET (1959) The theory of the growth of the firm. Wiley, New York

62. Rosenberg N (1982) Inside the black Box: technology and economics. Cambridge University Press, Cambridge

63. Rosenberg N (1994) Exploring the black Box: technology, economics and history. Cambridge University Press, Cambridge

64. Rosenkopf L, Nerkar A (2001) Beyond local research: boundary-spanning, exploration, and impact in the optical disk industry. Strateg Manag J 22(4):287–306

65. Salter A, McKelvey M (2016) Evolutionary analysis of innovation and entreprenuership: sidney G winter, recipient of the 2015 global award for entrepreneurship research. Small Bus Econ.

66. Scherer, F.M. (1965). 'Firm Size, Market Structure, Opportunity, and the Output of Patented Inventions', American Economic Review, LV, December, 1097–1125

67. Schumpeter J (1934) The theory of economic development. Harvard University Press, Cambridge

68. Schumpeter, J. A. (1942). Capitalism, Socialism and Democracy. Harper & Brothers. Reprint by George Allen & Unwin (Publishers Ltd)

69. Senker J (ed) (1999) Biotechnology and competitive advantage: Europe's firms and the US challenge. Edward Elgar, Cheltenham

70. Shane S (2000) Prior knowledge and the discovery of entrepreneurial opportunities. Organ Sci 11(4):448–469

71. Stankiewicz R (2002) The cognitive dynamics of biotechnology and the evolution of its technological systems. In: Carlsson B (ed) Technological systems in the Bio industries. Kluwer Academic Publishers, Boston, pp 35–52

72. Teece D (2007) Explicating dynamic capabilities: the nature of (sustainable) entreprise performance. Strateg Manag J 28(13):1319–1350

73. Teece DJ, Pisano G, Shuen A (1997) Dynamic capabilities and strategic management. Strateg Manag J 18(7):509–533

74. Utterback J (1994) Mastering the dynamics of innovation. Harvard Business School Press, Boston

75. Van den Bergh J, Gowdy J (2003) The microfoundations of macroeconomics: an evolutionary perspective. Camb J Econ 27:65–84

76. Vincenti WG (1990) What engineers know and how they know it. The Johns Hopkins University Press, Baltimore and London

77. Vincenti W (1994) 'Variation-selection in the innovation of the retractable airplane landing gear: the Northrop 'anomaly". Res Policy 23:575–582

78. Von Hippel E (1988) The sources of innovation. Oxford University Press, Oxford

79. Witt U (2010) How evolutionary is Schumpeter's theory of economic development. Ind Innov 9(2):7–22

9

CHINA'S STRUCTURAL TRANSFORMATION: REACHING POTENTIAL GDP IN THE FINANCIAL SERVICES SECTOR

Sara Hsu[1*] and Alba Carolina Melchor Simon[2]

[1] State University of New York at New Paltz, 600 Hawk Drive, JFT 804, New Paltz, NY 12561, USA.

[2] London School of Economics, London, England, UK.

ABSTRACT

China's economy faces the daunting challenge of shifting from a manufacturing-based economy to a service-based economy. Reforms in the services sector are slated to continue to take place in the coming years, including in the financial sector. In this paper, we explore China's success and challenges with structural change and then take a closer look at the financial services sector to find out where reforms have occurred, where the potential lies, and what the future will bring. We first describe structural change with regard to growth and TFP (total factor productivity), then as it applies to China. We examine China's financial services sector. Next, we calculate potential GDP of the financial services sector now and with the implementation of expected reforms. We find that, given even conservative estimates, the value added of the financial intermediation sector could double, as labor, capital, technology, and elasticity respond to liberalization policies. Whether potential GDP under reforms is reached is another question; therefore, we recommend that China both increase the pace of implementation, focusing in particular on reducing the oligopoly in the banking sector, increasing investment options by reforming its bond and equity markets, and enhancing innovation in the financial sphere while controlling for risk.

Keywords: China, Financial sector, Structural transformation, Banking

BACKGROUND

China's economy faces the daunting challenge of shifting from a manufacturing-based economy to a service-based economy. Reforms in the services sector are slated to continue to take place in the coming years, including in the financial sector. In this paper, we explore China's success and challenges with structural change, then take a closer look at the financial services sector to find out where reforms have occurred, where the potential lies, and what the future will bring. There is little written about the potential impacts of opening up China's financial sector on GDP and potential GDP, yet it is critical to understand the role that China's massive targeted structural change will have upon growth and other factors. This paper seeks to fill the gap in the literature on the economic impact China's financial service sector reforms can have.

Structural change is a complex process that transforms an economy in a basic manner. While China has been successful in transforming from an agricultural-based economy to a manufacturing-based economy, it is unclear to what extent China will be successful in moving to a service-based economy. China's financial sector in particular faces challenges since financial institutions are closely tied to the state, whose institutional structure has prevented improvements in efficiency.

Multiple reforms are expected to occur in the financial sector, but the current economic slowdown, coupled with enduring state interests, present barriers to change. Still, if the reforms were successful, they could potentially generate far more GDP than they do at present. Better productivity, greater employment, and more capital in the banking sector alone could lead to large economic gains. In what follows, we first describe structural change and TFP, as well as structural change as it applies to China, then examine China's financial services sector. Next, we calculate potential GDP of the financial services sector now and with the implementation of expected reforms. We conclude with policy recommendations.

Structural change, TFP, and growth

The relationship between economic growth, structural transformation and TFP has been examined to some extent in the literature. This relationship has been illustrated through different models and results in different conclusions depending on countries and sectors examined.

Bah and Brada (2009) estimate total factor productivity at the sectoral level, developing a model that estimates sectoral TFP from data on sectoral employment and GDP per capita, in order to examine structural change in Eastern Europe. The authors evaluate TFP in industry, service, and agriculture, finding that the former communist regimes in Eastern Europe have experienced structural change through the services sector, and that TFP is growing rapidly relative to that in Austria. Bah and Brada (2014) look at labor market developments in former communist nations of Eastern Europe and the Soviet Union, specifically studying the interaction between aggregate output and employment, and later analyzing the impact of privatization on employment outcomes in the context of sectoral restructuring.

Buera and Kaboski (2012) analyze the role of specialized high-skilled labor in service sector growth in the USA. The authors create a theory that reflects the shifting demand toward more skill-intensive output as productivity increases. This provides the link between skill accumulation and growth of the services sector.

Duarte and Restuccia (2010) examine sectoral labor productivity to explain structural transformation, finding that the productivity catch-up in industry, across countries and relative to the USA, explains about half the gains in productivity across countries. Using a general equilibrium model, the authors also conclude that low productivity in the services sector and lack of convergence explains stagnation observed across countries.

Ngai and Pissarides (2007) construct a model in which structural change is driven by sectoral labor reallocation dependent on rates of TFP growth. The authors find that on the balanced growth path, labor that produces consumer goods moves to sectors with low TFP growth rates, while employment shares of intermediate and capital goods remain constant. Acemoglu and Guerrieri (2008) analyze sectoral differences in factor proportions within a two-sector general equilibrium model, showing that as sectoral levels of TFP diverge or capital accumulates, structural change takes place. As in Ngai and Pissarides, Agemoglu, and Guerrieri show that structural change is driven by changes in the relative price of factors.

There is little written on the financial services sector per se and structural transformation. Much of the emphasis with respect to financial sector change is associated with regulatory reform and liberalization. This has been discussed with particular reference to developed economies, such as the USA, the UK, and Europe (see Volcker 2012, Bhatia 2007 and Riksbank 2015), especially in the wake of the global crisis, but not with reference to TFP or the structural transition to a service sector-based economy.

Structural change theory and application to China

Structural change is an essential, multi-faceted component of development. This is a broad term that implies some important assumptions. Most importantly, while stages of growth theories a la Rostow and others have been deemed too constricting in their approach, neglecting the variation, dynamics, and fluctuations experienced by developing economies, economists continue to view structural change as a movement from a primary sector-based economy to a manufacturing sector-based economy, and ultimately to a service-based economy, or from a traditional sector-based economy to a modern sector-based economy. The reason for this assumption is that structural change is thought to occur in conjunction with an upgrading of skills and capital, with a climb up the "ladder" of primary, secondary, and tertiary sectors largely coinciding with increasingly skill- and capital-intensive processes. This phenomenon has been applied to China in various ways.

Structural change in China has been analyzed across three sectors and across provinces, in the works of Fan, Fan and Robinson (2003), Fleisher and Yang (2003), Wu and Yao (2003), Heckman (2005), Au and Henderson (2006), Bhaumik and Estrin (2007), Bosworth and Collins (2008), and Gong and Lin (2008). Other works use a macroeconomic framework to describe reallocations between private firms and state-owned enterprises, as in Song et al. (2011) and Dekle and Vandenbroucke (2012).

China has successfully carried out the structural change from agriculture to industry, increasing total factor productivity in agriculture by 6.5 % annually between 1991 and 2009 (Cao and Birchenall 2013). Cao and Birchenall (2013) find that total factor productivity expansion in the agriculture sector explains most of the reorientation of output and employment toward rapid non-agricultural productivity growth. Movement away from a focus on the agricultural sector comprised an important stage of growth in most other countries. Reforms, which started with the agricultural sector, freed up agricultural labor as productivity rose.

Chen, Jefferson and Zhang (2011) use a stochastic frontier sectoral production function to examine total factor productivity growth and quantitative growth of inputs. The authors find that TFP growth exceeded quantitative growth of inputs since 1992, indicating a "structural bonus" as referred to in Timmer and Szirmai (2000), but that the contribution of TFP to output growth declines starting in 2001. Structural change embodied in reforms to factor markets and industrial structure heavily influenced the efficiency of factor allocation over the period in question. This is because factor markets were underdeveloped, and this became clear in particular after 2001. Industrial policies began to favor other, high-profit industries, such as high-tech and heavy industries, which were unable to absorb much labor.

Wang et al (2014) put forth a new structural decomposition analysis model, which interprets the changes in sectoral output production. The authors incorporate, among more traditional indicators of structural change, the ratio of final goods demand over total output. Analysis is applied to three periods, 1992–1997, a high growth phase, especially for the mechanical and electrical machinery sector; 1997–2002, a soft landing period, in which growth in the mechanical and electrical machinery sector slowed; and 2002–2006, an initial stage of a high growth period, which experienced a surge in the mechanical and electrical machinery sector, combined with declines in the contribution to growth of the agriculture and services sectors. Findings indicate that the driver of China's movement toward increased production of machinery and electrical equipment is external demand for export, while changes in production technology and import substitution have hindered structural change.

Jiang and Shi (2015) use an Eaton-Kortum model to discern total factor productivity differences across provinces. The authors find that different sectoral contributions by province indicate high migration barriers. They conclude that migration barriers actually expand the provincial manufacturing labor share, and that rich provinces gain less from inter-provincial trade than poor provinces.

Lee and Malin (2013) use a structural labor model of sector choice to find that 11 % of aggregate growth in output per worker between 1978 and 2004 can be explained by increased education, with most of the growth (9 %) stemming from sectoral reallocations of labor.

Relatedly, a sizeable literature exists on whether China has reached the Lewis turning point, moving from a period of surplus labor in the agricultural sector to a period of rising wages in the agricultural and industrial sectors. This literature indicates that China may have completed the first phase of development and moved into the second, modern sector stage. Scholars noticed in the late 2000s that wages were rising and that labor shortages in some coastal cities were presenting bottlenecks to production. This led to the rise of such literature, with some authors concluding that China has reached the turning point, and others finding that it has not. The discussion can be found in Zhang, Yang and Wang (2011), Zhu and Cai (2012), Cai and Du (2011), Golley and Meng (2011), Cai (2010), Yao and Zhang (2010), Minami and Ma (2010), and others.

While we do not discuss the Lewis turning point per se, the demographic implications of these studies are essential to understanding China's ability to undergo structural change to a service-based economy. What we can gather from these studies is that: (1) China's working age population has recently peaked; (2) demand for migrant workers remains high in the low-skilled modern urban sector; (3) China has entered a new stage of demographic transition, with an aging population, before it has become fully affluent or developed; and (4) improvements in human capital and technology are now more important than simple labor or capital inputs. China's financial sector is no exception to these conclusions. We next describe China's financial sector and discuss where it is heading.

China's financial sector

First, we must understand China's financial sector, its reform status, and where it is heading in order assess potential structural change in this industry. As is well known, China's financial sector continues to be dominated by a small number of major state-owned banks, while private banks play a minimal role. At the same time, demand for financing is high among underserved populations such as rural areas and small- and medium-sized enterprises. Financing constraints among the banking sector gave rise to the shadow banking sector after 2007, alternative methods of financing that sought to serve smaller and riskier borrowers. Leveling the playing field among banks and reducing regulations would increase competition and efficiency in this sector, and enhance the role of the financial industry in China's restructuring process. Not only would improving competition create employment in this sector, but reducing financing constraints would complement the growth of other industries.

China's Big Four banks, the Industrial and Commercial Bank of China, Bank of China, Agricultural Bank of China, and China Construction Bank, have far more market power over the financial industry than do the thousands of other financial institutions. The Big Four comprise 40–50 % of the bank loan market share and 93 % of banking sector market capital. The industry is therefore moderately oligopolistic. By contrast, foreign subsidiaries control only about 1 % of the market share. Barriers to entry in the financial sector are mainly explicit and implicit government preference.

The Big Four Banks, ironically, are less profitable, less efficient, and have lower asset quality than other types of banks (Lin and Zhang 2009; Fu and Heffernan 2009). In this way, these firms are atypical oligopolies as to some degree; they are tools of the state. China's banking structure contradicts the X-efficiency hypothesis, which says that more X-efficient banks have lower costs, higher profits, and larger market shares (Demsetz 1973, 1974). China's X-inefficiency increased between 1985 and 2002, especially among state-owned banks, indicating a rise in moral hazard (Fu and Heffernan 2009). China's banking structure also fails to support the relative scale-efficiency hypothesis, which finds that banks that are at the appropriate economy of scale will have lower costs and higher profits that can lead to greater market concentration (Lambson 1987).

Other banks include joint-stock commercial banks, policy banks, credit cooperatives, and urban commercial banks. All of these together comprise a little over half of lending activity in China. These institutions, along with the Big Four, are constrained by interest rate ceilings on deposits and lending quotas. Interest rate ceilings on deposits pinch the potential returns on savings that depositors may earn. In times of higher inflation, real returns on deposits have even turned out to be negative. Savers have few viable savings and investment outlets other than bank deposits, and the deposit interest rate ceiling reinforces their dissatisfaction with China's financial system. What is more, lending quotas may restrict the amount of loans that banks can lend.

In recent years, a sizeable shadow banking sector has grown up to serve institutions that cannot obtain loans from the formal banking sector. The shadow banking sector includes trust companies, internet lending platforms, credit guarantee companies, and other institutions, and products include wealth management and trust products, bankers' acceptance bills, and entrusted loans. Shadow banking encompasses means through which riskier and non-state firms can obtain loans, as the formal banking sector is constrained in its lending. Risks associated with the shadow banking sector are higher than in the banking system, as credit, liquidity, and solvency risks present substantial threats among institutions, products, and borrowers.

The bond market includes government and corporate bonds. Government bonds are issued by the MOF, and local governments and Central bank notes and Policy Bank bonds are most actively traded, but are purchased by state-owned banks. Corporate bonds incur large transaction costs during the issuance process and have been insufficiently rated by China's ratings agencies, leading to potential defaults of companies whose debt quality was overestimated. The stock market is the second largest in the world by equity value but is dominated by state-owned firms. Market prices are inefficient at present, as an asset price bubble looms.

Capital controls restrict interaction with the international financial sector. Controls over currency conversion and flows have been loosened, particularly in the current account, but persist in the capital account. The question is, however, to what extent do capital controls stand in the way of domestic financial reform? There are two answers to this: one is that allowing larger capital inflows for investment purposes would help to deepen China's financial system; while the other, contradicting, view, is that China's financial system is fragile and must be protected from larger capital inflows. Which argument would best support financial reform as measured by financial deepening?

Experience tells us that maintaining a fixed (even within a band) currency in conjunction with porous capital controls and a weak financial system can result in volatile capital flows, shocking the financial and then real economic sectors. However, if all of these elements are to be liberalized over time (and we do not underscore the many arguments in favor of liberalization here—see Eichengreen 2001 and Kose et al 2006 for discussion), there may be a period in which exposure to capital flows disrupts the economy. To combat this, economists have advocated for a proper order of financial liberalization. McKinnon (1993) is one of the heavyweights on the order of economic liberalization. He argues that one of the first orders of reform should be that interest rates are liberalized to reflect borrowing and lending costs, and that private debt contracts be enforced through the legal system. Chinn and Ito (2006) find that increasing financial openness contributes to the development of equity markets only after a threshold of strong legal systems and institutions is attained and after some development in the banking sector has also occurred. The authors also find that liberalization of cross-border goods is a precondition for liberalization of the capital account. In terms of order of capital and exchange rate liberalization, most scholars contend that first, the exchange rate and then the capital account should be liberalized (Eichengreen 2007). The argument is that liberalizing the exchange rate first can reduce speculative pressure.

Expanding flexibility of the exchange rate would ideally take place in periods of stability in exchange markets, and as a second best position, should occur when the domestic economy is strong and there are pressures for the currency to appreciate (Prasad, Rumbaugh, and Wang 2005, Eichengreen and Mussa 1998 and Agénor 2004).

Exchange rate liberalization will help to alleviate "hot money" inflows and outflows that increase as appreciation and depreciation expectations rise. However, there are dangers associated with this, including currency speculation, creation of adverse conditions for trade, fluctuation in the real value of foreign debt claims, and generation of inflation. The biggest challenge is maintaining financial stability and minimizing shocks. Currency speculations trigger a hostile environment of uncertainty. Investors will tend to shy away from investment. This uncertainty encourages consumer price volatility which is exacerbated by inflation. This is an adverse environment for trade and economic growth.

McKinnon (2006) points out that even (and especially) Chinese holders of US public debt may experience deterioration of their assets. Perhaps even more importantly, McKinnon and Schnabl (2012) state that China cannot fully float its currency since it will not be able to lend an amount sufficient to balance the trade surplus; the RMB would continue to appreciate unless the central bank stepped in to purchase dollars. China is seeking to expand lending in RMB through its Silk Road projects and participation in global lending institutions. Over time, this will provide China with further room in which to liberalize its exchange rate.

A more flexible exchange rate regime would permit China to support a more independent monetary policy, ensuring a buffer against domestic and external shocks that would reduce its vulnerability. In an ever more globalized world, where countries and economies are becoming more integrated, it is in China's own benefit to reduce its exposure to potential external macroeconomic shocks. The current overall exposure of the corporate sector and banks in China to foreign exchange risks appears to have been growing slowly as it has become an important player in the international arena. Prasad et al. (2005) however, advocate that China's banking system is "unlikely to be subject to substantial stress simply as a result of greater exchange rate flexibility."

China's titanic growth has been in great part a result of its trade flows and foreign direct investment (FDI) inflows. For this reason, many policymakers argue that a more flexible exchange rate would negatively influence these trade and FDI flows, hindering China's growth. On the other hand, studies from Clark, Tamirisa, and Wei (2004) believe that exchange rate volatility does not influence trade flows significantly. The renminbi's real value keeps a close eye on the dollar and maintains a stable exchange rate, whereas, with its other major trading counterparties, China allows greater exchange volatility. This behavior does not seem to prove an obstacle for China's expanding trade strategies in other countries. Furthermore, the benefits of enjoying macroeconomic stability that could emanate from increasing exchange rate flexibility could compensate and offset the effects of reduced trade flows. With a greater flexibility, the Chinese financial market would also grow deeper and stronger, together with the foreign exchange market.

It is important to note that China need not fully liberalize its exchange rate in order to create more room for a consumption and market-based economy. China may choose to follow the example of a nation like South Korea, which has a weakly managed float in place in order to smooth volatility rather than to manipulate exchange rates. China may reduce its control over the currency by decreasing intervention in the foreign exchange market.

Capital account liberalization will help to reduce interest rate differentials between China and other nations, but this may destabilize the economy where large interest rate differentials persist. Currency appreciation expectations may surge given rapid capital inflows, and some basic controls must be put into place to prevent this from occurring.

Barriers to reform of the financial system are many, but some of the most pressing include leveling the playing field to make banks outside the Big Four more competitive, fully allowing interest rates to reflect market forces and improving the credit scoring system. Measures to liberalize interest rates are under way; while the lending floor was lifted in July 2013 and a new prime lending rate was created in October 2013, steps to remove the deposit rate ceilings are under way. The PBOC implemented deposit insurance in May 2015 in order to ensure that once deposit interest rate ceilings are lifted, depositors are protected from risky competitive behavior engaged in by banks. China is also in the process of implementing a social credit score to rate individuals and firms based on the credit history and other data. This is expected to be rolled out in 2017. Local provincial governments are collecting credit information as well to improve lending at to local institutions.

Banks suffer from some issues with non-performing loans, although the Ministry of Finance is able to combat this problem by using asset management companies to purchase non-performing loans. Foreign competition is also restricted.

China's leadership is well aware of the need for changes and has laid out an ambitious reform agenda for the financial sector. China's reform agenda aims to:

open up the financial sector by allowing small private banks to emerge;

- promote bond and equity finance;
- improve insurance compensation process;
- bring about inclusive finance;
- promote financial innovation;
- increase exchange and interest rate liberalization;
- increase capital account liberalization;
- regulate capital flows within a macroprudential framework;
- enhance financial regulation; and
- reform financial institutions' exit mechanism.

Most banking reforms that have already been carried out have not radically changed the sector's market structure. Banking reforms include the following.

Small-scale reforms have also worked to provide finance to smaller borrowers in order to make finance more inclusive. Although some P2P firms have engaged in risky lending, other internet firms such as Eloan.cn have worked to provide small-scale finance to SMEs and rural borrowers.

Foreign entry into China's financial sector began in 2006 as part of China's commitment to the WTO agreement. Foreign bank activity is highly restricted by Chinese regulators. Limitations include lending and deposit constraints, foreign exchange constraints, large capital requirements, and murky regulatory framework (PWC 2014).

Date	Policy	Description
7/1/ 2013	Guidelines on Financial Support for Economic Restructuring, Transformation and Upgrading	Allows some changes in capital investment structure
7/26/ 2013	Guiding Opinions on Strengthening Financing Services to Support SMEs	Requires government agencies to enhance financing to SMEs
8/8/ 2013	Implementation Opinion on Providing Financial Support for Small and Micro Enterprises	Provides new financing options to SMEs
8/30/ 2013	Guidelines on Protecting Rights and Interests of Consumers	Requires banks to improve governance to protect consumer rights
9/27/ 2013	Measures on Consumer Finance Pilots	Creates 10 consumer finance business pilots
11/8/ 2013	Guidance on Commercial Banks Issuing Corporate Bonds to Replenish Capital	Allows listed commercial banks to issue corporate bonds
1/6/ 2014	Notice on Issues Concerning Strengthening the Supervision on Shadow Banking	Focuses on stabilizing shadow banking
2/14/ 2014	General Plan for the Qingdao Wealth Management Comprehensive Reform Pilot	Creates a pilot zone to encourage wealth management zone
2/14/ 2014	Measures for the Administration of Service Prices of Commercial Banks	Regulates commercial banks' service prices
2/19/ 2014	Circular on the Reapproval of Charging Standards of Supervision Fees for the Banking Sector	Changes standards on collecting fees for banks
2/20/ 2014	Administrative Measures for the Liquidity Risk of Commercial banks	Implements measure to assess liquidity risk
2/27/ 2014	Credit Industry Management Act	Calls for social credit information system
3/17/ 2014	Regulations on Financial Leasing Companies	Clarifies operating rules for financial leasing industry
3/27/ 2014	Opinions on Accelerating the Construction of Microenterprise and Rural Credit Systems	Creates credit risk system for micro and rural enterprises
7/24/ 2014	Notice on Improving and Innovating Loans to Small and Micro Enterprises to Improve the Financial Services to Small and Micro Enterprises	Improves loans to small enterprises
7/25/ 2014	CBRC Approvals to create Qianhai Weizhong Bank, Wenzhou Private Bank, and Tianjin Jincheng Private Bank	Establishes three private banks
9/26/ 2014	CBRC Approvals to create Shanghai Huarui Private Bank and Zhejiang Web Commercial Bank	Establishes private banks

The capital account has been opened to a limited extent under the QFII and QDII programs. Qualified Domestic Retail Investor (QDRI) and Qualified Domestic Individual Investor (QDII2) programs are also in the making. Under the Qualified Domestic Individual Investor scheme, individuals in Guangzhou and Shenzhen (at present) can purchase securities listed on the Hong Kong market. These investors are required to have at least 1.5 million RMB in financial assets. The Qualified Domestic Retail Investor program, still in the planning stage, would allow citizens to invest in overseas stocks and properties.

Through the Qualified Domestic Institutional Investor system, mainland institutions can invest in foreign exchange products. Approved financial institutions may purchase and sell foreign currency or RMB-denominated financial products to mainland investors. Such products include money market instruments, fixed income products, equity products, mutual funds, and structured products.

The Shanghai-Hong Kong Stock Connect which opened in April 2014 now allows cross-border stock investment between the Shanghai and Hong Kong stock exchanges, but had a limited impact. Funds will soon be added to sales of cross-border shares through the Shanghai-Hong Kong Stock Connect, and a Shenzhen-Hong Kong Stock connect is expected open at the end of 2015. However, strong deviation in prices for the same stocks sold in Shanghai and Hong Kong has revealed lack of market efficiency as well as lack of investor sophistication.

Some exchange rate reform has also been carried out. More substantive recent reform measures include reforming foreign exchange management under companies' capital accounts, expanding multinational use of foreign exchange, setting up pilot zones in which foreign companies can convert foreign capital into RMB (US-China Business Council 2015). Less impactful reforms include promotion of the foreign currency cash business, simplification of cross-border foreign exchange guarantee, providing instructions to government bodies on how to expand foreign trade, clarifying procedures in foreign exchange settlement, and allowing foreign invested banks to convert currency for operating capital.

The Shanghai Pilot Free Trade Zone is an example of one of China's initiatives to implement economic and social reforms in a controlled manner. As announced by the State Administration of Foreign Exchange (SAFE) Shanghai branch on 28 February 2014, the Shanghai Free Trade Zone will allow yuan convertibility and unrestricted foreign currency exchange. Furthermore, it will also permit a tax-free period of 10 years for the businesses in the area as a means to simplify the process of FDI and facilitate the management of capital accounts.

In a nutshell, the Shanghai FTZ's aim is to facilitate and encourage business. The main benefits entities within the Shanghai FTZ will benefit from are listed below (McBride 2014).

1. Simplified cross-border payment procedures—Shanghai FTZ entities can open capital accounts without prolonged government foreign exchange (FX) registration approvals, and banks are now authorized to carry out FX registration and Renminbi (RMB) cross-border settlement directly.

2. Free trade accounts—Shanghai FTZ entities can open free trade accounts (FTA) and transfer funds freely between FTAs, other offshore accounts, and onshore non-resident accounts.

3. Loosening of control over cross-border finance—controls over outbound security and FX finance have been relaxed so Shanghai FTZ entities may now borrow offshore RMB funds subject to

certain requirements (for example, limits on the use of such offshore RMB funds and maturity profile).

4. RMB convertibility—Shanghai FTZ entities enjoy full capital account RMB convertibility along with the benefits of future FX reforms (for example, FIEs can immediately convert foreign exchange into RMB and utilize RMB hedging, whereas a non-Shanghai FTZ FIE must wait until there is a commercial contract requiring hard currency payment before it can make the conversion).

5. Deposit rate liberalization—Shanghai FTZ entities may be offered higher interest rates for foreign exchange and RMB deposits with banks due to the loosening of the statutory interest rate limits.

However, there is some distance between the current reforms and reform targets and where the financial sector would be to maximize GDP growth. First, the Big Four banks' oligopoly should be ended by eliminating policy favoritism and implicit government guarantees. A much better information mechanism needs to be implemented to judge risk and return, particularly for small and medium sized enterprises, which provide most of China's economic growth but remain extremely credit constrained. These two banking-specific reforms in and of themselves would require massive reorientation of the banking sector to implement. Government projects should rely less on the Big Four banks for funding and seek other types of financing, including tax revenue funding, bond financing (in which bonds would be held by the public rather than mainly banks), and perhaps loans from designated institutions such as the Policy Banks. Breaking up the Big Four oligopoly is not even on the reform agenda, but reducing market share of these institutions would go a long way to freeing up finance for other types of firms.

Development of the bond market is also quite nascent and will take massive effort to truly marketize and expand. Well-functioning bond markets are prerequisites for relaxing capital controls and are channels of transmission for an interest rate-led monetary policy. China's bond market has been growing in leaps and bounds: bond issues are on the rise; market capitalization is expanding substantially; turnover in the secondary market is surging; and the number and variety of market participants and instruments are rapidly increasing. After more than 10 years of development, China's bond market is now the third largest in the world at about RMB 35.89 trillion, or about USD 4.24 trillion.

China has two bond markets: the interbank bond market, which is regulated by the People's Bank of China (PBOC), and the Exchange bond market, which is regulated by the China Securities Regulatory Commission (CSRC).

The interbank market plays the leading role, accounting for more than 95 % of total trading volume.

Commercial banks dominate trading activity in China's interbank bond market, accounting for around 70 % of trading volume (Goldman Sachs 2015). Foreign investors may access the Chinese bond market through two programs. The first program is the Qualified Foreign Institutional Investor (QFII) program, which allows foreign investors access to both the Exchange bond market and the interbank bond market. The other program was launched in 2010 to allow three types of offshore institutions to invest in China's largely closed interbank bond market. The qualified institutions include: foreign central banks, lenders in Hong Kong and Macao that have already conducted renminbi clearing, and overseas banks involved in renminbi cross-border trade settlement.

When taking a look at China's fiscal and social landscape, there is pressure to increase public expenditure to cover welfare benefits of an aging population. The population also demands higher investments in education, the health system, and labor protection. These expenditures cannot be financed merely through tax receipts. Thus, the supply of public bonds would need to rise to meet these demands (Aglietta 2007). In an attempt to boost demand for its bonds, China has also been allowing more foreign institutional investors to trade on its interbank market. The decision to eliminate quotas on interbank trading leads to opening up the bond market and the capital account, but much more will need to be done to truly develop China's financial markets. Essential reforms require better ratings of bonds and better information management.

An important feature of China's financial development is its stock market growth since 1991. The Chinese government is highly engaged in fostering a stock market that can compete with those of developed countries. In order to achieve this objective, the Chinese Government is committed to apply reforms that affect share issue privatization (SIP), the reform of non-tradable shares, the reform of firms' access to the capital market, the regulation of financial intermediaries, the refinement of the legal system governing the capital market, the convergence of Chinese accounting standards with IFRS (International Financial Reporting Standards), and audit market reforms.

According to Megginson and Netter, 2001; Gupta, 2005; Shleifer, 1998, share issue privatization (SIP), in which the government sells shares in state-owned enterprises (SOEs) to private investors, has been the most profitable and successful method of privatization since it has contributed to increase firm's efficiency.

The development and growth of the Chinese stock market must be studied in the context of the "partial privatization" of SOEs in the 1990s. At the beginning of the 1980s, the Chinese Government launched the SOE reform aiming to decentralize the central government's managerial decision rights in SOEs. In the following decade, the SOEs became partially privatized and began to issue new and minority shares to individual investors, who could trade their shares freely on the newly developed Shanghai and Shenzhen stock markets (set up in early 1990 and 1991, respectively).

The idea was to give birth to a stock market that was representative of the different geographical regions and industries in China. The central government decided which subset of SOEs was to be selected and listed. Due to this partial privatization process, the government could no longer sell controlling stake in the firms. The shares held by public investors became freely tradable on the stock market, while the shares held by the state and legal persons were still not tradable.

Lu and Fu (2014) describe China's privatization strategy as a two-step approach. The first step is "partial" privatization, which involves SOEs selling a minority stake to public investors which are listed on the stock market, while the majority of stakes are still owned by the State. The second step is known as "complete" privatization, in which the government sells its controlling rights in selected SOEs to private investors. Chinese listed companies can be grouped into SOEs controlled by state asset management bureaus (SAMBs), SOEs affiliated to the central government, and SOEs affiliated to the local government (Chen, Firth, and Xu, 2009).

The question of capital account opening is difficult to answer—to what extent must the capital account be opened to induce growth without bringing on too much financial fragility? The banking system continues to be underdeveloped and is unable to effectively handle risk and return. If the capital account is liberalized and foreign capital surges into the banking system, there is a good chance that excessive risk will build up in this sector since channels for obtaining information on borrowers are insufficient. The same is true for capital inflows into the bond and equity markets, which continue to be controlled in the types of firms that can finance through these means, which is not based on risk and return per se. Capital outflows may result in the collapse of the banking system, which is dependent on funding from deposits.

If the banking, equity, and bond markets were not constrained, the foreign financial inflows may help to boost growth by funding promising projects. Even so, foreign capital inflows can also result in currency overvaluation under a liberalized exchange rate regime and repress export growth. Further, even though economic theory states that foreign finance will expand the funds available for investment and growth in a developing country, the relationship between external finance and growth is in practice not guaranteed. For example, Aizenmann, Pinto and Radziwill (2004) find that for the 1990s, countries that self-financed enjoyed higher growth rates than countries that had lower levels of self-financing. Prasad, Rajan, and Subramanian (2007) provide evidence that developing countries that rely more on foreign finance have not grown faster in the long run. The question of capital controls and their growth-distance from capital account liberalization remains unresolved and we can choose to leave it out of the equation.

It is possible that capital account and exchange rate liberalization can generate growth but also uncertainty and volatility, which may present negative shocks. We therefore examine the potential GDP in China's financial sector while focusing on assessing and increasing domestic production inputs while leaving opening up reforms to later research. We now turn to the model to assess potential growth in the financial sector, given the present reform trajectory.

Methods: modeling financial sector potential

We calculate potential GDP of the financial sector at present and compare it to the current GDP to find the output gap at the current level of reform. We also calculate potential GDP based on assumptions for labor, capital, and TFP given current reforms and then draw a comparison between the "before" and "after" reform scenarios.

To calculate potential GDP, we use the production function approach followed by CBO (2001) and Roeger (2006) (and many others) which is rooted in economic theory. This uses a combination of factor inputs multiplied with the technological level. We use the Cobb-Douglas production function to illustrate potential GDP.

$$Y = (U_L L E_L)^{\alpha}(U_K L K)^{1-\alpha} = L^{\alpha}K^{1-\alpha} * \text{TFP} \quad (1)$$

where labor L and capital K, checked by excess capacity U_L, U_K and adjusted for efficiency E_L, E_K determine production Y. Total factor productivity, TFP, is given by

$$\text{TFP} = (E_L^{\alpha} E_K^{1-\alpha})(U_L^{\alpha} U_K^{1-\alpha}). \quad (2)$$

This equation shows to what extent factors of production are used as well as their efficiency or technological level.

We use total wage bill for the financial intermediation sector as a measure of labor input, assuming that the wage bill reflects a real measure of work rather than greed. While we do know the number of employees for the financial intermediation sector and could calculate the hours worked based on this, this would also be an estimate as we would have to assume weeks and hours worked per year and week, respectively. Also, when we compare the two figures, TFP for analysis using the wage bill is more realistic than for hours worked.

For simplicity, we assume constant returns to scale, which reflects China's banking sector reality, as rigorously tested in Fu and Heffernan (2008). We use numbers from Chow and Li (2002) and Chow (2008) for the Chinese economy as a whole, which shows that elasticity of labor α is 0.4 and elasticity of capital 1-α is 0.6.

For the capital stock, we use the Penn World Tables Capital Stock table for China which assumes a 3.1 % rate of depreciation. This uses the perpetual inventory method as the capital stock becomes a weighted sum of previous capital stock investments. We must still determine the capital stock in the financial sector. We approximate this by multiplying the capital stock by the ratio of the financial sector output to total output (GDP).

$$I = is * YPOT \tag{3}$$

$$K = I + (1 - dep)K(-1)^2 \tag{4}$$

RESULTS

Using figures from 2011, we find that TFP is 1.0345 if the capital stock is proportionately used (proportion of capital stock used by the financial sector is found in terms of the ratio financial sector value added to GDP), 1.563 if half the proportional capital stock is used, and 2.3767 if one quarter the proportional capital stock is used. The capital stock estimate includes not only machinery but also computers and software, which are intensively used in the financial sector. Therefore, we do not believe the capital stock is lower than ¼ the proportional capital stock.

Since we are working only with the financial sector rather than with the economy as a whole, we can make various estimations of total potential financial labor force without using the NAIRU and labor force projections for the economy as a whole. Still, we must come up with a rational projection for the financial sector. Current statistics state that there were 5,053,000 employees in financial intermediation in 2011. These employees are mainly college educated.

The rate of unemployment in China is low. Still, among college graduates, unemployment is relatively higher than among other demographic groups (about 7 million graduates). If 1/20 of these college graduates (say) were employed in the financial sector, an additional 350,000 workers could be added if the jobs were available. For capital, we assume that ½ the proportionate capital is currently utilized and that if all proportionate capital were utilized, the potential capital stock would be twice as large. TFP is therefore assumed to be 1.563.

We can then use these equations to calculate potential GDP in China's financial sector, and find that it is 3,782,925 million RMB under our assumptions.

The next step is to determine how further reforms would affect potential GDP in the financial sector. The reform with the largest impact includes encouraging financial innovation, if risks are appropriately controlled for. The impact of other reforms depends on how they are carried out. First, opening up the financial sector by allowing small private banks to emerge will likely have little impact on any factors unless many small private banks are allowed to emerge.

Second, bond and equity finance has a long way to go in terms of truly boosting value added of the financial industry, so it is unlikely that it will contribute very much in the short run. Over time, it is possible that the bond market in particular can be overhauled (the equity market is currently taking backward steps after government intervention). Third, bringing about inclusive finance may be successful if it promotes employment and output of SMEs, and this may result in increasing labor elasticity to some degree. Fourth, promoting financial innovation may increase the elasticity of labor and capital, and will also likely enhance total factor productivity if it introduces more productivity than risk.

Fifth, increasing exchange rate, capital account, and interest rate liberalization may have varied effects. Exchange rate and capital account liberalization will depend very much on whether they properly control for risk and do not remove value added rather than contributing to it. How much these would contribute to labor, capital, and overall value added in China's domestic economy is really a question. There is less debate about interest rate liberalization, as it appears that more market-based interest rates would increase efficiency of the financial sector.

Sixth, regulating capital flows within a macroprudential framework, enhancing financial regulation, and reforming financial institutions' exit mechanism may increase the efficiency of labor and capital and also prevent losses that might otherwise occur.

In order to calculate potential GDP under the implementation of reforms, we assume slightly increasing returns for labor and capital combined and somewhat larger labor and capital values. We can also assume a small increase in total factor productivity. Suppose that structural change allows for more people to be employed in the financial sector as more jobs are created, and along with them, the capital stock is built up. We assume that structural change boosts labor, capital, and TFP by 10 %, and that elasticity of capital and labor rise by 0.01 %. This seems reasonable based on the current reform agenda, as quantity and quality of productive inputs are likely to be increased if all reforms are carried out.

After performing calculations, we find that potential GDP of China's financial sector under these conditions is 5,780,761 million RMB. This is a 53 % increase over the current potential GDP and a 132 % increase over the current actual GDP.

We do not capture indirect value created by the financial sector in this article. However, we note that the financial sector is a core component of the economy because it provides financial capital to the rest of the economy, which multiplies through the economy as wages are paid and consumed. The larger impact of the financial sector is even greater, such that a 53 or 132 % increase in GDP created within the financial sector will result in even greater value added.

DISCUSSION AND POLICY RECOMMENDATIONS

China is on the road to financial reform, albeit at a gradual pace. If the nation were to implement all of its planned reforms in the financial sector, it could increase GDP and boost the contribution of services to output. Still, China has yet to implement many of the reforms, and must increase its pace in order to accomplish its target outcomes.

First, China should focus on reducing the oligopoly of its largest banks in order to increase competition and efficiency within the banking sector. As a result of this, smaller private banks can be encouraged and have a greater chance of survival. This can also help to promote inclusive finance. Marketization of the banking sector can also be further enhanced by liberalizing deposit interest rates, allowing banks to pay consumers properly for their savings. This is critically important as alternative savings and investment channels are opened up to consumers, and will help banks to maintain their deposit holdings.

Second, China must attempt to increase investment options by reforming its bond and equity sectors. As we have seen from the equity market boom and bust in the summer of 2015, which was fraught with government intervention, the market is not rational and also does not sufficiently reflect firms that provide the greatest sources of growth. Many changes must be made in the bond and equity markets before these can become viable sources of yield.

Third, innovation can be an important source of growth, but can also risky. Proper risks must be controlled for as financial regulation is enhanced, and as failing financial institutions are given a proper exit mechanism. This will help to check risk in the financial sector and allow reforms to flourish.

Without the implementation of these planned reforms, as we can see from our model, output creation in the financial sector will remain relatively low. China's slow progress in the direction of these reforms is positive, but at this pace, the full financial reform agenda will not be realized in the near future.

CONCLUSIONS

China is going through a large structural change. Part of the process includes reforming the oligopolistic banking sector and other aspects of the financial system. While the reform agenda is ambitious, relatively slow progress has been made on this list.

In this paper, we have modeled China's current GDP and potential GDP contribution of the financial sector, as well as its potential GDP, given planned reforms. We find that, given even conservative estimates, the value added of the financial intermediation sector could double, as labor, capital, technology, and elasticity respond to liberalization policies. Whether potential GDP under reforms is reached is another question; therefore, we recommend that China both increase the pace of implementation, focusing in particular on reducing the oligopoly in the banking sector, increasing investment options by reforming its bond and equity markets, and enhancing innovation in the financial sphere while controlling for risk.

Further study may include analysis of ways in which the manufacturing sector can benefit from financial sector liberalization, and analyses of the potential impacts of other service subsector liberalization on potential GDP.

DECLARATIONS

Competing interests

The authors declare that they have no competing interests.

Authors' contributions

SH conceived and drafted the manuscript, AS helped draft the manuscript. Both authors read and approved the final manuscript.

REFERENCES

1. Acemoglu D, Guerrieri V (2008) Capital deepening and nonbalanced economic growth. J Pol Econ 116(3):467–498
2. Agénor P-R (2004) "Orderly Exits from Adjustable Pegs and Exchange Rate Bands: Policy Issues and Role of Capital Flows", Global Development Finance Report 2004 Background Study. World Bank, Washington
3. Aglietta M, Maarek P (2007) Developing the bond market in China: The next step forward in financial reform. Economie Internationale 3(111):29–53.
4. Aizenman J, Brian P, Artur R (2004) Sources for financing domestic capital—is foreign saving a viable option for developing countries? Working Paper 10624. National Bureau of Economic Research (July), Cambridge, Mass
5. Au and Henderson (2006) How migration restrictions limit agglomeration and productivity in China. J Dev Econ 80: 350-388
6. Bah E-h, Brada J (2009) Total factor productivity growth, structural change and convergence in transition economies. Comp Econ Stud 51:421–446
7. Bah E-h, Brada J (2014) Labor markets in the transition economies: an overview. Eur J Comp Econ 11(1):3–53
8. Bhatia AV (2007) N ew landscape, new challenges: structural change and regulation in the U.S. financial sector. IMF Working Paper 07/195
9. Bhaumik and Estrin (2007) How transition paths differ: enterprise performance in Russia and China. J Dev Econ 82(2): 374-392
10. Bosworth and Collins (2008) Accounting for growth: comparing China and India. J Econ Perspect 22(1): 45-66
11. Buera FJ, Kaboski JP (2012) The rise of the service economy. Am Econ Rev 102(6):2540–69
12. Cai F (2010) Demographic transition, demographic dividend, and Lewis turning point in China. China Econ J 3(2):107–119
13. Cai F, Yang D (2011) Wage increases, wage convergence, and the Lewis turning point in China. China Econ Rev 22:601–610
14. Cao KH, Birchenall JA (2013) Agricultural productivity, structural change, and economic growth in post-reform China. J Dev Econ 104:165–180

15. CBO (2001) CBO's method for estimating potential output: an update., CBO Paper, http://www.cbo.gov/sites/default/files/potentialoutput.pdf

16. Chen G, Firth M, Xu L (2009) Does the type of ownership control matter? Evidence from China's listed companies. J Bank Finance 33:171–181.

17. Chinn MD, Ito H (2006) What matters for financial development? Capital controls, institutions, and interactions. J Dev Econ 81(1):163–192

18. Chow GC (2008) Another look at the rate of increase in TFP in China. J Chin Econ Bus Stud 6(2):219–24

19. Chow GC, Li K-W (2002) China's economic growth: 1952-2010. Econ Dev Cult Change 51(1):247–56

20. Clark P, Tamirisa N, Wei SJ (2004) Exchange Rate Volatility and Trade Flows - Some New Evidence. IMF Working Paper May 2004

21. Dekle R, Vandenbroucke G (2012) A quantitative analysis of China's structural transformation. J Econ Dyn Control 36(1):119–135

22. Demsetz H (1973) Industry structure, market rivalry, and public policy. J Law Econ 16:1–9

23. Demsetz H (1974) Two systems of belief about monopoly. In: Goldschmid H (ed) Industrial Concentration: The New Learning. Little, Brown, Boston

24. Duarte M, Restuccia D (2010) The role of the structural transformation in aggregate productivity. Q J Econ 125(1):129–173

25. Eichengreen BJ (2001) Capital account liberalization: what do the cross-country studies tell us? World Bank Econ Rev 15:341–66

26. Eichengreen B, Michael M (1998) "Exit Strategies: Policy Options for Countries Seeking Greater Exchange Rate Flexibility," IMF Occasional Paper No. 168. International Monetary Fund, Washington, DC

27. Eichengreen B, China's Exchange Rate Regime: The Long and Short of It (2007) Chapter in calomiris, Charles W. China's financial transition at a crossroads. Columbia University Press, New York

28. Fan, Zhang and Robinson (2003) Structural change and economic growth in China. Rev Dev Econ 7(3): 360-377

29. Fleisher and Yang (2003) Labor laws and regulations in China. China Econ Rev 14(4): 426-433

30. Fu X, Heffernan S (2008) Economies of scale and scope in China's banking sector. Appl Financ Econ 18(5):345–356

31. Fu X, Heffernan S (2009) The effects of reform on China's bank structure and performance. J Bank Finance 33(2009):39–52

32. Golley J, Meng X (2011) Has China run out of surplus labour? China Econ Rev 22:555–572

33. Gong and Lin (2008) Deflationary expansion: an overshooting perspective to the recent business cycle in China. China Econ Rev 19(1): 1-17

34. Goldman S (2015) FAQ: China's Bond Market. Global Liquidity Management Report, First Half 2015

35. Gupta N (2005) Partial Privatization and Firm Performance, Journal of Finance 60, 987–1015

36. Heckman (2005) China's human capital investment. China Econ Rev 16(1): 50-70

37. Jiang Z and Shi H (2015) Sectoral technological progress, migration barriers, and structural change in China. J Comp Econ 43(2):257–273

38. Kose, M. A., E. Prasad, K. Rogoff, and S. J. Wei. 2006. Financial globalization: a reappraisal. Working Paper No. 12484, Natl Bureau Econ Res

39. Lambson VE (1987) Is the concentration–profit correlation partly an artefact of lumpy technology? Am Econ Rev 77:731 733

40. Lee S, Malin BA (2013) Education's role in China's structural transformation. J Dev Econ 101:148–166

41. Lin X, Zhang Y (2009) Bank ownership reform and bank performance in China. J Bank Finance 33:20–29

42. Lu, Haitian and Fu, Jiajia (2014) Structural changes in the Chinese stock market: a review of empirical research. China Account Finance Rev 16(2)39–65

43. McKinnon RI (1993) The order of economic liberalization. Johns Hopkins University Press, Baltimore, MD

44. McKinnon, Ronald I (2006) China's exchange rate trap: Japan redux? Stanford institute for economic policy research, April

45. McKinnon RI, Schnabl G (2012) China and its dollar exchange rate: a worldwide stabilizing influence? World Econ 35(6):667–693

46. McBride P (2014) China opening more doors with the Shanghai Free Trade Zone. http://www.kwm.com/en/es/ knowledge/ insights/china-opening-more-doors-with-the-shanghai-free-tradezone-20141014

47. Megginson WL, Netter JM (2001) From State to Market: A Survey of Empirical Studies on Privatization. J Econ Lit 39(2):321–389

48. Minami R, Ma X (2010) The Lewis turning point of Chinese economy: comparison with Japanese experience. China Econ J 3(2):163–179

49. Ngai LR, Pissarides CA (2007) Structural change in a multisector model of growth. Am Econ Rev 97(1):429–443

50. Prasad E, Rumbaugh T, Wang Q (2005) Putting the Cart Before the Horse? Capital Account Liberalization and Exchange Rate Flexibility in China. IMF Policy Discussion Paper

51. Prasad ES, Rajan RG, Subramanian A (2007) Foreign Capital and Economic Growth. NBER Working Paper 13619

52. PWC (2014) Foreign banks in China 2013., www.pwccn.com

53. Riksbank S (2015) Structural changes in the Swedish financial system. Riksbank Studies, February

54. Roeger W (2006) The production function approach to calculating potential growth and output gaps: estimates for EU Member States and the US. Paper prepared for the workshop on Perspectives on potential output and productivity growth, organised by Banque de France and Bank of Canada

55. Song Z, Storesletten K, Zilibotti F (2011) Growing like China. Am Econ Rev 101(1):201–241

56. Shleifer A (1998) State Versus Private Ownership. J Econ Perspect 12:133–150

57. Timmer MP, Szirmai A (2000) Productivity growth in Asian manufacturing: the structural bonus hypothesis reexamined. Struct Change Econ Dyn 11:371–392

58. US-China Business Council (2015) USCBC China Economic Reform Scorecard—"Mixed Signals."., https://www.uschina.org/reports/china-economic-reform-scorecard-february-2015

59. Volcker P (2012) Unfinished business in financial reform. Int Finance 15(1):125–135

60. Wang F, Dong B, Yin X, An C (2014) China's structural change: a new SDA model. Econ Model 43:256–266

61. Wu and Yao (2003. Intermigration and intramigration in China: a theoretical and empirical analysis. China Econ Rev 14(4): 371-385

62. Yang Y, Zhang K (2010) Has China passed the Lewis turning point? A structural estimation based on provincial data. China Econ J 3(2):155–162

63. Zhang X, Jin Y, Shenglin W (2011) China has reached the Lewis turning point. China Econ Rev 22(Issue 4):542–554

64. Zhu A, Cai W (2012) The Lewis turning point in China and its impacts on the world economy. AUGUR Working Paper, February 2012 (WP #1)

10

APPROACHING A NEOCLASSICAL SCENARIO: THE LABOR MARKET IN CHINA AFTER THE LEWIS TURNING POINT

Fang Cai

Institute of Population and Labor Economics, Chinese Academy of Social Sciences, Beijing 100732, China

ABSTRACT

As China passes through its Lewis turning point characterized first by the appearance of a labor shortage and a constant increase in wages, its labor market shows both features of the dual economy and neoclassical growth. This paper first depicts the trend of population as a root cause of the labor market transition from dual economy to neoclassical scenario. It then reveals the changed labor market profile - the labor shortage and wage increase. By examining three major groups of employment, namely, migrant workers, university graduates, and urban vulnerable workers, it tries to explore those unique characteristics of the labor market in such a transitional period and draws policy implications.

Keywords: Demographic transition Lewis turning point Labor market institutions

INTRODUCTION

The three chief characteristics of a neoclassical scenario of the labor market, which I contrast with a dualistic scenario of the labor market such as described by Lewis (1954), are (1) wage is determined by marginal productivity of labor, (2) the labor market can correct its own disequilibrium in labor supply and demand over the long run, and (3) there are only three basic types of unemployment - cyclical, frictional, and structural - all of which need to be addressed with macroeconomic and labor market policies.

For some time, the Chinese economy has exemplified a dual economy characterized by unlimited labor supply, subsistence wages, and the existence of institutional barriers to labor mobility, as well as the resultant difficulty in labor market clearing. Consequently, employment issues in China were understood exclusively in Lewisian, and never in neoclassical terms. Since the implementation of reform and opening, and in particular China's entry into the WTO in the new millennium, an enormous number of surplus laborers from rural areas have migrated to coastal cities to take up non-agricultural jobs. It was not until very recently that the Lewis turning point arrived, signaled by widespread labor shortage and constant wage increases, particularly for unskilled workers, and facilitated by both demand and supply factors, such as demographic trends and strong growth of employment in urban areas.

While China is moving away from an unlimited supply of labor and toward a neoclassical labor market scenario, today's employment problems show both neoclassical and dual economy characteristics. Some of the more prominent of these problems are (1) underemployment in the agricultural sectors has yet to be alleviated, (2) the worsening of cyclical unemployment, especially among migrant workers, (3) a higher degree of vulnerability among young people and older workers in urban areas than other groups to forms of natural unemployment, including structural and frictional unemployment, and (4) inadequate protection for workers' rights, including those relating to wage negotiation and labor disputes.

This paper illustrates how China's recent demographic trends, together with fast economic growth and employment expansion, have reshaped the country's employment landscape, which is characterized no longer by unlimited supply but by a near-equilibrium one. In response to this shift, we must also fundamentally change the way we understand China's employment problems and the challenges policy-makers face. In addition to promoting employment, increasingly, policies must try to address problems of cyclical and natural unemployment, particularly among those who have been hardest hit by the transition and as such are especially vulnerable.

In this paper we highlight key employment issues in China by looking closely at three distinct groups: migrant workers, college graduates, and the urban working vulnerable. Each of these groups faces its own set of employment-related difficulties. Migrant workers are prone to be affected by cyclical unemployment because when the urban labor markets tighten due to economic slowdowns, many of them end up returning to agriculture work, which is a form of underemployment. College graduates are most vulnerable to structural and frictional unemployment, which partly explains why unemployment rates are often higher among this group than among some other groups. Thirdly, the vulnerability of vulnerable workers in urban areas is due largely to inadequate education and skill, a situation for which there are deep historical reasons.

This last problem points toward major challenges in institution building, and we will discuss it in some detail in this paper. As a result of the widespread awakening to their rights and entitlements among ordinary workers, brought about by the arrival of the Lewis turning point and the continuing stress the labor market is under, labor disputes have been on the rise. The government has been quick to respond to this trend by passing legislations and implementing policies. This is in fact yet another sign that China's labor market is on track to turn from Lewisian, where it has been to some time, to neoclassical.

The demographic trend and its impacts on labor supply

Thanks to its strict implementation of the one-child policy, China has been able to complete in a very short time a demographic transition that took most developed countries much longer to complete. Since reform began, China's demographic profile has gone through the following stages: a sharp decline in fertility rate, then in the number of young people as a percentage of the total population, a decreasing growth rate for people of working age, and then the rapid aging of the Chinese population. When the percentage of young people contracted at a higher rate than the growth rate of the percentage of elderly people, China began to see a sufficient labor supply, a result of productive population structure. As these demographic trends continue, the working age population will grow more slowly, while the aging process will pick up speed. These trends will surely raise many challenges.

Despite the dramatic decline in the total fertility rate (TFR) in China throughout the 1970s from 5.8 to 2.3, by the early 1980s, China's TFR was still above the replacement level. The drastic reduction in the fertility rate that China has been able to achieve owes very much to socioeconomic development on one hand and wide adoption of family planning on the other during the reform period. These circumstances were highly effective in arresting high fertility rates. By the dawn of the twenty-first century, not only had China successfully carried out the transition toward a modern population growth pattern, but it was also able to be in less than 30 years.

By comparison, it took many industrialized countries of comparable income levels almost a century to do the same.

There have long been disagreements among scholars and official authorities about China's TFR. Figure 1 shows China's TFR from 1950 to 2009. All of the pre-1998 figures had government sources and were as such 'official', but scholars treat only those for the years after 1998 to be genuinely trustworthy. In Figure 1, one can see that the TFR in China has been below 1.5 for many years, which is quite low by international comparison (Gu and Li 2010).

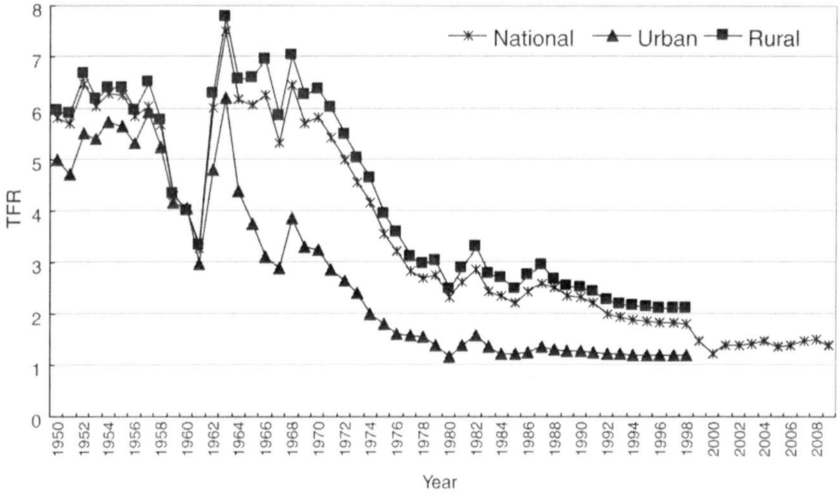

Figure 1. Reduction in total fertility rates: aggregate, rural, and urban. Source: Regional TFR for the period before 1998 was calculated using data from the China Center for Population Information database; national TFR post-1998 is calculated on the basis of various population surveys and/or census data.

As the Chinese government gradually began to distance itself from this position, i.e., that TFR in China has been below 1.5 for many years according to census data from the National Bureau of Statistics, the United Nations put China's TFR for 2006 at 1.4 in its newly published *World Fertility Pattern, 2009*, thereby placing the country among those with low fertility rates (United Nations 2010). We may yet be hit by a consequent decline in labor supply, which will happen quite unannounced.

One repercussion of persistently low fertility rates is a change in the age composition of a population. Since about 1980, the growth of the elderly population has accelerated, while that of the population of people of working age has decelerated, and the population of young people has shrunk altogether. We can conclude that under the condition of persistently low fertility rates, the growth of the working age population will slow before stopping altogether. These trends will eventually lead to labor shortages. According to one forecast based on the latest available statistics (United Nations Department of Economic and Social Affairs, Population Division 2011), the number of Chinese between the ages of 15 and 64 will peak in 2015, after which it will begin to decrease (Figure 2).

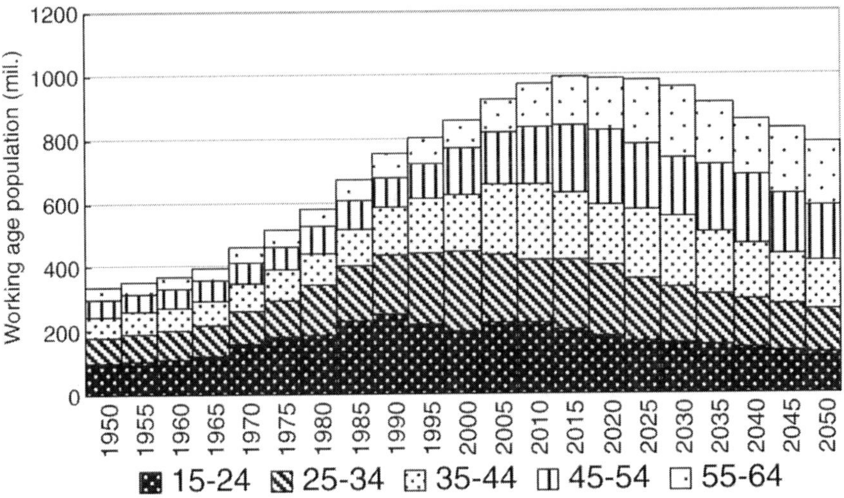

Figure 2. Changing age composition of working age population. Source: United Nations Department of Economic and Social Affairs, Population Division (2011).

Trends such as those just described will lead to concomitant changes to the age structure of China's population. Our argument is based on two assumptions. First, we assume continual rise in enrollment in higher education and have left those aged 15 to 19 outside the purview of these analyses. Second, we assume that there will be little or no increase in the rate of labor force participation for people 65 or older and have included in our analysis only people between the ages of 20 and 64. In the next decade, we expect to see a rise in the average age of people of working age, a slight decrease in the population size of the very young, a more significant decrease in the population size of people of ages between those of the previous two groups, and the elderly to account for 32% of the nation's total population by 2020.

As many previous studies have shown, among rural laborers, those with a more favorable demographic profile, e.g., those who are better educated and younger, are more likely to migrate and to settle in places farther from home and for longer periods (Du and Wang 2010). Since non-agricultural labor supply is closely linked to rural–urban labor migration, and except in cases where sufficiently strong incentives intrinsic to the labor market or the prospects for professional growth exist, people of working age tend to become less mobile as they get older. Moreover, since older urban workers tend to face greater risks for structural and frictional unemployment, and the enrollment rate in higher education has continued to rise, an older labor force also means a reduction in labor force participation rates.

Consequences for the labor market

An aging population presents two huge challenges to any society. On one hand, it poses a threat to the sustainability of the pension system and elderly care infrastructure, and on the other hand, it reduces labor supply. In the period of reform, when there existed underemployment in both rural and urban sectors, the Chinese government has actively helped promote employment by developing the labor market and reallocating people among different sectors and between rural and urban areas. Therefore, China's economic growth is on one hand partly attributable to the massive supply of labor and on the other the reallocative efficiency gained by labor mobility from agricultural to non-agricultural sectors, which constitutes the demographic dividend of total factor productivity growth (World Bank 1997; Cai and Wang 19992005). As China enters a new demographic era, the impact on the labor market will be enormous. These changes will shape the course of China's future development.

Labor supply and demand: basic characteristics

Even though past forecasts for the annual increase in the number of new entrants to the nation's workforce never put the number above 20 million, official figures for the number of new jobs needed each year to absorb the addition workers have been consistently larger. According to calculations from the Ministry of Human Resources and Social Security, there are a total of more than 24 million people in the labor reserve. They arrive at this number by adding up the numbers for three groups of people: more than ten million new entrants to the labor market, each year; more than eight million people currently unemployed who are looking for work; and over six million laid-off workers who need work (Zhang 2008).

This calculation method is problematic, however. First of all, it is missing a temporal dimension and creates the false impression of timelessness. While the landscape of China's labor demand and supply has changed significantly in recent years, some of the basic categories assumed in this calculation no longer exist. For example, what used to be called 'laid-off workers' were renamed in 2005 and are now referred to as the 'registered unemployed'.

This means that, at least officially, there were no longer any laid-off workers in China but a total of 80 million registered unemployed in 2008. The second problem with this calculation is that it is based on the questionable assumption that all of the unemployed must be absorbed. But this intention is neither necessary nor feasible. According to mainstream theories of employment, insofar as there is such a thing as natural unemployment rate, it tends to stay fairly stable over the long run.

The demographic and economic trends described above have led to a changed relationship between labor supply and demand. Take the annual increase in the number of people between the ages of 16 and 64 on the supply side and the annual increase in the number of urban workers on the demand side. When the two trends are examined together, the changing dynamics of the labor market become obvious. Since the number of agricultural workers has been falling while that of non-agricultural workers in rural areas is not expected to expand, we may treat the increases in the number of urban workers, migrant workers included, as representative of the magnitude of the overall labor demand of the Chinese economy.

In what follows, we take a closer look at the general employment situation in China by comparing the demand and the supply of labor for urban sectors. There are two parts to the statistical data on urban employment in China. The first includes the total number of urban employees, which is published by the National Bureau of Statistics (NBS). This number does not, however, cover most migrant workers in urban areas. According to estimation on the basis of microdata from 2009, only 12.5% of thc total of 310 million urban employees were migrant workers. The second part includes the total number of people classifiable as migrant workers according to the NBS official definition. According to that definition, an individual qualifies as a 'migrant worker' if s/he has been away from the town or township of their household registration for 6 months or more. Surveys have shown that of all migrant workers, 95.6% work and live in cities of varying sizes. Factoring in the overlap between these two numbers, we can calculate the actual number of urban workers inclusive of both registered urban residents and migrant workers. We can then compare this number with the total number of people of working age in the country (Table 1).

Between 2001 and 2011, labor demand of urban sectors, which encompasses employment among both urban residents and the migrants, grew at an annual rate of 3.2%. During the same period, labor supply, measured by the number of people of working age, grew by an annual rate of only 1.1%. For the purpose of this study, we have excluded people older than 60 from working age population because, given China's retirement age - 60 for men and 55 for women - they by default stand little chance of

Table 1. Increases in demand for and supply of labor force (million, %)

	Urban resident workers		Migrant workers		Working age population	
	Numbers	Growth rate	Numbers	Growth rate	Numbers	Growth rate
2001	236	-	80	-	885	-
2002	241	2.1	100	24.7	901	1.7
2003	246	2.0	109	8.8	914	1.5
2004	250	1.8	113	3.8	929	1.6
2005	254	1.7	120	6.4	944	1.6
2006	259	2.0	126	5.0	952	0.9
2007	265	2.1	131	3.7	960	0.8
2008	268	1.3	134	2.5	968	0.8
2009	272	1.4	139	3.5	974	0.7
2010	277	1.6	146	5.3	981	0.7
2011	280	1.0	152	3.7	986	0.6

Source: Authors' own calculations based on *China Statistical Yearbook* (various years), *China Yearbook of Rural Household Survey* (various years), and *China Population Yearbook* (various years), and Du and Hu (unpublished memo).

finding a job in the present labor market. A look at people between the ages of 15 and 59 shows that this population had begun to shrink by 2010. This suggests, among other things, that the problem of high rates of underemployment in both the rural and the urban labor markets was finally easing. As such, constant surplus of supply relative to demand no longer accurately describes China's labor market after the arrival of the Lewis turning point.

Wage increases for unskilled workers

Wages have been growing continuously in China since the late 1990s, when a huge number of workers were laid off in urban areas and labor productivity increased as a consequence. Since the beginning of this century, the average wage in major urban sectors has been rising at an annual rate of over 8%, which is unrivaled by any group anywhere in the world. However, understanding China's official statistical data on wages can be a challenge because of the complex ways in which they are collected and calculated. For example, data on urban wage cover only workers formally employed in formal sectors and leave out information on temporary workers and those who work in informal sectors; therefore, such data cannot be relied upon completely if one wants to understand the dynamics of the situation in China with respect to wages. However, wage increases for migrant workers warrant close examination since they not only make up one third of urban employment but also account for a large percentage of informal workers in non-agricultural sectors,

Until 2004, wages for migrant workers had shown little growth even though wages for urban workers who are local residents had begun to rise. In 2004, the country was hit by the first migrant labor shortage, which triggered a rapid increase in wages. As can be seen in Figure 3, wages for all sectors, including those dominated by migrant workers (such as manufacturing and construction), have been increasing constantly, while the wage increase for migrant workers has been particularly impressive. We conclude, therefore, that observed wage increases are mainly attributable to changes in labor demand and supply. We have included here the figures for wage increases in select agricultural sectors as further evidence for the validity of this claim. Indeed, strong wage growth in agricultural sectors signals the decline of the dual economy, which, according to Lewis, is an economy characterized by surplus labor in agriculture.

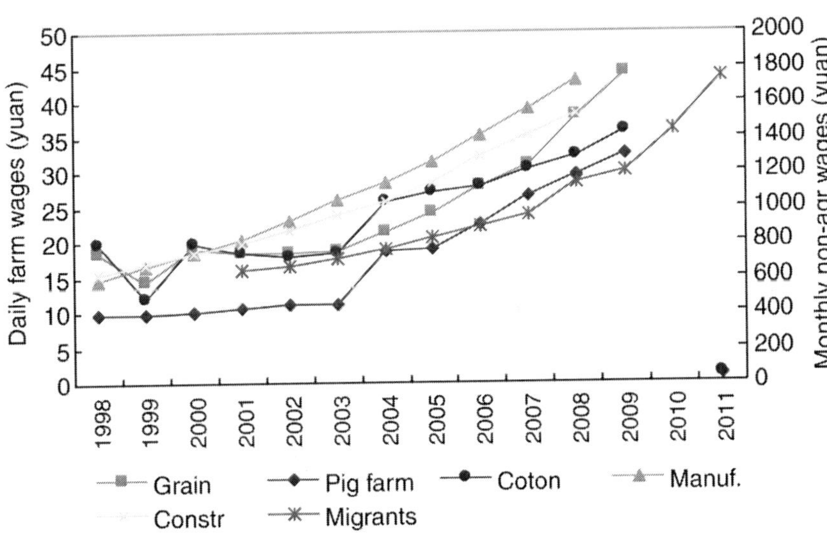

Figure 3. Wage increases in select sectors. Source: Data on the daily wages for workers in grain and cotton production and on hog farms with more than 50 hogs are from *Compilation of national farm product cost-benefit data*, monthly wages of manufacturing and construction are from *China Labor Statistics* (various years), and monthly wages of migrant workers are from *NBS Statistical Report* (various years).

Wages for migrant workers have been rising continuously since 2004, as a result of migrant labor shortages. Even the global financial crisis did not interrupt this trend. A survey done by the NBS shows that the average real monthly wage of migrant workers was 1,221 yuan in 2009, which was 90% higher than what it was in 2001. The real wage of migrant workers increased by 19% in 2010 and further increased by 21% in 2011. Other surveys and reports besides the one by NBS have put the figures for migrant labor wage increases even higher. For example, according to a survey conducted in early 2010 by the People's Bank of China, China's central bank, the average wage for migrant workers was 1,783.2 yuan in 2009, 17.8% higher than the year before (Department of Survey and Statistics, People's Bank of China (DSS-PBC) 2010).

In fact, because urban local workers and migrant workers tend to differ considerably with respect to their hours and pay structures, a comparative analysis of the wages for the two groups must factor in both wage rates and working hours. According to a 2010 survey ('China Urban Labor Survey' or CULS[a]), migrant workers work for an average of 27% longer than do urban local workers per week, and their hourly wage rates were on average 88.2% of the average wage rate for local urban workers. This means that the reason the average monthly earning for migrant workers was higher (by 5.6% higher) than the number for urban local workers was that the former make up for lower hourly wage rates with longer hours worked.

Moreover, as the demographic profile of this population evolves, so do working habits. For example, younger workers today tend to work fewer hours than their older counterparts used to previously. Findings from CULS show that in 2010, migrant workers worked an average of almost 12.4 h less than did migrant workers in 2005. This means that the increase in total monthly earning for migrant workers is a reflection of substantial surge in wage rate (i.e., hourly rate).

Rise in labor disputes

In recent years, particularly after 2008, the year in which several labor-related laws were passed or updated, heightening workers' awareness of rights and entitlements[b], the incidence of labor disputes in China has increased sharply. According to official records, the total number of labor disputes in 2010 was twice what it was in 2003. Moreover, the number of incidents of severe unrest triggered by conflicts in labor relations has grown too. That is not necessarily a sign of worsening trend in labor relations, but may be more of an indication of stronger demand for labor market institutions.

In his seminal work, Hirschman (1970) named three mechanisms, namely, exit, voice, and loyalty, by which citizens, consumers, and workers can express their dissatisfaction with conditions in the market. Here, we borrow those expressions to describe changed labor relations in China after the arrival of the Lewis turning point. As laborers in general and migrant workers in particular (especially in China) enjoy more employment opportunities, there has also been greater room for them to exercise their rights by 'voting with their feet', i.e., by choosing 'exit'.

How individual migrant workers use their power of choice depends on what jobs they hold. For example, workers who are dissatisfied with their jobs in small companies with poor growth prospects may simply quit since the odds are fairly good that they can find a better job elsewhere. But for workers who are dissatisfied with but reluctant to leave their jobs in sizable companies with some industry recognition and growth potential, efforts to seek higher pay and better working conditions may take the form of overt actions such as vocal complaints, collective bargaining, and, in more extreme cases, strikes.

Figure 4 shows the level of labor dispute in different provinces such as measured by the ratio between the number of reported cases and total employment. We can see that they happen more often in the more developed coastal regions than they do elsewhere. Of the total number of labor disputes in China in 2008, a vast majority, or 74.8%, took place in eastern provinces.

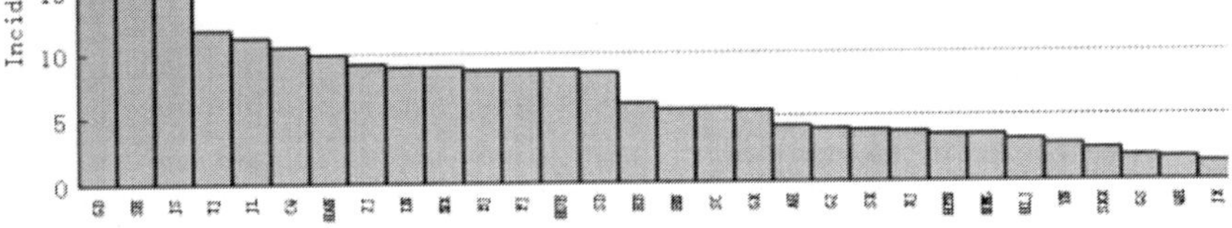

Figure 4. Incidence of labor dispute by province. According to China's official categorization, more developed provinces (the eastern region) include Beijing (BJ), Shanghai (SH), Tianjin (TJ), Jiangsu (JS), Zhejiang (ZJ), Guangdong (GD), Shangdong (SD), Fujian (FJ), Liaoning (LN), Hainan (HAN), and Hebei (HB). Developmentally intermediate provinces (the central region) include Hunan (HUN), Hubei (HUB), Henan (HN), Jilin (JL), Heilongjiang (HLJ), Jiangxi (JX), Shanxi (SX), and Anhui (AH). Least developed provinces (the western region) include Guangxi (GX), Shaanxi (SXX), Gansu (GS), Guizhou (GZ), Inner Mongolia (NMG), Xinjiang (XJ), Yunnan (YN), Ningxia (NX), Qinghai (QH), Sichuan (SC), Chongqing (CQ), and Tibet (XZ, omitted from the figure due to data unavailability). Source: NBS, *China Labor Statistical Yearbook, 2009*.

There are several reasons for these regional variations in the occurrence of labor disputes. They are (1) the Lewis turning point came to the more developed region earlier than it did elsewhere, (2) the more developed region is also where migrant workers are most concentrated[c], and (3) since migrant workers are more vulnerable to abuse, they are correspondently more likely to initiate actions in defense of their rights. The rise in labor disputes and the uneven geographical distribution of their occurrence both suggest that there has been a sharp increase both in worker awareness about rights and in the demand for the institutionalization of their protection.

Three vulnerable groups

In studying unemployment, scholars in macroeconomics and labor economics have mostly focused on two types of unemployment: cyclical unemployment and natural unemployment (which includes frictional and structural unemployment). In a typical labor market and under normal conditions, macroeconomic fluctuations are associated with temporary changes in the relationship between labor demand and supply, which generate cyclical unemployment. By contrast, natural unemployment, either in the form of frictional or structural employment, is the effect of a mismatch between the employment objectives of workers on one hand and employment opportunities employers can offer on the other. More specifically, such a mismatch can reflect either the time cost of job search or changes in skill requirements.

As market mechanism plays an increasingly prominent role in labor allocation and macroeconomic business cycles occur in China, both cyclical and natural unemployment have been present. According to one estimate (Cai et al. 2004), during the period between 1995 and 2002, roughly 60% to 80% of urban unemployment in China that had been observed was not the result of macroeconomic fluctuations and should be classified as natural unemployment.

According to Lewis (1954), as a dual economy grows, excess labor supply in agriculture is increasingly absorbed by expanding non-agricultural sectors. It is widely believed that 30% to 40% of China's agricultural labor force during the period between the mid-1980s and the late 1990s constituted excess supply (Taylor 1993; Carter et al. 1996). Similarly, as a legacy of a planned economy, 30% to 40% of total employees of state-owned enterprises (SOEs) in urban areas were deemed dispensable (Zhang 2008). Both of these forms of underemployment, affecting rural and urban sectors, respectively, are tantamount to a kind of hidden unemployment. We can distinguish, therefore, three different forms of unemployment: cyclical, natural (frictional and structural), and hidden, and discuss changes in them separately.

When economic reform began in China, the Chinese economy was a typical dual economy characterized by a sharp rural–urban dichotomy and high rates of hidden unemployment in both spheres. At the same time, both natural unemployment and cyclical unemployment have existed in China. The former is due to a combination of pervasive underdevelopment, inadequate public employment services, and the prevalence of mismatch between job skills and requirements. The latter is due to macroeconomic fluctuations, which happened throughout the reform period. In order to be able to focus our analytical attention on how the transition away from a dual economy reduced hidden unemployment, the effects of urban employment policy reform, and the breakup of the 'iron rice bowl' at SOEs, we shall assume that cyclical unemployment and natural unemployment stay relatively constant.

From Figure 5, a sketch map, one can see that since the beginning of China's reform policies, as the migration of surplus rural labor into urban areas and the reallocation of redundant urban workers continued, hidden unemployment shrank substantially in terms of both aggregate scale and percentage of total 'unemployment'. A number of empirical studies have shown that the massive flows of labor force from agricultural to non-agricultural sectors and from rural to urban areas have contributed tremendously to the reduction in the amount of excess labor in agriculture (for example, Cai and Wang 2008). Since 2004, when the first nationwide labor shortage took place, the wage rates for ordinary workers have been rising continuously. This was by definition a Lewis turning point.

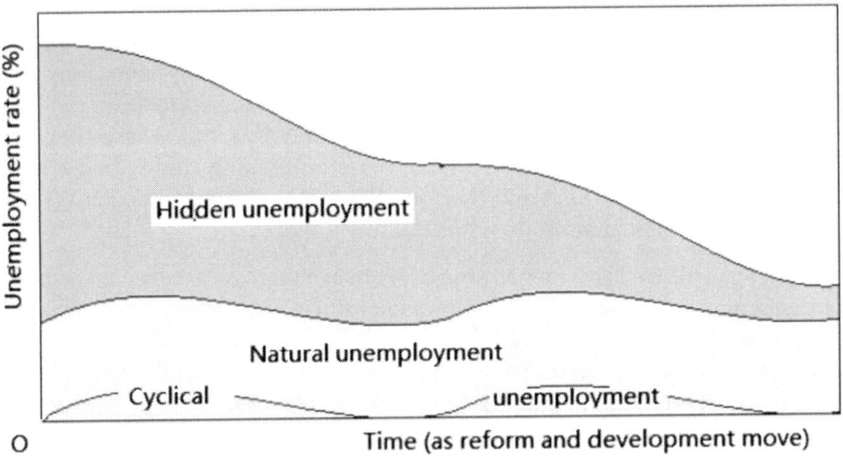

Figure 5. Unemployment types and their changing trends.

The urban labor market has been experiencing painful adjustments since the late 1990s, and a total of 40 million workers were laid off up to 2002. As the economy continues to grow and the labor market to evolve, people who had been laid off and were officially registered as unemployed have either found new jobs or retired. It seems, therefore, that while these kinds of adjustments help eliminate hidden unemployment in urban areas, older workers are more vulnerable to frictional and structural unemployment.

Both the government and the public recognize three subpopulations in China as being particularly vulnerable with respect to employment. These are migrant workers, college graduates, and urban vulnerable workers who are relatively old and poorly educated, who suffer from unemployment or difficulty of finding jobs from time to time. By taking a closer look at each of these groups, one can begin to understand better the new challenges China is facing in this transition toward a neoclassical labor market.

In Chinese, a migrant worker is, literally, a 'farmer turned worker'. Much of this population is made up of surplus labor from rural areas. One's status as a migrant worker does not necessarily mean that s/he is unwanted for agricultural production. More often, agricultural workers who choose to migrate into the cities do so because they better satisfy the personal conditions for migration than others. In other words, in comparison with those who stay behind, rural migrants have some notable advantages.

First, a higher percentage of migrants, who are mostly between the ages of 20 and 30, would have had some formal education. Many would have completed 9 years of free education legally mandated in China. As such, this population is suitably prepared for most of the unskilled and/or semiskilled jobs available in urban areas. Second, because they invariably lack access to social protections, including employment assistance, they can ill afford to stay unemployed and have no income. As a result, they tend to have a higher level of tolerance for poor pay and poor working conditions and have a high rate of labor participation. Third, since this population tends to suffer from spatial distance between where they live and where they can find a job, institutional exclusion from decision-making, and informational asymmetry between them and their employers, they tend to be cut off to a certain extent from market demand.

Today, agriculture is no longer able to reabsorb migrant returnees from the cities when urban labor demand crashes during an economic downturn. There are two major reasons for this. First, agricultural production has changed greatly from what it was in earlier times, in part as a result of the great labor hemorrhage. Second, the demand for migrant workers in urban areas is now relatively inelastic. They are, therefore, no longer a reserve labor force but rather the pillar of the urban labor market. However, since they tend to receive weaker institutional protections and enjoy less of a social safety net, they are more likely to become victims of labor market volatility caused by macroeconomic fluctuations. As the macroeconomy goes through cycles of boom-and-bust, high rates of cyclical unemployment among migrant workers and migrant worker shortages take place alternately.

The difficulties in finding a job facing university graduates are a relatively new phenomenon. Before the massive expansion of university enrollment, university graduates were a scarce human resource and tended to be highly valued in the labor market. Even though the system of job placement had largely been phased out by the end of the 1990s, as a group, college graduates had relatively little difficulty securing jobs and the unemployment rate among them remained low. This began to change, however, when the first graduates from the classes of enlarged enrollment entered the labor market. In 2001, when this group of students was yet to graduate from universities, the share of new entrants in the total unemployed who used publicly run employment services was 16.5%. By contrast, in 2002, when the graduates from the first class of enlarged enrollment who had spent 3 years or longer in colleges entered the labor market, that number increased to 20.1%. In 2011, it reached 23.9%. Of these unemployed new entrants, 40.6% were that year's university graduates. A 2005 national survey shows that the unemployment rate was 8% among 3-year college graduates and 6.1% for university graduates. Both these numbers were significantly higher than the urban average of 5.2% (Cai and Wang 2009; Wang and Cai 2009).

While the higher unemployment rate and the employment difficulties facing university graduates are no doubt in part caused by macroeconomic cycles of boom-and-bust, to a higher degree, they are a case of frictional and structural unemployment. As human capital, university graduates in general have a higher value than and are at an advantage relative to other groups, including migrant workers, (older) urban workers, and new entrants into the labor market with fewer years of formal education. They are, therefore, more likely to work in the formal sectors, to be better paid, and to enjoy more job security. However, since their training is more in specific skills than that of other groups, the job search for university graduates requires more time and a more sophisticated matching mechanism. As a result, they are more likely to face the risk of structural and frictional unemployment.

Among urban laborers, human capital deficiency is typically associated with older age, less formal education, poorer health, and outdated skills. This is another population that faces greater risks for natural unemployment. Let us consider the effect of education, for example. According to one study (Wang and Niu 2009), for those in the 24 to 64 age range, each additional year in age difference corresponds to a 10.2% drop in educational attainment. The correlation becomes more pronounced among older workers. For those in the 44 to 64 age range, each additional year in age difference represents a 16.1% reduction in the level of educational attainment. Suppose there is a critical minimum to human capital - say (and not unreasonably), 9 years of formal education, which is required for all Chinese citizens - the demarcation separating those who meet it and those who do not would be the age of 33[d].

Therefore, this group of laborers is subject not only to the risks of layoffs induced by the campaign to break the iron rice bowl of SOEs but also to the risks of frictional and structural unemployment. One silver lining for them, however, is that since most of them have urban *hukou*, or household registrations, and are already living in urban communities, they tend to be counted properly in official statistics in regard to their employment status. By contrast, migrant workers are often discounted, undercounted, or uncounted altogether. This is evidenced by the fact that they have consistently accounted for a large share of the registered unemployed in official records. On the one hand, since the difficulties those laborers face are long-standing and persistent, registered unemployment in urban areas has been relatively insensitive to macroeconomic fluctuations. But on the other hand, they are also relatively well protected by the urban social security system and safety net.

CONCLUSIONS AND POLICY IMPLICATIONS

Thanks to rapid economic growth, fundamental changes in society, and strict implementation of family planning policies since the early 1980s, China has achieved a population transition, changing from one characterized by 'high birth rate, low mortality rate, and high growth rate' to one of 'low birth rate, low mortality rate, and low growth rate', and has done so within a very short time. There have been a number of concomitant demographic changes, most notably with respect to age structure, which in particular has generated a demographic dividend during much of this period but that began to dissipate in the early twenty-first century. The labor market has responded to these developments, which can be clearly seen in the nationwide labor shortage and steep rises in worker wage.

According to the literature of development economics, these phenomena signal the arrival of the Lewis turning point. Since this point marks a separation between a dual economic labor market and a neoclassical one, China faces new and fundamentally different tasks and challenges in its effort to maintain good order in its labor market and to keep unemployment rates low. In particular, instead of focusing exclusively on promoting employment, employment policies in China should also address problems of cyclical and natural unemployment and in ways that uniquely suit the situation in China.

First, the household registration (or *hukou*) system, a unique institution that makes a sharp distinction between the rural and urban labor markets, is a key target for reform if China's labor market is to see greater development. More specifically, one important part of this reform is to allow migrants to apply to be granted urban resident status so they can have full access to social services. This can not only help keep the labor supply adequately large and stable but can also help reduce the negative effects of cyclical unemployment for migrant workers.

Second, education and training are areas in which more profound visions and more assertive government actions are urgently needed. In China, one serious problem is that wage convergence tends to generate a disincentive to complete schooling. To counter this tendency, heavier public spending toward education and better coordination between the education system and the labor market are imperative. Boosting labor force participation through, say, increasing the retirement age can only be effective if accompanied by systematic increases in continuing education and job training for older workers.

Third, the construction of labor market institutions is now of critical importance. Lessons from the experiences of either advanced countries or those of middle-income level suggest that labor market institutions, including industrial relations legislation, minimum wage regimes, laws governing collective bargaining, and unemployment protection, are instrumental for coordinating the demands of different groups and for maintaining social cohesion.

ENDNOTES

[a]China Urban Labor Survey or CULS is a series of surveys conducted by the Institute of Population and Labor Economics, Chinese Academy of Social Sciences in 2001, 2005, and 2010, respectively. It representatively sampled laborers in urban households and migrant households and surveyed both individual laborers and households in Shanghai, Wuhan, Shenyang, Fuzhou, and Xi'an.

[b]In the year 2008 alone, three labor-related laws began implementation, of which the *Employment Contract Law* emphasizes on enhancing employment security and on providing better protection for migrant workers and the urban working vulnerable, the *Employment Promotion Law* clearly claims the responsibility of governments in promoting employment and in eliminating various kinds of labor market discrimination, and *Labor Disputes Mediation and Arbitration Law* is intended to provide a legal framework for improving labor relations.

[c]In 2004, for example, 70% of Chinese migrant workers were in the eastern region (Sheng and Peng 2006).

[d]The critical age here is estimated based on data of the country as a whole. Because the educational attainment level in rural areas is lower than that in urban areas, it may postpone a little bit if we examine the urban working age population. The conclusion holds unchanged - that is, the older the less educated and the critical point of 9 years of compulsory education arrives much before the official retirement age. For a related analysis on education

attainments and returns to human capital in both rural and urban areas, see Wang (2009).

Authors' information

FC, born in 1956, graduated from Renmin University of China and Graduate School of Chinese Academy of Social Sciences (CASS). He holds a Ph. D. degree in economics. Currently, he serves as a Member of the Standing Committee and Agricultural and Rural Committee of the National People's Congress of China, a Fellow of the Chinese Academy of Social Sciences, and the Director of the Institute of Population and Labor Economics, CASS. He is also a Member of the Global Agenda Council on Ageing and a Member of the Population and the Planet Working Group, Royal Society. He published *The Chinese Economy* and *The Lewis Turning Point*, and he has been editing the *Greenbook Series of Population and Labor.*

DECLARATIONS

Competing interests

The author declares that he has no competing interests.

REFERENCES

1. Cai F, Wang D: The sustainability of China's economic growth and the contributions of labor. Econ Res J 1999, 10: 62–68.
2. Cai F, Wang D: China's demographic transition: implications for growth. In The China boom and its discontents. Edited by: Garnaut R, Ligang S. Canberra: Asia Pacific Press; 2005:34–52.
3. Cai F, Wang M: A counterfactual analysis on unlimited surplus labor in rural China. China World Econ 2008,16(1):51–65.
4. Cai F, Wang M: The Chinese employment situation and youth employment difficulties. The sustainability of economic growth from the perspective of human resources, vol 10. In The China population and labor yearbook. Edited by: Cai F. Beijing: Social Sciences Academic Press; 2009:27–43.
5. Cai F, Du Y, Gao W: Employment elasticity, NAIRU and macroeconomic policies. Econ Res J 2004,39(9):5–18.
6. Carter C, Zhong F, Cai F: China's ongoing reform of agriculture. Institute, San Francisco; 1996.

7. Department of Survey and Statistics, People's Bank of China (DSS-PBC) : The fifth monitoring report on migrant workers. In The China population and labor yearbook volume 11: labor market challenges in the post-crisis era. Edited by: Cai F. Beijing: Social Sciences Academic Press; 2010:35–47.

8. Du Y, Wang M: New estimate of surplus rural labor force and its implications. J Guangzhou U (Soc Sci Edition) 2010,9(4):17–24.

9. Gu B, Li J: The debate on China's population policy in the 21st century. Beijing: Social Sciences Academic Press; 2010.

10. Hirschman A: Exit, voice, and loyalty: responses to decline in firms, organizations, and states. Cambridge: Harvard University Press; 1970.

11. Lewis A: Economic development with unlimited supply of labor. Manch Sch 1954, 22: 139–191.

12. Sheng L, Peng L: Current situation of rural migrant laborers: quantity, components and individual characteristics. In The China population and labor yearbook volume 7: demographic transition and its social and economic consequences. Edited by: Cai F. Beijing: Social Sciences Academic Press; 2006:44–57.

13. Taylor JR: Rural employment trends and the legacy of surplus labor, 1978–1989. In Economic trends in Chinese agriculture: the impact of post-Mao reforms. Edited by: Kueh YY, Ash RF. New York: Oxford University Press; 1993:352.

14. United Nations: World fertility patterns. 2010. . Accessed 22 Dec 2011 http://www.un.org/esa/population/publications/worldfertility2009/worldfertility2009.htm

15. United Nations Department of Economic and Social Affairs: Population Division. The 2010 revision. CD-ROM Edition, 2011: World population prospects; 2011.

16. Wang M: Universal high school and mass higher education. In The China population and labor yearbook volume 10: the sustainability of economic growth from the perspective of human resources. Edited by: Cai F. Beijing: Social Sciences Academic Press; 2009:163–174.

17. Wang D, Cai F: The education and employment of rural and urban youth in China. In The China population and labor yearbook volume 10: the sustainability of economic growth from the perspective of human resources. Edited by: Cai F. Beijing: Social Sciences Academic Press; 2009:44–64.

18. Wang G, Niu J: Composition and development of the Chinese education system. In The China population and labor yearbook

volume 10: the sustainability of economic growth from the perspective of human resources. Edited by: Cai F. Beijing: Social Sciences Academic Press; 2009:104–123.

19. World Bank: China 2020: development challenges in the new century. Washington, D.C: World Bank; 1997.

20. Zhang X: The reforms and developments of the Chinese employment. China Labor and Social Security. Beijing: Press; 2008.

11

INTERGENERATIONAL MOBILITY AND INTERPERSONAL INEQUALITY IN AN AFRICAN ECONOMY

Sylvie Lambert[a], Martin Ravallion[b], Dominique van de Walle[c a]

[a] Paris School of Economics, INRA, France

[b] Georgetown University, USA

[c] The World Bank, USA

ABSTRACT

How much economic mobility is there across generations in a poor, primarily rural, economy? How much do intergenerational linkages contribute to current inequality? We address these questions using original survey data on Senegal that include a sub-household measure of consumption for cells within the household. While intergenerational linkages are evident, we find a relatively high degree of mobility across generations, associated with the shift from farm to non-farm sectors and greater economic activity of women. Male-dominated bequests of land and housing bring little gain to consumption and play little role in explaining inequality, though they have important effects on sector of activity. Inheritance of non-land assets and the education and occupation of parents (especially the mother) and their choices about children's schooling are more important to adult welfare than property inheritance. Significant gender inequality in consumption is evident, though it is almost entirely explicable in terms of factors such as education and (non-land) inheritance. There are a number of other pronounced gender differences, with intergenerational linkages appearing through the mother rather than the father.

Keywords: Inheritance; Land; Mobility; Inequality; Gender

1. INTRODUCTION

Traditional agrarian economies are often thought to have limited intergenerational mobility and (hence) highly persistent inequality. However, while intergenerational mobility has long been a subject of research in developed countries, the issue has received relatively little attention in poor, primarily agrarian, economies.[1] In particular, we know very little about how much of the inequality seen in such economies is associated with the linkages across generations through inheritance of assets and occupations, bequests, parental choices on schooling and parental characteristics. Inheritance of agricultural land—the main non-labor factor of production—is probably the first mechanism one thinks of for the intergenerational transmission of inequality in such settings. However, education could well be at least as important, especially in facilitating diversification into more remunerative non-farm activities. Are these economies characterized by a high degree of intergenerational persistence of poverty and affluence, or is there churning associated with successes and failures for adults taking up new economic opportunities? How much do intergenerational linkages and parental characteristics matter to adult living standards and economic activities?

We also know very little about inter-personal inequality in living standards, including between men and women. This reflects a long-standing limitation of the available survey data on consumption, namely that these data are almost invariably collected at the household level. Inequality and poverty measures typically assume equality within households. Since adult women are generally married, it is difficult to separate their own welfare from that of their husbands on the basis of household data. However, gender dimensions of inequality are considered important. Male control over land and its inheritance has long been an issue in development studies.[2] Maternal education and work experience might also be expected to play a role. It has often been argued that maternal education has an important influence on children's health, nutritional status and schooling.[3] There might also be implications for adult welfare and economic activity, though there has been less research on this intergenerational linkage.

This paper helps fill this gap in our knowledge on intergenerational mobility and the transmission of inter-personal inequality in a poor, primarily rural, economy. The central question we address is how important various intergenerational linkages are to consumption inequality among adults. The paper takes advantage of an unusual new data set for Senegal that measures consumption at a relatively disaggregated level within the household, so that we can build a measure that is closer to individual adult consumption than is usually available, to be matched with individualized data on inheritance and various control variables. The data also allow us to distinguish intergenerational linkages by gender.

We model our measure as a function of various intergenerational linkages, including land inheritance, education and parental characteristics (including occupation), with controls for other individual characteristics. In keeping with past literature, we treat inheritance as conditionally exogenous (conditional on our controls).[4] However, that assumption can be questioned. While we have limited scope for identification we offer one test of robustness to relaxing exogeneity, under the assumption that the father's death more than two years before is excludable from the consumption regressions, i.e., that the past death only matters via inheritance.

We use our model of consumption to attribute overall consumption inequality to these explanatory factors. Here we use the Shorrocks's (1982) "natural decomposition," as adapted to a linear regression function following Fields (2003). Using the same regression models and identification strategy, the paper also examines the role of intergenerational linkages in occupational and geographic mobility between parents and their offspring.

We find negligible consumption gain from land inheritance. Other sources of intergenerational linkages such as parental education and occupation, as well as parental investments in children's education, appear to play a much bigger role in raising consumption. These factors also emerge as significant determinants of the intergenerational transition from farm to non-farm activity and geographic mobility—both likely to be linked with higher consumption. Land inheritance makes it more likely that one will remain a farmer and stay in rural areas. In general, formal schooling brings higher returns in consumption terms than the inheritance of physical assets. Nevertheless, it is only for men that education is correlated with a higher probability of engaging in non-farm activities and moving away from the parental location of residence. Overall, the inheritance of physical assets (land and housing) plays little role in explaining consumption inequality, even among rural households.

These results lead us to question the traditional model of a developing economy with imperfect credit markets in which privately-owned land is a marketable asset generating an income stream exclusively for the designated individual owner. But our results are easier to understand in the light of richer models of rural economies with limited market development. We already know from the literature (in anthropology as well as economics) that market failures and non-market allocation processes play an important role in how land is used. Agricultural land inheritance in much of Africa is typically filtered through customary land allocation processes involving kinship or community groups.[5]Inheritance signals a change in responsibility, such that the recipient of land inherits obligations as well as an asset, and it is an asset that is not easily monetized to support other productive investments.

The impacts of inheritance will naturally reflect how the "dynastic family" allocates its resources, given the market and institutional environment. In principle at least, the extended family has the ability to attain any desired distribution of consumption, independently of the formal assignment of ownership rights. Indeed, it is an open question in this setting whether there is any net impact on the inheritor of a land bequest within the family.

Our results suggest that other mechanisms for the intergenerational transmission of inequality—notably related to parental education including assortative matching, and children's schooling—are more important than land inheritance in explaining interpersonal economic welfare and economic activities. Even in very poor settings, parental background can influence the schooling, expectations, and general life chances, of children in ways that matter to the realized living standards of adults. Our results support this view, echoing other findings in the literature.[6] Some degree of intergenerational correlation in occupational choices can be expected, for which we find supportive evidence.

In the following section, we begin by discussing what is currently known about intergenerational linkages in developing economies. We then describe our data for Senegal and the setting in Section 3. Section 4 briefly examines occupational mobility. The methods of analysis and our empirical results on the intergenerational effects on consumption, economic activity and geographic mobility are discussed in the next two sections, while Section 7 explores various tests of robustness. Section 8 examines the implications for understanding inter-personal inequality and a final section concludes.

2. INTERGENERATIONAL LINKAGES IN A DEVELOPING ECONOMY

The role of parental choices in creating intergenerational linkages has received some attention in the literature. A still small but growing literature has studied how parents go about assigning various assets among their children in developing countries. Estudillo et al. (2001) and Quisumbing et al. (2004) explore the parental allocation decision over land transfers and investments in education, from the point of view of gender equity. Using data for the Philippines, Sumatra and Ghana, they argue that parents aim to equalize economic well-being across their offspring, which may well result in unequal inheritance of specific assets given gender differences in returns. Intergenerational transfers thus reflect parents' expectations of returns to land and human capital assets and allow multiple sources of linkages and substitution. La Ferrara and Milazzo (2012) also document how parents strategize and substitute land and education transfers to their offspring in Ghana. They examine how a reform in inheritance law alters the transmission of human capital investments and land from parents to sons and daughters. As posited by the authors, the relaxation of matrilineal rules of descent results in a reallocation away from schooling and toward land transfers that is more pronounced for boys and only evident for matrilineal (Akan) households. Akan sons are also found to be significantly more likely to be farmers post reform.

Although not our immediate focus in this paper, a strand of the literature has also focused on spousal inheritance at divorce or widowhood, and impacts thereof (Cooper and Bird, 2012, Kumar and Quisumbing, 2012a, Kumar and Quisumbing, 2012b and Peterman, 2012). For example, Kumar and Quisumbing (2012b) investigate the impact of changes in Family Law and land registration procedures favorable to women in Ethiopia on married women's perceptions of asset and child custody allocations in the event of divorce. Reform induced changes in attitudes are found not only to have increased women's well-being but also led to intergenerational linkages through increased investments in child schooling.

Intergenerational transmission mechanisms are also emphasized in the literature documenting the role of property ownership, most prominently land, in enhancing women's status and bargaining power within the household with spillover effects on child human and physical capital (for example, Quisumbing, 2009 and Quisumbing and Maluccio, 2003). Such female control over assets is often obtained through parental bequests.

There has been a lacuna of research on intergenerational mobility in Africa. Indeed, we know of only one paper addressing the issue, focusing on the intergenerational mobility between agricultural and non-agricultural occupations in five countries, namely Côte d'Ivoire, Ghana, Guinea, Madagascar and Uganda. In explaining the revealed variance in intergenerational occupational mobility across the countries, Bossuroy and Cogneau (2013) emphasize educational immobility in Madagascar and the pronounced duality in the spatial distribution of employment in the other countries, which the authors link to the countries' respective colonial histories.

The assignment of land ownership is naturally expected to play a role in any rural economy and this has been a theme in the development literature.

Private ownership of land (with or without a formal title) is typically viewed as a form of private wealth, which is expected to deliver exclusively to its owner an income stream derived from the productive capacity of the owned land. In the context of a mainly rural market-based economy, one thus expects land ownership to play an important role in determining the individual's standard of living. Land inheritance is one way of acquiring ownership. Thus land inheritance should be important to the intergenerational transmission of inequality and also to economic activity, including diversification into non-farm production, especially when credit is unavailable. Development policy debates often focus on inheritance laws, especially reforms aiming to improve women's rights.[7]

Taxation policies have also emphasized land ownership as a basis for assigning taxes, including in poor rural economies. Taxes on land are found in almost all countries. Also, transfers and various direct interventions are often targeted according to land holding, defined by ownership. These include policies aiming to redistribute land itself. Tenure security is traditionally defined in terms of individual titles of private ownership. There have been many efforts (often supported by external development assistance) to foster individual ownership through land titling, with expected benefits to the government in efforts to tax land value, and also expected gains in both efficiency (promoting land investment through greater tenure security and access to credit) and equity (notably in promoting women's empowerment).[8]

However, it is far from clear how relevant this standard model of land as a form of marketable and productive wealth is to poor rural economies where land markets are thin or non-existent and imperfect (and asymmetric) information and long-established social institutions play an important role in how land is allocated and used. The benefits from efforts to foster individual ownership titles are known to be uncertain when individual titling is introduced in an indigenous system of tenure, which is probably why the evidence that such efforts have had their expected benefits appears to be mixed.[9]

Inheritance of the family farm may well bring enhanced individual power within the family—interpretable as a non-pecuniary gain—but it undoubtedly also comes with responsibilities and constraints. Past observations about African agriculture lead one to question the extent of the gains to the inheritor of land, who may have to take on various obligations. These naturally include responsibility for the family as an economic unit, but they may also extend well beyond the immediate, and even the extended, family. Anthropologists have emphasized the social responsibilities that come with acquired wealth such as through land ownership. As Shipton and Goheen (1992, p. 311) note with reference to land in rural Africa, "Rights often entail duties. Cultivation and grazing rights may entail obligations to share farm products beyond the domestic group." Similarly, with reference to the Luo people of Kenya, Shipton (1992,

p. 361) argues that "Rights of individuals [over land] were not thought sacrosanct, but instead they interlocked with the rights of others, and overlapped with those of families and wider groups." Individual responsibilities within a village economy are often embedded in broader social ties, interpretable as means of enforcing cooperative equilibria that bring collective benefits (Platteau, 2000). Whether such responsibilities come with a consumption incentive is unclear on a priori grounds, given that there are also likely to be non-pecuniary benefits and costs.

In much of Africa, the local state and community governance are involved in land allocation, as are traditional, customary, non-market kin-based allocation processes. In particular, land that is not kept in use and looked after appropriately risks appropriation by the community in many rural economies: the lineage or household head is thus in charge of making sure this doesn't happen so as to insure the family's long-term security. Further, membership of an (potentially large) extended family often conveys rights to work the family's land holding and/or share in its bounty. These arrangements can mean that individual land ownership conveys obligations and associated costs to the owner, especially if he or she is also the head of household. As noted by Ensminger (1997) "Lineages are not just kinfolk…they cooperate in labor, risk management, and investment. Fundamental to the high level of trust and cooperation that such systems enjoy are basic guarantees of subsistence in the short run – through access to land – and the long run through inheritance of that land" (p. 165). One cannot even rule out consumption losses to the inheritor. Without a land market it will be hard for the recipient to "cash in" the land to finance some other (non-farm) investment. The lack of a land market may then create occupational stickiness, whereby the bequest of land inhibits the recipient's transition to non-farm activities (though possibly enhancing the scope for such a transition by others in the family). Land-market failures may even entail that the (say) eldest son who gets the land and the responsibilities of being the head of household ends up trapped in farming, while his siblings see new opportunities for diversification into non-farm activities.

Indeed, inheriting the land but without the responsibilities of headship may allow the recipient to leave the land to take up some non-farm activity. As already noted, given weak market and governmental institutions for risk-sharing, the family farm is known to serve a social security role in traditional societies. The recipient of the land bequest may then effectively transfer the right to other family members (the mother, spouse, and children). Their security (at some minimal level) is thus assured, and the son is free to seek work or start an enterprise elsewhere, such as in an urban area. However, one can also imagine situations in which non-market factors in the allocation of command over the product of land can discourage agriculture, even for the household head, in favor of other (non-farm) activities possibly outside the village economy. This can happen when the non-market allocation rules require a sharing of the product of land,

and that the sharing rule entails that inheriting extra land reduces the marginal product of the owner's effort in farming relative to other uses of labor time, thus generating a substitution toward non-farm activities. This is a distortion to inter-sectoral allocation, in the sense that marginal products of labor become unequal between activities. In principle, such an inefficiency could be avoided if the family is well informed about other (non-farm) income sources, so allowing sharing rules based on total income.

Finally, it is worth underlining that land inheritance can be accompanied by learning within kinship groups—a source of specific human capital that may play an important role in the welfare gains from inheritance. It is widely believed that traditional farming practices in developing countries are characterized by a high degree of farm-specific knowledge, accumulated through experience farming the same land. Rosenzweig and Wolpin (1985) have emphasized the role of family-specific information in explaining intergenerational and intra-household land transfers, including inheritance; they find support for the claim that specific-knowledge about the family farm means that land is kept within the family rather than being sold. This could also explain why land markets are often thin or non-existent and also why the extended family is so common in poor rural economies, given that the older generation will have accumulated greater knowledge about the family farm. As long as the extended family can share knowledge there will be little economic loss at the death of the head of the household, though one can imagine circumstances (including unanticipated deaths) when that is not the case.

We have seen that in the context of a poor rural economy, and in the African context more specifically, land inheritance may be a mixed blessing. The same is true of the other main intergenerational linkage, namely parental investments in their children's education. It is well understood that the parental decision to favor one son (say) with extra schooling comes with an implicit (and sometimes quite explicit) contract for that son to share a steady stream of his subsequent earnings. These arrangements, and the redistributive pressures on economically successful household members, as synthetized by Platteau (2006), are thought to be common in Africa and there is supportive anecdotal evidence for Senegal (Boltz and Villar, 2014). The son's own consumption gain from schooling is then reduced according to how much is to be sent home, or shared within the larger family group if the son remains resident. (Identifying the individual consumption gain in this case may also require data on consumption within the household.)

The upshot of these observations is that inheritance of land and educational attainments can have ambiguous effects on welfare and economic activities. The linkages may well be quite weak. The rest of this paper will address these issues empirically using an unusual data set for Senegal.

3. SETTING AND DATA

The data used here come from an original survey entitled Pauvreté et Structure Familiale (Poverty and Family Structure, henceforth PSF) conducted in Senegal in 2006/2007. The PSF survey stems from the cooperation between a team of French researchers and the National Statistical Agency of Senegal.[10] The survey is described in detail in De Vreyer et al. (2008).

The PSF covers a sample of over 1800 households spread over 150 clusters drawn randomly from the census districts so as to insure a nationally representative sample. About 1750 household records can be exploited, covering 14,450 individuals. The survey describes a population of which the majority (57%) live in rural areas, 48% are male and 95% are Muslim—statistics that accord well with other sources (World Bank, 2009). Despite more than half of the country's close to 12.5 million inhabitants in 2009 being rural, the contribution of agriculture to GDP amounts to only 18%. Like other African countries, Senegal has seen considerable population urbanization; at the time of independence in 1960 rural areas were the home of 77% of the population. Urbanization over time is evident in the survey in that among those adults who had a father in rural areas, 22% now live in urban areas. A similar percentage of those whose mother lived in rural areas also do so.

Senegalese households are large, with slightly more than eight members on average in the PSF. The families are typically multigenerational and extended both horizontally and vertically, with 36% of household members that are neither the head, nor one of his wives or children. Two thirds of households include such "extended" family members. Polygamous unions are common, with 24% of married men and 37% of married women engaged in such unions. Most of these comprise a husband and two wives (only 20% of polygamous unions have more than two wives). We find that 31% of polygamous men have non-cohabiting wives. In half of these cases, the husband is either considered the head of both households, or of one, while one of the wives is considered head of the other household. In the other half, a married polygamous woman lives in a separate household headed by a relative (mainly her father, brother or son).

In addition to the usual information on individual characteristics, the survey collected details on each household's structure and budgetary arrangements. To best reflect intra-household structure and resource allocation, each household was divided into groups or "cells" according to the following rules: the head of household and unaccompanied dependent members, such as his widowed parent or his children whose mothers do not live in the same household, are grouped together. Any unmarried brothers of the head would also be considered in his cell. Each wife of the head and her children and any other dependents then form separate cells.

Other women with children or other dependents and whose husbands are not present, are also considered cell heads. The same goes for any other family nucleus such as a married child of the household head with his/her spouse and children, or a sister of the household's head residing in the household with her children (after divorce or while her husband looks for a job). This disaggregation emerged from field interviews as being the relevant way to split the household into its component groups. Enumerators saw this as a natural way to divide households and had no difficulty collecting the data accordingly.

Consumption expenditures are recorded in several parts: first all common expenditures are collected (housing, electricity bills etc.). Food expenditures are compiled based on a detailed account of who shares which meal and how much money is specifically used to prepare the meal. These are the "DQ" or "dépenses quotidiennes" — the name the Senegalese give to the amount of money a woman has at her disposal to buy fresh ingredients for the meals of the day. Next individual consumption is collected at the group level (such as clothing, mobile phone, transportation, and food outside the home expenditures). Finally, expenditures that are shared between several cells are collected.

A measure of per capita consumption can then be constructed at the cell level allowing us to identify unequal consumption levels within households. Subgroups also emerge that take some or all of their meals separately (in 17% of households), thus widening the possibility for differences in nutritional intake among household members. Thanks to these data we can construct a relatively individualized measure of consumption, which is almost never available in household surveys. This is what we will use to better assess individual economic welfare. The measure we use here is the amount of expenditures specific to the cell and not shared with any other cell *plus* the cell's imputed share of the household's joint expenditures.

We will restrict our study to individuals who are heads of their cells. For consumption purposes, they are assumed to be the decision makers at the cell level.[11] We are therefore left with 4401 observations, of which 56.8% are women. 75% of cell heads are household heads or the head's spouse, 7.5% are daughters of the head, and 3% are daughters-in-law. The average number of cells per household is 2.51. The range is from 1 to 12; 81% of the sampled households have more than one cell.

In this sample, average per capita total consumption amounts to about 276,000 CFA francs per year, which corresponds to nearly $925 US in 2005 PPP exchange rates for consumption, or about $2.50 per day. When looking at total expenditures, inequalities within the household are evident: the ratio between the expenditures of the richest and the poorest cell within a household can be as high as 18 and is still equal to 4.4 after trimming off the 5% most unequal households. Computing an inequality index for the distribution of cash expenditures in the population, we find a Gini index of

59.8% if we attribute to each person the average per capita consumption level in his or her household. The index is 62.7% if instead each individual is attributed the per capita consumption in his cell (i.e. the sum of the per capita expenditures specific to the cell and of the cell's share of common household expenditures, distributed on a per capita basis within the cell). The Gini index of inequality in the distribution of the cell-specific component of cash expenditures (ignoring the joint consumption within the household) is 77.9%.

The consumption data also reveal a sizeable gender gap. Regressing the log of cell consumption on gender, the regression coefficient (the difference in mean log consumption) is 0.57 and is significant at the 1% level ($t = 14.92$).

Importantly for the purpose of our paper, these data include information on parental characteristics and inheritance. If the parent has died, the survey asked whether he or she left any inheritance and then, for each person, whether they obtained any inheritance in the form of land, housing, money, durable goods or productive capital. No valuation of these inheritances was obtained.[12] In particular, we do not know how much land was inherited. For this reason we use a dummy variable indicating whether land was inherited or not (and likewise for the other forms of inheritance). This may affect the size and significance of our estimates, although the endogeneity concerns (which we return to) would clearly be even greater using amounts of inherited land rather than simply the incidence of inheritance.

On paper, agricultural land is allocated through local community level administrative processes in Senegal. Since 1964, most of the land (between 95 and 98%) has been owned by the state and part of what is called the national domain (Boone, 2007 and Caveriviére, 1986). Allocation and use are reserved for those who belong to the local community or kinship group (Boone, 2007). Land use rights are attributed by local land committees on the basis of needs and capacity to farm. This land cannot be sold and in theory cannot be bequeathed either. As a result, rural land markets are very weak. A land reform aiming to strengthen the security of use rights and to facilitate market transfers was attempted in 2004. Following extensive consultations with rural producers and civil society, the Law for Agro-Sylvo-Pastoral Development (LOASP) was finally enacted in 2004 but its land component was dropped due to a lack of consensus. The fear was that communities would be at risk of being dispossessed of lands not yet formally attributed by the local land committees. Land reform is still being discussed.

The unequal access to land across gender is also a source of concern in Senegal. The legal system has recently changed to try to reduce this gender inequality. The constitution of 2001 finally granted women the right to own land. They have only been allowed to be on the local land committees in charge of the attribution of use rights since May 2010. Hence, in the past, women very rarely received land through this allocation mechanism. There has been little progress in the last decade. In its 2011 report on land policy in West Africa, the Economic Commission for Africa still emphasizes Senegalese women's very poor access to land (UNECA, 2011).

Despite the legal setting described above, the reality on the ground is that land bequests are common. Our survey data indicate that, in our sample of cell heads, 32% of men and 43% of those whose fathers have died, but only 17% (28%) of women, report that they inherited land. Looking at all forms of inheritance (including housing, durables, money and productive assets) 54% of men in the sample inherited something, while 38% of women did so. In practice, heirs are given priority over land use rights relative to other potential users. Hence, inheritance of paternal lineage land is an important means of access to ownership. We observe very few changes in land ownership over the five years preceding the survey. Nevertheless, half of the cases where the amount of land owned increased are due to inheritance.

Several inheritance laws that give different treatment to women coexist in Senegal. Individuals can choose which law to abide by before their death.[13] The French inspired ("modern") system of inheritance dictates that wealth be shared equally among children, whatever their gender. By contrast, Islamic inheritance law (which is by far the most common choice) limits the inheritance of daughters to half of that of sons.[14] In addition, entrenched tradition favors sons for inheriting land (with a small exception in Basse Casamance where there is slightly more access to land for women, due to strong tradition in women-dominated rice cultivation). Since daughters typically move to their husband's abode, they are supposedly compensated by their brothers with money or other forms of wealth such as their imputed yearly share of the harvest, for what would have otherwise been their share of land inheritance.

Inheritance is not always shared immediately after a father's death. The heirs may carry on living in the parental house, using the parental land, without a formal sharing having taken place. During this period – which can last for years – the heirs who do not partake in the use right (typically daughters) because they live somewhere else, are not compensated. Although they are, in practice, owners of their share, they cannot cash it in. In this paper, we do not consider pre-mortem gifts as inheritance. These do not appear to be prevalent. Sons may receive some money to help pay the bride price and to settle down upon getting married. However, such transfers are not taken into account in the sharing of inheritance.

As can be seen in Table 1, 72% of the heads of cells report that their deceased father left some form of inheritance to his children and 32% of them received land bequests. In contrast, only 22% of the heads of cells indicate that their deceased mothers transmitted any inheritance, while 2% received land. Fathers bequeath their wealth to their sons more often than to their daughters, particularly when it is in the form of land. Mothers treated sons and daughters roughly equally in this respect, although they also favored sons with the little land they bequeathed. The Statistical Addendum provides probits for inheritance (both land and any form of inheritance) with a wide range of controls for individual and parental characteristics. Even with these controls, we continue to find that men are more likely to inherit than women. Conditional on the controls, being male adds 0.11 to 0.13 to the conditional probability of receiving any inheritance, while it adds 0.08 to the probability of inheriting land.

Table 1. Inheritance, by gender.

Among individual heads of cells whose father or mother is dead	Men	Women	All	t-Test of the difference (women-men)
Father has left any form of inheritance	75.34% (987)	68.26% (974)	71.65%	−4.12
Father has transmitted land to this person	40.61% (588)	24.74% (410)	32.14%	−9.58
Mother has left any form of inheritance	21.23% (173)	22.49% (190)	21.87%	0.62
Mother has transmitted land to this person	2.62 (38)	1.75% (29)	2.16%	−1.67

Note: number of observations in brackets. Estimates are based on sampled cell heads' reporting inheritance from their deceased mother or father.

The data reveal that very few women (about 2%) have any land to transfer to their heirs when they die, while more than a third of men leave some land. Note that the large discrepancy between the above noted 17% of women reporting that they inherited land and the 2% leaving land is largely explained by the fact that women's land use rights are highly revocable when their marital situations change. A woman loses access to her family land when she marries, and often loses access to her husband's land in the event of widowhood or divorce. She may well also lose control over any land she has inherited over her lifetime. In addition, she has no decision power over its transmission: a deceased woman's land is first returned to her husband (or his family) or to her brothers, and eventually transferred to children only at their father's death.

In these respects, Senegal is not unusual within Sub-Saharan Africa (Cooper, 2008 and Cooper, 2010). The rights of women to land are mainly indirect (Platteau et al., 2000) and contingent on marital status. As a daughter living in her father's household, a woman will work on the family land and eventually obtain use rights to a plot. As a wife, she'll work on the land of her husband's family and might also have use rights on her personal plot. If she is in neither of these positions, she simply won't have access to land. This in part explains the high remarriage rate following widowhood or divorce.

The complex nature of households in Senegal – reflecting households' extended, multigenerational character, the prevalence of polygamy, as well as of widowhood and divorce followed by widespread remarriage, and of child fostering – together with inheritance customs, means that it is important to control for household structure in examining intergenerational mobility and interpersonal inequality outcomes. For example, a child's inheritance will be a function not only of his gender but also of the gender and number of competing siblings as well as whether they share the same father and mother, or just the same mother, or the same father. The interaction of gender and birth order may also play a determining role. We will control for these factors in our regressions.

Despite net primary schooling rates now reaching 78%, the average education in the adult population is still low. In the sample of cell heads we are using (hence excluding the youngest cohorts who have benefitted from the expansion of schooling), 30% have some formal (non-Koranic) education. This is the case for only 11% of those living in rural areas (47% in urban areas). In addition, in rural areas, 75% of people with some education never went beyond primary schooling. The gender gap is also quite sizeable: only 25% of women have ever had any formal schooling, while 35% of men have. The gap increases with the level of education. Less than 40% of women with some education reached at least the secondary level, while this is true for half of the men who attended a formal school. Women in rural areas cumulate both disadvantages and only 8% of them have ever been to a formal school. In all cases our education variable is defined as a dummy for whether the individual has some formal education.

A statistical addendum is available from the authors providing summary statistics on the main PSF variables.

4. OCCUPATIONAL MOBILITY

The first form of intergenerational linkage we consider is in occupations. Do sons of farmers tend to be farmers? What about daughters? Are there links with mothers' occupation? Information was collected on the occupation and education of each parent for each individual. The last place of the mother and father's residence is also known allowing us to determine whether an individual resides in the same village as his parents.

Occupation has been classified under four categories: agriculture, non-agriculture, other, or inactive. 'Other' contains individuals who reported that they were active but not employers, wage workers, or self-employed. As their activities are not known to us, we are unable to classify them into farm/non-farm and so have kept them as a separate group.[15] Inactive includes "housewives," students, and those unable to work due, for example, to disability. Table 2 gives the joint distribution of occupations for parents and their children, for men and women.[16] We find that 36% of individuals had a father working in agriculture, while 22% declare that their mother was in agriculture. Note that women who manage a plot of land on the side to make some extra cash (as is common for Senegalese women in both rural and urban areas) do not define themselves as farmers. It is thus likely that mothers were identified as housewives even when they did a modest amount of agricultural work, so that those who report being active in agriculture probably dedicated considerable time to this occupation, suggesting relatively poor households. When the mother is declared a farmer, in 72% of the cases, the father is also in farming. More generally, parents' sectors of activity are highly correlated.

Table 2. Sectoral occupational mobility across generations for men and women.

No. observations (% of all individuals)	Men					Women				
	Farm	Non-farm	Inactive	Other	Total	Farm	Non-farm	Inactive	Other	Total
Father's occupation										
Farm	219 (12.41)	314 (17.79)	28 (1.59)	76 (4.31)	637 (36.09)	229 (9.74)	276 (11.73)	267 (11.35)	121 (5.14)	893 (37.97)
Non-farm	53 (3.00)	421 (23.85)	53 (3.00)	27 (1.53)	554 (31.39)	49 (2.08)	403 (17.13)	358 (15.22)	19 (0.81)	829 (35.25)
Inactive	175 (9.92)	279 (15.81)	50 (2.83)	40 (2.27)	544 (30.82)	107 (4.55)	183 (7.78)	280 (11.90)	41 (1.74)	611 (25.98)
Other	1 (0.06)	10 (0.57)	5 (0.28)	14 (0.79)	30 (1.70)	1 (0.04)	6 (0.26)	6 (0.26)	6 (0.26)	19 (0.81)
Total	448 (25.38)	1024 (58.02)	136 (7.71)	157 (8.90)	1765 (100.00)	386 (16.41)	868 (36.90)	911 (38.73)	187 (7.95)	2352 (100.00)
Cramer's V					0.204					0.194
Odds-ratio (farm and non-farm only)					5.54					6.82
Mother's occupation										
Farm	154 (8.67)	134 (7.54)	13 (0.73)	50 (2.81)	351 (19.75)	187 (7.97)	173 (7.37)	89 (3.79)	104 (4.43)	553 (23.56)
Non-farm	19 (1.07)	208 (11.71)	20 (1.13)	13 (0.73)	260 (14.63)	22 (0.94)	218 (9.29)	155 (6.60)	14 (0.60)	409 (17.43)
Inactive	268 (15.08)	684 (38.49)	103 (5.80)	58 (3.26)	1113 (62.63)	172 (7.33)	476 (20.28)	652 (27.78)	53 (2.26)	1353 (57.65)
Other	5 (0.28)	7 (0.39)	2 (0.11)	39 (2.19)	53 (2.98)	4 (0.17)	6 (0.26)	5 (0.21)	17 (0.72)	32 (1.36)
Total	446 (25.10)	1033 (58.13)	138 (7.77)	160 (9.00)	1777 (100.00)	385 (16.40)	873 (37.20)	901 (38.39)	188 (8.01)	2347 (100.00)
Cramer's V					0.289					0.265
Odds-ratio (farm and non-farm only)					12.59					10.71

Women have been moving out of an almost exclusive focus on (or self-identification with) household work over time. We find that 38% of sampled women were coded as "inactive" but that this was true of 58% of their mothers. Over one third of those with inactive mothers went into the non-farm sector, with far fewer (13%) going into farming. Very few women have a mother whose occupation is classified as "other," but the reproduction over time is quite strong. Over half of those women are themselves classified in other. This is quite understandable if as we believe, the category consists mostly of traditional non-farm occupations that are caste or lineage-based (and not gender-differentiated) and that require skills and possibly reputations built up and transmitted across generations.

Table 2 suggests considerable intergenerational mobility out of farming. Only one third of the one third of men whose fathers worked in agriculture stayed in the sector, though there is somewhat stronger persistence with respect to mother's sector with 43% of the men (33% of the women) who declared that their mother was working in agriculture doing so as well. One explanation for this is that poorer farm households are both more likely to have had a mother in farming and to be less mobile. Participation in the non-farm sector was more persistent across generations, with nearly three-quarters of those men whose fathers worked in the non-farm sector being also recorded as working in that sector. A significant amount of persistence is also apparent with respect to "other" for mothers and their sons (74% of sons with mothers in "other" were also classified that way) as well as their daughters (53%). There is little occupational stickiness for fathers engaged in "other" and daughters, although close to half of sons followed in their footsteps.

How does the persistence in occupations across generations compare to that found in other developing countries? A common measure of mobility is the odds ratio (widely used in quantitative sociology), which has the advantage that it can be compared with similar calculations for other countries. To help assure comparability with Bossuroy and Cogneau (2013) we confine our calculations to the odds ratio given by the ratio of the odds of the son being in the non-farm (*NF*) sector when his father was in that sector to the odds of the son having switched to *NF* when the father was in the farm (*F*) sector. [17] The odds ratio is then[18]:

$$OR = \frac{p(y = NF|x = NF)/[1-p(y = NF|x = NF)]}{p(y = NF|x = F)/[1-p(y = NF|x = F)]}. \tag{1}$$

Here $p(.)$ denotes the empirical probability of the term in parentheses where $x = k$ denotes that the father is in sector k (= NF,F) and $y = k$ denotes this for the son.

Table 2 gives the results. The OR for fathers and sons of 5.5 might suggest a relatively high degree of immobility; the odds of being in the non-farm sector given that your father was in that sector is 5.5 times higher than if your father had been a farmer. However, it turns out that among the nine developing countries for which results are reported in Bossuroy and Cogneau (2013), Senegal is the third most mobile (behind Ghana and Uganda). At the other extreme, India is the least mobile with an odds ratio of 32, which may well reflect occupational rigidities associated with the caste system.

Bossuroy and Cogneau (2013) only give results for fathers and sons, but we can repeat the calculation for mothers and daughters and the cross-effects, as given in Table 2. We find that women are less mobile than men, with a "mothers–daughters" odds ratio of 10.7. We also find that there is more occupational mobility for daughters relative to their father's sector than there is for sons relative to their mother's sector.

5. INTERGENERATIONAL EFFECTS ON ADULT CONSUMPTION

We regress the log of cell-specific consumption expenditure on dummy variables for having inherited land, housing and other assets (finance, consumer durables and physical capital). The regressions also include a large number of control variables to account for the heterogeneity in individual and household characteristics, including parental characteristics. Specifically we control for gender, age and age squared, age at first marriage, whether one is the first born of a given gender among siblings with the same mother and same father, whether one is the first born among all children with the same mother and father, whether the first born sibling from the same mother and father is a boy, number of brothers from the same father and mother, number of brothers from the same father only and same mother only, and the same three variables for sisters, ethnic group, being Muslim relative to other religions, having some formal education (henceforth referred to as "education"), whether fostered as a child, and whether fostered at a young age (prior to two years of age, which typically implies a permanent move for the child in the Senegal context). There are also controls for parental characteristics (education, occupation, place of residence, whether the father died in the last two years) and some demographic variables describing the household (log household size) and the individual's cell (log cell size, share of adults and share of children age 5 and under). We begin by following past literature in assuming the exogeneity of inheritance; we test robustness to relaxing this in Section 7.

Table 3, Table 4 and Table 5 give results for (log) cell expenditure per person; recall that this combines the cell-specific expenditures with imputed values for the cell's share of jointly consumed items within the household. Table 3 first presents the coefficients on inheritance estimated without any controls. This is followed by coefficients estimated by adding various correlates, which we do in two steps: adding controls for geographic effects alone, and then adding the controls for individual, household and parental characteristics. We next give results with all controls for the full sample, and for both an urban–rural stratification and gender stratification in Table 4 and Table 5.[19]

Without any controls, inheriting land has a strong negative correlation with consumption (Table 3): those who inherited land have consumption that is lower by about 28%.[20] But this is considerably attenuated when one controls for location, reflecting the fact that rural households tend to be both poorer and more likely to inherit land. The negative effect is further reduced with the addition of other controls, remaining close to 7%. Inheriting a house is strongly positively correlated with consumption without controlling for location or other individual and household characteristics. Here again, the effect is reduced, but remains significantly positive when the full set of controls is added (of the order of 7%). Finally, a positive effect of other (non-land, non-housing) forms of inheritance emerges when conditioning on location alone.

This finding of a small negative effect of land in the full sample with controls loses statistical significance in the various strata (urban/rural, male/female and the gender/location interaction) (Table 4 and Table 5). Here and elsewhere, we cannot rule out the possibility that the small or insignificant estimated impacts of land inheritance are due to the fact that the variable is measured as a dummy variable as opposed to land area or value, and hence does not capture sufficient variation. Given our data, we are unable to test this.

Housing inheritance has a positive effect in the full sample and for urban women. The significant effects of other types of inheritance are confined to the urban stratum and to men. When we stratify by the interaction of gender with urban–rural residence, a sharper picture emerges on the adult consumption gains from other forms of inheritance, namely that they are confined to men (Table 5). Recall that we find a sizeable gender gap in consumption. Strikingly, this gender gap in consumption largely vanishes when we add our controls. Ceteris paribus then, adult male heads of cells (who are typically, though not always, the overall household head as well) do not have higher consumption than females (Table 4). Note, however, that our controls include variables such as schooling, which are unequal between genders. So our finding can be interpreted as indicating that the gender gap in consumption can be explained by the gender difference in individual and household characteristics.

Table 3. Estimated effects of inheritance on log cell per capita consumption with and without controls.

	(1) No controls	(2) Rural location and department dummies	(3) As in (2) + controls for individual and household characteristics
Inherited land	-0.324^{***}	-0.0978^{**}	-0.0740^{*}
	(0.0541)	(0.0430)	(0.0449)
Inherited house	0.196^{***}	0.0733^{**}	0.0736^{**}
	(0.0438)	(0.0361)	(0.0368)
Other inheritance	0.0234	0.0889^{**}	0.0642
	(0.0494)	(0.0424)	(0.0419)
Constant	12.53^{***}	13.01^{***}	12.95^{***}
	(0.0276)	(0.247)	(0.285)
Observations	4339	4339	3392
R^2	0.014	0.325	0.465

Note: Robust standard errors in parentheses, clustered at the household level. Controls included in the regression reported in column 3 are: rural location, the cell head's gender, age and age squared, age at first marriage, whether the first born of a given gender among siblings with the same mother and same father, whether the first born among all children with the same mother and father, whether the first born sibling from the same mother and father is a boy, number of brothers from the same father and mother, number of brothers from the same father and same mother only, and the same three variables for sisters, ethnic group, whether Muslim relative to other religions, whether has some formal education, whether fostered as a child, and whether fostered under two years of age; parent's characteristics (education, farm, non-farm or other occupation, last place of residence, whether the father died in the last two years, whether the mother died in the last two years); log household size, log cell size, cell's share of adults and share of children age 5 and under and regional (department) dummies.

*** $p < 0.01$.

** $p < 0.05$.

* $p < 0.1$.

Table 4. Regressions for log cell expenditure per capita.

	(1) Full sample	(2) Rural	(3) Urban	(4) Men	(5) Women
Male	−0.00550	−0.0400	0.0249	–	–
	(0.0409)	(0.0614)	(0.0564)		
Age	−0.00281	−0.00575	0.00327	0.00602	−0.0148*
	(0.00623)	(0.00755)	(0.00993)	(0.0101)	(0.00829)
Age squared	−2.31e−06	1.56e−06	−2.95e−05	−9.40e−05	0.000139
	(6.24e−05)	(7.56e−05)	(9.89e−05)	(9.50e−05)	(8.74e−05)
Muslim	0.0649	−0.0934	0.123	0.0975	0.0409
	(0.0968)	(0.199)	(0.106)	(0.128)	(0.105)
Serere ethnicity	−0.191***	−0.209*	−0.181***	−0.259***	−0.131*
	(0.0630)	(0.122)	(0.0685)	(0.0845)	(0.0697)
Poular ethnicity	−0.0475	0.0687	−0.104	−0.0828	−0.0139
	(0.0521)	(0.0852)	(0.0646)	(0.0682)	(0.0542)
Diola ethnicity	−0.158	−0.163	−0.111	0.0259	−0.264***
	(0.0995)	(0.373)	(0.102)	(0.154)	(0.0978)
Mandingue ethnicity	−0.110	0.152	−0.256***	−0.175*	−0.0590
	(0.0867)	(0.159)	(0.0804)	(0.102)	(0.0957)
Sarakole ethnicity	−0.0853	0.0782	−0.104	−0.171	−0.00624
	(0.127)	(0.235)	(0.167)	(0.175)	(0.146)
Mandiaque ethnicity	−0.443**	−0.585	−0.390**	−0.181	−0.554***
	(0.181)	(0.380)	(0.193)	(0.217)	(0.200)
Other ethnicities	−0.0103	0.152	−0.128	0.0880	−0.101
	(0.108)	(0.180)	(0.115)	(0.142)	(0.116)
Brothers same father	−0.000649	−0.0113	0.00398	0.000877	−0.00205
	(0.00782)	(0.0106)	(0.0114)	(0.0135)	(0.00969)
Brothers same parents	0.000895	0.00962	−0.00638	0.0159	−0.0134
	(0.00940)	(0.0129)	(0.0132)	(0.0147)	(0.0117)
Sisters same father	0.0114	0.0201*	0.00548	0.00171	0.0200**
	(0.00794)	(0.0121)	(0.0107)	(0.0139)	(0.00980)
Sisters same parents	0.0195**	0.0285**	0.0157	0.0123	0.0306***
	(0.00908)	(0.0142)	(0.0122)	(0.0143)	(0.0117)
Brothers same mother	0.0459**	0.0325	0.0496**	0.0753***	0.0271
	(0.0180)	(0.0317)	(0.0219)	(0.0257)	(0.0230)
Sisters same mother	−0.0287	−0.0246	−0.0251	−0.0374	−0.0246
	(0.0206)	(0.0270)	(0.0294)	(0.0291)	(0.0287)
First same gender	0.00358	0.0408	−0.0323	−0.00374	0.0180
	(0.0321)	(0.0449)	(0.0448)	(0.0604)	(0.0452)
First of siblings	0.0122	−0.0154	0.0463	−0.0337	0.0749
	(0.0382)	(0.0521)	(0.0538)	(0.0661)	(0.0627)
First born is male	0.0561*	0.106**	−0.0113	0.0334	0.0931**
	(0.0310)	(0.0435)	(0.0413)	(0.0628)	(0.0415)
Father died recently	−0.0188	−0.00483	−0.0176	0.0161	−0.0428
	(0.0534)	(0.0760)	(0.0740)	(0.100)	(0.0585)
Father in farming	0.0932**	0.0567	0.123*	0.0672	0.0986**
	(0.0418)	(0.0534)	(0.0660)	(0.0573)	(0.0490)
Mother in farm	−0.0738	−0.0967	0.00610	−0.0922	−0.0672
	(0.0449)	(0.0589)	(0.0669)	(0.0619)	(0.0538)
Father in non-farm	0.168***	0.154**	0.177***	0.198***	0.134***
	(0.0426)	(0.0701)	(0.0560)	(0.0609)	(0.0511)
Mother in non-farm	−0.118***	−0.0516	−0.136**	−0.164**	−0.0793
	(0.0441)	(0.0686)	(0.0574)	(0.0696)	(0.0525)
Father in 'other'	0.400***	0.139	0.573**	0.422**	0.369
	(0.151)	(0.181)	(0.250)	(0.205)	(0.250)
Mother in 'other'	−0.223**	−0.184*	0.0543	−0.186	−0.313*
	(0.0960)	(0.104)	(0.255)	(0.128)	(0.161)
Father's schooling	0.0744	−0.0656	0.0984*	0.152*	0.0356
	(0.0493)	(0.0905)	(0.0561)	(0.0802)	(0.0592)
Mother's schooling	0.165***	0.0987	0.228***	0.0371	0.245***
	(0.0630)	(0.0959)	(0.0816)	(0.0879)	(0.0893)
Father rural	0.00560	−0.0166	−0.0160	0.0498	−0.0292
	(0.0510)	(0.0799)	(0.0667)	(0.0911)	(0.0584)
Mother rural	−0.0659	−0.0394	−0.0707	−0.114	−0.0274
	(0.0515)	(0.0821)	(0.0677)	(0.0909)	(0.0583)
Log hh size	−0.305***	−0.289***	−0.315***	−0.286***	−0.327***
	(0.0362)	(0.0626)	(0.0416)	(0.0487)	(0.0415)
Log cell size	−0.112***	−0.170***	−0.100***	−0.141***	−0.0553
	(0.0271)	(0.0397)	(0.0366)	(0.0505)	(0.0438)
Share of cell aged <5	−0.194**	−0.224*	−0.126	−0.349*	−0.159
	(0.0962)	(0.132)	(0.143)	(0.202)	(0.113)
Share of cell adults	0.438***	0.245**	0.553***	0.381***	0.478***
	(0.0769)	(0.115)	(0.105)	(0.145)	(0.0997)
Has formal schooling	0.274***	0.160**	0.322***	0.229***	0.288***
	(0.0361)	(0.0638)	(0.0438)	(0.0535)	(0.0461)
Fostered	0.102**	0.126*	0.0987	0.159**	0.0256
	(0.0521)	(0.0767)	(0.0714)	(0.0785)	(0.0648)
Fostered young	−0.00118	−0.0452	−0.00601	−0.150	0.117
	(0.0669)	(0.103)	(0.0904)	(0.118)	(0.0828)
Age at first marriage	−7.50e−05	0.00329	−0.00165	−0.00315	0.00450
	(0.00276)	(0.00419)	(0.00362)	(0.00403)	(0.00379)
Inherited land	−0.0740*	−0.0266	−0.0897	−0.102	−0.0366
	(0.0449)	(0.0691)	(0.0586)	(0.0622)	(0.0539)
Inherited house	0.0736**	0.0601	0.0862*	0.0617	0.0883*
	(0.0368)	(0.0614)	(0.0448)	(0.0535)	(0.0452)
Other inheritance	0.0642	0.0330	0.114*	0.159***	−0.0186
	(0.0419)	(0.0558)	(0.0614)	(0.0566)	(0.0508)
Rural	−0.298***	–	–	−0.322***	−0.291***
	(0.0607)			(0.0842)	(0.0653)
Constant	12.95***	13.41***	12.46***	13.69***	13.52***
	(0.285)	(0.484)	(0.326)	(0.512)	(0.366)
Observations	3392	1756	1636	1479	1913
R^2	0.465	0.279	0.415	0.471	0.463

Note: Robust standard errors in parentheses, and are clustered at the household level. The variables 'First same gender', 'First of siblings' and 'First born is male' all refer to children of the same father, same mother. Regressions also contain regional (department) dummies. The reference variables are Wolof ethnicity, all other religions, occupation 'inactive', share of cell members 5–15, no and non-formal schooling.

*** $p < 0.01$.

** $p < 0.05$.

* $p < 0.1$.

Table 5. Regressions for log cell expenditure per capita by gender and rural/urban residence.

	(1) Rural men	(2) Rural women	(3) Urban men	(4) Urban women
Age	−0.0110	−0.00852	0.0310**	−0.0216
	(0.0138)	(0.00866)	(0.0148)	(0.0134)
Age squared	2.80e−05	5.68e−05	−0.000290**	0.000245*
	(0.000129)	(8.85e−05)	(0.000140)	(0.000140)
Muslim	−0.261	−0.00343	0.269*	0.0682
	(0.232)	(0.196)	(0.150)	(0.127)
Serere ethnicity	−0.186	−0.237**	−0.271***	−0.0591
	(0.161)	(0.120)	(0.0938)	(0.0925)
Poular ethnicity	0.0758	0.0565	−0.168*	−0.0575
	(0.103)	(0.0914)	(0.0948)	(0.0680)
Diola ethnicity	0.308	−0.394	0.0561	−0.193*
	(0.485)	(0.391)	(0.167)	(0.104)
Mandingue ethnicity	0.238	0.126	−0.414***	−0.160*
	(0.164)	(0.184)	(0.126)	(0.0863)
Sarakole ethnicity	−0.0774	0.285	−0.155	−0.0299
	(0.322)	(0.287)	(0.239)	(0.171)
Mandiaque ethnicity	−0.481	−0.678*	0.00144	−0.477**
	(0.408)	(0.383)	(0.262)	(0.225)
Other ethnicity	0.326	0.0227	0.0234	−0.220*
	(0.209)	(0.198)	(0.166)	(0.129)
Brothers same father	−0.0216	0.00527	0.0154	−0.0113
	(0.0191)	(0.0138)	(0.0191)	(0.0146)
Brothers same parents	0.0341	−0.0161	0.00828	−0.0173
	(0.0233)	(0.0153)	(0.0190)	(0.0172)
Sisters same father	0.0134	0.0215	−0.00529	0.0208
	(0.0199)	(0.0157)	(0.0190)	(0.0134)
Sisters same parents	0.00783	0.0522***	0.00588	0.0244
	(0.0217)	(0.0173)	(0.0188)	(0.0162)
Brothers same mother	0.0401	0.0185	0.0845***	0.0224
	(0.0509)	(0.0392)	(0.0296)	(0.0299)
Sisters same mother	0.0419	−0.0602**	−0.0728**	0.00366
	(0.0686)	(0.0243)	(0.0288)	(0.0467)
First same gender	0.0263	0.0615	0.0461	−0.0491
	(0.0822)	(0.0630)	(0.0864)	(0.0636)
First of siblings	−0.0861	0.0691	−0.0309	0.0769
	(0.0942)	(0.0897)	(0.0964)	(0.0866)
First born is male	0.106	0.152***	0.00555	−0.00539
	(0.0886)	(0.0581)	(0.0894)	(0.0599)
Father died recently	0.0760	−0.0227	−0.00617	−0.0561
	(0.140)	(0.0920)	(0.153)	(0.0752)
Father in farming	−0.0529	0.145**	0.239***	0.00457
	(0.0754)	(0.0607)	(0.0916)	(0.0818)
Mother in farm	−0.0828	−0.0999	−0.0873	0.0945
	(0.0856)	(0.0651)	(0.0891)	(0.0885)
Father in non-farm	0.0849	0.206**	0.279***	0.0802
	(0.0947)	(0.0875)	(0.0795)	(0.0697)
Mother in non-farm	−0.134	0.0652	−0.169*	−0.124*
	(0.101)	(0.0902)	(0.0917)	(0.0668)
Father in 'other'	0.147	0.0268	0.586*	0.398
	(0.240)	(0.232)	(0.322)	(0.386)
Mother in 'other'	−0.119	−0.287	0.401	0.0399
	(0.136)	(0.209)	(0.301)	(0.421)
Father's schooling	−0.242*	0.121	0.230**	0.0305
	(0.142)	(0.112)	(0.0948)	(0.0680)
Mother's schooling	0.0382	0.109	0.0969	0.292***
	(0.158)	(0.143)	(0.117)	(0.111)
Father rural	−0.0790	0.00103	−0.0576	−0.0394
	(0.159)	(0.0894)	(0.110)	(0.0822)
Mother rural	−0.167	0.0439	−0.0132	−0.0626
	(0.165)	(0.0870)	(0.112)	(0.0845)
Log hh size	−0.207**	−0.359***	−0.332***	−0.310***
	(0.0872)	(0.0636)	(0.0537)	(0.0557)
Log cell size	−0.255***	−0.0863	−0.0880	−0.0756
	(0.0776)	(0.0616)	(0.0664)	(0.0606)
Share of cell aged <5	−0.631**	−0.0906	0.123	−0.254
	(0.286)	(0.152)	(0.303)	(0.173)
Share of cell adults	0.104	0.309**	0.602***	0.503***
	(0.218)	(0.137)	(0.196)	(0.148)
Has formal schooling	0.111	0.142	0.278***	0.359***
	(0.0876)	(0.0871)	(0.0704)	(0.0552)
Fostered	0.209*	0.0131	0.181	0.0178
	(0.112)	(0.0953)	(0.118)	(0.0861)
Fostered young	−0.299	0.108	−0.112	0.128
	(0.182)	(0.118)	(0.157)	(0.114)
Age at first marriage	0.00241	0.00461	−0.00861	0.00613
	(0.00641)	(0.00586)	(0.00552)	(0.00501)
Inherited land	−0.0875	0.0363	−0.127	−0.0600
	(0.0898)	(0.0845)	(0.0921)	(0.0697)
Inherited house	0.0298	0.0785	0.105	0.100*
	(0.0799)	(0.0768)	(0.0752)	(0.0576)
Other inheritance	0.176**	−0.100	0.166*	0.0458
	(0.0727)	(0.0636)	(0.0888)	(0.0786)
Constant	14.28***	12.44***	11.78***	13.20***
	(0.811)	(0.534)	(0.530)	(0.384)
Observations	758	998	721	915
R^2	0.292	0.309	0.419	0.413

Note: Robust standard errors in parentheses, clustered at the household level. The variables 'First same gender', 'First of siblings' and 'First born is male' all refer to children of the same father, same mother. Regressions also contain regional (department) dummies. The reference variables are Wolof ethnicity, all other religions, occupation 'inactive', share of cell members 5–15, no and non-formal schooling.

*** $p < 0.01$.
** $p < 0.05$.
* $p < 0.1$.

Along with the gender differences in characteristics, which (as we have seen) account for the gender disparity in consumption, there are also gender differences in returns to characteristics. A Chow test rejects the null hypothesis of equality of the coefficients across the regressions for men and women ($F(72,1498) = 1.84$; Prob. $> F < 0.00005$).

Both own education and mother's education are significant in the full sample consumption regressions. Strikingly, *maternal* education has a much stronger effect—a change of 0.17 in log consumption—than paternal education, and this is due to its effect in urban areas and for women. But note that only 7.5% of mothers have some formal education.

Other parental characteristics matter. Having a father (but not a mother) who worked in the non-farm sector has a large and significant effect on log consumption of 0.30; having a father in farming has a smaller effect (0.17). (The left out category is inactive.) These effects are stronger for men than for women. It is clear that parental characteristics matter, even though land and housing inheritance do not.

Being fostered out as a child is associated with higher adult consumption; the effect is confined to men, and is stronger for those living in urban areas. This result is consistent with the previously noted fact that the common practice of fostering is often associated with investment in the human capital of the child. Notice, however, that having been fostered out young (under age 2) has an offsetting effect for men. The positive effect on adult welfare is for those who were not fostered young.[21]

To throw some light on the costs and benefits to adult offspring of parental sorting by sector and schooling, Table 6 presents the total effect on log consumption of various combinations of fathers' and mothers' characteristics using the full sample estimates. The results suggest that whatever the education of one's parents, having both parents in the non-farm sector yields higher consumption than having both in farming. That is probably what one would expect. However, there is a more surprising and interesting effect of having parents from different sectors. The mixed combination of a father in a non-farm and a mother in a farm-related occupation provides the highest welfare gain to a child at any given combination of parental education—a higher gain than having had both in non-farm activities. This could well reflect longer-term benefits from a more dynamic and diversified family background. But notice that this only holds when it is the father who is in the non-farm sector; the reverse parental combination (father in farming; mother in non-farm work) yields the lowest consumption gain at whatever education combination is considered—even lower than having both parents in farming.

Table 6. Returns to log per capita consumption of parental characteristics.

	Formal schooling			
	Neither	Father yes/ mother no	Father no/ mother yes	Both
Same sector				
Both farm	0.019	0.093	0.184	0.258
Both non-farm	0.050	0.124	0.215	0.289
Mixed sectors				
Father farm/mother non-farm	−0.025	0.049	0.140	0.214
Father non-farm/mother farm	0.094	0.168	0.259	0.333

Note: Based on the coefficients estimated for total log consumption per capita given in Table 4, column 1.

At any given combination of parental occupation, the consumption gains are largest when both parents have had some formal schooling (Table 6). Furthermore, for any parental farm and non-farm occupational combination, having better schooled parents is better for the offspring's adult living standards. Positive parental matching on education is beneficial while positive sorting on sector is not (holding education and all else constant). Finally, mothers' formal education is more welfare enhancing than fathers' education whatever the parents' combination of occupational sectors.

6. INTERGENERATIONAL EFFECTS ON ECONOMIC ACTIVITIES AND GEOGRAPHIC MOBILITY

We now turn to the question of how much intergenerational linkages matter to the sector of economic activity and location. Table 7 summarizes the key marginal effects from probits for agricultural self-employment. Again, parental characteristics matter, though in some possibly surprising ways. Having a father in farming does not have a significant effect, but having a mother who was a farmer makes it more likely one will be a farmer. This is so for men and women, but is significantly larger for men in rural areas (consistent with the effect of having a mother in farming on the probability of inheriting land being positive and stronger for men). Having had either parent (and more so a mother) in the non-farm sector makes it less likely that one will be a farmer in rural areas, with a far more pronounced effect for men.

Table 7. Marginal effects of inheritance, schooling and parental characteristics on agricultural employment.

	(1) All	(2) Rural	(3) Urban	(4) Men	(5) Women	(6) Rural men	(7) Rural women	(8) Urban men	(9) Urban women
Father in farming	0.0169	0.0141	0.00740	0.0120	0.0198	−0.00175	0.0353	0.0218	−0.00463
	(0.0168)	(0.0324)	(0.0104)	(0.0271)	(0.0191)	(0.0485)	(0.0409)	(0.0196)	(0.00294)
Mother in farm	0.0770***	0.116***	0.0175	0.112***	0.0567**	0.192***	0.0692	−0.0209**	0.0500
	(0.0240)	(0.0396)	(0.0185)	(0.0377)	(0.0241)	(0.0588)	(0.0426)	(0.00932)	(0.0313)
Father in non-farm	−0.0235	−0.0765*	−0.00121	−0.0523	−0.0213	−0.180***	−0.0226	0.00792	−0.0109
	(0.0198)	(0.0450)	(0.0103)	(0.0325)	(0.0243)	(0.0653)	(0.0634)	(0.0152)	(0.00724)
Mother in non-farm	−0.0541***	−0.159***	−0.00426	−0.105***	−0.0262	−0.237***	−0.106*	−0.0129	−0.000300
	(0.0208)	(0.0483)	(0.00923)	(0.0325)	(0.0237)	(0.0679)	(0.0588)	(0.0119)	(0.00306)
Father in 'other'	−0.112***	−0.244***	–	−0.142***	–	−0.289**	–	–	–
	(0.0239)	(0.0827)		(0.0451)		(0.118)			
Mother in 'other'	−0.104***	−0.221***	–	−0.150***	−0.0773***	−0.276***	−0.174***	–	–
	(0.0177)	(0.0490)		(0.0276)	(0.0184)	(0.0789)	(0.0578)		
Father's schooling	0.0273	0.0795	−0.00209	0.0200	0.0103	0.0148	0.0803	0.00639	−0.000983
	(0.0301)	(0.0819)	(0.00978)	(0.0516)	(0.0321)	(0.121)	(0.103)	(0.0194)	(0.00279)
Mother's schooling	−0.0147	−0.0963	0.00123	−0.0849*	0.0356	−0.145	−0.0947	−0.0307***	0.0353
	(0.0384)	(0.0776)	(0.0159)	(0.0454)	(0.0530)	(0.107)	(0.0872)	(0.00879)	(0.0275)
Own schooling	−0.0203	−0.0673	−0.00524	−0.0656**	0.0354	−0.0902	0.0136	−0.0542***	0.00835*
	(0.0181)	(0.0451)	(0.00802)	(0.0282)	(0.0243)	(0.0633)	(0.0621)	(0.0170)	(0.00474)
Inherited land	0.0557**	0.0801*	0.00998	0.00373	0.114***	−0.00998	0.171***	0.00312	0.0118
	(0.0218)	(0.0412)	(0.0128)	(0.0304)	(0.0343)	(0.0571)	(0.0643)	(0.0158)	(0.0100)
Inherited house	0.00825	0.0128	0.0148	0.00210	0.0153	−0.0298	0.0769	0.0196	−0.000619
	(0.0180)	(0.0371)	(0.0117)	(0.0273)	(0.0218)	(0.0515)	(0.0528)	(0.0144)	(0.00375)
Inherited other	−0.0404**	−0.0669*	−0.0157**	−0.0402	−0.0255	−0.0519	−0.0438	−0.0142	−0.00492*
	(0.0160)	(0.0343)	(0.00723)	(0.0260)	(0.0186)	(0.0490)	(0.0442)	(0.0114)	(0.00270)
Observations	3407	1761	1565	1479	1843	752	957	675	725
Pseudo R^2	0.306	0.222	0.240	0.318	0.348	0.234	0.285	0.314	0.433

Notes: Robust standard errors in parentheses, clustered at the household level. Marginal effects are reported. The regressions include controls listed in Table 3 notes. The 'other' occupation drops out of the urban regressions as it is found only in rural areas.

*** $p < 0.01$.

** $p < 0.05$.

* $p < 0.1$.

Parental schooling effects on the probability of being a farmer seem weak, though for urban men there is a significant negative effect of mother's schooling. Own formal schooling makes it less likely men will be in farming (particularly urban men), but makes this slightly more likely for urban women.

We find that inheriting land makes farming more likely though this effect is confined to women in rural areas. Endogeneity is a concern here; as women rarely inherit land, those who remained in the same village as their parents and are in farming are more likely to be the ones who inherit land. Inheriting land does not make it more likely that men will be farmers. We find no significant effects of inheriting a house. Other (non-land, non-housing) forms of inheritance are associated with lower probabilities of an adult being in agricultural self-employment. This effect is found in both rural and urban areas, though it is stronger for rural areas (Table 7).

Analogous results for non-farm occupations are found in Table 8. For rural men, having a father in the rural non-farm sector enhances the probability of being in that sector. On the other hand, having a mother who farms or whose occupation is 'other' significantly reduces that likelihood for rural men. A mother in the non-farm sector significantly enhances the probability of an adult working in the non-farm sector, although not for rural women. Higher own schooling increases the probability for men (and it is a larger effect for men in rural areas) but not for women. Fathers' schooling has no influence, while mothers' formal education is positively associated with rural men's off-farm work.

Table 8. Marginal effects of inheritance, schooling and parental characteristics on non-agricultural employment.

	(1) All	(2) Rural	(3) Urban	(4) Men	(5) Women	(6) Rural men	(7) Rural women	(8) Urban men	(9) Urban women
Father in farming	0.0122	−0.00256	0.0333	0.0355	−0.00763	0.0202	−0.0255	0.0330	0.0430
	(0.0273)	(0.0301)	(0.0381)	(0.0373)	(0.0339)	(0.0469)	(0.0340)	(0.0411)	(0.0602)
Mother in farm	−0.0350	−0.0388	0.0275	−0.131***	0.0354	−0.148***	0.0245	−0.0146	0.0493
	(0.0308)	(0.0322)	(0.0464)	(0.0448)	(0.0378)	(0.0497)	(0.0368)	(0.0581)	(0.0686)
Father in non-farm	0.0377	0.106**	−0.00258	0.0979**	0.00573	0.199**	0.0636	0.0383	−0.0144
	(0.0283)	(0.0440)	(0.0334)	(0.0429)	(0.0366)	(0.0774)	(0.0559)	(0.0393)	(0.0506)
Mother in non-farm	0.140***	0.157***	0.133***	0.168***	0.128***	0.222**	0.0961	0.103***	0.144***
	(0.0302)	(0.0544)	(0.0296)	(0.0482)	(0.0379)	(0.0899)	(0.0631)	(0.0328)	(0.0455)
Father in 'other'	−0.111	0.0334	−0.201	−0.0914	−0.134	0.106	–	−0.398*	−0.0866
	(0.113)	(0.122)	(0.172)	(0.175)	(0.108)	(0.152)		(0.214)	(0.188)
Mother in 'other'	−0.201***	−0.173***	0.0144	−0.308***	0.0325	−0.270***	0.0117	−0.129	0.160
	(0.0761)	(0.0432)	(0.250)	(0.107)	(0.145)	(0.0607)	(0.112)	(0.238)	(0.312)
Father's schooling	−0.0303	−0.0765	0.0245	−0.0107	−0.0350	−0.0377	−0.0619	0.0401	−0.000904
	(0.0326)	(0.0549)	(0.0348)	(0.0603)	(0.0384)	(0.118)	(0.0617)	(0.0445)	(0.0493)
Mother's schooling	−0.00922	0.172*	−0.0652	0.0655	−0.0489	0.284**	0.100	−0.0215	−0.0856
	(0.0476)	(0.0889)	(0.0530)	(0.0835)	(0.0510)	(0.124)	(0.106)	(0.0774)	(0.0683)
Own schooling	0.0560**	0.0919**	0.0375	0.166***	0.00599	0.278***	0.0378	0.118***	−0.0172
	(0.0258)	(0.0437)	(0.0290)	(0.0364)	(0.0321)	(0.0682)	(0.0504)	(0.0350)	(0.0412)
Inherited land	−0.0323	−0.0161	0.00446	0.00839	−0.0209	0.0656	−0.0615	−0.0307	0.0576
	(0.0305)	(0.0359)	(0.0434)	(0.0429)	(0.0397)	(0.0566)	(0.0409)	(0.0494)	(0.0604)
Inherited house	0.0225	−0.00491	0.0173	−0.00856	0.0324	−0.0278	0.0152	−0.0163	0.0285
	(0.0269)	(0.0344)	(0.0331)	(0.0382)	(0.0335)	(0.0528)	(0.0441)	(0.0375)	(0.0453)
Inherited other	0.0464*	0.00324	0.121***	0.0170	0.0855**	−0.0120	0.0297	0.0752**	0.174***
	(0.0272)	(0.0316)	(0.0335)	(0.0362)	(0.0354)	(0.0467)	(0.0398)	(0.0341)	(0.0499)
Observations	3385	1732	1646	1479	1906	741	974	718	921
Pseudo R^2	0.208	0.154	0.156	0.262	0.175	0.233	0.148	0.148	0.141

Notes: Robust standard errors in parentheses, clustered at the household level. Marginal effects are reported. The regressions include controls listed in Table 3 notes.
*** $p < 0.01$.
** $p < 0.05$
* $p < 0.1$.

We find no evidence that inheriting land has a significant effect on the likelihood of doing non-farm activities (Table 8) (although, as we will see, this changes when we allow land to be endogenous). However, inheritance of other (non-land, non-housing) assets makes it more likely that women overall, and men and women in urban Senegal, will be employed in the non-farm sector (Table 8).

A number of effects on geographic mobility—identified by whether an adult lives in the same place as his or her parents—are evident in Table 9. Having a farmer for a father makes a child's mobility more likely in the full sample. The effect is much attenuated and only significant at the 10% level for the rural and all male and female samples. Having a father who worked in the non-farm sector has the opposite effect—increasing the likelihood of living in the same place, though the effect is only significant for rural areas, and is larger for rural women. A mother who was engaged in a non-agricultural activity also has a significant effect on living in the same place, but in this case, not for daughters. Children with parents occupied in 'other' are also more likely to be where their parents resided. Having a father with formal schooling makes mobility more likely for urban men; a mother with schooling makes it more likely that rural men will live in the same place as their parents. Own formal schooling makes mobility more likely, though the effect is only significant for men. These results underline the fact that the intergenerational occupational mobility discussed in the last section implies geographical mobility more often when parents are farmers than when they are in a non-farm activity and hence, less likely to have a rural location.

Table 9. Marginal effects of inheritance, schooling and parental characteristics on living in the same residence.

	(1) All	(2) Rural	(3) Urban	(4) Men	(5) Women	(6) Rural men	(7) Rural women	(8) Urban men	(9) Urban women
Father in farming	−0.0730***	−0.0541*	−0.0448	−0.0630*	−0.0619*	−0.0296	−0.0483	−0.0412	−0.0643
	(0.0259)	(0.0325)	(0.0522)	(0.0359)	(0.0339)	(0.0200)	(0.0458)	(0.0774)	(0.0667)
Mother in farm	−0.00612	0.00221	0.000699	0.0239	−0.0299	0.0316*	−0.0441	0.00264	0.0229
	(0.0289)	(0.0352)	(0.0649)	(0.0397)	(0.0369)	(0.0189)	(0.0480)	(0.104)	(0.0853)
Father in non-farm	0.0755**	0.125***	0.0438	0.0634*	0.0693*	0.0536***	0.182***	0.0214	0.0451
	(0.0298)	(0.0429)	(0.0427)	(0.0378)	(0.0389)	(0.0170)	(0.0700)	(0.0654)	(0.0535)
Mother in non-farm	0.120***	0.150***	0.105***	0.121***	0.0681*	0.0567***	0.123	0.175**	0.0676
	(0.0297)	(0.0441)	(0.0398)	(0.0385)	(0.0378)	(0.0162)	(0.0817)	(0.0723)	(0.0474)
Father in 'other'	0.192**	–	0.0547	0.0656	0.268**	–	–	−0.117	0.119
	(0.0878)		(0.149)	(0.103)	(0.128)			(0.213)	(0.187)
Mother in 'other'	0.248***	0.131*	0.322**	0.170**	0.249**	0.0461**	0.144	0.116	0.280
	(0.0685)	(0.0747)	(0.127)	(0.0693)	(0.108)	(0.0227)	(0.160)	(0.165)	(0.187)
Father's schooling	−0.0282	0.0846	−0.0667*	−0.0644	−0.0321	0.0248	0.0326	−0.120**	−0.0278
	(0.0360)	(0.0693)	(0.0393)	(0.0514)	(0.0440)	(0.0410)	(0.113)	(0.0606)	(0.0497)
Mother's schooling	0.0740	0.146**	−0.0159	0.0781	0.0249	0.0509***	0.183	0.0182	−0.0531
	(0.0452)	(0.0608)	(0.0554)	(0.0654)	(0.0583)	(0.0171)	(0.113)	(0.119)	(0.0625)
Own schooling	−0.0457*	−0.0606	−0.0698**	−0.0762**	−0.00579	−0.105**	0.0352	−0.107*	−0.0672
	(0.0277)	(0.0536)	(0.0343)	(0.0383)	(0.0356)	(0.0504)	(0.0705)	(0.0581)	(0.0436)
Inherited land	−0.0213	0.0288	−0.0948**	0.0221	−0.0810**	0.0349	0.0244	−0.0574	−0.120**
	(0.0283)	(0.0387)	(0.0419)	(0.0383)	(0.0389)	(0.0233)	(0.0613)	(0.0703)	(0.0556)
Inherited house	0.0459*	0.00788	0.0469	0.0562*	0.0250	0.0408*	−0.0449	0.0618	0.0291
	(0.0245)	(0.0365)	(0.0349)	(0.0321)	(0.0328)	(0.0227)	(0.0563)	(0.0564)	(0.0438)
Inherited other	0.0170	0.0239	0.000188	0.0242	−0.0220	0.0258	−0.00785	0.0282	−0.0218
	(0.0257)	(0.0351)	(0.0422)	(0.0342)	(0.0349)	(0.0211)	(0.0537)	(0.0692)	(0.0537)
Observations	3407	1736	1646	1436	1921	701	994	702	921
Pseudo R^2	0.180	0.279	0.330	0.346	0.109	0.366	0.183	0.426	0.309

Notes: Robust standard errors in parentheses, clustered at the household level. Marginal effects are reported. The regressions include controls listed in Table 3 notes.
*** $p < 0.01$.
** $p < 0.05$.
* $p < 0.1$.

Inheriting land does not have any significant effect on the probability of moving to a location different from where one's father resided in the sample as a whole (Table 9). However, there is a sign that inheriting land actually encourages such mobility for urban women. Inheriting a house makes it more likely that a man living in rural areas will have the same residence as his parents—in a rather obvious way since the one son who will inherit the house is the one who intends to live in it (or already does)—but there are no other significant effects of this form of inheritance. Nor are there any significant effects of other (non-land, non-housing) inheritance.

7. TESTS OF ROBUSTNESS

Possibly the effect of inheritance is diluted by including in the sample cell heads whose parents are still alive, and cannot (of course) be a source of inheritance. We tested this possibility by only including cases where either the father or the mother is dead or both are dead. (Details are found in the Statistical Addendum.) In all three cases, the coefficients and standard errors were very similar to the results presented in Table 3. Again we found no significant effect of inheriting land on consumption. There were only minor differences for Table 4.[22]

We also tested sensitivity to allowing for an interaction effect between inheritance and the time since the father died; for those with a dead father, the mean time since death is 22 years (the median is 19). It is not clear on a priori grounds what one would expect. The inherited asset may have a positive rate of return allowing for capital accumulation, though other factors may come into play; for example, there were clearly fewer options to farming for those who inherited the land a long time ago. Also, assets (including land) depreciate in value over time. Our tests involved simply adding an interaction effect between inheritance and years since the death of the father to the preceding regressions.[23] For cell consumption per capita, there was a negative interaction effect though only among urban men, for which the effect was significant at the 5% level. The total effect was positive up to about 30 years, though not significant even when the father died recently. For agricultural self-employment the interaction effect was often positive though generally not significant, except for urban men; for non-farm employment the pattern switched, with a negative interaction effect, though again not strong. However, allowing for such an interaction effect does not change the main findings reported above.

Yet another variation is to allow for "cross-effects" of inheritance and education of the spouse (for example, including the inheritance of a woman's husband in the regression for her consumption or economic activity). We found no significant cross-effects of inheritance or education on consumption for either men or women. Nor were there any significant effects of a husband's inheritance on the wife's sector of work.[24] There were signs that a wife's inheritance increased the likelihood of men in rural areas being farmers, and made it more likely that urban men would be inactive. One significant cross-effect was that having an educated husband made mobility more likely for women, as measured by whether she lived in the same village as her parents. This was found in both urban and rural areas.

Another possible concern is that some of our regressors may be considered endogenous. The main results on the effects of inheritance on the various dependent variables were found to be robust to dropping other potentially endogenous variables, namely own-schooling, being fostered as a child and age at first marriage. (The endogeneity concern here is that these variables may be jointly determined with land inheritance.) One change of note is that dropping own education revealed even weaker effects of parental education on sector of employment.

Our assumption that past inheritance is exogenous to current living standards can be questioned. Choices about who inherits the land may be influenced by factors that are unobserved by us, but observed by the parents or other stakeholders—factors that are also correlated with the economic activity and economic welfare of the child on reaching adulthood. It may be decided by the family group that one of the sons is best suited to taking charge of the family farm on the father's death. This may reflect a latent interest or ability at farming, revealed while growing up. Or it may be that other sons show more aptitude for non-farm work. Parents may also have gender preferences in their choices about inheritance and schooling—choices that are influenced by both market and non-market parameters.[25] Another potential source of endogeneity is the fact that children could possibly decline the inheritance, in particular of land, if taking care of it is not compatible with their preferred activity or if, being themselves economically successful, they feel that their siblings have a greater need for it.

In testing the robustness of our results to treating inheritance as endogenous, the key identifying assumption we make is that the death of the father or mother only matters to an individual adult's current economic welfare via inheritance of land or other assets. It is hard to see why parental death sometime in the past would matter to current adult consumption except via inheritance and (hence) wealth. Possibly the shock of parental death will have an impact, but then we control for a father's recent death (within the last two years) in all our regressions.

For the purpose of testing robustness to allowing for endogenous land inheritance we assume that parents first decide who gets the land, and on that basis then determine the assignment of non-land inheritance, education, and fostering. We also assume that age at marriage is endogenous, and determined in part by whether one inherited the land. Thus we treat these variables as unidentified functions of land inheritance and the remaining regression controls, so that we can solve for the outcomes of interest as functions of only land-inheritance and those controls. Thus we are able to treat land inheritance as endogenous using parental death as the only available IV.[26]

The Statistical Addendum gives the first-stage regressions. Unsurprisingly, the death of either parent significantly increased the probability of inheritance, and the coefficients are considerably higher for paternal death.

Table 10 gives the IV estimates, treating land inheritance as endogenous, for each of the dependent variables.[27] (Note that the estimator is not feasible for the sub-sample for which the father is dead.) Our results on land inheritance are reasonably robust to relaxing the exogeneity assumption. In particular, we still find that land inheritance does not convey any significant consumption benefit.

Table 10. IV estimates for all dependent variables for the total, men only and women only samples.

	(1)	(2)	(3)	(4)	(5)	(6)	(7)	(8)	(9)	(10)	(11)	(12)
	Log per cap expenditures			Farm employment			Non-farm			Same residence as parents		
	All	Men	Women	All	Men	Women	All	Men	Women	All	Men	Women
Inherited land	0.119	0.0475	0.214	−0.0394	−0.159**	0.0510	0.124**	0.178**	0.0650	0.0373	0.0756	−0.0316
	(0.110)	(0.151)	(0.164)	(0.0449)	(0.0714)	(0.0602)	(0.0611)	(0.0856)	(0.0914)	(0.0614)	(0.0751)	(0.0934)
Father in farming	0.0849**	0.0537	0.0955**	0.0103	0.00756	0.0167	0.0192	0.0364	0.000268	−0.0589***	−0.0404*	−0.0636**
	(0.0404)	(0.0568)	(0.0474)	(0.0195)	(0.0289)	(0.0226)	(0.0218)	(0.0305)	(0.0277)	(0.0208)	(0.0239)	(0.0304)
Mother in farming	−0.0611*	−0.0840	−0.0936*	0.0965***	0.113***	0.0791***	−0.0333	−0.105***	0.0221	−0.00340	0.0230	−0.0235
	(0.0440)	(0.0631)	(0.0523)	(0.0248)	(0.0346)	(0.0285)	(0.0239)	(0.0358)	(0.0300)	(0.0239)	(0.0280)	(0.0328)
Father in non-farm	0.210***	0.226***	0.181***	−0.0217	−0.0651**	−0.0135	0.0575**	0.122***	0.0241	0.0668***	0.0552*	0.0648*
	(0.0442)	(0.0626)	(0.0547)	(0.0172)	(0.0291)	(0.0201)	(0.0238)	(0.0359)	(0.0326)	(0.0253)	(0.0317)	(0.0354)
Mother in non-farm	−0.0990**	−0.135**	−0.0678	−0.0285*	−0.0695**	−0.0235	0.108***	0.105***	0.113***	0.106***	0.115***	0.0609*
	(0.0436)	(0.0679)	(0.0533)	(0.0157)	(0.0293)	(0.0185)	(0.0247)	(0.0372)	(0.0336)	(0.0256)	(0.0327)	(0.0346)
Father's schooling	0.170***	0.263***	0.129**	0.0138	0.0109	0.00273	−0.0175	0.00455	−0.0240	−0.0114	−0.0430	−0.00684
	(0.0503)	(0.0784)	(0.0610)	(0.0152)	(0.0277)	(0.0177)	(0.0262)	(0.0395)	(0.0357)	(0.0296)	(0.0383)	(0.0381)
Mother's schooling	0.193***	0.0571	0.278***	0.00894	−0.0399	0.0293	−0.0210	0.0420	−0.0618	0.0543	0.0764	0.0140
	(0.0638)	(0.0874)	(0.0863)	(0.0248)	(0.0432)	(0.0264)	(0.0373)	(0.0607)	(0.0453)	(0.0361)	(0.0503)	(0.0492)
Constant	13.73***	12.97***	13.79***	0.149	0.789***	0.537***	0.386**	0.0374	0.201	0.608***	0.623***	0.752***
	(0.308)	(0.412)	(0.363)	(0.197)	(0.161)	(0.148)	(0.197)	(0.179)	(0.135)	(0.135)	(0.210)	(0.228)
Observations	3571	1554	2017	3587	1561	2026	3587	1561	2026	3587	1561	2026
R^2	0.449	0.461	0.437	0.286	0.306	0.326	0.242	0.278	0.212	0.218	0.393	0.147

Notes: Linear IV coefficients for (4)-(12). Robust standard errors in parentheses, clustered at household level. The regressions exclude own education, whether fostered and age at first marriage; other controls are as listed in Table 3 notes.
*** $p < 0.01$
** $p < 0.05$.
* $p < 0.1$.

However, we now find that land inheritance tends to encourage a male to only shift from farm to non-farm work, suggesting that there was a downward bias in the earlier estimates. When we stratify according to whether the man is the household head or not we find that this effect is far stronger in size and only statistically significant for those who are *not* household heads. Table 11 gives a split of the results for farm and non-farm activities (as well as for the other dependent variables) according to whether or not the cell head is also the overall household head.[28] The IV coefficients on land inheritance in the non-farm regression are 0.133 (s.e. = 0.105) for male heads of household and 0.457 (s.e. = 0.151) for male non-heads. Likewise, the significant negative impact of inheriting land on being a farmer is only present for non-household heads. The latter sub-sample tends to be comprised of married brothers of household heads. Finally, and in line with the above findings, land inheritance also makes it significantly more likely that male heads live where their parents lived, and less likely for non-heads. When land inheritance comes *without* the responsibilities of headship it appears to be an important factor in encouraging diversification into non-farm activities.

Table 11. IV estimates for all dependent variables for the sample of men only.

	(1)	(2)	(3)	(4)	(5)	(6)	(7)	(8)
	Log expenditure per capita		Farm employment		Non-farm employment		Same residence as parents	
	Heads	Non-heads	Heads	Non-heads	Heads	Non-heads	Heads	Non-heads
Inherited land	0.168	−0.307	−0.127	−0.283**	0.133	0.457***	0.224**	−0.200*
	(0.200)	(0.261)	(0.0896)	(0.115)	(0.105)	(0.151)	(0.107)	(0.111)
Father in farming	0.0950	−0.154	0.00702	−0.0133	0.0278	0.115	−0.0504*	−0.0463
	(0.0654)	(0.119)	(0.0306)	(0.0650)	(0.0330)	(0.0808)	(0.0275)	(0.0566)
Mother in farming	−0.137**	0.272*	0.0512	0.305***	−0.0676*	−0.210**	0.0297	0.0134
	(0.0698)	(0.146)	(0.0351)	(0.0861)	(0.0378)	(0.0985)	(0.0314)	(0.0744)
Father in non-farm	0.309***	−0.0705	−0.0717**	−0.0784	0.0907**	0.330***	0.0483	0.0387
	(0.0716)	(0.146)	(0.0321)	(0.0612)	(0.0391)	(0.0885)	(0.0378)	(0.0641)
Mother in non-farm	−0.105	−0.0622	−0.0803**	−0.0459	0.128***	0.0409	0.112**	0.119**
	(0.0828)	(0.110)	(0.0353)	(0.0451)	(0.0440)	(0.0699)	(0.0435)	(0.0464)
Father's schooling	0.331***	0.0554	0.0423	−0.0976*	−0.00891	0.0890	−0.0566	−0.0118
	(0.0991)	(0.119)	(0.0329)	(0.0512)	(0.0451)	(0.0939)	(0.0501)	(0.0616)
Mother's schooling	−0.0147	0.258*	−0.0658	−0.000177	0.0688	−0.00361	0.0863	−0.00846
	(0.122)	(0.153)	(0.0504)	(0.0590)	(0.0662)	(0.116)	(0.0678)	(0.0717)
Constant	13.73***	13.26***	0.199	−0.245	0.431	0.110	0.938***	0.931***
	(0.483)	(0.856)	(0.245)	(0.361)	(0.278)	(0.574)	(0.209)	(0.328)
Observations	1193	361	1198	363	1198	363	1198	363
R^2	0.451	0.505	0.327	0.452	0.309	0.340	0.372	0.358

Notes: Linear IV coefficients for (3)–(8). Robust standard errors in parentheses, clustered at the household level. The regressions exclude own education, whether fostered and age at first marriage; other controls are as listed in Table 3 notes.
*** $p < 0.01$.
** $p < 0.05$.
* $p < 0.1$.

8. IMPLICATIONS FOR EXPLAINING INEQUALITY

It is clear from these results that bequests can play little role in perpetuating consumption inequality. However, other parental characteristics clearly do matter, both directly and via a child's characteristics at adulthood, notably education. To quantify the contributions of the various additive factors we have identified above, we follow Shorrocks (1982) in identifying the contribution of the kth explanatory variable to total inequality by its share of variance, with equal sharing of the interaction terms stemming from correlations among the factors. (Shorrocks terms this the "natural decomposition" and shows that, under certain conditions, it is also relevant to other inequality measures besides the variance.) Following Fields (2003), when the "income" variable y is given by its linear regression on a vector x, this gives:

$$c_k = \frac{\beta_k \operatorname{cov}(x_k, y)}{\operatorname{var}(y)} \qquad (2)$$

where

$$y_i = \sum_{k=1}^{m} \beta_k x_{ik}. \qquad (3)$$

And x_{ik} is the kth predictor (x_{im} can be taken to be an error term, with $\beta_m = 1$). Thus the contribution of the kth explanatory variable to inequality in y is simply the product of the partial regression coefficient of y on x_k (holding all other variables constant) with the total regression coefficient of x_k on y (holding nothing else constant). Note that the decomposition is unchanged if y is the log of income (Fields, 2003).

Table 12 presents decompositions of consumption inequality implied by the regressions in Table 4. As expected, the inheritance variables (land, housing or other assets) contribute very little. Far more important to inequality than these forms of inheritance is "own schooling," which contributes 9% to overall consumption inequality (almost one fifth of the explained component) and 11% in urban Senegal. The share is even higher for women but is much lower in rural areas. The father's sector of employment is important, with the incidence of non-farm parental work contributing almost 6%, while the incidence of farm employment among fathers reduced inequality. Demographics, especially cell size and the proportion of adults, also emerge as large contributors to inequality, especially in rural areas. In the national sample, almost half of the explained inequality is attributable to rural–urban location.

Table 12. Inequality decomposition for log consumption per person implied by Table 4.

	Share of inequality attributable to each source (%)				
	All	Rural	Urban	Men	Women
Male	−0.07	−1.03	0.60	–	–
Age	−0.65	0.39	1.11	−0.07	−2.81
Age squared	0.05	−0.05	−0.89	0.66	2.44
Muslim	−0.05	−0.11	0.00	−0.11	−0.03
Serere	0.79	3.40	−0.28	1.14	0.54
Poular	0.26	0.63	1.02	0.84	0.03
Diola	0.04	0.94	−0.01	0.02	0.30
Mandingue	0.25	−0.10	1.10	0.55	0.07
Sarakole	−0.06	0.41	−0.06	−0.08	−0.01
Mandiaque	0.05	0.91	0.36	−0.09	0.32
Other ethnicity	−0.01	0.36	−0.08	0.17	0.00
Brothers same father	0.001	−0.08	0.19	0.09	−0.03
Brothers same parents	0.01	0.26	0.00	0.43	0.00
Sisters same father	0.39	0.62	0.24	0.01	0.82
Sisters same parents	0.34	0.70	0.20	0.15	0.91
Brothers same mother	0.55	0.44	0.52	0.87	0.38
Sisters same mother	−0.17	0.12	−0.08	−0.12	−0.26
First same gender	0.004	0.03	−0.02	0.01	0.06
First of siblings	0.06	0.00	0.36	−0.05	0.36
First born is male	0.34	2.04	−0.08	0.06	0.03
Father dead recently	0.01	0.03	0.02	0.01	0.04
Father in farming	−1.60	−0.50	−0.87	−0.84	−2.12
Mother in farming	1.42	2.74	−0.04	1.49	1.48
Father in non-farm	4.45	1.19	3.41	4.90	4.03
Mother in non-farm	−0.48	−0.01	0.68	−0.15	−0.64
Father in 'other'	0.02	−0.27	1.01	−0.28	0.15
Mother in 'other'	0.65	0.96	−0.03	0.80	0.67
Father's schooling	1.08	−0.08	1.59	2.17	0.57
Mother's schooling	1.08	0.33	1.99	0.10	2.61
Father rural	−0.23	0.04	0.20	−1.83	1.20
Mother rural	2.46	0.13	0.74	4.07	1.15
Log hh size	13.82	17.98	19.20	13.95	13.87
Log cell size	4.16	13.65	5.83	4.75	1.28
Share of cell aged <5	1.59	3.04	1.29	2.13	1.03
Share of cell adults	9.25	8.99	14.39	5.47	8.62
Has formal schooling	9.02	1.27	11.02	6.92	9.76
Fostered	0.65	0.47	0.79	0.79	0.19
Fostered young	−0.001	0.01	−0.02	−0.29	0.51
Age at first marriage	−0.07	0.98	−0.56	−0.55	0.91
Inherited land	0.60	−0.07	0.38	1.80	0.16
Inherited house	0.45	0.32	0.66	−0.15	0.92
Other inheritance	0.03	0.10	1.04	−0.47	−0.01
Rural	14.43	–	–	15.25	14.88
Total share explained	46.50	27.90	41.50	47.00	46.20

Note: The sources do not add to the total share explained due to the omission of the share of inequality due to department of residence.

9. CONCLUSIONS

We find evidence of significant intergenerational linkages in this setting. This is evident in the correlations between parents' and children's sectors of occupation, which persist on adding controls for heterogeneity in other respects. Nonetheless, there is considerable intergenerational mobility, both across sectors and residentially. This is primarily associated with the transition from farm to non-farm activities. Only one third of the sons of farmers stayed in farming. Father–son mobility between farm and non-farm sectors is high in Senegal relative to other developing countries for which comparable estimates are available. And adult women in our sample are far more economically active than were their mothers, although there is still less occupational mobility for women.

Our results suggest that gender plays an important role. There is consumption inequality between men and women, though this is largely accountable to differences in observable factors such as education. The intergenerational linkages through the mother appear to be stronger than through the father, including on the son's economic activity. Educated mothers are more likely to have sons in the non-farm sector. While women with formal schooling are no more likely to be in non-farm employment and (slightly) more likely to be farmers, it is their sons who are more likely to find their way into the non-farm sector.

Assuming conditional exogeneity of inheritance (and with a wide range of controls), inheriting the land makes it more likely that a woman will stay a farmer, but this is not so for men. Inheriting other (non-land, non-housing) assets appears to strongly help get urban women into non-farm work, but the effect is less significant and smaller for urban men and not present in rural areas. However, endogeneity bias might partly account for those results. As a robustness test, we allow for the possible endogeneity of land inheritance by assuming that the death of a parent only matters via inheritance (though allowing for the short-term shock of parental death). With only one instrumental variable we are only able to identify the causal effect of land inheritance, subject to the aforementioned exclusion restriction. We find evidence that land inheritance does play a role in facilitating diversification from farm into non-farm activities, although this is only present for men who do not also inherit the responsibilities of being the overall head of the household. The potential wealth effect of inheritance on activity choice seems to be inhibited by the obligations attendant to household headship.

On average, inheriting the land or house brings no significant gain to an adult's consumption. It appears that intra-household allocation across generations comes fairly close to equalizing consumption between otherwise identical individuals, only one of whom takes on the responsibility for the family's land and housing assets. However, we find that there are significant gains from inheriting other (non-land and non-housing) assets. In particular, formal schooling appears to yield much higher returns.

In short, while intergenerational linkages clearly matter, there still appears to be considerable intergenerational mobility in this setting. Inheritance of land or housing contributes very little to overall inequality, and does not appear to be an important channel for enhancing economic efficiency through transfers of ownership. Non-land inheritance, schooling and parental characteristics (especially the mother's) appear to play a far more important role.

REFERENCES

1. Akresh et al., 2010Akresh, Richard, Chen, Joyce J., Moore, Charity, 2010. Altruism, cooperation and intrahousehold allocation: agricultural production in polygynous households. Mimeo, University of Illinois, Urbana-Champaign.
2. Anderson and Genicot, 2014Siwan Anderson, Garance Genicot**Suicide and property rights in India** NBER Working Paper No. 19978 (2014) (March)
3. Barrows and Roth, 1990 R. Barrows, M. Roth **Land tenure and investment in African agriculture: theory and evidence**J. Mod. Afr. Stud., 28 (2) (1990), pp. 265–297
4. Beck et al., 2014
5. Simon Beck, Philippe De Vreyer, Sylvie Lambert, Karine Marazyan, Abla Safir **Child fostering in Senegal** J. Comp. Family Stud. (2014) (forthcoming)
6. Behrman and Rosenzweig, 2002 Jere Behrman, Mark Rosenzweig **Does increasing women's schooling raise the schooling of the next generation?** Am. Econ. Rev., 92 (1) (2002), pp. 323–334
7. Besley, 1995 Timothy Besley **Property rights and investment incentives: theory and evidence from Ghana** J. Polit. Econ., 103 (5) (1995), pp. 903–937
8. Blau and Duncan, 1967 Peter M. Blau, Otis Dudley Duncan **The American Occupational Structure** Wiley and Sons, New York (1967)
9. Boltz and Villar, 2014 Marie Boltz, Paola Villar **Mobilité Géographique et Transferts: Les Liens au Ménage d'Origine: Etude de Cas au Sénégal** L'argent des migrations, Autrepart, n°68 (2014) (forthcoming)

10. Boone, 2007 Catherine Boone **Property and constitutional order: land tenure reform and the future of the African state** Afr. Aff., 106 (425) (2007), pp. 557–586

11. Bossuroy and Cogneau, 2013 Thomas Bossuroy, Denis Cogneau **Social mobility in five African countries** Rev. Income Wealth, 59 (2013), pp. S84–S110

12. Caveriviére, 1986 Monique Caveriviére**Incertitudes et Devenir du Droit Foncier Sénégalais** Rev. Int. Droit Comparé, 38 (1) (1986), pp. 95–115

13. Cooper, 2008 Elizabeth Cooper **Inheritance Practices and the Intergenerational Transmission of Poverty: A Literature Review and Annotated Bibliography** Overseas Development Institute (ODI) and Chronic Poverty Research Center (CPRC), London (2008)

14. Cooper, 2010 Elizabeth Cooper **Inheritance and the Intergenerational Transmission of Poverty in Sub-Saharan Africa: Policy Considerations** Chronic Poverty Research Center (CPRC) (2010)

15. Cooper and Bird, 2012 Elizabeth Cooper, Kate Bird **Inheritance: a gendered and intergenerational dimension of poverty** Dev. Policy Rev., 30 (5) (2012), pp. 527–541

16. Coppolctta ct al., 2011 Coppoletta, Rosalinda, De Vreyer, Philippe, Lambert, Sylvie, Safir, Abla. 2011. The long term impact of child fostering in Senegal: adults fostered in their childhood. Mimeo, Paris School of Economics.

17. De Vreyer et al., 2008 Philippe De Vreyer, Sylvie Lambert, Abla Safir, Momar B. Sylla **Pauvreté et Structure Familiale, Pourquoi une Nouvelle Enquête?** Stateco, 102 (2008), pp. 261–275

18. Deininger, 2003 Klaus Deininger **Land Policies for Growth and Poverty Reduction** World Bank, Washington DC (2003)

19. Deininger et al., 2013 Klaus Deininger, Aparajita Goyal, Hari Nagarajan **Women's inheritance rights and intergenerational transmission of resources in India** J. Hum. Resour., 48 (1) (2013), pp. 114–141

20. Dumas and Lambert, 2011 Christelle Dumas, Sylvie Lambert **Children's education in Senegal: how does family background influence achievement?** J. Afr. Econ., 20 (1) (2011), pp. 1–26

21. Ensminger, 1997 Jean Ensminger **Changing property rights: reconciling formal and informal rights to land in Africa** John Drobak, John V.C. Nye (Eds.), The Frontiers of the New Institutional Economics, Academic Press, San Diego (1997), pp. 165–196

22. Estudillo et al., 2001 Jonna P. Estudillo, Agnes R. Quisumbing, Keijiro Otsuka **Gender differences in land inheritance and schooling investments in the rural Philippines** Land Econ., 77 (1) (2001), pp. 130–143

23. Feder and Noronha, 1987 Gershon Feder, Raymond Noronha **Land rights systems and agricultural development in sub-Saharan Africa** World Bank Res. Obs., 2 (2) (1987), pp. 143–169

24. Citing articles (118) Ferreira and Gignoux, 2010 Francisco Ferreira, Jérémie Gignoux **The measurement of inequality of opportunity: theory and an application to Latin America** Policy Research Working Paper 4659, Washington DC, World Bank (2010)

25. Fields, 2003 Gary Fields **Accounting for income inequality and its change: a new method, with application to the distribution of earnings in the United States** Res. Labor Econ., 22 (2003), pp. 1–38

26. Goldthorpe, 1987 J.H. Goldthorpe **Social Mobility and Class Structure in Modern Britain** (2nd ed.)Clarendon Press, Oxford (1987)

27. Gray and Kevane, 1999 Leslie Gray, Michael Kevane **Diminished access, diverted exclusion: women and land tenure in sub-Saharan Africa** Afr. Stud. Rev., 42 (2) (1999), pp. 15–39

28. Citing articles (49) Hallward-Driemeier and Gajigo, 2011 Mary Hallward-Driemeier, Ousman Gajigo **Strengthening economic rights and women's occupational choice: the impact of reforming Ethiopia's family law** Paper Presented at 25th Conference of Center for the Study of African Economies, University of Oxford (2011)

29. Haveman and Wolfe, 1995 Robert Haveman, Barbara Wolfe **The determinants of children's attainments: a review of methods and findings** J. Econ. Lit., 33 (4) (1995), pp. 1829–1878

30. Hill and King, 1995 Anne M. Hill, Elizabeth King **Women's education and economic well-being** Fem. Econ., 1 (2) (1995), pp. 21–46

31. Holden et al., 2009 Stein T. Holden, Klaus Deininger, Hosaena Hagos Ghebru **Impacts of low-cost land certification on investment and productivity** Am. J. Agric. Econ., 91 (2) (2009), pp. 359–373

32. Jacoby and Minten, 2007 Hanan Jacoby, Bart Minten**Is Land Titling in Sub-Saharan Africa Cost-Effective? Evidence from Madagascar** World Bank Econ. Rev., 21 (3) (2007), pp. 461–485

33. Kumar and Quisumbing, 2012a Neha Kumar, Agnes Quisumbing **Inheritance practices and gender differences in poverty and well-being in rural Ethiopia** Dev. Policy Rev., 30 (5) (2012), pp. 573–595

34. Kumar and Quisumbing, 2012b Neha Kumar, Agnes Quisumbing **Beyond "death do us part": the long-term implications of divorce perceptions on women's well-being and child schooling in rural Ethiopia** World Dev., 40 (12) (2012), pp. 2478–2489

35. La Ferrara and Milazzo, 2012mLa Ferrara, Eliana, Milazzo, Annamaria, 2012. Customary norms, inheritance, and human capital: evidence from a reform of the matrilineal system in Ghana. Mimeo, Bocconi University.

36. Lesorogol et al., 2011Carolyn Lesorogol, Gina Chowa, David Ansong **Livestock or the pen: the effects of inheritance and education on poverty among pastoralists** Working Paper 188, Chronic Poverty Research Centre, University of Manchester (2011)

37. Peterman, 2012 Amber Peterman **Widowhood and asset inheritance in sub-Saharan Africa: empirical evidence from 15 countries**Dev. Policy Rev., 30 (5) (2012), pp. 543–571

38. Platteau, 2000 Jean-Philippe Platteau **Institutions, Social Norms and Economic Development** Harwood Academic Publishers, Amsterdam (2000)

39. Platteau, 2006 Jean-Philippe Platteau **Solidarity norms and institutions in village societies: static and dynamic considerations** Handbook on the Economics of Giving, Reciprocity and Altruism, Elsevier, Amsterdam (2006)

40. Platteau et al., 2000 Jean-Philippe Platteau, A. Abraham, A. Braselle, F. Gaspart, A. Niang, J. Sawadogo, L. Stevens **Marriage System, Access to Land, and Social Protection for Women, Part One: The Case of Senegal** Centre de Recherche en Economie du Développement, Namur University, Belgium (2000)

41. Quisumbing, 2009 Agnes Quisumbing **Investments, bequests, and public policy: intergenerational asset transfers and the escape from poverty** Tony Addison, David Hulme, Ravi Kanbur (Eds.), Poverty Dynamics Interdisciplinary Perspectives, Oxford University Press, Oxford (2009), pp. 267–289 (Chapter 12)

42. Quisumbing and Maluccio, 2003 Agnes Quisumbing, John Maluccio **Resources at marriage and intra-household allocation: evidence from Bangladesh, Ethiopia, Indonesia, and South Africa** Oxf. Bull. Econ. Stat., 65 (3) (2003), pp. 283–328

43. Quisumbing et al., 2004 Agnes Quisumbing, Jonna P. Estudillo, Keijiro Otsuka **Land and Schooling: Transferring Wealth Across Generations** Johns Hopkins University Press for the International Food Policy Research Institute, Baltimore and London (2004)

44. Rosenzweig and Wolpin, 1985 Mark Rosenzweig, Kenneth Wolpin **Specific experience, household structure, and intergenerational transfers: farm family land and labor arrangements in developing countries** Q. J. Econ., 100 (1985), pp. 961–987

45. Roy, 2011 Sanchari Roy **Empowering women: inheritance rights and female education in India** Paper Presented at 25th Conference of Center for the Study of African Economies, University of Oxford (2011)

46. Shipton, 1992 Parker Shipton **Debts and trespasses: land, mortgages, and the ancestors in western Kenya** Afr. J. Int. Afr. Inst., 62 (3) (1992), pp. 357–388

47. Shipton and Goheen, 1992 Parker Shipton, Mitzi Goheen **Understanding African land-holding: power, wealth, and meaning** Afr. J. Int. Afr. Inst., 62 (3) (1992), pp. 307–325

48. Shorrocks, 1982 Anthony Shorrocks **Inequality decomposition by factor components** Econometrica, 50 (1) (1982), pp. 193–212

49. Sow, 1992 Fatou Sow **Femmes et Tenure Foncière au Sénégal** Université Cheikh Anta Diop, Dakar, Sénégal (1992)

50. UNECA, 2011 UNECA **Land Policy in Africa: West Africa Regional Assessment AUC-ECA-AFDB Consortium, 2011, Addis Ababa, Ethiopia** (2011)

12

ENDOGENOUS TIME-VARYING RISK AVERSION AND ASSET RETURNS

Michele Berardi

Economics, School of Social Sciences, The University of Manchester, Manchester, Lancashire, UK

ABSTRACT

Stylized facts about statistical properties for short horizon returns in financial markets have been identified in the literature, but a satisfactory understanding for their manifestation is yet to be achieved. In this work, we show that a simple asset pricing model with representative agent is able to generate time series of returns that replicate such stylized facts if the risk aversion coefficient is allowed to change endogenously over time in response to unexpected excess returns under evolutionary forces. The same model, under constant risk aversion, would instead generate returns that are essentially Gaussian. We conclude that an endogenous time-varying risk aversion represents a very parsimonious way to make the model match real data on key statistical properties, and therefore deserves careful consideration from economists and practitioners alike.

Keywords: Risk aversion, Returns, Asset prices, Financial markets

1 INTRODUCTION

The statistical analysis of price variations in financial markets has attracted a lot of attention, both from practitioners and academic economists, in an attempt to find regularities that could help us understand and possibly predict the evolution of prices in such markets. Such extensive analysis has led to the identification of a number of statistical properties for financial returns that seem to hold across markets and over time, and that can be summarized in the following set of empirical stylized facts (see, e.g., Cont 2001 and Tseng and Li 2011): i) the distribution of returns is not Gaussian but presents instead fat tails; ii) there is no serial correlation in returns; iii) there is positive correlation in absolute returns, with slow decay; iv) returns show strong volatility clustering, with large fluctuations that tend to cluster together.

Though there is agreement among researchers on such empirical observations, we still lack a clear understanding of their causes. We suggest in this work that a common origin could be identified in the time-varying nature of the risk aversion coefficient for investors, and show that an otherwise standard, rational expectations asset pricing model, once enhanced with such a feature, can generate time series for returns that replicate very closely the main stylized facts identified in the empirical literature.

A growing body of literature has recently tried to use adaptive learning to improve the empirical performance of asset pricing models. Examples include Branch and Evans (2010, 2011), Adam et al. (2015), Carceles-Poveda and Giannitsarou (2008), Bullard and Duffy (2001), Brock and Hommes (1998) and Timmermann (1993, 1996). The main success of these works has been in generating models able to show excess volatility similar to that observed in financial markets, but they have not focused on the same array of short-horizon stylized facts that we consider here.

An important attempt at explaining such short-run stylized facts comes instead from models based on stochastic interactions among traders. These models are borrowed and adapted from the physics literature, where they have been known for being able to generate data that display scaling laws regularities similar to those found in financial markets.[1] While the spirit of these works is similar to the motivation of this paper, our study would fit perhaps better in the behavioral economics literature, as we try to remain as close as possible to a standard economics framework, while departing from it only in the way a behavioral characteristic, risk aversion, is modeled. The advantage of this approach with respect to models based on stochastic interacting particles is that the economic interpretation remains clearer. While stochastic models of interacting agents seem to be able to replicate facts such as fat tails and volatility clustering, in fact, they tend to lack microfoundations and do not explicitly provide an economic justification for the behavior of agents.

The backbone model that we use for our analysis is a simple, standard, present value asset pricing model with stochastic dividends, as presented, for example, by De Long et al. (1990). Such a model, as it stands, does a poor job in matching stylized facts about financial returns, as it implies that returns are normally distributed and independent over time. Our main contribution is to show that a simple behavioral modification of this model can generate returns that match key statistical properties of historical data for financial markets. The risk aversion coefficient for investors is usually assumed, in the standard economics and finance literature, to be a primitive of the model, a feature that is hard wired into the brain of people when they are born and that does not change. We believe instead that there is scope for modelling the attitude of agents towards risk as a feature that depends on the environment in which agents make their decisions, and that evolves with it.

For example, narrative evidence suggests that many people, who had been very cautious up to that point with their investment decisions and mainly kept their savings in government securities or similar activities, during the stock market bubble of the late nineties and early 2000 abandoned their safe investments and moved their money into more risky assets. Observing high rates of returns on stock markets, those people became more willing to take on risky activities in an attempt to join in and share the high profits that were realized on financial markets at the time. In a sort of herd-like behavior induced by their decreased risk aversion, previously cautious investors entered into the stock market. When prices then started to fall and returns decreased, those same investors became afraid of losses, their risk aversion increased and they fled financial markets, selling their assets and fuelling a sharper decrease in prices.

Alan Greenspan, on this point, said in a speech at the Federal Reserve Bank of Kansas City (Greenspan, 2005; Italics added):

> "Thus, this vast increase in the market value of asset claims is in part the indirect result of *investors accepting lower compensation for risk*. [...] Any onset of *increased investor caution* elevates risk premiums and, as a consequence, lowers asset values and promotes the liquidation of the debt that supported higher asset prices."

Greenspan suggests in his speech that changes in market values depend, partly, on changes in risk premia required by agents, which in turn depend on the attitude of investors towards risk. In this paper we make formal this argument and show that adding this feature to an otherwise standard model changes completely the statistical properties of simulated asset returns, making them similar to those observed in real markets.

Time-varying risk aversion is not new in economics. In consumption-based asset pricing models, for example, Brandt and Wang (2003) propose a time-varying risk aversion coefficient that responds to news about consumption growth and inflation, while Li (2007) studies asset prices under the assumption of a countercyclical risk aversion. We propose instead a process for risk aversion that depends on unexpected excess returns: agents adapt their attitude towards risk on the basis of the unexpected excess gains that they observe from risky activities.

While in standard economics risk aversion is a feature that depends solely on the curvature of the utility function being maximized by agents, the form of which is assumed constant over time, in behavioral economics Kahneman and Tversky (1979)'s prospect theory argues that expected utility maximization is a poor representation of how people make choices under risk, and suggests instead an alternative framework where people's attitude towards risk is situation dependent. We will continue to use here the expected utility maximization framework, but modify it to allow for the curvature of the utility function, and therefore the risk attitude of agents, to evolve over time endogenously. An evolutionary justification for changes in attitudes towards risk is provided by Netzer (2009), who shows that, from an evolutionary perspective, the utility function of agents, and therefore their risk aversion, should depend on the probability distribution of alternatives about which agents need to make decisions. In our context, such alternatives are represented by returns from risky versus risk-free activities, and agents adapt their perceptions about the distribution of such alternatives using observations about unexpected excess returns on the stock market.

The plan of the paper is as follows: in Section 1.1 we discuss the literature related to our work, while in Section 1.2 we discuss more in detail the statistical properties of financial returns by looking at the S&P500 index as a representative case. Section 2 introduces the basic model, Section 2.1 discusses endogenous time-varying risk aversion and Section 2.2 derives the equilibrium solution for the model. Section 3 presents results from simulations of the model with constant and with endogenous time-varying risk aversion, and compares the resulting series for returns with those from real data. Section 4 discusses the results, and Section 5concludes.

1.1 Related literature

Two main lines of research are relevant to our work, one based on bounded rationality and learning, and the other based on behavioral models of human decisions.

In terms of the first strain of literature, Branch and Evans (2010) show that real time learning dynamics, in an otherwise standard consumption based asset pricing model, calibrated to U.S. stock data, is capable of reproducing regime-switching returns and volatilities. Branch and Evans (2011) introduce learning about risk and returns in the De Long et al. (1990) framework and show that escape dynamics emerge that look like stock market crashes, even though the escape route is not from a bubble high but from the equilibrium fundamental value. Hommes and Zhu (2014) use the concept of stochastic consistent expectations equilibrium to explain excess volatility in a standard present value asset pricing model with stochastic dividends similar to the one we consider here. Adam et al. (2015) show how adaptive learning can generate excess volatility in a consumption based asset pricing model and present an estimated version of the model to US data that can replicate some asset price puzzles such as stock price volatility, the persistence of the price-dividend ratio and the predictability of long-horizon returns. All these works mainly focus on the long-horizon properties of asset prices returns, while we will focus our attention on trying to explain and replicate statistical properties of returns in the short run.

As for the second strain of literature, Lux (2009) provides an extensive surveys on behavioral asset pricing models based on interacting agents. He divides such literature into four groups, and we follow here his classification in our discussion. A first class of models is focused on interactions between fundamentalists and chartists, where the disaggregation of markets is limited to the distinction between two classes of agents that form their demand according to different rules. Early contributions are Beja and Goldman (1980), Day and Huang (1990) and Chiarella (1992). The interaction between these two classes of agents is able to generate a mix of centripetal and centrifugal forces that can lead to rich dynamics in prices. More recently, Chiarella and He (2002, 2003) propose a model where there is heterogeneity in risk aversion between fundamentalists and trend chasers, coupled with learning about future returns, and find that the dynamics of asset prices are affected by the relative risk attitudes of different types of investors.

A second class of models is built on local stochastic interactions, based on the seminal work of Kirman (1993) on herding: here the departure from traditional economics models is more marked, with agents' demand being determined by a local interaction mechanism by which agents are recruited by neighbors on a particular strategy. Kirman and Teyssière (2002) show that such a feature can generate long-term dependence in absolute and squared returns.

A third class of models tries to capture non-local interactions through field effects, as for example in Lux (1995, 1998): the main feature here is that traders are assumed to be influenced not by other individual agents, but by the overall mood of the market. Such models can generate fads or herding in the market that lead to autoregressive dependence in higher moments.

Finally, some authors have explored the importance of the topology of interactions on financial markets. Bouchaud and Cont (2000), for example, build on the percolation model popular in statistical mechanics and place traders on a lattice with interactions among neighboring agents forming clusters: the ensuing distribution of returns shows fat tails but higher moments are uncorrelated, thus failing to match one key stylized fact of financial markets. Subsequent works have tried to improve on this framework: for example, Iori (2002), using a different network structure, has been able to generate time series that more closely match those observed in financial markets.

Among these approaches based on stochastic interactions among agents, we believe the mechanism at work in our framework is closer in spirit to the one used in models with field effects, where individual decisions are affected by aggregate features of the economy. In our case the (individual) demand for the risky asset depends on the risk aversion coefficient, which changes endogenously in response to changes in excess returns, an aggregate feature of the market. Despite the similar interpretation, the way we model such effects, from the aggregate to the individual level and back, differs sharply, as in our case the link from macro to micro goes through an explicitly identified and endogenous response of agents' preferences to their environment. We believe that, compared to models with field effects, our approach is more intuitive from an economic perspective.

A key feature of our model will be the time-varying nature of risk aversion. This is not new in the literature. Brandt and Wang (2003) present a model in which the coefficient of risk aversion changes in response to news about consumption growth and inflation, and find empirical support for the hypothesis that aggregate risk aversion varies in response to news about inflation. Li (2007), instead, assumes a countercyclical risk aversion that drives a pro-cyclical risk premium in asset prices, but finds that such a feature may not help explain important facts such as the predictability of long-horizon stock returns or the univariate mean-reversion of stock prices. Park (2014) proposes a model of heterogeneous risk aversion, where fundamentalists have constant risk aversion while chartists' risk aversion varies over time due to psychological factors: the time variation in risk attitudes increases price fluctuations and generates chaotic dynamics. Finally, Smith and Whitelaw (2009) find empirical evidence in support of the hypothesis that risk aversion moves countercyclically.

An important theoretical paper for our modelling choice of risk aversion is Netzer (2009), who proposes a model of the evolution and adaptation of hedonic utility and provides an evolutionary explanation for risk attitudes that adapt according to changes in the perceived distribution of possible alternatives. We will discuss this point at length in Section 2.1.1.

In terms of evidence about short-horizon returns on financial markets, stylized facts are presented in a number of papers in the literature, such as Cont (2001) and Tseng and Li (2011). Both works show that the same stylized facts discussed in Section 1.2 below hold for a large number of financial time series, including Standard & Poor's 500 Index, NASDAQ Composite Index and Hang Seng Index, series for individual stock prices such as IBM, Microsoft and BMW, and even series for exchange rates.

1.2 Stylized facts

As we mentioned before, the main stylized facts identified for short-horizon returns on financial markets are: i) the distribution of returns is not Gaussian, and presents instead fat tails; ii) there is no correlation in returns; iii) there is positive correlation (with slow decay) in absolute returns; iv) returns show volatility clustering, i.e., large fluctuations tend to cluster together.

Such stylized facts hold for returns computed from many asset price series (see, e.g., Tseng and Li, 2011). As an example, we report here statistics for the S&P500 index, for the period 02/01/1957 until 12/04/2012,[2]

Returns are computed as

$$r_t = \frac{p_t - p_{t-1}}{p_{t-1}},$$

where p_t is the price of the asset or index at time t. It is also common practice to normalize returns as follows

$$nr_t = \frac{r_t - \mu}{\sigma},$$

where μ and σ are the mean and standard deviation of returns. Absolute returns are then defined as

$$ar_t = |r_t|.$$

For the S&P500 index, $\mu_r = 0.000294$ and $\sigma_r = 0.0100$ and returns and normalized returns are plotted in Fig. 1. It is clearly evident the volatility clustering of returns, with large movements that tend to cluster together at particular times.

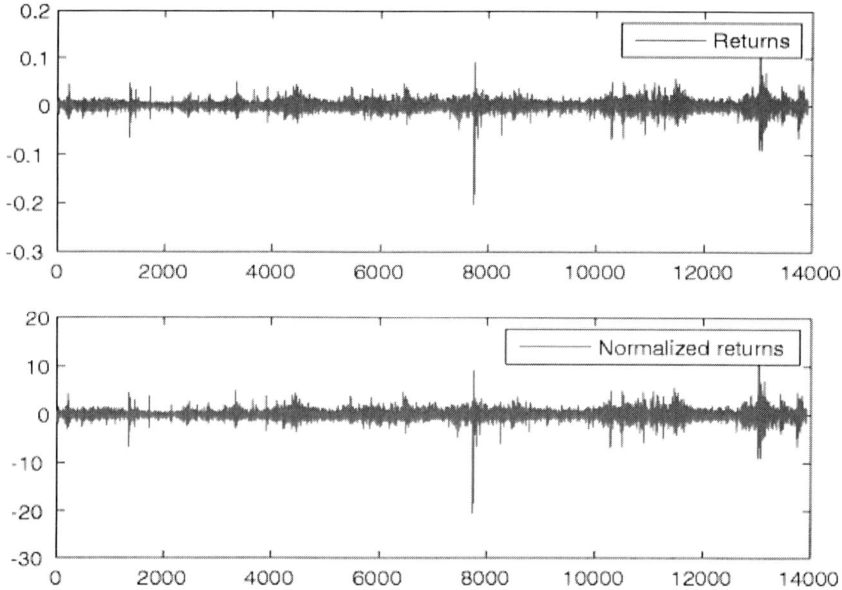

Figure 1. Returns and normalized returns for the S&P500 index

We compute then the empirical probability density function (pdf) for normalized returns and overlay it with the analytical normal pdf for comparison (Fig. 2): it is evident that the distribution of returns deviates from normality. Non-normality is also confirmed by the 4th moment of the distribution, kurtosis, which in the data is 24.378, while the value for a Gaussian distribution is 3, and by the Jarque-Bera test, which rejects at 5 % significance level the null hypothesis that the sample comes from a normal distribution with unknown mean and variance. Note that the estimated tail index for returns, which represents the order of the highest finite absolute moment, is 3.1083 , so the estimate for the fourth moment of the distribution is not reliable, which is consistent with previous evidence on asset returns (Cont 2001). The tail index conveys information about the tail of a distribution: the lower the index, the fatter the tails.[3]

As for the correlation of returns and absolute returns over time, the serial correlation of returns is usually analyzed by computing the autocorrelation function (ACF). For the S&P500, the ACF for returns drops to zero after one period, while it stays positive for absolute returns at long lags, being still above .1 at 100 lags (See Fig. 3).[4] This is a typical finding in financial markets: returns have short-memory and present exponentially decaying autocorrelations, while absolute (or squared) returns display long-memory and are characterized by hyperbolic exponential decline in autocorrelation.

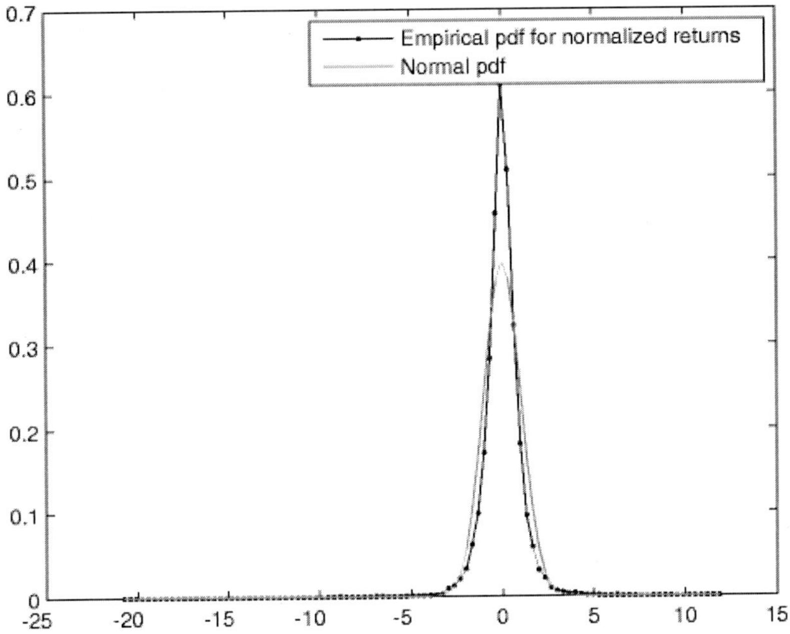

Figure 2. Empirical pds of normalized returns and normal fit

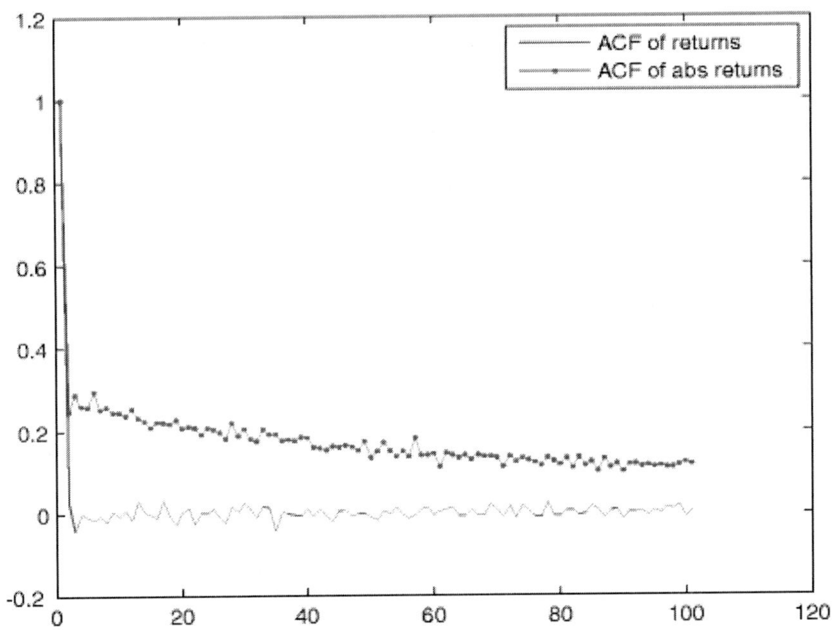

Figure 3. ACFs for returns and absolute returns for the S&P500 index

We have presented in this section a brief exposition of the main stylized facts concerning statistical regularities in financial returns. We now develop a simple model that will be able to replicate closely all such facts.

2 THE MODEL

We start with a standard, present value asset pricing model with stochastic dividends. There are two types of assets: a risk free one, elastically supplied, with a gross rate of return $R = \beta^{-1}$, where β is the discount factor; and a risky asset, the price of which is p_t and pays a stochastic dividend d_t. The supply of the risky asset is exogenous and stochastic.

The dynamic equation for wealth (W_t) is then represented by

$$W_{t+1} = RW_t + (p_{t+1} + d_{t+1} - Rp_t)z_t^d$$

where zdtztd is the demand for the risky asset.

Agents are myopic mean variance maximizers, and therefore maximize

$$E_t\left[\alpha_t E_t W_{t+1} - \alpha_t^2/2Var_t(W_{t+1})\right] \quad (1)$$

where E_t and Var_t are the conditional expectation and variance of wealth based on the subjective probability distribution of agents, and $\alpha_t \in R$ is the coefficient of absolute risk aversion.

The coefficient of risk aversion has a time t subscript, to make it explicit that we will allow such parameter to evolve over time: the specification of its endogenous dynamics will be given in the next section. Though risk aversion evolves over time, at each time t agents take such a coefficient as given in their maximization problem, only to revise it in the following period on the basis of new evidence. Moreover, by assuming such a parameter as fixed, agents also implicitly disregard the feedback from time-varying risk aversion on asset price volatility, and maintain this parameter constant in their maximization problem. In this respect, agents in our setting implement an anticipated utility model in the spirit of Kreps (1998). Such a modeling strategy has been largely adopted in the macroeconomics literature on bounded rationality and learning (e.g., Sargent 1993, 1999 and Evans and Honkopohja 2001) and we believe it can represent a good approach also in the present context where behavioral parameters rather than beliefs evolve over time.

Note also that risk aversion is allowed to become negative, thus making agents risk lovers: this will happen in our setting when there is a long series of large and unexpected profits in the stock market, so that investors become, in effect, willing to gamble in financial markets. [5]

From the above setting, it follows that the optimal demand for the risky asset is given by

$$z_t^d = \frac{E_t(p_{t+1} + d_{t+1}) - \beta^{-1} p_t}{\alpha_t \sigma_t^2}, \tag{2}$$

where σ2tσt2 is agents' conditional variance of excess returns $p_{t+1} + d_{t+1} - Rp_t$ and is given by

$$\sigma_t^2 = E_t\left[(p_{t+1} + d_{t+1}) - E_t(p_{t+1} + d_{t+1})\right]^2. \tag{3}$$

Equating demand and supply, denoted by zstzts, we obtain the pricing equation

$$p_t = \beta E_t(p_{t+1} + d_{t+1}) - \beta \alpha_t \sigma_t^2 z_t^s. \tag{4}$$

The exogenous process for dividends is assumed to be given by

$$d_t = d_0 + u_t, \tag{5}$$

where d_0 is a constant and u_t is an i.i.d., zero mean, normally distributed disturbance.

We also assume that supply follows the exogenous random process

$$z_t^s = s_0 + v_t, \tag{6}$$

where s_0 is a constant and v_t is an i.i.d., zero mean, normally distributed disturbance uncorrelated with u_t.

2.1 Endogenous time-varying risk aversion (ETVRA)

The coefficient of absolute risk aversion, α_t, is modelled as time-varying and endogenous, depending on unexpected (excess) returns in the stock market: higher returns than expected make agents more willing to take on the risk involved in investing in the stock market. Specifically, we postulate a process of the form

$$\alpha_t = \alpha_{t-1} - \gamma_\alpha \pi_t, \tag{7}$$

where $\gamma_\alpha \geq 0$ and

$$\pi_t = p_t + d_t - E_{t-1}(p_t + d_t), \qquad (8)$$

i.e., risk aversion decreases when excess profits in the financial market are higher than expected.[6] Parameter γ_α represents the sensitivity of risk aversion to unexpected returns: with $\gamma_\alpha = 0$, we have the standard case of constant risk aversion over time, while positive values of γ_α mean that agents are willing to take on more risk when they see excess returns in the stock market compared to what they expected (and vice-versa). Such endogenous dynamics for the coefficient of risk aversion will make the reduced form parameters in the solution for prices be time-varying.

2.1.1 An evolutionary justification to ETVRA

The postulated process for risk aversion dynamics, represented by Eq. 7, might seem ad-hoc at first. In reality, it has a simple and intuitive justification under an evolutionary framework for the derivation of the utility function of agents coupled with learning dynamics.

From an evolutionary perspective, it can be shown (Netzer 2009) that, if individual decisions are guided by hedonic utility, i.e., if agents, given a set of alternatives, prefer the one that promises the greatest pleasure, then a utility function can be considered as a reward system to induce agents to make optimal choices, and its slope can be interpreted as the degree of attention devoted to the available alternatives. The shape of the utility function therefore determines where agents put more attention in their choices. Evolutionary forces would shape the utility function to make it responsive to the decision environment and, in particular, to the distribution of alternatives available for choice, in order to devote more attention to areas where the decision is more critical. If the properties of such distribution are not known a-priori, agents would have to learn them from the environment, and the evolution of agents' beliefs about such distribution would then affect the shape of their utility function, making it time-varying in a way that is well represented by our ETVRA dynamics.

In our setting, the distribution of excess returns from the risky activity is unknown, and agents adapt their beliefs about it over time by moving in the direction indicated by unexpected returns. Equation 7 can, therefore, be interpreted as a simple adaptive learning rule with constant gain, through which agents keep track of the evolution of returns on the stock market by adjusting their beliefs in the direction suggested by forecast errors. A shift in probability is signalled by π_t, a realization of unexpected excess returns on the stock market. Parameter γ_α represents a behavioral feature that captures the degree of adjustment of agents' perceived distribution of excess returns to evidence about unexpected realizations. As beliefs about the distribution of returns adapt, so does risk aversion. In particular, a decrease in the estimate of α, which corresponds to a shift in probability mass to alternatives with larger payoffs, reduces risk aversion.

2.2 Equilibria

In this section, we solve the model for an equilibrium under constant risk aversion, and then introduce time-varying risk aversion dynamics. Under rational expectations (RE) and constant risk aversion, two possible equilibria exist: a fundamental equilibrium, where pice dynamics are affected only by the fundamental features of the economy, and a bubble solution, which admits sunspot components. For a number of reasons discussed below, we will focus only on the fundamental equilibrium.

2.2.1 Constant risk aversion

Under RE, with constant risk aversion ($\alpha_t \equiv \alpha$), it is well known that Eqs. 4–6 admit two possible equilibria, the fundamental solution and the bubble one.

The price equation in the fundamental equilibrium is represented by

$$p_t = \beta (1 - \beta)^{-1} \left(d_0 - \alpha s_0 \sigma^2 \right) - \beta \alpha \sigma^2 v_t, \tag{9}$$

while, in the bubble equilibrium, it is given by

$$p_t = \alpha \sigma^2 s_0 - d_0 + \beta^{-1} p_{t-1} - \alpha \sigma^2 v_{t-1} + \xi_t, \tag{10}$$

where ξ_t is a martingale difference sequence that opens the door to sunspot variables affecting prices. It is also known (see, e.g., Branch and Evans, 2011) that the fundamental equilibrium is adaptively learnable by agents, while the bubble one is not. Moreover, since β<1, the process for p_t in the bubble equilibrium is not stable.

2.2.2 ETVRA

With a time-varying risk aversion, the solution to the model must be enriched to include an equation for the evolution of risk aversion and for the variance of returns. We stress again here that agents in our setting, in the spirit of the anticipated utility model of Kreps (1998), solve at each point in time their maximization problem (and we, as modeler, find the equilibrium) as if risk aversion and the conditional variance of dividends were constant, but then modify their attitudes towards and perception of risk as new evidence on unexpected excess returns comes available next period.

For the fundamental equilibrium, the evolution of the system is therefore represented by

$$p_t = \beta(1-\beta)^{-1}\left(d_0 - \alpha_t s_0 \sigma_t^2\right) - \beta\alpha_t\sigma_t^2 v_t \tag{11}$$

$$\alpha_{t+1} = \alpha_t - \gamma_\alpha \pi_t, \tag{12}$$

$$\pi_t = -\beta\alpha_t\sigma_t^2 v_t + u_t \tag{13}$$

$$\sigma_t^2 = \frac{1 \pm \sqrt{1 - 4\alpha_t^2\beta^2\sigma_v^2\sigma_u^2}}{2\alpha_t^2\beta^2\sigma_v^2} \tag{14}$$

where Eq. 13 for unexpected excess returns comes from computing (8) in the fundamental equilibrium. Expression (14) for the conditional variance of excess returns is obtained from Eq. 3 by substituting in the equations for prices and dividends.

By substituting into expression (12) for α_{t+1} those for π_t and σ2tσt2, it is possible to see that the dynamics for the risk aversion coefficient are represented by a non linear difference equation that depends on parameters β and γ_α and on the variances and realizations of the two processes u_t and v_t:

$$\alpha_{t+1} = \alpha_t - \gamma_\alpha\left[u_t - \beta\alpha_t\frac{1 \pm \sqrt{1 - 4\alpha_t^2\beta^2\sigma_v^2\sigma_u^2}}{2\alpha_t^2\beta^2\sigma_v^2}v_t\right].$$

Simulations will be done with the (-) root, as this is the one that Branch and Evans (2011) show to be stable under learning. It is also the one that ensures that simulated prices follow a smooth process without unrealistic and sudden large jumps.

In the bubble equilibrium, instead, the evolution of the system under ETVRA is described by

$$\begin{aligned} p_t &= \left(\alpha_{t-1}\sigma_{t-1}^2 s_0 - d_0\right) + \beta^{-1}p_{t-1} - \alpha_{t-1}\sigma_{t-1}^2 v_{t-1} + \xi_t, \\ \alpha_{t+1} &= \alpha_t - \gamma_\alpha \pi_t, \\ \pi_t &= u_t \\ \sigma_t^2 &= \sigma_u^2 + \sigma_\xi^2. \end{aligned}$$

It is easy to see that, in this case, α_t simply follows a random walk process

$$\alpha_{t+1} = \alpha_t - \gamma_\alpha u_t.$$

In a bubble equilibrium, therefore, asset prices diverge, unexpected excess returns from the risky activity are white noise and the ETVRA follows a random walk: for all these reasons, we do not focus on such equilibrium in this work. In a fundamental equilibrium, instead, asset prices follow a stationary process, but unexpected excess returns depend on risk aversion of agents and the dynamics for the ETVRA coefficient are highly nonlinear. These features, we will show, impact significantly on the implied nature of returns from the risky asset, and are able to generate dynamics that in many dimensions closely resemble those observed in real financial markets.

3 SIMULATIONS AND STATISTICAL ANALYSIS

In order to compare the statistical properties of observed returns on financial markets with those that come from our model, we simulate price dynamics in the fundamental RE equilibrium, first with constant risk aversion and then with ETVRA. From such series, we compute returns and analyze their properties in comparison with the stylized facts reported in Section 1.2.

The baseline calibration for the model is as follows: $\beta = .95$, $s_0 = 1$, $d_0 = 5$, σ2v=.5σv2=.5, σ2u=.9σu2=.9. These parameter values are taken from Branch and Evans (2011), apart from d_0 which we have set to a higher value in order to avoid prices hitting the zero lower bound.[7] We also set the initial value for risk aversion, α_0, equal to 0.75, which is the value used by Branch and Evans (2011) for their constant risk aversion. Sensitivity analysis results regarding these parameters are reported in Section 3.3. The key new parameter γ_α is instead calibrated to 0.025: extensive investigations have shown that the higher is γ_α, the further away from normality is the distribution of returns. We will discuss further this point later on when reporting results from simulations.

3.1 Asset returns with constant risk aversion

Under constant risk aversion, it is clear from Eq. 9 that returns follow a normal distribution. For comparison with subsequent statistics under ETVRA, we simulate our model with constant risk aversion and compute returns from the resulting time series for asset prices. Mean and standard deviation of simulated returns, μ~tμ~t and σ~tσ~t, are, respectively, 0.000119 and 0.0156, in line with those found in real data.

Normality of simulated returns is confirmed by the Jarque-Bera test, which can not reject at 5 % significance level the null hypothesis that the sample comes from a normal distribution with unknown mean and variance, and by the estimated kurtosis, which is 3.0049. Moreover, computing the ACFs for simulated returns and their absolute value we find that, in both series, the autocorrelation function drops to zero quickly, in contrast to what real returns show.

All the above evidence on simulated returns under constant risk aversion clearly indicates that the model with constant risk aversion is not able to replicate the key stylized facts that have been consistently observed in series for returns on real financial markets.

3.2 Asset returns with ETVRA

We simulate now the model with endogenous time-varying risk aversion and compute returns from the resulting time series for asset prices. Mean and standard deviation of simulated returns, μ~tμ~t and σ~tσ~t, are, respectively, 0.000090 and 0.0110, in line with those found in real data.

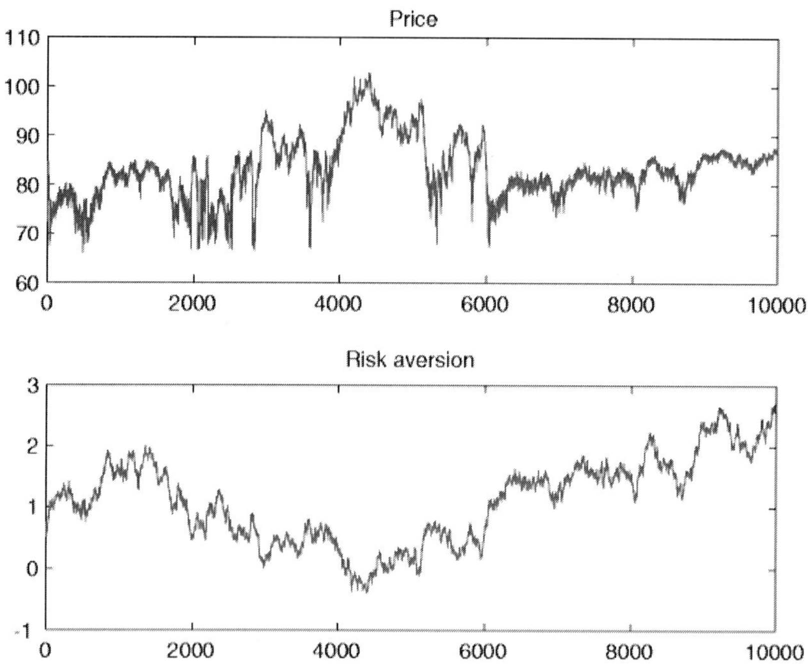

Figure 4. Evolution of prices and risk aversion under ETVRA. Parameter values and initial conditions as follows: $\beta = .95, s_0 = 1, d_0 = 5, \sigma_v^2 = .5, \sigma_u^2 = .9, \alpha_0 = 0.75$

We first show in Fig. 4 the time series of prices and risk aversion coefficient under time-varying risk aversion for a representative run of simulated data. It is possible to see that ETVRA introduces persistence in prices, which with constant risk aversion would simply be white noise around the fundamental equilibrium price - see Eq. 9.

We then plot returns from the same representative run of simulated data in Fig. 5, together with their normalized counterpart. It is evident now that ETVRA generates volatility clustering in returns.

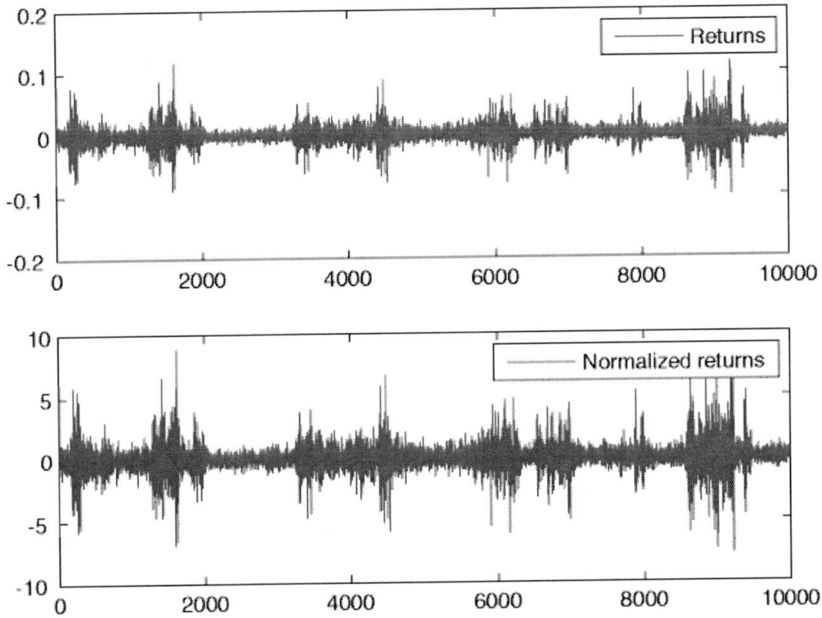

Figure 5. Returns and normalized returns for the simulated series with ETVRA. Parameter values and initial conditions as follows: $\beta = .95, s_0 = 1, d_0 = 5, \sigma_v^2 = .5, \sigma_u^2 = .9, \alpha_0 = 0.75$

In Fig. 6, we compute the empirical pdf for the simulated normalized returns and overlay it with the analytical normal pdf for comparison: it seems evident that the distribution of returns under ETVRA differs significantly from a Gaussian and shows instead characteristics similar to those observed for returns in real financial markets. This impression is confirmed by the Jarque-Bera test, which this time rejects at 5 % significance level the null hypothesis that the sample comes from a normal distribution with unknown mean and variance. Also, in terms of kurtosis, we find a value of 21.48, in line with the one estimated for S&P500 returns and much higher than the one, close to 3, obtained under constant risk aversion and consistent with a Gaussian distribution. Note, though, that the estimated tail index is 2.88, so the estimated fourth moment of the distribution is not reliable.

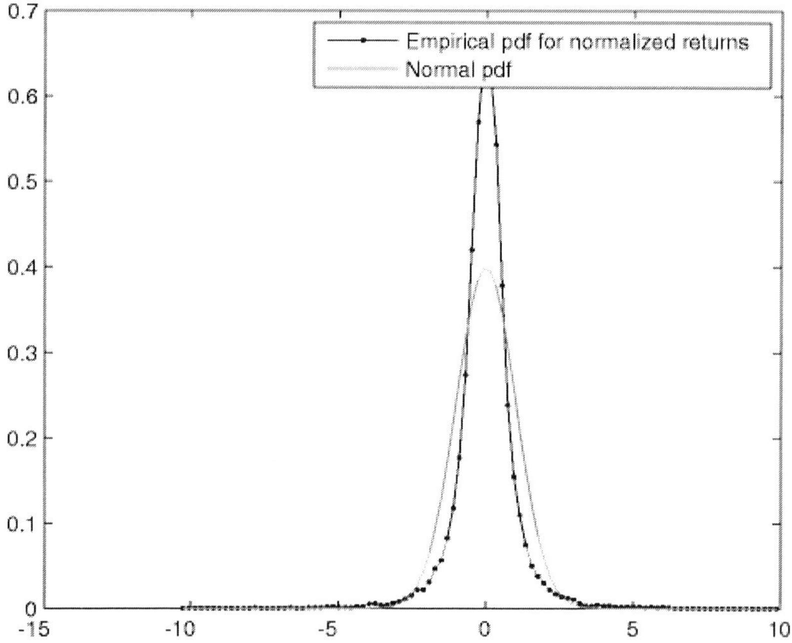

Figure 6. Empirical pds of simulated normalized returns and normal fit

We note here that estimated kurtosis for the distribution of simulated returns is sensitive to the value of γ_α: higher values of γ_α imply higher kurtosis, as the distribution of returns drifts further away from normality.[8] As risk aversion becomes more sensitive to unexpected excess returns from the risky asset, the feedback effect from returns to asset demand and therefore prices is strengthened, making the distribution of returns more heavy tailed. Figure 7 plots the ACFs for simulated returns under ETVRA and for their absolute value: we can see that, while there is no serial correlation in returns, absolute returns show positive correlation with slow decay, very similar to that observed in S&P500 returns. All the above evidence on simulated returns with ETVRA shows that simply introducing an endogenous risk aversion coefficient that responds to unexpected excess returns from the risky activity in an otherwise standard asset pricing model fundamentally changes the statistical properties of simulated returns, and makes them strikingly resemble those observed in real financial markets.

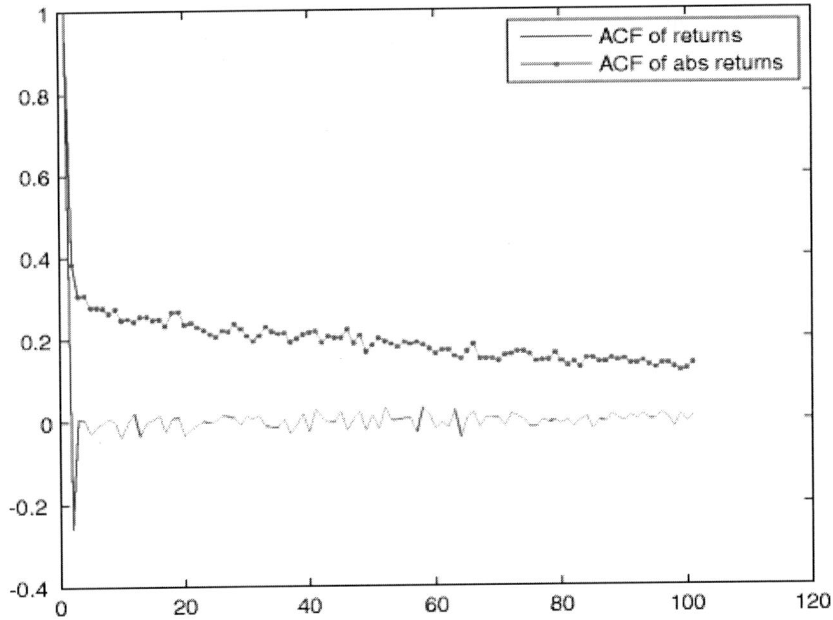

Figure 7. ACFs for returns and absolute returns for the simulated series with ETVRA

3.3 Robustness check

In order to investigate the sensitivity of our results to the specific values assumed for the parameters in the model, we run now extensive simulations under different parameterization: reported statistics are computed as averages over 100 simulations, each of 10,000 time periods.

Model Parameterization	Mean	Std. Dev.	Kurtosis	Tail index	ACFs (1/5 lags)
Baseline*	8.5910×10^{-5}	0.0115	23.1789	2.8815	0.4166/0.3346
$\gamma_a = .005$	8.1076×10^{-5}	0.0113	7.1184	4.6997	0.3778/0.2300
$\gamma_a = .1$	1.5112×10^{-4}	0.0146	74.8951	2.2048	0.5184/0.4329
$s_0 = 5$	9.7316×10^{-5}	0.0118	21.5593	2.8856	0.4132/0.3191
$d_0 = 1$	-3.48×10^{-2}	20.5120	5.2203×10^{3}	1.1202	0.0388/0.0423
$\sigma_u^2 = .1$	6.1165×10^{-7}	0.0011	5.1893	5.4159	0.3430/0.1786
$\sigma_u^2 = .5$	3.5291×10^{-5}	0.0075	12.1375	3.5280	0.3972/0.2945
$\sigma_v^2 = .1$	2.4291×10^{-4}	0.0200	54.9828	2.6201	0.4039/0.3240
$\sigma_v^2 = .9, \sigma_u^2 = .1$ **	1.7943×10^{-6}	0.0016	5.5993	5.0826	0.3591/0.1931

*Baseline parameterization: $\beta = .95$, $s_0 = 1$, $d_0 = 5$, $\gamma_a = .025$, $\sigma_u^2 = .9$, $\sigma_v^2 = .5$. Each raw differs from baseline parameterization only in the element indicated

** σ_u^2 had to be adjusted in order to avoid σ_ε^2 from Eq. 14 to become a complex number

The first thing to notice is that results for the baseline parameterization reported in the previous section are confirmed when averaged across 100 simulations: mean returns are effectively zero, with a variance around .01 and kurtosis close to the value found in empirical data.

In terms of the effect of different parameter values on the properties of simulated returns, a few comments are necessary. First, in terms of the variances of the stochastic terms in the model, the variance of dividends (σ2uσu2) needs to be high enough to generate kurtosis and tail indexes in line with those observed in the data: low values of σ2uσu2 in fact generate thinner tails. The variance of risky asset supply (σ2vσv2) also needs to be sufficiently high but not too high: in this case, though, low values of σ2vσv2 generate the opposite problem, i.e., fatter tails (but note that the product of the two variances must be such that σ2tσt2 remains real). The different impact of the two variances can be understood by looking at Eq. 14 for the conditional variance of dividends. While σ2uσu2 enters at the numerator with a multiplicative effect on the time varying risk aversion, the main effect of σ2vσv2 comes from the term it the denominator (again with a multiplicative effect on α_t): while higher values for the first thus enhance the impact of unexpected returns (see also Eq. 13) on risk aversion and thus demand, higher values for the second dampen the effect.

Second, in terms of the constants in the model, s_0 (average supply) is fairly irrelevant, while d_0(average dividends) needs to remain high enough (roughly above 2) to avoid negative prices and ensuing unrealistic statistics.

An important thing to note, also, is that all these parameterizations imply distributions of returns that pass the JB Test for non-normality (i.e., the null of normality is rejected at 5 % significance level). Estimated tail indexes are also in general between two and five, consistent with evidence on asset returns.[9] ACFs of absolute returns also remain positive and significant at long lags, and tend to be higher with parameterizations that generate fatter tails.

We have already discussed the effect of γ_α, but it is worth stressing here the point once again. This parameter represents the degree of adjustment of risk aversion to unexpected excess returns. When equal to zero, we have the standard model with constant risk aversion and simulated results are as reported in Section 3.1; as γ_α increases, the endogenous character of risk aversion is strengthened and the tails of the return distribution gets fatter, which is reflected in a higher kurtosis and smaller tail index. Interpreting Eq. 7 as a simple adaptive learning rule, this means that γ_α represents a constant gain coefficient in the learning algorithm. Milani (2011), in a model of business cycles where agents need to learn about inflation, output and interest rates, has estimated a gain coefficient of about 0.02.[10] A similar value was estimated also in Milani (2007). Though in these works the learning algorithm is more complex than the one we use here, as it is basically a recursive least squares algorithm with constant gain, similar values for the gain in our setting seem to generate returns with characteristics that best resemble those found in real data.

4 DISCUSSION

Comparing simulations of returns with a constant and a time varying risk aversion, the differences in the statistical properties of the generated time series are remarkable. With a constant risk aversion, returns are essentially normally distributed, and fail to show any of the properties identified as stylized facts for returns on financial markets. In contrast, with ETVRA, the generated returns match surprisingly well the statistical properties of actual returns.

Our simulations thus suggest that ETVRA could be an important factor in understanding financial markets. An endogenous risk aversion coefficient that responds to excess returns introduces a reinforcement effect from market returns to asset demand and prices, and can, therefore, generate fat tail distributions for returns. We have also shown that as such a reinforcement effect is strengthened (i.e., as γ_α is increased) and the impact of excess returns on asset demand increased, the tails of the distribution get fatter.

In light of the literature discussed in the Introduction, we believe the mechanism at work in our setting could be considered a sort of field effect, in the sense that it introduces a feedback loop from the aggregate to individual decisions. In models with field effects, individual behavior is affected by some aggregate feature of the economy, giving rise to herds: in a similar way here, unexpected excess returns, by decreasing risk aversion, impact individual demand and result in a herd-like behavior: when asset prices rise more than expected, demand increases and, as a consequence, prices are increased even further, reinforcing the feedback effect and generating heavy tails in the distribution of returns.

Such a feedback effect from unexpected returns to demand can explain the correlation in absolute returns paired with an absence of correlation in returns. Absolute returns are, in fact, a measure of volatility, so the fact that they are correlated while returns are not means that there is predictability in the volatility of returns but not in returns themselves. The endogenous time-varying risk aversion in our model does not affect expected returns (which are still zero), but generates volatility clustering as periods of high volatility (low risk aversion) and of low volatility (high risk aversion) alternate. Low risk aversion generates higher volatility because it amplifies the impact of prices on demand, as can be seen in Eq. 2. This mechanism is thus able to generate fat tails in the distribution of returns and correlation in their volatility by endogenizing the demand through a link to the unexpected component of returns.

From a technical point of view, time-variation of risk aversion transforms the baseline additive stochastic framework into a doubly stochastic, multiplicative process that is able to generate fat tailed distributions. [11]

5 CONCLUSIONS

We have proposed in this paper a possible unifying explanation for many stylized facts about returns on financial markets that had so far eluded a common understanding. Our suggestion is that features such as volatility clustering, non-normality of distribution and heavy tails, absence of correlation in returns but positive correlation (with slow decay) in their absolute value, can all emerge in an otherwise standard, present value model of asset prices with stochastic dividends if an endogenous time-varying risk aversion is introduced. Simulations of the model with a coefficient of risk aversion that is allowed to change endogenously in response to unexpected excess returns in the risky activity produced returns that are surprisingly close, in all these dimensions, to real data, while simulated returns from the same model under constant risk aversion display normality of distribution, absence of volatility clustering and lack of correlation both in returns and in their absolute value. We conclude that endogenous time-varying risk aversion represents a very parsimonious way to explain key stylized facts in financial markets and deserves careful consideration from economists and practitioners alike.

FOOTNOTES

[1] An extensive survey of these models is provided in Lux (2009).

[2] Data are freely available at: http://research.stlouisfed.org/fred2/series /SP500?cid=32255

[3] The tail index is computed using the Hill estimator (Hill 1975), based upon the upper 2.5 % tail of the half sample. Estimates of the tail index are dependent on the sample fraction used: we choose to report here the statistics based on the half sample after experimenting with different fractions, always getting values between 2 and 4.

[4] Lux (2009) reports that, in fact, the ACF for the S&P500 absolute returns has been found to remain positive over 2500 lags.

[5] Note that such a feature is not essential for our results. We tried a different specification where risk aversion is constrained to remain positive and all the results of the paper carried through.

[6] Note that $E_{t-1}\beta p_{t-1} = \beta p_{t-1}$, so these terms drop out of Eq. 8.

[7] Branch and Evans (2011) avoid such a problem by modelling supply slightly differently from us and allowing it to become endogenous when prices sharply decline: this is meant to capture the drying up of asset float in financial markets that perform poorly. We chose not to use such a mechanism here, but simulations showed that it would not affect our results.

[8]The case with constant risk aversion corresponds to $\gamma_\alpha = 0$, and we have seen in Section 3.1that it implies normality of returns and a kurtosis close to 3.

[9]Again, the main exception being for $d_0 = 1$, which, as noted before, generates unrealistic statistics.

[10]More precisely, he estimated a value of 0.0196, with a 95 % credible interval between 0.015 and 0.025.

[11]The general formal framework for such processes was first studied by Kesten (1973).

REFERENCES

1. Adam K, Marcet A, Nicolini JP (2015) Stock market volatility and learning. J Financ. forthcoming
2. Beja A, Goldman MB (1980) On the dynamic behavior of prices in disequilibrium. J Financ 35:235–248
3. Bouchaud J-P, Cont R (2000) Herd behaviour and aggregate fluctuations in financial market. Macroecon Dyn 2:170–196
4. Branch WA, Evans GW (2010) Asset return dynamics and learning. Rev Financ Stud 23:1651–1680
5. Branch WA, Evans GW (2011) Learning about risk and return: a simple model of bubbles and crashes. American Economic Journal: Macroeconomics 3:159–191
6. Brandt MW, Wang KQ (2003) Time-varying risk aversion and unexpected inflation. J Monet Econ 50:1457–1498
7. Brock W, Hommes C (1998) Heterogeneous beliefs and routes to chaos in a simple asset pricing model. J Econ Dyn Control 22:1235–1274
8. Bullard J, Duffy J (2001) Learning and excess volatility. Macroecon Dyn 5:272–302
9. Carceles-Poveda E, Giannitsarou C (2008) Asset pricing with adaptive learning. Rev Econ Dyn 11:629–651
10. Chiarella C (1992) The dynamics of speculative behavior. Ann Oper Res 37:101–123
11. Chiarella C, He X-Z. (2002) Heterogeneous beliefs, risk and learning in a simple asset pricing model. Comput Econ 19:95–132

12. Chiarella C, He X-Z (2003) Heterogeneous beliefs, risk and learning in a simple asset pricing model with a market maker. Macroecon Dyn 7:503–536

13. Cont R (2001) Empirical properties of asset returns: stylized facts and statistical issues. Quant Finan 1:223–236

14. Day RH, Huang W (1990) Bulls, bears, and market sheep. J Econ Behav Organ 14:299–329

15. De Long JB, Shleifer A, Summers LH, Waldmann J (1990) Noise trader risk in financial markets. J Polit Econ 98:703–38

16. Evans GW, Honkapohja S (2001) Learning and Expectations in Macroeconomics. Princeton University Press, Princeton

17. Greenspan A (2005) Reflections on Central Banking. Speech, Federal Reserve Bank of Kansas City Jackson Hole Symposium, Jackson Hole, p 2005. http://www.federalreserve.gov/boarddocs/speeches/2005/20050826/default.htm

18. Hill BM (1975) A simple general appraoch to inference about the tail of a distribution. Ann Stat 3:1163–1174

19. Hommes C, Zhu M (2014) Learning under misspecification: a behavioral explanation of excess volatility in stock prices and persistence in inflation. J Econ Theory 150:778–814

20. Iori G (2002) A micro-simulation of traders' activity in the stock market: The role of heterogeneity of agents' interactions and trade-friction. J Econ Behav Organ 49:269–285

21. Kahneman D, Tversky A (1979) Prospect theory: an analysis of decision under risk. Econometrica 47:263–291

22. Kesten H (1973) Random difference equations and renewal theory for products of random matrices. Acta Mathematica 131:207–248

23. Kirman A (1993) Ants, rationality, and recruitment. Q J Econ 108:137–156

24. Kirman A, Teyssière G (2002) Microeconomic models for long memory in the volatility of financial time series. Studies in Nonlinear Dynamics & Econometrics 5:137–156

25. Kreps D (1998) Anticipated Utility and Dynamic Choice. In: Jacobs DP, Kalai E, Kamien M (eds) Frontiers of Research in Economic Theory. Cambridge University Press, Cambridge, pp 242–74

26. Li G (2007) Time-varying risk aversion and asset prices. Journal of Banking and Finance 31:243–257

27. Lux T (1995) Herd behaviour, bubbles and crashes. Econ J 105:881–896

28. Lux T (1998) The socio-economic dynamics of speculative markets: Interacting agents, chaos, and the fat tails of return distributions. J Econ Behav Organ 33:143–165

29. Lux T (2009) Stochastic behavioral asset pricing models and the stylized facts. In: Hens T, Schenk-Hoppé K (eds) Handbook of Financial Markets: Dynamics and Evolution. Amsterdam, North-Holland, pp 161–215

30. Milani F (2007) Expectations, learning and macroeconomic persistence. J Monet Econ 54:2065–2082

31. Milani F (2011) Expectation shocks and learning as drivers of the business cycle. Econ J 121:379–401

32. Netzer N (2009) Evolution of time preferences and attitudes towards risk. Am Econ Rev 2009:937–955

33. Park B-J (2014) Time-varying, heterogeneous risk aversion and dynamics of asset prices among boundedly rational agents. Journal of Banking and Finance 43:150–159

34. Robson AJ (2001) The biological basis of economic behavior. J Econ Lit 39:11–33

35. Sargent TJ (1993) Bounded Rationality in Macroeconomics. Clarendon Press, Oxford

36. Sargent TJ (1999) The Conquest of American Inflation. Princeton University Press, Princeton

37. Smith DR, Whitelaw RF (2009) Does risk aversion change over time? Mimeo

38. Timmermann A (1993) How learning in financial markets generates excess volatility and predictability in stock prices. Q J Econ 108:1135–1145

39. Timmermann A (1996) Excess volatility and predictability of stock prices in autoregressive dividend models with learning. Rev Econ Stud 63:523–557

40. Tseng J-J, Li S-P (2011) Asset returns and volatility clustering in financial time series. Physica A 390:1300–1314

INDEX